Please remember that this is a library book,
and that it belongs only temporarily to each
person who uses it. Be considerate. Do
not write in this, or any, library book.

Modern Movements in Educational Philosophy

Van Cleve Morris
University of Illinois
at Chicago Circle

Houghton Mifflin Company · Boston
New York · Atlanta · Geneva, Ill. · Dallas · Palo Alto

Preface

I have always had my doubts about the value of anthologies and books of readings. In the sphere of educational philosophy, the concepts are often so subtle, and the development of a position so tenuous, that only a single author can bring all the loose ideas together and sustain a coherent line of argument in comparing several points of view. Indeed, this is the conventional manner in which textbooks in educational philosophy have been written.

Of course, this one-author method has its faults. For one thing, unless the author is thoroughly grounded in each position he treats, unless he has the fine ear to hear the idiomatic phrasing of a point of view, he cannot possibly be an authentic interpreter of it. But there is another difficulty with the one-author method which no amount of learned scholarship is likely to overcome, namely, the necessity of any author to work from a private base of understanding as to what he considers worth discussing in any work on educational philosophy. What this means is that any book, no matter how "fair" and "objective," must legislate for the student what it is he should pay attention to and, in doing so, must orient the student's thinking to a certain way of studying educational theory. This unavoidable process of orientation, in and by itself, may be sufficient to prejudice a majority of readers in favor of an author's way of going about things.

With all of these disquieting reservations rolling around in my head, I have gradually come around to the view that an anthological *pot pourri*, if tightly organized, might achieve the best of two worlds. We can offer the student a systematic treatment of the subject but spoken from the standpoints of the practicing theorists at work in the field.

This book is the result of this intra-personal dialectic which I have watched, rather like a badly played tennis game, going on within my own mind over the past few years. The volume is intended, as the foregoing implies, as a book to be studied with the day-by-day assistance of an instructor. It is so organized that either selected portions or the entire volume might be covered in any course in educational theory.

A glance at the table of contents will reveal one other important feature of this book. The positions examined do not include the standard "isms" of an earlier epoch of educational philosophy—no Idealism, Realism, Neo-Thomism. I consider these rubrics not entirely suitable for the contemporary study of philosophical tendencies in educational thought. They were appropriate in a day when educational theory building was a new and developing art, when a few relatively discrete classifications were needed to polarize—for the purpose of analysis and comparison—a tangle of opinions, impressions and prejudices as to what education was for in an open and ostensibly democratic society. Now that the lines have been drawn, and sometimes *over*drawn, now that identifiable "schools of thought" have been labeled and been provided *intellectis personae* in the scenario of contemporary social movements, we discover that nobody actually fits these positional descriptions. They have served their purpose as artificially contrived analytic categories around which educational argument can take place, but we no longer need them as a program to tell the "good guys" from the "bad guys" in educational thinking.

Instead, we need to move on to the consideration of tendencies in contemporary philosophical thinking which have not yet coalesced into "schools of thought." What are the brethren up to these days? What are the lines of argument which seem to be getting the biggest play? What are the theoretical arguments which most awaken the attention of the thoughtful educator? And how is he using these ideas in the conduct of his own work?

Accordingly, after a brief section on the uses of philosophy, PART ONE establishes a background for our study: *Scientific philosophy in educational thought.* There can be little argument that the scientific philosophers—Pragmatists, Instrumentalists, Experimentalists, Operationalists, Progressivists, and others of like mind—now represent the prevailing persuasion in educational philosophy. It is against this background that we can best understand the newer movements in educational theory, since they are all outgrowths of or demurrers from this conventional base.

Three such movements are examined in PART TWO: *Philosophical anthropology, analytic philosophy, and existential philosophy.* We look over the shoulders of major thinkers at work in these specialties. Then, in a companion section for each group, we see how educational theorists respond to the ideas presently under development in these workshops.

Following each selection, both philosophical and educational, I have inserted a short comment which is intended to lead the student with his instructor "toward dialogue" with these authors. These entries, together with the inevitable queries and curiosities of the reader, will serve to make this a *teaching book*, that is, a work whose chief aim is not to "tell" something to the student but to "engage" him in active consideration of important ideas.

In preparing this volume, I have incurred debts to many individuals. Of course, my main thanks go to those authors who have consented to appear in this collection. But also, regarding the "production" stage of this undertaking, I am grateful to my wife, Eloise, and my colleague, Charles Tesconi, for their helpful criticism of the book's plan and of those portions of the writing which are my own. Finally, may I recognize Mrs. Flora Costea whose stenographic assistance was both efficient and good-natured.

No book is a one-man job—certainly not this one. But someone must be prepared to answer the mail if faults are—as they inevitably are—to be found. Since the book is, after all, my idea, I gladly accept this responsibility.

Van Cleve Morris
Evanston, Illinois

Contents

PART TWO *Modern Movements in Educational Philosophy*

3 Philosophical Anthropology in Educational Thought

1

The
Uses
of
Philosophy

What's The Use of Philosophy?

Philosophy to the ordinary man has customarily seemed the most splendidly useless of subject matters. To be philosophical, he thinks, is to be very high-minded and profound, but essentially "out of it." To be philosophical is to ask deep and thoughtful but ultimately unanswerable questions—like, What is truth? or, Do moral principles exist in the real world? or, What is the meaning of life? Who, asks our ordinary man, would want to spend any time, much less an entire academic career, fooling with such opaque imponderables?

Some individuals, though, are attracted to such questions; they want to get acquainted with them, see what they involve, and test what difference it makes how one thinks about them. These individuals want to see if they can think about the unthinkable!

Assuming that most of us in the profession of education lean toward the latter, unordinary class, what uses do we find in such activity? I suggest two: the esthetic and the directive uses of philosophy.

For some people, philosophy is primarily esthetic. They engage in it merely because they enjoy it. Perhaps we could dub this "the Mallory syndrome." Lord George Mallory, a turn-of-the-century British adventurer, was asked why he wanted to climb Mount Everest. "Because it is there!" he replied; and felt that he had provided enough of an explanation. I suspect that our present-day programs of space travel are motivated by something of the same impulse. We must voyage to the moon and beyond merely to see if we can do it! We enjoy and are excited by the attempt itself.

1

Thus it is with some people's fascination for philosophy. They want to conquer "inner space," the mysterious workings of the human mind. They are challenged and excited by a problem or question which remains unresolved. They push into their curiosities for the sheer enjoyment of seeing how far their own logic will carry them.

No one should deprecate this philosophizing-for-its-own-sake attitude. It certainly has as much to be said for it as any other form of human effort carried on for its own enjoyment—from auto racing to playing a hand of bridge to sculpturing forms out of stone.

There is, however, more to philosophy than that, and most professionals, I suspect, would wish to justify their existence on a firmer foundation than the proposition that theirs is a pursuit which is its own reason for being pursued. Most of them would claim another, more decisive, rationale for philosophy. Let us call this the directive purpose. Philosophy guides and directs practical affairs. It does not specify and prescribe practice, but it does orient and rationalize. Philosophy is to practice what a road atlas is to an automobile trip. The atlas provides the larger context in which the movements are to be made. It rationalizes the procedures of travel. It shows the way without specifying the way; in this limited sense, it directs the traveler. Likewise, philosophy shows us the main features of the terrain of our thought; it provides a general scheme of ideas in relation to which we can make our way progressively to the analysis and solution of human problems.

John Dewey once put the argument in somewhat more sophisticated language:

> It is of assistance to connect philosophy with thinking in its distinction from knowledge. Knowledge, grounded knowledge, is science; it represents objects which have been settled, ordered, disposed of rationally. Thinking, on the other hand, is prospective in reference. It is occasioned by an unsettlement and it aims at overcoming a disturbance. Philosophy is thinking what the known demands of us— what responsive attitude it exacts.[1]

". . . what the known demands of us—what responsive attitude it exacts." Please note the two important variables in that statement: "the known" and "responsive attitude." What is "the known?" Each philosopher has his own private opinion. Some say that we know only what science can find out: if it hasn't been scientifically verified, it isn't knowledge. Others are more open, believing that we can know something of the human spirit which transcends the boundaries of science. It goes without saying that if we begin with a variety of notions of what is "known," we are bound to wind up with a variety of "responsive attitudes."

But what do we mean by "responsive attitudes?" This is the area in which philosophy exercises it directive power. To return to our atlas analogy—when the motorist consults the road map he sees there "the

[1] John Dewey, *Democracy and Education* (New York: Macmillan, 1916), pp. 380–381.

known" concerning the topographical features of the terrain he wishes to cover. He sees the variety of roads that might be taken. But his "responsive attitude," the choice of route, will always be a function of these "knowns" together with the ends he has in mind—where he wants to go, how variably interested he may be in speed, scenery, or freedom from traffic congestion. In a somewhat similar way, the philosopher provides the intellectual map by which our thinking can be ordered and rationalized; he establishes the ground against which our problems can be bracketed and analyzed. Then, considering the various ends sought by his fellow citizens—moralists, political scientists, social critics, and educational theorists—and the kind of society they hope to build, he recommends responsive attitudes to the human problems of our time. He does not offer solutions; he offers, rather, an understanding of what a solution would look like and what lines of thinking are most likely to lead to it.

This book is concerned with the way in which philosophical map-making can assist the educational theorist. We wish to see how the different philosophical atlases portray the human condition, and what responsive attitudes these several portrayals summon forth from the educator.

What (If Anything) to Expect from Today's Philosophers

There is an old saying that philosophy bakes no bread. It is perhaps equally true that no bread would ever have been baked without philosophy. For the act of baking implies a decision on the philosophical issue of whether life is worthwhile at all. Bakers may not have often asked themselves the question in so many words. But philosophy traditionally has been nothing less than the attempt to ask and answer, in a formal and disciplined way, the great questions of life that ordinary men might put to themselves in reflective moments.

The world has both favored and feared the philosophers' answers. Thomas Aquinas became a saint, Aristotle was tutor to Alexander the Great, and Voltaire was a confidant of kings. But Socrates was put to death, and Giordano Bruno was burned at the stake. Nowadays, Historian Will Durant has noted, no one would think of doing that—"not

From *Time*, January 7, 1966, pp. 24–25. By permission from *Time*, The Weekly Newsmagazine; Copyright Time Inc. 1966.

because men are more delicate about killing, but because there is no need to kill that which is already dead."

Philosophy dead? It often seems so. In a world of war and change, of principles armed with bombs and technology searching for principles, the alarming thing is not what philosophers say but what they fail to say. When reason is overturned, blind passions are rampant, and urgent questions mount, men turn for guidance to scientists, psychiatrists, sociologists, ideologues, politicians, historians, journalists—almost anyone except their traditional guide, the philosopher. Ironically, the once remote theologians are in closer touch with humanity's immediate and intense concerns than most philosophers, who today tend to be relatively obscure academic technicians. No living U.S. philosopher has the significance to the world at large that John Dewey or George Santayana had a generation or two ago. Many feel that philosophy has played out its role in the history of human culture; the "queen of sciences" has been dethroned.

Once all sciences were part of philosophy's domain, but gradually, from physics to psychology, they seceded and established themselves as independent disciplines. Above all, for some time now, philosophy itself has been engaged in a vast revolt against its own past and against its traditional function. This intellectual purge may well have been necessary, but as a result contemporary philosophy looks inward at its own problems rather than outward at men, and philosophizes about philosophy, not about life. A great many of his colleagues in the U.S. today would agree with Donald Kalish, chairman of the philosophy department at U.C.L.A., who says: "There is no system of philosophy to spin out. There are no ethical truths, there are just clarifications of particular ethical problems. Take advantage of these clarifications and work out your own existence. You are mistaken to think that anyone ever had the answers. There are no answers. Be brave and face up to it."

REVOLT OF THE LOGICIANS

Before such chilling views took hold, philosophers always were men who thought, says Yale's Professor Emeritus Brand Blanshard, that "they could sit down in their studies and arrive by reasoning at a knowledge of the ultimate nature of the world." Perhaps in no other age had philosophers greater confidence in their capacity to do this than in the 19th century. Hegel tried to encompass all aspects of life within his dialectical logic of thesis-antithesis-synthesis, in 18 ponderous tomes. His idealistic principle that the material world exists only in relation to the Absolute mind led to the metaphysics of F. H. Bradley, who denied—even during the course of an hour's conversation in an Oxford chamber—that time or space had objective reality.

By the turn of the century, science and common sense alike dictated a shift away from idealism. "Damn the Absolute," roared William James, and the American pragmatists turned from principles and categories to results and facts. But the most effective rebellion against Hegelianism was carried out by two groups—the analytic philosophers, who prevail in U.S. and British universities, and the partisans of phenomenology and existentialism, who predominate in Western Europe. On some U.S. campuses, they are known as "the logicians and the lotus-eaters."

The analytic revolt began with two convictions: first, that experience contradicted the idealistic theory that material objects are not in themselves "real"; second, that philosophy could not compete with science as a way of studying the real world and thus would have to turn to other tasks. The analytic thinkers decided that philosophy's true job was to answer that old Socratic question "What does it mean?"

The study of meaning takes many forms. One stems from G. E. Moore of Cambridge, who argued that the business of philosophy was simply the analysis and clarification of common sense beliefs. Moore's colleague Bertrand Russell tried to eliminate fallacies by using an artificial language of symbols into which the truths of science and ordinary descriptive statements could be translated in order to test their accuracy. The "Vienna Circle" of logical positivists—who carried their ideas to Britain and the U.S. in the 1930s—declared that the criterion of meaning was verifiability; if the meaning of a statement could not be verified by empirical procedures, it was literally nonsense. But, as Russell pointed out, this criterion was itself a philosophical principle.

Finally Ludwig Wittgenstein, an Austrian-born Cambridge don, and such Oxonians as J. L. Austin and Gilbert Ryle decided independently that philosophy was concerned not so much with meaning as with use, and should seek to establish the rules of the various "language games" that men played with ordinary words, describing when a word was used legitimately, and when it was not. About all the various analytic schools had in common was the beliefs that philosophy has nothing to say about the world and that clarity and straight thinking will dissolve most of the classical metaphysical problems.

THE RISE OF THE LOTUS-EATERS

On the Continent, the philosophical revolt took a different form. Germany's Edmund Husserl developed a "descriptive science" that he called phenomenology. His method was to examine and describe a particular experience—at the same time mentally blocking off any speculations about its origin or significance, any memories of similar experiences. By this act of epoche, a deliberate suspension of judgment, Husserl felt that the mind could eventually intuit the essence of the object being studied. Husserl's bafflingly difficult approach influenced such modern existentialist philosophers as Martin Heidegger and Jean-Paul Sartre.

What the existentialists emphasize about man is that he alone among other beings, is a decision-making creature blessed, or cursed, with the freedom to choose among a variety of possibilities in an absurd and mysterious existence: to be truly human, man must accept this freedom and conquer the anxiety and despair that threaten it by "commitment" to a way of life. This message can be bracing, notably in the religious version of existentialism, in which the commitment is directed toward a spiritual goal. It can also be nihilistic, notably in the atheistic version, in which commitment is demanded for its own sake only and the despair of the human situation is emphasized more than its conquest.

Both movements, the logicians as well as the lotus-eaters, appear to do away with what has usually been considered the very heart of philosophy: metaphysics, the attempt to comprehend through reason the nature of reality. In *The Conditions of Philosophy*, a current examination of the discipline, Mortimer Adler charges that the analytic thinkers abandon "first-order questions" that metaphysics used to ask—such as the nature of being, causation, free will—and are concerned mostly with second-order problems of method. The existentialists, on the other hand, continue to ask large-size questions, but because of their man-centered approach they are indifferent to systematic thinking. Thus, for both movements, a question such as "What is truth?" becomes impossible to answer. The logical positivist would say that a particular statement of fact can be declared true or false by empirical evidence; anything else is meaningless. A language philosopher would content himself with analyzing all the ways the word true can be used. The existentialist would emphasize what is true for a person in a particular situation.

THE WAR OF THE SCHOOLS

Both movements have turned philosophy into a private game for professionals. Laymen glancing at the June 10, 1965, issue of the *Journal of Philosophy* will find a brace of learned analysts discussing whether the sentence "There are brown things and there are cows" is best expressed by the formula $(\exists x)Exw \cdot (\exists x)Exy$ or by $(\exists x)Bx \cdot (\exists x)Cx$. And while the existentialists speak dramatically enough about the condition of man in novels and plays, their philosophical writing is so dense that Brandeis' Henry Aiken complains: "Reading Heidegger is like trying to swim through wet sand." One typical passage of Heidegger's alleged masterwork, *Being and Time*, reads: "If the Being of everyday Being-with-one-another is already different in principle from pure presence-at-hand—in spite of the fact that it is seemingly close to it ontologically—still less can the Being of the authentic Self be conceived as presence-at-hand."

Philosophy cannot and need not make sense to the layman in every detail; excerpts from Aristotle or Hegel (or, for that matter, Einstein) may also seem like gibberish to the uninitiated. But it is significant that the analytic and phenomenological thinkers don't even understand one another.

As a result, philosophy today is bitterly segregated. Most of the major philosophy departments and scholarly journals are the exclusive property of one sect or another. Harvard, U.C.L.A. and Cornell are oriented toward analytic thinking, for example, while Penn State and Northwestern are among the minority leaning toward phenomenology. Despite much academic talk about the horrors of conformity, some philosophy departments are rigidly conformist. Instructors or students with the "wrong" approach are forced out. The attitude at U.C.L.A., for instance, is that "a lot of nice young people who might be wholesome philosophers of the nonanalytic kind can't get through our requirements."

Many students who do make the grade in analytic courses are disappointed because they had expected more from philosophy. To some, the analytic approach is now old hat, while the older, unfashionable philosophies take on a new excitement. There are many older-line philosophers left in the U.S. who belong to neither of the two warring sides, including Yale's Paul Weiss, Chicago's Richard McKeon, the University of Texas' Charles Hartshorne, and Michigan's Abraham Kaplan, who states wryly: "The word philosophy means the love of wisdom. And the love of wisdom, I suppose, is like any other sort of love—the professionals are the ones who know least about it."

There are signs that, hesitantly and sometimes unintentionally, professional philosophers are beginning to take such reproaches to heart. At long last, philosophy may have stopped attacking the Hegelian bogey and be about ready to put its analytic tools to work on the real issues facing man.

Suggesting the glimmer of a *détente*, French Phenomenologist Paul Ricoeur now teaches a course in linguistic analysis at the University of Paris. Yale's John Wild recently published an article suggesting that the *lebenswelt*, the "life world" of experience that phenomenology investigates, is the world of "ordinary language" that the linguistic philosophers are studying.

Some analytic philosophers are even daring to "do metaphysics" again. P. F. Strawson, one of the most respected of Oxford's analytic philosophers, boldly subtitled his latest book, *Individuals, An Essay in Descriptive Metaphysics*. The book is partly concerned with the difference between material objects and human beings, a highly technical question that, by extension, has to do with the very real problem of whether man can be explained like a flesh-and-blood object or whether he is an organism with a purpose. Another, younger Oxonian, Anthony Quinton, is completing a philosophical treatise, grandly titled *The Nature of Things*, that starts from the problem of identity and reference: Is a given object simply a bundle of qualities, or is it something more than that? Quinton points out that the question is as old as Aristotle, who grappled with the meaning of "substance." Strawson, as well as such U.S. figures as Harvard's Morton White, emphasizes that analytic technique is a means rather than an end.

The early analytic thinkers believed that with the clarifying of language the old questions of philosophy would simply disappear, but their intellectual offsprings are wiser. "Once you see that language permeates the world," says Morris Kaplan, a Ph.D. candidate at Yale, "all the problems you had with the world come back." Strawson agrees that "the insatiable appetite of philosophers for generality has reasserted itself." In other words, the philosophers are beginning to re-invent philosophy.

In Britain, philosophers are newly concerned over such ancient issues as the relationship of body to mind and the problem of causation in human behavior. David Wiggins of Oxford is currently exploring "the entire concept of event identity—what makes it right to say that event A is the same as event B?" An American illustrates Wiggins' problem with a homely example: "Is my act of flipping on the light switch the same act as my act of alerting the prowler, if in fact by flipping on the switch and illuminating the room, I do alert the prowler?" Although the question sounds as relevant as the medieval puzzler about how many angels can dance on a pinhead, Wiggins notes that it has highly practical implications in fixing intention and responsibility, and theoretical ones in helping to solve the age-old puzzler of free will *v.* determinism. Free will is back in philosophical style, and Wiggins concedes that the traditional way of stating that problem "wasn't after all in quite such a mess as had recently been supposed."

TIME TO WAKE UP

In the Middle Ages, the questions that philosophy asked were determined largely by theology; today major philosophical issues are posed by science. Says Chicago's McKeon: "The new priests come from the lab and hand us the tablet—how do we handle it?" Philosopher Hubert Dreyfus of M.I.T. is wondering about the possibility of creating a computer that would be completely determined by programming but would behave as if it were a free, intelligent agent. "If something that we knew was just a machine could behave intelligently," he muses, "it would tend to suggest that maybe we are just machines." Would such computers have to be considered conscious beings? Would they raise a civil liberties problem? To some, such questions suggest that science is creating more problems than philosophy can readily cope with; and concepts like antimatter and the expanding universe make some philosophers quite nervous.

Chances are, however, that philosophy will learn to coexist with science and (in Mortimer Adler's phrase) reach its delayed maturity, provided it resolutely insists on being a separate discipline dealing publicly and intelligibly in first-order questions. Caution is bound to remain. Instead of one-man systems, philosophy in the future will probably consist of a dialogue of many thinkers, each seeking to explore to the fullest one aspect of a common problem. Says Oxford's James Urmson, a visiting professor at the University of Michigan: "It is just like Galileo experimenting with little balls on inclined planes before he addressed the heavens."

The question remains: Will philosophy ever again address the heavens? Will it contribute anything to man's vision, rather than merely clarifying it? Caution and confusion are not necessarily signs of disaster, and even Hegel remarked that "the owl of Minerva spreads its wings only with the falling of the dusk." But the shadows are deep and the time for an awakening is at hand.

ISAIAH BERLIN

A 'Dangerous But Important Activity'

Philosophy is the critical examination not of what exists or has existed or will exist—this is dealt with by ordinary opinion and the natural sciences—but of the ways in which they are viewed or conceived; not of the items of experience but of the categories in terms of which they are conceived and classified.

Philosophy is not an empirical study; nor is it a kind of formal deduction as mathematics or logic is. Its subject matter is the permanent or semi-permanent categories in terms of which experience is conceived. Purpose versus mechanical causality; organism versus mere amalgams; systems versus mere togetherness; spatio-temporal order versus timeless being; duty versus appetite; and value versus fact—these are categories, models, spectacles. Some of these are as old as human experience itself; others are more transient. In politics, for example, men tried to conceive of their social existence by analogy with various models: Plato tried to frame his system of human nature, its attributes and goals, following a geometrical pattern, since he thought it would explain all there was.

So, too, the biological pattern of Aristotle; the many Christian images with which the writings of the Fathers as well as the Old and New Testaments abound; the notion of a great human orchestra in which every man has a particular score, for which he is a particular instrument; the analogy of the family, which casts light upon human relations not provided by a mechanical model (such as that of Hobbes); the notion of an army on the march with its emphasis on such virtues as loyalty, dedication, obedience, needed to overtake and crush the enemy (with which so much play has been made in the Soviet Union); the notion of the state as a traffic policeman and night-watchman preventing collisions and looking after property, which is at the back of much individualist

Reprinted with permission from University: A Princeton Quarterly, Spring 1966. Copyright © Isaiah Berlin 1966.

and liberal thought; the notion of the state as much more than this—as a great cooperative endeavor with individuals seeking to fulfil a common end and therefore entitled to enter into every nook and cranny of human experience, that animates much of the "organic" thought of the 19th century—all these are models in terms of which human beings—solitary thinkers as well as groups and societies and cultures—have conceived of their experience.

These models often collide; some are rendered inadequate by failing to account for too many aspects of experience, and are in their turn replaced by other models which emphasize what these last have omitted, but in their turn may obscure what the others had rendered clear. The task of philosophy, and it is often a difficult and painful one, is to extricate and bring to light the hidden categories and models in terms of which human beings think, to analyse clearly what is obscure or contradictory in them, to discern the conflicts between them that prevent the construction of more adequate ways of organizing and explaining experience (for all explanation involves some models in terms of which explaining is done); and then, at a still more abstract level, to examine the nature of this explaining activity itself, and to bring to light the concealed models that operate in the second order activity itself.

If it is objected that all this seems very abstract and remote from daily experience, something too little concerned with the central interests, the happiness and misery and ultimate fate of ordinary men, the answer is that this charge is false. Men cannot live without seeking to explain the universe to themselves. The models they use in these explanations must deeply affect their lives, not least when they are unconscious; much of the misery and frustration of men is due to the mechanical or unconscious, as well as deliberate, application of models where they do not work. It is difficult to estimate how much misery has been caused by the organic model in politics, or the analogy of the state with a work of art, in our own times, or, in previous ages, by the exaggerated application of metaphors and models fashioned after the patterns of paternal authority within a family to the relations between rulers of states to their subjects, or of priests to the laity.

If there is to be any hope of a rational order on earth, or of a just appreciation of the many various interests that divide diverse groups of human beings, required for any attempt to balance them and find viable compromises through which men may continue to live and satisfy their desires without thereby crushing the equally central desires and needs of others, it lies in the bringing to light of these models, the examination of whether they are adequate to their task.

The perennial task of philosophers is to examine categories, concepts, models, ways of thinking or acting, and particularly ways in which they clash with one another with a view to constructing other, less internally contradictory, images and systems of categories. It is certainly a reasonable hypothesis that one of the principal causes of misery and fear is blind adherence to outworn notions, irrational suspicions of any form of critical self-examination, frantic efforts to prevent any degree of rational analysis of what we live by and for.

This dangerous but important activity is the work of philosophers, whether they deal with the natural sciences or moral or political or purely personal issues. The goal of philosophy is always the same: to assist men to understand themselves and thus operate in the open and not wildly, in the dark.

The Prevailing Persuasion

2

Scientific Philosophy in Educational Thought

Scientific Philosophy

William James once remarked that Pragmatism was not really a philosophy but merely a method of dealing with life. The earlier philosophies, from Plato to Hegel, had been principally concerned with metaphysical questions and a total theory of all creation, but the new Pragmatism had virtually nothing to say about the construction of the universe. Instead, it settled for developing a way to manage human experience.

The Pragmatists hoped to invent a method of thinking which would apply human reason to life's difficulties. Thus, reason, which had been allowed an arcane aloofness, would now be brought into the workaday world and into the direct service of people's needs. In this role, reason might better be labeled intelligence, that is, thought applied to action. The genuinely educated man, asserted the Pragmatists, was not the man of superb speculative reason, as we had always been told, but the man of intelligent, reflective behavior.

The man who started it all—at least the American strain—was Charles Sanders Peirce, a relatively little-known philosopher active during the latter years of the 19th century. In two famous articles, "The Fixation of Belief,"[1] and "How to Make Our Ideas Clear,"[2] Peirce put

[1] Justus Buchler, ed., *The Philosophy of Peirce—Selected Writings* (London: Routledge and Kegan Paul, 1940), pp. 5–22.
[2] *Ibid.*, pp. 23–41.

15

forward a relatively unorthodox notion: the meaning of an idea cannot be determined merely by turning it over in one's mind or by defining the words with which it is expressed, but rather by the application of the idea to action, by acting on it and seeing what happens. Thus, if I say "It's raining," I find the meaning of this remark not in some internal process of conceptualization but in the observable phenomena empirically related to it—darkening skies, drops of water on the window, puddles in the streets. "Consider what effects, that might conceivably have practical bearings, we conceive the object of our conception to have. Then, our conception of these effects is the whole of our conception of the object."[3]

William James picked up this idea and moved it to a new level. Not only the meaning of an idea is to be found in its practical effects, but its truth or falsity as well. "What difference," he said, "would it practically make to any one if this notion rather than that notion were true?"[4] If to believe an idea is to have experience made more comprehensible and manageable, that is, if an idea seems to explain and rationalize the phenomena to which it relates, then the idea is true. This James metaphorically called the "cash value" of an idea. An idea gets its truth from the results of acting on it. A check which we write to a merchant is not good just because we write it; it is made good—it is verified as cash —by the bank holding our checking account. Likewise, we must cash in our ideas at the bank of experience to see if they work, to see if they are made good by subsequent events. If they are, then they are true.

Putting Peirce and James together, we see that a great many philosophical problems are not really problems. The ancient puzzler about how many angels can dance on the head of a pin is not to be solved by taking careful measurements of the pinhead nor by reminding everybody that angels are disembodied. The problem can be dismissed entirely, because no matter what answer is given to the question, it can make no practical difference to anybody. Turning this proposition around, we see that only those questions whose answers make a real difference in the way we deal with the world are now considered legitimate questions. These questions and answers, taken in their entirety, are what we call science.

John Dewey carried the argument one step further. If ideas have their meanings in practical effects—are made true or false by the consequences of acting on them—then ideas have a prospective function; once verified by their consequences, ideas can be used to bring about those consequences. Ideas are thus tools of action or "instruments," prompting Dewey to label his own point of view "Instrumentalism." It is this instrumental feature of scientific logic which earns for science the ability to predict and control events.

[3] *Ibid.*, p. 31.
[4] *Pragmatism* (Cleveland: The World Publishing Company, Meridian Books, original copyright 1907), p. 42.

As this kind of logic has developed, it has acquired a number of different names. Educators frequently use the term "Experimentalism"; Anatol Rapoport, from whom we hear next, uses the term "Operationalism."

Rapoport's essay is followed by two selections from John Dewey, the first a general discussion of the processes of human thinking, the second a detailed analysis of the special form of thinking which we call "reflective," and which is the primary concern of the scientifically oriented educator. Included is one of Dewey's most widely acclaimed theoretical formulations, the "Complete Act of Thought."

Finally, does a scientific outlook pervade an entire culture? If science becomes the ruling ethic, the secular god, of a whole people, what effect does it have on the way they live? Kouwenhoven tells us in his essay, "What's 'American' about America?"

ANATOL RAPOPORT

Operational Philosophy

The topics discussed in this book are as old as philosophy: How do we know what we know? How ought we to behave? What is it all about? The *approach* to these questions which we will use here is not old, certainly not more than a century old. Yet this approach, which we will call "operationalism," has roots stretching far back in the history of Western thought.

The nominalists of the twelfth century in their critique of the "reality of universals" carried the germ of the operational idea.[1] Roger Bacon (*ca.* 1212–*ca.* 1294), the earliest outspoken champion of the experimental method, appears as a prophet of the future philosophy of action among the scholasticists of his day. The line carries on through da Vinci, Galileo, Newton, and Huygens, through the English empiricists and the

[1] The argument was between the "nominalists" and the "realists," two opposing schools in scholastic philosophy. The realists maintained that only "universals" were real, that is, what existed primarily were categories, such as House, Man, or Tree, and that the individual houses, men, and trees were only secondary manifestations of the universals. The nominalists, on the contrary, held that the individual things only were real, the universal categories being mere *names* applied to classes of things (hence the label "nominalists"). The nominalists thus were already leaning toward what is known in general semantics as the "extensional orientation."

From *Operational Philosophy*, (New York: Harper and Bros., Publishers, 1953), pp. vii–viii and 3–4.

French Encyclopedists into the nineteenth century. Historically, operationalism has been the way of science. But in our day it has acquired a special significance. Today operationalism is *being aware* of the way of science—the philosophy of science.

The philosophy of science is a comparatively new field of inquiry. In the old days, science *was* philosophy. That is to say, the sort of knowledge which science has always pursued—knowledge of "general principles," of the "why" of things—was supposed to be embodied in the works of professional thinkers, philosophers. The other kind of knowledge which today goes under the name of "know-how," the knowledge of obtaining desirable results in specific, concrete situations, was practiced by a different class of people, the professional workers—artists, craftsmen, even slaves.

About the time of the Renaissance there occurred in Western Europe a union of these two—systematic thinking, recorded and accumulated, and purposeful activity toward preconceived desired ends. This union of "know how" and "know why" can be taken to be the beginning of our scientific age. It also marks the separation of science and philosophy, in which science switched its allegiance from "eternal truths" to immediate "brute facts."

Thereafter many philosophers turned their backs on science, impatient with its preoccupation with detail, and many scientists turned away from philosophy and forgot their heritage. They forgot that were it not for the intellectual fountainhead of philosophic thought, they would have nothing to investigate. As Alfred North Whitehead put it, scientists were living on the intellectual capital of the seventeenth century.

Near the end of the nineteenth century, this capital was nearing exhaustion. A new intellectual outlook was needed. It could not have come from the then existing philosophy, which had divorced itself from science. So science created its own philosophy, a reexamination of its own methods and foundations. This philosophy appears in the works of Whitehead, of Poincaré, of Russell, of Vaihinger, and of many others all clustering in the first quarter of this century. All these works reflect a growing preoccupation of science with *itself*, an increasing self-awareness of science. Out of such self-awareness, particularly in the light of the new theory of meaning (semantics), operationalism has crystallized.

The newest developments, particularly in the United States, are attempts to extend operationalism so as to make it a method for dealing with human affairs. In particular, the school of thought founded by Alfred Korzybski (1879–1950) has had many followers. The impetus of Korzybski's ideas gave rise to numerous popularizations of operationalism. Although the difficulties of scientific philosophy are largely passed over in these popularizations, they nevertheless have played an important part in establishing an intellectual climate in which such a philosophy can flourish. The existence of such a climate is of prime importance in our day when public opinion has much more weight than formerly in influencing educational policies.

* * *

Traditionally, philosophy courses offered in universities have been concerned with the study of various philosophical systems. Such studies are sometimes purely descriptive (simply noting what each philosopher has said); sometimes they are historical (noting how the ideas of one system of philosophy have stemmed from those of another); sometimes comparative (noting how various systems of philosophy are like or unlike each other). What is usually lacking in the conventional academic approach to philosophy is an extensive inquiry into the relations between *thinking* and *doing*. How does the framework in which people think about the world influence what they do about the world and (what is even more important) vice versa?

There have been thinkers who were keenly concerned with such problems and who have offered theories to deal with them. One such thinker was Marx. He tried to show how what people do in the economic structure of their society influences (we are toning him down here —Marx actually believed *determines*) what they think about the nature of society, about right and wrong, and even about the physical world.

Another such thinker was Freud. He tried to explain the formation of the individual personality in terms of the individual's early "sexual" experience. It is natural to extend this point of view to a theory of the relation of a world outlook to primitive sexual experience.

And still another such thinker (although this has not been commonly recognized) was Einstein. He actually showed by mathematical reasoning how what one "does" determines what one "means." His investigations have been confined to simple kinds of meaning and action, and for this reason his results have been more lucid and precise than those of Marx and Freud. Einstein showed, for example, that if our reasoning about events in time and space is to make sense, we must always keep in mind that "time" and "space" mean not what we *say* or *think* about them, but what we *do* about them—they acquire meaning from the operations we must perform in measuring them and have no meaning *apart* from these operations. Thus Einstein's contribution has to do with the relation between thought and action and as such has something in common with the contributions of Freud and Marx.

Marx, Freud, and Einstein are not often thought of as "philosophers," at least not in the same way as Plato, Hegel, and Bergson are. Perhaps this is so because Marx, Freud, and Einstein fixed their attention on "events" (such as "price fluctuations," "impotence," "propagation of electromagnetic waves") instead of on "ideas" (such as "the soul," "the Absolute," "the Vital Force") as the philosophers who are universally recognized as philosophers do. Yet there is an abundance of ideas in the theory of surplus value, in the notion of the Oedipus complex, and in the definition of space-time curvature. The difference between thinkers like Plato, Hegel, and Bergson on the one hand and Marx, Freud, and Einstein on the other is that one can trace the ideas put forward by the latter to some sort of *action* or some set of "operations," both with regard to where the ideas come from and to what can be done with them. Operational philosophy . . . stems from an attempt to treat the sort of problems which occupied people like Marx, Freud, and Einstein.

Toward Dialogue

Rapoport is saying that theories grow out of observable events. Thus Marx developed his dialectical materialism out of observations of the price market, Freud his conception of the subconscious out of female hysteria, and Einstein his "relativity" out of electromagnetic waves. Likewise, Toynbee has worked out theories of history from the fortunes and misfortunes of twenty-one civilizations, Bruner the laws of cognition from the thinking behavior of youngsters, and McLuhan his understanding of media from the way we use telephones and television.

Where, however, are we going to put theories not so generated—Paul Tillich's idea, for example, that the religious impulse at base is the striving for "the courage to be," or Martin Buber's "theory" that "all real living is meeting"? What is the status of these ideas? And at what point in their growth and development can we say that they have come of age and bear listening to?

In Rapoport's own language, are there some ideas for which there are no operations to be taken in their behalf? Is there possibly a zone of idea formation—what the psychologist calls "conceptualization"—which runs beyond the operationalist boundary, where what you think does not necessarily link with what you do?

JOHN DEWEY

What Is Thinking?

DIFFERENT MEANINGS OF THOUGHT

The Best Way of Thinking

No one can tell another person in any definite way how he *should* think, any more than how he ought to breathe or to have his blood circulate. But the various ways in which men *do* think can be told and can be described in their general features. Some of these ways are better than others; the reasons why they are better can be set forth. The person who understands what the better ways of thinking are and why they are better can, if he will, change his own personal ways until they become more effective; until, that is to say, they do better the work that thinking can do and that other mental operations cannot do so well. The better way of thinking that is to be considered in this book is called reflective thinking: the kind of thinking that consists in turning a subject over in the mind and giving it serious and consecutive consideration. Before we take up this main theme, we shall, however, first take note briefly of some other mental processes to which the name *thought* is sometimes given.

The 'Stream of Consciousness'

All the time we are awake and sometimes when we are asleep, something is, as we say, going through our heads. When we are asleep we call that kind of sequence 'dreaming.' We also have daydreams, reveries, castles built in the air, and mental streams that are even more idle and chaotic. To this uncontrolled coursing of ideas through our heads the name of 'thinking' is sometimes given. It is automatic and unregulated. Many a child has attempted to see whether he could not 'stop thinking' —that is, stop this procession of mental states through his mind—and in vain. More of our waking life than most of us would care to admit is whiled away in this inconsequential trifling with mental pictures, random recollections, pleasant but unfounded hopes, flitting, half-developed impressions. Hence it is that he who offers 'a penny for your thoughts' does not expect to drive any great bargain if his offer is taken; he will only find out what happens to be 'going through the mind' and what 'goes' in this fashion rarely leaves much that is worth while behind.

From *How We Think,* 2nd ed. (Boston: D. C. Heath and Company, 1933), pp. 3–16.

Reflective Thought Is a Chain

In this sense, silly folk and dullards *think*. The story is told of a man in slight repute for intelligence, who, desiring to be chosen selectman in his New England town, addressed a knot of neighbors in this wise: "I hear you don't believe I know enough to hold office. I wish you to understand that I am thinking about something or other most of the time." Now, reflective thought is like this random coursing of things through the mind in that it consists of a succession of things thought of, but it is unlike in that the mere chance occurrence of any chance 'something or other' in an irregular sequence does not suffice. Reflection involves not simply a sequence of ideas, but a *con*-sequence—a consecutive ordering in such a way that each determines the next as its proper outcome, while each outcome in turn leans back on, or refers to, its predecessors. The successive portions of a reflective thought grow out of one another and support one another; they do not come and go in a medley. Each phase is a step from something to something—technically speaking, it is a *term* of thought. Each term leaves a deposit that is utilized in the next term. The stream or flow becomes a train or chain. There are in any reflective thought definite units that are linked together so that there is a sustained movement to a common end.

Thinking Usually Restricted to Things Not Directly Perceived

The second meaning of thinking limits it to things not sensed or directly perceived, to things *not* seen, heard, touched, smelt, or tasted. We ask the man telling a story if he saw a certain incident happen, and his reply may be, "No, I only thought of it." A note of invention, as distinct from faithful record of observation, is present. Most important in this class are successions of imaginative incidents and episodes that have a certain coherence, hang together on a continuous thread, and thus lie between kaleidoscopic flights of fancy and considerations deliberately employed to establish a conclusion. The imaginative stories poured forth by children possess all degrees of internal congruity; some are disjointed, some are articulated. When connected, they simulate reflective thought; indeed, they usually occur in minds of logical capacity. These imaginative enterprises often precede thinking of the close-knit type and prepare the way for it. In this sense, a thought or idea is a mental picture of something not actually present, and thinking is the succession of such pictures.

Reflective Thinking Aims at a Conclusion

In contrast, reflective thinking has a purpose beyond the entertainment afforded by the train of agreeable mental inventions and pictures. The train must lead somewhere; it must tend to a conclusion that can be substantiated outside the course of the images. A story of a giant may satisfy merely because of the story itself; a reflective conclusion that a giant lived at a certain date and place on the earth would have to have some justification outside of the chain of ideas in order to be a valid or sound conclusion. This contrasting element is probably best conveyed in the ordinary saying: "Think it *out.*" The phrase suggests an entanglement to be straightened out, something obscure to be cleared up through the application of thought. There is a goal to be reached, and this end sets a task that controls the sequence of ideas.

Thinking as Practically Synonymous with Believing

A third meaning of thought is practically synonymous with *belief.* "I think it is going to be colder tomorrow," or "I think Hungary is larger than Jugo-Slavia" is equivalent to "I believe so-and-so." When we say, "Men used to think the world was flat," we obviously refer to a belief that was held by our ancestors. This meaning of thought is narrower than those previously mentioned. A belief refers to something beyond itself by which its value is tested; it makes an assertion about some matter of fact or some principle or law. It means that a specified state of fact or law is accepted or rejected, that it is something proper to be affirmed or at least acquiesced in. It is hardly necessary to lay stress upon the importance of belief. It covers all the matters of which we have no sure knowledge and yet which we are sufficiently confident of to act upon and also the matters that we now accept as certainly true, as knowledge, but which nevertheless may be questioned in the future—just as much that passed as knowledge in the past has now passed into the limbo of mere opinion or of error.

There is nothing in the mere fact of thought as identical with belief that reveals whether the belief is well founded or not. Two different men say, "I believe the world is spherical." One man, if challenged, could produce little or no evidence for thinking as he does. It is an idea that he has picked up from others and that he accepts because the idea is generally current, not because he has examined into the matter and not because his own mind has taken any active part in reaching and framing the belief.

Such 'thoughts' grow up unconsciously. They are picked up—we know not how. From obscure sources and by unnoticed channels they insinuate themselves into the mind and become unconsciously a part of our mental furniture. Tradition, instruction, imitation—all of which depend upon authority in some form, or appeal to our own advantage, or fall in with a strong passion—are responsible for them. Such thoughts are prejudices; that is, prejudgments, not conclusions reached as the result of personal mental activity, such as observing, collecting, and examining evidence. Even when they happen to be correct, their correctness is a matter of accident as far as the person who entertains them is concerned.

Reflective Thinking Impels to Inquiry

Thus we are brought again, by way of contrast, to the particular kind of thinking that we are to study in this volume, *reflective thinking.*

Thought, in the two first senses mentioned, may be harmful to the mind because it distracts attention from the real world, and because it may be a waste of time. On the other hand, if indulged in judiciously these thoughts may afford genuine enjoyment and also be a source of needed recreation. But in either case they can make no claim to truth; they cannot hold themselves up as something that the mind should accept, assert, and be willing to act upon. They may involve a kind of emotional commitment, but not intellectual and practical commitment. Beliefs, on the other hand, do involve precisely this commitment and consequently sooner or later they demand our investigation to find out upon what grounds they rest. To think of a cloud as a whale or a camel—in the sense of to 'fancy'—does not commit one to the conclusion that the person having the idea would ride the camel or extract oil from the whale. But when Columbus 'thought' the world was round, in the sense of 'believed it to be so,' he and his followers were thereby committed to a series of other beliefs and actions: to beliefs about routes to India, about what would happen if ships traveled far westward on the Atlantic, etc., precisely as thinking that the world was flat had committed those who held it to belief in the impossibility of circumnavigation, and in the limitation of the earth to regions in the small civilized part of it Europeans were already acquainted with, etc.

The earlier thought, belief in the flatness of the earth, had some foundation in evidence; it rested upon what men could see easily within the limits of their vision. But this evidence was not further looked into; it was not checked by considering other evidence; there was no search for new evidence. Ultimately the belief rested on laziness, inertia, custom, absence of courage and energy in the investigation. The later belief rests upon careful and extensive study, upon purposeful widening of the area of observation, upon reasoning out the conclusions of alternative conceptions to see what would follow in case one or the other were adopted for belief. As distinct from the first kind of thinking there was an orderly chain of ideas; as distinct from the second, there was a controlling purpose and end; as distinct from the third, there was personal examination, scrutiny, inquiry.

Because Columbus did not accept unhesitatingly the current traditional theory, because he doubted and inquired, he arrived at his thought. Skeptical of what, from long habit, seemed most certain, and credulous of what seemed impossible, he went on thinking until he could produce evidence for both his confidence and his disbelief. Even if his conclusion had finally turned out wrong, it would have been a different sort of belief from those it antagonized, because it was reached by a different method. *Active, persistent, and careful consideration of any belief or supposed form of knowledge in the light of the grounds that support it and the further conclusions to which it tends* constitutes reflective thought. Any one of the first three kinds of thought may elicit this type; but once begun, it includes a conscious and voluntary effort to establish belief upon a firm basis of evidence and rationality.

THE CENTRAL FACTOR IN THINKING

The Suggestion of Something Not Observed

There are, however, no sharp lines of demarcation between the various operations just outlined. The problem of attaining correct habits of reflection would be much easier than it is, did not the different modes of thinking blend insensibly into one another. So far, we have considered rather extreme instances of each kind in order to get the field clearly before us. Let us now reverse this operation; let us consider a rudimentary case of thinking, lying between careful examination of evidence and a mere irresponsible stream of fancies. A man is walking on a warm day. The sky was clear the last time he observed it; but presently he notes, while occupied primarily with other things, that the air is cooler. It occurs to him that it is probably going to rain; looking up, he sees a dark cloud between him and the sun, and he then quickens his steps. What, if anything, in such a situation can be called thought? Neither the act of walking nor the noting of the cold is a thought. Walking is one direction of activity; looking and noting are other modes of activity. The likelihood that it will rain is, however, something *suggested*. The pedestrian *feels* the cold; first he *thinks* of clouds, then he looks and perceives them, and then he thinks of something he does not see: a storm. This *suggested possibility* is the idea, the thought. If it is believed in as a genuine possibility which may occur, it is the kind of thought which falls within the scope of knowledge and which requires reflective consideration.

Up to a certain point there is the same sort of situation as when one who looks at a cloud is reminded of a human figure and face. Thinking in both of these cases (the cases of belief and of fancy) involves noting or perceiving a fact, followed by something else that is not observed but that is brought to mind, suggested by the thing seen. One thing reminds us, as we say, of the other. Side by side, however, with this factor of agreement in the two cases of suggestion is a factor of marked disagreement. We do not *believe* in the face suggested by the cloud; we do not consider at all the probability of its being a fact. There is no *reflective* thought. The danger of rain, on the contrary, presents itself to us as a genuine possibility—a fact of the same nature as the observed coolness. Put differently, we do not regard the cloud as meaning or indicating a face, but merely as suggesting it, while we do consider that the coolness may *mean* rain. In the first case, on seeing an object, we just happen, as we say, to think of something else; in the second, we consider the *possibility and nature of the connection between the object seen and the object suggested*. The seen thing is regarded as in some way *the ground or basis of belief* in the suggested thing; it possesses the quality of *evidence*.

The Function of Signifying

This function whereby one thing signifies or indicates another, thus leading us to consider how far the one may be regarded as warrant for belief in the other, is, then, the central factor in all reflective or distinctively intellectual thinking. By calling up various situations to which such terms as *signifies* and *indicates* apply, the student will realize for himself the actual facts denoted. Synonyms for these terms are: points to, tells of, betokens, prognosticates, represents, stands for, implies.[1] We also say one thing portends another, is ominous of another, or a symptom of it, or a key to it, or (if the connection is quite obscure) that it gives a hint, clue, or intimation. Reflection is not identical with the mere fact that one thing indicates, means, another thing. It commences when we begin to inquire into the reliability, the worth, of any particular indication; when we try to test its value and see what guarantee there is that the existing data *really* point to the idea that is suggested in such a way as to *justify* acceptance of the latter.

Reflection Implies Belief on Evidence

Reflection thus implies that something is believed in (or disbelieved in), not on its own direct account, but through something else which stands as witness, evidence, proof, voucher, warrant; that is, as *ground of belief.* At one time, rain is actually felt or directly experienced; at another time, we *infer* that it has rained from the appearance of the grass and trees, or that it is going to rain because of the condition of the air or the state of the barometer. At one time, we see a man (or suppose we do) without any intermediary fact; at another time, we are not quite sure what we see, and hunt for accompanying facts that will serve as signs, indications, tokens of what we are to believe.

Thinking, for the purposes of this inquiry, is accordingly defined as *that operation in which present facts suggest other facts (or truths) in such a way as to induce belief in what is suggested on the ground of real relation in the things themselves,* a relation between what suggests and what is suggested. A cloud *suggests* a weasel or a whale; it does not *mean* the latter, because there is no tie, or bond, in the things themselves between what is seen and what is suggested. Ashes not merely suggest a previous fire, but they signify there has been a fire, because ashes are produced by combustion and, if they are genuine ashes, only by combustion. It is an objective connection, the link in actual things, that makes one thing the ground, warrant, evidence, for believing in something else.

PHASES OF REFLECTIVE THINKING

We may carry our account further by noting that *reflective* thinking, in distinction from other operations to which we apply the name of thought, involves (1) a state of doubt, hesitation, perplexity, mental difficulty, in which thinking originates, and (2) an act of searching, hunting,

---

[1] *Implies* is more often used when a principle or general truth brings about belief in some other truth; the other phrases are more frequently used to denote the cases in which a fact or event leads us to believe in some other fact or in a law.

inquiring, to find material that will resolve the doubt, settle and dispose of the perplexity.

The Importance of Uncertainty and of Inquiry

In our illustration, the shock of coolness generated confusion and suspended belief, at least momentarily. Because it was unexpected, it was a shock or an interruption needing to be accounted for, identified, or placed. To say that the abrupt occurrence of the change of temperature constitutes a problem may sound forced and artificial; but if we are willing to extend the meaning of the word *problem* to whatever—no matter how slight and commonplace in character—perplexes and challenges the mind so that it makes belief at all uncertain, there is a genuine problem, or question, involved in an experience of sudden change.

The turning of the head, the lifting of the eyes, the scanning of the heavens, are activities adapted to bring to recognition facts that will answer the question presented by the sudden coolness. The facts as they first presented themselves were perplexing; they suggested, however, clouds. The act of looking was an act to discover whether this suggested explanation held good. It may again seem forced to speak of this looking, almost automatic, as an act of research, or inquiry. But once more, if we are willing to generalize our conceptions of our mental operations to include the trivial and ordinary as well as the technical and recondite, there is no good reason for refusing to give this title to the act of looking. For the result of the act is to bring facts before the mind that enable a person to reach a conclusion on the basis of evidence. In so far, then, as the act of looking was deliberate, was performed with the intention of getting an external basis on which to rest a belief, it exemplifies in an elementary way the operation of hunting, searching, inquiring, involved in any reflective operation.

Another instance, commonplace also, yet not quite so trivial, may enforce this lesson. A man traveling in an unfamiliar region comes to a branching of the road. Having no sure knowledge to fall back upon, he is brought to a standstill of hesitation and suspense. Which road is right? And how shall his perplexity be resolved? There are but two alternatives: he must either blindly and arbitrarily take his course, trusting to luck for the outcome, or he must discover grounds for the conclusion that a given road is right. Any attempt to decide the matter by thinking will involve inquiring into other facts, whether brought to mind by memory, or by further observation, or by both. The perplexed wayfarer must carefully scrutinize what is before him and he must cudgel his memory. He looks for evidence that will support belief in favor of either of the roads—for evidence that will weight down one suggestion. He may climb a tree; he may go first in this direction, then in that, looking, in either case, for signs, clues, indications. He wants something in the nature of a signboard or a map, and *his reflection is aimed at the discovery of facts that will serve this purpose.*

The foregoing illustration may be generalized. Thinking begins in what may fairly enough be called a *forked-road* situation, a situation that is ambiguous, that presents a dilemma, that proposes alternatives. As long as our activity glides smoothly along from one thing to another, or as long as we permit our imagination to entertain fancies at pleasure, there is no call for reflection. Difficulty or obstruction in the way of reaching a belief brings us, however, to a pause. In the suspense of uncertainty, we metaphorically climb a tree; we try to find some standpoint from which we may survey additional facts and, getting a more commanding view of the situation, decide how the facts stand related to one another.

The Regulation of Thinking by Its Purpose

Demand for the solution of a perplexity is the steadying and guiding factor in the entire process of reflection. Where there is no question of a problem to be solved or a difficulty to be surmounted, the course of suggestions flows on at random; we have the first type of thought described. If the stream of suggestions is controlled simply by their emotional congruity, their fitting agreeably into a single picture or story, we have the second type. But a question to be answered, an ambiguity to be resolved, sets up an end and holds the current of ideas to a definite channel. Every suggested conclusion is tested by its reference to this regulating end, by its pertinence to the problem in hand. This need of straightening out a perplexity also controls the kind of inquiry undertaken. A traveler whose end is the most beautiful path will look for other signs and will test suggestions on another basis than if he wishes to discover the way to a given city. *The nature of the problem fixes the end of thought*, and *the end controls the process of thinking*.

SUMMARY

We may recapitulate by saying that the origin of thinking is some perplexity, confusion, or doubt. Thinking is not a case of spontaneous combustion; it does not occur just on 'general principles.' There is something that occasions and evokes it. General appeals to a child (or to a grown-up) to think, irrespective of the existence in his own experience of some difficulty that troubles him and disturbs his equilibrium, are as futile as advice to lift himself by his boot-straps.

Given a difficulty, the next step is suggestion of some way out—the formation of some tentative plan or project, the entertaining of some theory that will account for the peculiarities in question, the consideration of some solution for the problem. The data at hand cannot supply the solution; they can only suggest it. What, then, are the sources of the suggestion? Clearly, past experience and a fund of relevant knowledge at one's command. If the person has had some acquaintance with similar situations, if he has dealt with material of the same sort before, suggestions more or less apt and helpful will arise. But unless there has been some analogous experience, confusion remains mere confusion. Even when a child (or a grown-up) has a problem, it is wholly futile to urge him to think when he has no prior experiences that involve some of the same conditions.

There may, however, be a state of perplexity and also previous experience out of which suggestions emerge, and yet thinking need not be reflective. For the person may not be sufficiently *critical* about the ideas that occur to him. He may jump at a conclusion without weighing the grounds on which it rests; he may forego or unduly shorten the act of hunting, inquiring; he may take the first 'answer,' or solution, that comes to him because of mental sloth, torpor, impatience to get something settled. One can think reflectively only when one is willing to endure suspense and to undergo the trouble of searching. To many persons both suspense of judgment and intellectual search are disagreeable; they want to get them ended as soon as possible. They cultivate an over-positive and dogmatic habit of mind, or feel perhaps that a condition of doubt will be regarded as evidence of mental inferiority. It is at the point where examination and test enter into investigation that the difference between reflective thought and bad thinking comes in. To be genuinely thoughtful, we must be willing to sustain and protract that state of doubt which is the stimulus to thorough inquiry, so as not to accept an idea or make positive assertion of a belief until justifying reasons have been found.

Toward Dialogue

Dewey concludes with the general thesis that the most productive kind of thinking always begins in doubt. If we take that criterion to its ultimate limit, the greatest doubter of them all—Descartes—would belong in the scientific tradition. Descartes began by doubting everything—the existence of the world, the tree outside his window, even his own existence. But, he said, I cannot doubt the existence of one thing: my doubting. Thus, with the primitive and self-affirming proposition "I doubt (think)," Descartes proceeded to the next step, i.e., ". . . therefore, I am."

Peirce, Dewey's predecessor, ruled out this Cartesian, "wholesale" doubt, claiming that nobody actually started thinking this way except Descartes. No one genuinely doubts his own existence and it is pointless to argue the necessity for doing so. We do, however, have little "retail" doubts—doubts one at a time about this or that feature of our experience —and it is these day–by–day doubts, Peirce said, that generate thinking.

One wonders, though, if Dewey and Peirce are entirely right about this. Doubting one's existence may not be a promising starting place. But how about other nagging, less "retail" doubts that all of us have?

Who am I? Am I important to anyone? Am I capable of loving others? What is the meaning of my life; why am I here? What is the meaning of human existence? What, if anything, is the point of it all? Where do these questions fit in the Dewey–Peirce scheme?

JOHN DEWEY

Analysis of Reflective Thinking

FACTS AND IDEAS

When a situation arises containing a difficulty or perplexity, the person who finds himself in it may take one of a number of courses. He may dodge it, dropping the activity that brought it about, turning to something else. He may indulge in a flight of fancy, imagining himself powerful or wealthy, or in some other way in possession of the means that would enable him to deal with the difficulty. Or, finally, he may face the situation. In this case, he begins to reflect.

Reflection Includes Observation

The moment he begins to reflect, he begins of necessity to observe in order to take stock of conditions. Some of these observations are made by direct use of the senses; others by recollecting observations previously made either by himself or by others. The person who had the engagement to keep, notes with his eyes his present location, recalls the place where he should arrive at one o'clock, and brings back to mind the means of transportation with which he is acquainted and their respective locations. In this way he gets as clear and distinct a recognition as possible of the nature of the situation with which he has to deal. Some of the conditions are obstacles and others are aids, resources. No matter whether these conditions come to him by direct perception or by memory, they form the '*facts* of the case.' They are the things that are *there*, that have to be reckoned with. Like all facts, they are stubborn. They cannot be got out of the way by magic just because they are disagreeable. It is no use to *wish* they did not exist or were different. They must be taken for just what they are. Hence observation and recollection must be used to the full so as not to glide over or to mistake important features. Until the habit of thinking is well formed, facing the situation to

From *How We Think*, 2nd ed. (Boston: D. C. Heath and Company, 1933), pp. 102–118.

discover the facts requires an effort. For the mind tends to dislike what is unpleasant and so to sheer off from an adequate notice of that which is especially annoying.

Reflection Includes Suggestions

Along with noting the conditions that constitute the facts to be dealt with, suggestions arise of possible courses of action. Thus the person of our illustration thinks of surface cars, elevated trains, and the subway. These alternative suggestions compete with one another. By comparison he judges which alternative is best, which one is the more likely to give a satisfactory solution. The comparison takes place indirectly. The moment one thinks of a possible solution and holds it in suspense, he turns back to the facts. He has now a point of view that leads him to new observations and recollections and to a reconsideration of observations already made in order to test the worth of the suggested way out. Unless he uses the suggestion so as to guide to new observations instead of exercising suspended judgment, he accepts it as soon as it presents itself. Then he falls short of truly reflective thought. The newly noted facts may (and in any complex situation surely will) cause new suggestions to spring up. These become clews to further investigation of conditions. The results of this survey test and correct the proposed inference or suggest a new one. This continuous interaction of the facts disclosed by observation and of the suggested proposals of solution and the suggested methods of dealing with conditions goes on till some suggested solution meets all the conditions of the case and does not run counter to any discoverable feature of it.

Data and Ideas Are Correlative and Indispensable
Factors in Reflection

A technical term for the observed facts is *data*. The data form the material that has to be interpreted, accounted for, explained; or, in the case of deliberation as to what to do or how to do it, to be managed and utilized. The suggested solutions for the difficulties disclosed by observation form *ideas*. Data (facts) and ideas (suggestions, possible solutions) thus form the two indispensable and correlative factors of all reflective activity. The two factors are carried on by means respectively of *observation* (in which for convenience is included memory of prior observations of similar cases) and *inference*. The latter runs beyond what is actually noted, beyond what is found, upon careful examination, to be actually present. It relates, therefore, to what is *possible*, rather than to what is actual. It proceeds by anticipation, supposition, conjecture, imagination. All foresight, prediction, planning, as well as theorizing and speculation, are characterized by excursion from the actual into the possible. Hence (as we have already seen) what is inferred demands a double test: first, the process of forming the idea or supposed solution is checked by constant cross reference to the conditions observed to be actually present; secondly, the idea *after* it is formed is tested by *acting* upon it, overtly if possible, otherwise in imagination. The consequences of this action confirm, modify, or refute the idea.

We shall illustrate what has been said by a simple case. Suppose you are walking where there is no regular path. As long as everything goes smoothly, you do not have to think about your walking; your already formed habit takes care of it. Suddenly you find a ditch in your way. You think you will jump it (supposition, plan); but to make sure, you survey it with your eyes (observation), and you find that it is pretty wide and that the bank on the other side is slippery (facts, data). You then wonder if the ditch may not be narrower somewhere else (idea), and you look up and down the stream (observation) to see how matters stand (test of idea by observation). You do not find any good place and so are thrown back upon forming a new plan. As you are casting about, you discover a log (fact again). You ask yourself whether you could not haul that to the ditch and get it across the ditch to use as a bridge (idea again). You judge that idea is worth trying, and so you get the log and manage to put it in place and walk across (test and confirmation by overt action).

If the situation were more complicated, thinking would of course be more elaborate. You can imagine a case in which making a raft, constructing a pontoon bridge, or making a dugout would be the ideas that would finally come to mind and have to be checked by reference to conditions of action (facts). Simple or complicated, relating to what to do in a practical predicament or what to infer in a scientific or philosophic problem, there will always be the two sides: the conditions to be accounted for, dealt with, and the ideas that are plans for dealing with them or are suppositions for interpreting and explaining the phenomena.

In predicting an eclipse, for example, a multitude of observed facts regarding position and movements of earth, sun, and moon, comes in on one side, while on the other side the ideas employed to predict and explain involve extensive mathematical calculations. In a philosophic problem, the facts or data may be remote and not susceptible of direct observation by the senses. But still there will be data, perhaps of science, or of morals, art, or the conclusions of past thinkers, that supply the subject matter to be dealt with and by which theories are checked. On the other side, there are the speculations that come to mind and that lead to search for additional subject matter which will both develop the proposed theories as ideas and test their value. Mere facts or data are dead, as far as mind is concerned, unless they are used to suggest and test some idea, some way out of a difficulty. Ideas, on the other hand, are *mere* ideas, idle speculations, fantasies, dreams, unless they are used to guide new observations of, and reflections upon, actual situations, past, present, or future. Finally, they must be brought to some sort of check by actual given material or else remain ideas. Many ideas are of great value as material of poetry, fiction, or the drama, but not as the stuff of knowledge. However, ideas may be of intellectual use to a penetrating mind even when they do not find any immediate reference to actuality, provided they stay in the mind for use when new facts come to light.

THE ESSENTIAL FUNCTIONS OF REFLECTIVE ACTIVITY

We now have before us the material for the analysis of a complete act of reflective activity. In the preceding chapter we saw that the two limits of every unit of thinking are a perplexed, troubled, or confused situation at the beginning and a cleared-up, unified, resolved situation at the close. The first of these situations may be called *pre*-reflective. It sets the problem to be solved; out of it grows the question that reflection has to answer. In the final situation the doubt has been dispelled; the situation is *post*-reflective; there results a direct experience of mastery, satisfaction, enjoyment. Here, then, are the limits within which reflection falls.

Five Phases, or Aspects, of Reflective Thought

In between, as states of thinking, are (1) *suggestions*, in which the mind leaps forward to a possible solution; (2) an intellectualization of the difficulty or perplexity that has been *felt* (directly experienced) into a *problem* to be solved, a question for which the answer must be sought; (3) the use of one suggestion after another as a leading idea, or *hypothesis*, to initiate and guide observation and other operations in collection of factual material; (4) the mental elaboration of the idea or supposition as an idea or supposition (*reasoning*, in the sense in which reasoning is a part, not the whole, of inference); and (5) testing the hypothesis by overt or imaginative action.

We shall now take up the five phases, or functions, one by one.

The First Phase, Suggestion

The most 'natural' thing for anyone to do is to go ahead; that is to say, to *act* overtly. The disturbed and perplexed situation arrests such direct activity temporarily. The tendency to continue *acting* nevertheless persists. It is diverted and takes the form of an idea or a suggestion. The *idea* of what to do when we find ourselves 'in a hole' is a substitute for direct action. It is a vicarious, anticipatory way of acting, a kind of dramatic rehearsal. Were there only one suggestion popping up, we should undoubtedly adopt it at once. But where there are two or more, they collide with one another, maintain the state of suspense, and produce further inquiry. The first suggestion in the instance recently cited was to jump the ditch, but the perception of conditions inhibited that suggestion and led to the occurrence of other ideas.

Some inhibition of *direct* action is necessary to the condition of hesitation and delay that is essential to thinking. Thought is, as it were, conduct turned in upon itself and examining its purpose and its conditions, its resources, aids, and difficulties and obstacles.

The Second Phase, Intellectualization

We have already noted that it is artificial, so far as thinking is concerned, to start with a ready-made problem, a problem made out of whole cloth or arising out of a vacuum. In reality such a 'problem' is simply an assigned *task*. There is not at first a situation *and* a problem, much less just a problem and no situation. There is a troubled, perplexed, trying situation, where the difficulty is, as it were, spread throughout the entire situation, infecting it as a whole. If we knew just what the difficulty was and where it lay, the job of reflection would be much easier than it is. As the saying truly goes, a question well put is half answered. In fact, we know what the problem *exactly* is simultaneously with finding a way out and getting it resolved. Problem and solution stand out *completely* at the same time. Up to that point, our grasp of the problem has been more or less vague and tentative.

A blocked suggestion leads us to reinspect the conditions that confront us. Then our uneasiness, the shock of disturbed activity, gets stated in some degree on the basis of observed conditions, of objects. The width of the ditch, the slipperiness of the banks, not the mere presence of a ditch, is the trouble. The difficulty is getting located and defined; it is becoming a true problem, something intellectual, not just an annoyance at being held up in what we are doing. The person who is suddenly blocked and troubled in what he is doing by the thought of an engagement to keep at a time that is near and a place that is distant has the suggestion of getting there at once. But in order to carry this suggestion into effect, he has to find means of transportation. In order to find them he has to note his present position and its distance from the station, the present time, and the interval at his disposal. Thus the perplexity is more precisely located: just so much ground to cover, so much time to do it in.

The word 'problem' often seems too elaborate and dignified to denote what happens in minor cases of reflection. But in every case where reflective activity ensues, there is a process of *intellectualizing* what at first is merely an *emotional* quality of the whole situation. This conversion is effected by noting more definitely the conditions that constitute the trouble and cause the stoppage of action.

The Third Phase, the Guiding Idea, Hypothesis

The first suggestion occurs spontaneously; it comes to mind automatically; it *springs* up; it "pops," as we have said, "into the mind"; it flashes upon us. There is no direct control of its occurrence; the idea just comes or it does not come; that is all that can be said. There is nothing *intellectual* about its occurrence. The intellectual element consists in *what we do with it,* how we use it, *after* its sudden occurrence as an idea. A controlled use of it is made possible by the state of affairs just described. In the degree in which we define the difficulty (which is effected by stating it in terms of objects), we get a better idea of the kind of solution that is needed. The facts or data set the problem before us, and insight into the problem corrects, modifies, expands the suggestion that originally occurred. In this fashion the suggestion becomes a definite supposition or, stated more technically, a *hypothesis.*

Take the case of a physician examining a patient or a mechanic inspecting a piece of complicated machinery that does not behave properly. There is something wrong, so much is sure. But how to remedy it cannot be told until it is known *what* is wrong. An untrained person is likely to make a wild guess—the suggestion—and then proceed to act upon it in a random way, hoping that by good luck the right thing will be hit upon. So some medicine that appears to have worked before or that a neighbor has recommended is tried. Or the person fusses, monkeys, with the machine, poking here and hammering there on the chance of making the right move. The trained person proceeds in a very different fashion. He *observes* with unusual care, using the methods, the techniques, that the experience of physicians and expert mechanics in general, those familiar with the structure of the organism or the machine, have shown to be helpful in detecting trouble.

The idea of the solution is thus controlled by the diagnosis that has been made. But if the case is at all complicated, the physician or mechanic does not foreclose further thought by assuming that the suggested method of remedy is certainly right. He proceeds to act upon it tentatively rather than decisively. That is, he treats it as a guiding idea, a working hypothesis, and is led by it to make more observations, to collect more facts, so as to see if the *new* material is what the hypothesis calls for. He reasons that *if* the disease is typhoid, *then* certain phenomena will be found; and he looks particularly to see if *just* these conditions are present. Thus both the first and second operations are brought under control; the sense of the problem becomes more adequate and refined and the suggestion ceases to be a *mere* possibility, becoming a *tested* and, if possible, a *measured* probability.

The Fourth Phase, Reasoning (in the Narrower Sense)

Observations pertain to what exists in nature. They constitute the facts, and these facts both regulate the formation of suggestions, ideas, hypotheses, and test their probable value as indications of solutions. The ideas, on the other hand, occur, as we say, in our heads, in our minds. They not only occur there, but are capable, as well, of great development there. Given a fertile suggestion occurring in an experienced, well-informed mind, that mind is capable of elaborating it until there results an idea that is quite different from the one with which the mind started.

For example, the idea of heat in the third instance in the earlier chapter* was linked up with what the person already knew about heat—in his case, its expansive force—and this in turn with the contractive tendency of cold, so that the idea of expansion could be used as an explanatory idea, though the mere idea of heat would not have been of any avail. Heat was quite directly suggested by the observed conditions; water was felt to be hot. But only a mind with some prior information about heat would have reasoned that heat meant expansion, and then used the idea of expansion as a working hypothesis. In more complex cases, there are long trains of reasoning in which one idea leads up to another idea known by previous test to be related to it. The stretch of links brought to light by reasoning depends, of course, upon the store of knowledge that the mind is already in possession of. And this depends not only upon the prior experience and special education of the individual who is carrying on the inquiry, but also upon the state of culture and science of the age and place. Reasoning helps extend knowledge, while at the same time it depends upon what is already known and upon the facilities that exist for communicating knowledge and making it a public, open resource.

A physician to-day can develop, by reasoning from his knowledge, the implications of the disease that symptoms suggest to him as probable in a way that would have been impossible even a generation ago; just as, on the other hand, he can carry his observation of symptoms much farther because of improvement in clinical instruments and the technique of their use.

Reasoning has the same effect upon a suggested solution that more intimate and extensive observation has upon the original trouble. Acceptance of a suggestion in its first form is prevented by looking into it more thoroughly. Conjectures that seem plausible at first sight are often found unfit or even absurd when their full consequences are traced out. Even when reasoning out the bearings of a supposition does not lead to its rejection, it develops the idea into a form in which it is more apposite to the problem . . . Suggestions at first seemingly remote and wild are frequently so transformed by being elaborated into what follows from them as to become apt and fruitful. The development of an idea through reasoning helps supply intervening or intermediate terms which link together into a consistent whole elements that at first seemingly conflict with each other, some leading the mind to one inference and others to an opposed one.

MATHEMATICS AS TYPICAL REASONING. Mathematics affords the typical example of how far can be carried the operation of relating ideas to one another, without having to depend upon the observations of the senses. In geometry we start with a few simple conceptions, line, angle, parallel, surfaces formed by lines meeting, etc., and a few principles de-

---

* [An illustration of reflective thinking concerning the expansion and then contraction of air in drinking tumblers after they have been washed in hot soapsuds and placed mouth downward on a plate.]

fining equalities. Knowing something about the equality of angles made by parallel lines when they intersect a straight line, and knowing, by definition, that a perpendicular to a straight line forms two right angles, by means of a combination of these ideas we readily determine that the sum of the interior angles of a triangle is equal to two right angles. By continuing to trace the implications of theorems already demonstrated, the whole subject of plane figures is finally elaborated. The manipulation of algebraic symbols so as to establish a series of equations and other mathematical functions affords an even more striking example of what can be accomplished by developing the relation of ideas to one another.

When the hypothesis indicated by a series of scientific observations and experiments can be stated in mathematical form, that idea can be transformed to almost any extent, until it assumes a form in which a problem can be dealt with most expeditiously and effectively. Much of the accomplishment of physical science depends upon an intervening mathematical elaboration of ideas. It is not the mere presence of measurements in quantitative form that yields scientific knowledge, but that particular kind of mathematical statement which can be developed by reasoning into other and more fruitful forms—a consideration which is fatal to the claim to scientific standing of many educational measurements merely because they have a quantitative form.

The Fifth Phase, Testing the Hypothesis by Action

The concluding phase is some kind of testing by overt action to give *experimental corroboration*, or *verification*, of the conjectural idea. Reasoning shows that *if* the *idea* be adopted, certain consequences follow. So far the conclusion is hypothetical or conditional. If when we look we find present all the conditions demanded by the theory, and if we find the characteristic traits called for by rival alternatives to be lacking, the tendency to believe, to accept, is almost irresistible. Sometimes direct observation furnishes corroboration . . . In other cases, . . . experiment is required; that is, *conditions are deliberately arranged in accord with the requirements of an idea or hypothesis to see whether the results theoretically indicated by the idea actually occur.* If it is found that the experimental results agree with the theoretical, or rationally deduced, results, and if there is reason to believe that *only* the conditions in question would yield such results, the confirmation is so strong as to induce a conclusion—at least until contrary facts shall indicate the advisability of its revision.

Of course, verification does not always follow. Sometimes consequences show failure to confirm instead of corroboration. The idea in question is refuted by the court of final appeal. But a great advantage of possession of the habit of reflective activity is that failure is not *mere* failure. It is instructive. The person who really thinks learns quite as much from his failures as from his successes. For a failure indicates to the person whose thinking has been involved in it, and who has not come to it by mere blind chance, what further observations should be made. It suggests to him what modifications should be introduced in the hypothesis upon which he has been operating. It either brings to light a new problem or helps to define and clarify the problem on which he has been engaged. Nothing shows the trained thinker better than the use he makes of his errors and mistakes. What merely annoys and discourages a person not accustomed to thinking, or what starts him out on a new course of aimless attack by mere cut-and-try methods, is a stimulus and a guide to the trained inquirer.

The Sequence of the Five Phases Is Not Fixed

The five phases, terminals, or functions of thought, that we have noted do not follow one another in a set order. On the contrary, each step in genuine thinking does something to perfect the formation of a suggestion and promote its change into a leading idea or directive hypothesis. It does something to promote the location and definition of the problem. Each improvement in the idea leads to new observations that yield new facts or data and help the mind judge more accurately the relevancy of facts already at hand. The elaboration of the hypothesis does not wait until the problem has been defined and adequate hypothesis has been arrived at; it may come in at any intermediate time. And as we have just seen, any particular overt test need not be final; it may be introductory to new observations and new suggestions, according to what happens in consequence of it.

There is, however, an important difference between test by overt action in practical deliberations and in scientific investigations. In the former the practical commitment involved in overt action is much more serious than in the latter. An astronomer or a chemist performs overt actions, but they are for the sake of knowledge; they serve to test and develop his conceptions and theories. In practical matters, the main result desired lies outside of knowledge. One of the great values of thinking, accordingly, is that it defers the commitment to action that is irretrievable, that, once made, cannot be revoked. Even in moral and other practical matters, therefore, a thoughtful person treats his overt deeds as experimental so far as possible; that is to say, while he cannot call them back and must stand their consequences, he gives alert attention to what they teach him about his conduct as well as to the nonintellectual consequences. He makes a problem out of consequences of conduct, looking into the causes from which they probably resulted, especially the causes that lie in his own habits and desires.

In conclusion, we point out that the five phases of reflection that have been described represent only in outline the indispensable traits of reflective thinking. In practice, two of them may telescope, some of them may be passed over hurriedly, and the burden of reaching a conclusion may fall mainly on a single phase, which will then require a seemingly disproportionate development. No set rules can be laid down on such matters. The way they are managed depends upon the intellectual tact and sensitiveness of the individual. When things have come out wrong, it is, however, a wise practice to review the methods by which the unwise decision was reached, and see where the misstep was made.

One Phase May Be Expanded

In complicated cases some of the five phases are so extensive that they include definite subphases within themselves. In this case it is arbitrary whether the minor functions are regarded as parts or are listed as distinct phases. There is nothing especially sacred about the number five. For example, in matters of practical deliberation where the object is to decide what to do, it may be well to undertake a scrutiny of the underlying desires and motives that are operating; that is, instead of asking what ends and means will best satisfy one's wish, one may turn back to the attitudes of which the wish is the expression. It is a matter of indifference whether this search be listed as an independent problem, having its own phases, or as an additional phase in the original problem.

Reference to the Future and to the Past

Again, it has been suggested that reflective thinking involves a look into the future, a forecast, an anticipation, or a prediction, and that this should be listed as a sixth aspect, or phase. As a matter of fact, every intellectual suggestion or idea is anticipatory of some possible future experience, while the final solution gives a definite set toward the future. It is both a record of something accomplished and an assignment of a future method of operation. It helps set up an enduring habit of procedure. When a physician, for example, has diagnosed a case, he usually makes also a *prognosis*, a forecast, of the probable future course of the disease. And not only is his treatment a verification—or the reverse—of the idea or hypothesis about the disease upon which he has proceeded, but the result also affects his treatment of future patients. In some cases, the future reference may be so important as to require special elaboration. In this case, it may be presented as an added, distinct phase. Some of the investigations of an astronomical expedition to watch an eclipse of the sun may be directly intended, for example, to get material bearing on Einstein's theory. But the theory, itself, is so important that its confirmation or refutation will give a decided turn to the future of physical science, and this consideration is likely to be uppermost in the minds of scientists.

Of equal importance is the reference to the *past* involved in reflection. Of course, suggestions are dependent in any case upon one's past experience; they do not arise out of nothing. But while sometimes we go ahead with the suggestion without stopping to go back to the original experience of which it is the fruit, at other times we go consciously over the past experience in considerable detail as part of the process of testing the value of the suggestion.

For example, it occurs to a man to invest in real estate. Then he recalls that a previous investment of this kind turned out unfortunately. He goes over the former case, comparing it bit by bit with the present, to see how far the two cases are alike or unlike. Examination of the past may be the chief and decisive factor in thought. The most valuable reference to the past is likely, however, to come at the time the conclusion is reached. We noted earlier the importance of a final survey to secure a net formulation of the exact result and of the premises upon which it logically depends. This is not only an important part of the process of *testing*, but, as was stated in the earlier discussion, is almost necessary if good habits are to be built up. Ability to *organize* knowledge consists very largely in the habit of reviewing previous facts and ideas and relating them to one another on a new basis; namely, that of the conclusion that has been reached. A certain amount of this operation is included in the testing phase that has been described. But its influence upon the attitude of students is so important that it may be well at times so to emphasize it that it becomes a definite function, or phase, on its own account.

Toward Dialogue

On page 33, Dewey remarks that "many ideas are of great value as material of poetry, fiction, or the drama, but not as the stuff of knowledge." Notice here the confinement which the scientific philosopher wishes to place upon the term 'knowledge.' Some of us have difficulty accepting this confinement. Suppose I remark to someone, "We live in a time of alienation—of feeling estranged from our government, from our institutions, from our fellow citizens, even sometimes from ourselves." And suppose he and I both agree that this is, as we say, "common knowledge." Is the term 'knowledge' accurately used in this case?

Dewey would probably say no. If one proceeds through the several steps of the account he gives, it would not be easy to specify the kinds of evidence which would count as documenting the existence of "alienation." On the other hand, a feeling of alienation does undoubtedly prevail in the hearts and minds of many people. Moreover, such a theme frequently finds its way into "poetry, fiction, or the drama." Indeed, it is often only through these media that such a truth can be brought to our awareness.

It is disturbing to learn that the insights that come to us off the pages of a novel or over the footlights are not knowledge of the most human sort.

JOHN A. KOUWENHOVEN

What's "American" About America

The discovery of America has never been a more popular pastime than it is today. Scarcely a week goes by without someone's publishing a new book of travels in the bright continent. Magazines here and abroad provide a steady flow of articles by journalists, historians, sociologists, and philosophers who want to explain the United States to themselves, or to itself, or to others.

The discoverers of America have, of course, been describing their experiences ever since Captain John Smith wrote his first book about America almost three hundred and fifty years ago. But as Smith himself noted, not everyone "who hath bin at Virginia, understandeth or knows what Virginia is." Indeed, just a few years ago the Carnegie Corporation, which supports a number of college programs in American Studies, entitled its quarterly report "Who Knows America?" and went on to imply that nobody does, not even "our lawmakers, journalists, civic leaders, diplomats, teachers, and others."

There is, of course, the possibility that some of the writers who have explored, vicariously or in person, this country's past and present may have come to understand or know what America really is. But how is the lay inquirer to judge which accounts to trust? Especially since most of the explorers seem to have found not one but two or more antipodal and irreconcilable Americas. The Americans, we are convincingly told, are the most materialistic of peoples, and, on the other hand, they are the most idealistic; the most revolutionary, and, conversely, the most conservative; the most rampantly individualistic, and, simultaneously, the most gregarious and herdlike; the most irreverent toward their elders, and, contrariwise, the most abject worshipers of "Mom." They have an unbridled admiration of everything big, from bulldozers to bosoms; and they are in love with everything diminutive, from the "small hotel" in the song to the "little woman" in the kitchen.

Maybe, as Henry James thought when he wrote *The American Scene*, it is simply that the country is "too large for any human convenience," too diverse in geography and in blood strains to make sense as any sort of unit. Whatever the reason, the conflicting evidence turns up wherever you look, and the observer has to content himself with some sort of pluralistic conception. The philosopher Santayana's way out was to say that the American mind was split in half, one half symbolized by the skyscraper, the other by neat reproductions of Colonial mansions (with surreptitious modern conveniences). "The American will," he concluded, "inhabits the skyscraper; the American intellect inhabits the Colonial mansion." Mark Twain also defined the split in architectural terms, but more succinctly: American houses, he said, had Queen Anne fronts and Mary Ann behinds.

And yet, for all the contrarieties, there remains something which I think we all feel to be distinctively American, some quality or characteristic underlying the polarities which—as Henry James himself went on to say—makes the American way of doing things differ more from any other nation's way than the ways of any two other Western nations differ from each other.

I am aware of the risks in generalizing. And yet it would be silly, I am convinced, to assert that there are certain things which are more American than others. Take the New York City skyline, for example— that ragged man-made Sierra at the eastern edge of the continent. Clearly, in the minds of immigrants and returning travelers, in the iconography of the admen who use it as a backdrop for the bourbon and airplane luggage they are selling, in the eyes of poets and of military strategists, it is one of the prime American symbols.

Let me start, then, with the Manhattan skyline and list a few things which occur to me as distinctively American. Then, when we have the list, let us see what, if anything, these things have in common. Here are a dozen items to consider:

1. The Manhattan skyline
2. The gridiron town plan
3. The skyscraper
4. The Model-T Ford
5. Jazz
6. The Constitution
7. Mark Twain's writing
8. Whitman's *Leaves of Grass*
9. Comic strips
10. Soap operas
11. Assembly-line production
12. Chewing gum

Here we have a round dozen artifacts which are, it seems to me, recognizably American, not likely to have been produced elsewhere. Granted that some of us take more pleasure in some of them than in others—that many people prefer soap opera to *Leaves of Grass* while others think Mark Twain's storytelling is less offensive than chewing gum—all twelve items are, I believe, widely held to be indigenous to our culture. The fact that many people in other lands like them too, and that some of them are nearly as acceptable overseas as they are here at home, does not in any way detract from their obviously American character. It merely serves to remind us that to be American does not mean to be inhuman—a fact which, in certain moods of self-criticism, we are inclined to forget.

What, then, is the "American" quality which these dozen items share? And what can that quality tell us about the character of our culture, about the nature of our civilization?

SKYLINES AND SKYSCRAPERS

Those engaged in discovering America often begin by discovering the Manhattan skyline, and here as well as elsewhere they discover apparently irreconcilable opposites. They notice at once that it doesn't make any sense, in human or aesthetic terms. It is the product of insane politics, greed, competitive ostentation, megalomania, the worship of false gods. Its by-products, in turn, are traffic jams, bad ventilation, noise, and all the other ills that metropolitan flesh is heir to. And the net result is, illogically enough, one of the most exaltedly beautiful things man has ever made.

Perhaps this paradoxical result will be less bewildering if we look for a moment at the formal and structural principles involved in the skyline. It may be helpful to consider the skyline as we might consider a lyric poem, or a novel, if we were trying to analyze its aesthetic quality.

Looked at in this way, it is clear that the total effect which we call "the Manhattan skyline" is made up of almost innumerable buildings, each in competition (for height, or glamour, or efficiency, or respectability) with all of the others. Each goes its own way, as it were, in a carnival of rugged architectural individualism. And yet—as witness the universal feeling of exaltation and aspiration which the skyline as a whole evokes—out of this irrational, unplanned, and often infuriating chaos, an unforeseen unity has evolved. No building ever built in New York was placed where it was, or shaped as it was, because it would contribute to the aesthetic effect of the skyline—lifting it here, giving it mass there, or lending a needed emphasis. Each was built, all those now under construction are being built, with no thought for their subordination to any over-all effect.

What, then, makes possible the fluid and ever-changing unity which does, in fact, exist? Quite simply, there are two things, both simple in themselves, which do the job. If they were not simple, they would not work; but they are, and they do.

One is the gridiron pattern of the city's streets—the same basic pattern which accounts for Denver, Houston, Little Rock, Birmingham, and almost any American town you can name, and the same pattern which, in the form of square townships, sections, and quarter sections, was imposed by the Ordinance of 1785 on an almost continental scale as what Wolfgang Langewiesche has called "a diagram of the idea of the Social Contract," a blueprint for a future society in which men would live each in his own domain, free and equal, each man's domain clearly divided from his neighbor's.

Whatever its shortcomings when compared with the "discontinuous patterns" of modern planned communities, this artificial geometric grid —imposed upon the land without regard to contours or any preconceived pattern of social zoning—had at least the quality of rational simplicity. The section lines, along which roads and fences run due north-south and due east-west, and which are so clearly visible from a plane over most of the U.S.A., make most of the nation exactly what an airplane pilot wants country to be: graph paper. As Langewiesche, the pilot, has said: "You can time your [plane's] shadow with a stop-watch across two lines, and get your exact speed. You can head the airplane down a section line and check your compass. But you hardly need a compass. You simply draw your course on the map and see what angle it makes. Then you cross the sections at the same angle. You can't miss. If you want to go exactly west, you get on a fence and follow it." And this simple gridiron pattern, mimicked in the city's streets, horizontally controls the spacing and arrangement of the isolated rectangular shafts which go to make up the skyline.

The other thing which holds the skyline's diversity together is the structural principle of the skyscraper. When we think of individual buildings, we tend to think of details of texture, color, and form, of surface ornamentation or the lack of it. But as elements in Manhattan's skyline, these things are of little consequence. What matters there is the vertical thrust, the motion upward; and that is the product of cage, or skeleton, construction in steel—a system of construction which is, in effect, merely a three-dimensional variant of the gridiron street plan, extending vertically instead of horizontally.

The aesthetics of cage, or skeleton, construction have never been fully analyzed, nor am I equipped to analyze them. But as a lay observer, I am struck by fundamental differences between the effect created by height in the RCA building at Rockefeller Center, for example, and the effect created by height in Chartres cathedral or in Giotto's campanile. In both the latter (as in all the great architecture of the past) proportion and symmetry, the relation of height to width, are constituent to the effect. One can say of a Gothic cathedral, this tower is too high; of a Romanesque dome, this is top-heavy. But there is nothing inherent in cage construction to invite such judgments. A true skyscraper like the RCA building could be eighteen or twenty stories taller, or ten or a dozen stories shorter, without changing its essential aesthetic effect. Once steel cage construction has passed a certain height, the effect of transactive upward motion has been established; from there on, the point at which you cut it off is arbitrary and makes no difference.

Those who are familiar with the history of the skyscraper will remember how slowly this fact was realized. Even Louis Sullivan—greatest of the early skyscraper architects—thought in terms of having to close off and climax the upward motion of the tall building with an "attic" or cornice which should be, in its outward expression, "specific and conclusive." His lesser contemporaries worked for years on the blind assumption that the proportion and symmetry of masonry architecture must be preserved in the new technique. If with the steel cage one could go higher than with load-bearing masonry walls, the old aesthetic effects could be counterfeited by dressing the façade as if one or more buildings had been piled on top of one another—each retaining the illusion of being complete in itself. You can still see such buildings in New York: the first five stories perhaps a Greco-Roman temple, the next ten a neuter warehouse, and the final five or six an Aztec pyramid. That Aztec pyramid is simply a cheap and thoughtless equivalent of the more subtle Sullivan cornice. Both structures attempt to close and climax the upward thrust, to provide an effect similar to that of the *Katharsis* of Greek tragedy.

But the logic of cage construction requires no such climax. It has less to do with the inner logic of masonry forms than with that of the old Globe-Wernicke sectional bookcases, whose interchangeable units (with glass-flap fronts) anticipated by fifty years the modular unit systems of so-called modern furniture. Those bookcases were advertised in the nineties as "always complete but never finished"—a phrase which could with equal propriety have been applied to the Model-T Ford. Many of us remember with affection that admirably simple mechanism, forever susceptible to added gadgets or improved parts, each of which was interchangeable with what you already had.

Here, then, are the two things which serve to tie together the otherwise irrelevant components of the Manhattan skyline: the gridiron ground plan and the three-dimensional vertical grid of steel cage construction. And both of these are closely related to one another. Both are composed of simple and infinitely repeatable units.

THE STRUCTURE OF JAZZ

It was the French architect, Le Corbusier, who described New York's skyline as "hot jazz in stone and steel." At first glance this may sound as if it were merely a slick updating of Schelling's "Architecture . . . is frozen music," but it is more than that if one thinks in terms of the structural principles we have been discussing and the structural principles of jazz.

Let me begin by making clear that I am using the term jazz in its broadest significant application. There are circumstances in which it is important to define the term with considerable precision, as when you

are involved in discussion with a disciple of one of the many cults, orthodox or progressive, which devote themselves to some particular subspecies
of jazz. But in our present context we need to focus upon what all the
subspecies (Dixieland, Swing, Bop, or Progressive Jazz) have in common;
in other words, we must neglect the by no means uninteresting qualities
differentiating one from another, since it is what they have in common
which can tell us most about the civilization which produced them.

There is no definition of jazz, academic or otherwise, which does not
acknowledge that its essential ingredient is a particular kind of rhythm.
Improvisation is also frequently mentioned as an essential; but even if
it were true that jazz always involves improvisation, that would not distinguish it from a good deal of Western European music of the past.
It is the distinctive rhythm which differentiates all types of jazz from all
other music and which gives to all of its types a basic family resemblance.

It is not easy to define that distinctive rhythm. Winthrop Sargeant
has described it as the product of two superimposed devices: syncopa-
tion and poly-rhythm, both of which have the effect of constantly upsetting rhythmical expectations. Andre Hodeir, in his analytical study,
Jazz: Its Evolution and Essence, speaks of "an alternation of syncopa-
tions and notes played on the beat," which "gives rise to a kind of expectation that is one of jazz's subtlest effects."

As you can readily hear, if you listen to any jazz performance
(whether of the Louis Armstrong, Benny Goodman, or Dave Brubeck
variety), the rhythmical effect depends upon there being a clearly defined basic rhythmic pattern to enforce the expectations which are to be
upset. That basic pattern is the 4/4 or 2/4 beat underlying all jazz.
Hence the importance of the percussive instruments in jazz: the drums,
the guitar or banjo, the bull fiddle, the piano. Hence too the insistent
thump, thump, thump, thump which is so boring when you only half-
hear jazz—either because you are too far away, across the lake or in the
next room, or simply because you will not listen attentively. But hence
also the delight, the subtle effects of good jazz provides as the melodic
phrases evade, anticipate, and return to, and then again evade the steady
basic four-beat pulse which persists, implicitly or explicitly, throughout
the performance.

In other words, the structure of a jazz performance is, like that of
the New York skyline, a tension of cross-purposes. In jazz at its characteristic best, each player seems to be—and has the sense of being—on
his own. Each goes his own way, inventing rhythmic and melodic patterns which, superficially, seem to have as little relevance to one another
as the United Nations building does to the Empire State. And yet the
outcome is a dazzlingly precise creative unity.

In jazz that unity of effect is, of course, the result of the very thing
each of the players is flouting: namely, the basic 4/4 beat—that simple
rhythmic gridiron of identical and infinitely extendible units which holds
the performance together. As Louis Armstrong once wrote, you would

expect that if every man in a band "had his own way and could play as he wanted, all you would get would be a lot of jumbled-up, crazy noise." But, as he goes on to say, that does not happen, because the players know "by ear and sheer musical instinct" just when to leave the underlying pattern and when to get back on it.

What it adds up to, as I have argued elsewhere, is that jazz is the first art form to give full expression to Emerson's ideal of a union which is perfect only "when all the uniters are isolated." That Emerson's ideal is deeply rooted in our national experience need not be argued. Frederick Jackson Turner quotes a letter written by a frontier settler to friends back East, which in simple, unself-conscious words expresses the same reconciling of opposites. "It is a universal rule here," the frontiersman wrote, "to help one another, each one keeping an eye single to his own business."

One need only remember that the Constitution itself, by providing for a federation of separate units, became the infinitely extendible framework for the process of reconciling liberty and unity over vast areas and conflicting interests. Its seven brief articles, providing for checks and balances between interests, classes, and branches of the government, establish, in effect, the underlying beat which gives momentum and direction to a political process Richard Hofstadter has called "a harmonious system of mutual frustration"—a description that fits a jazz performance as well as it fits our politics.

The aesthetic effects of jazz, as Winthrop Sargeant long ago suggested, have as little to do with symmetry and proportion as have those of a skyscraper. Like the skyscraper, the total jazz performance does not build to an organically required climax; it can simply cease. The "piece" which the musicians are playing may, and often does, have a rudimentary Aristotelian pattern of beginning, middle, and end; but the jazz performance need not. In traditional Western European music, themes are developed. In jazz they are toyed with and dismantled. There is no inherent reason why the jazz performance should not continue for another 12 or 16 or 24 or 32 measures (for these are the rhythmic cages in jazz corresponding to the cages of a steel skeleton in architecture). As in the skyscraper, the aesthetic effect is one of motion, in this case horizontal rather than vertical.

Jazz rhythms create what can only be called momentum. When the rhythm of one voice (say the trumpet, off on a rhythmic and melodic excursion) lags behind the underlying beat, its four-beat measure carries over beyond the end of the underlying beat's measure into the succeeding one, which has already begun. Conversely, when the trumpet anticipates the beat, it starts a new measure before the steady underlying beat has ended one. And the result is an exhilarating forward motion which the jazz trumpeter Wingy Manone once described as "feeling an increase in tempo though you're still playing at the same tempo." Hence the importance in jazz of timing, and hence the delight and amusement of the so-called "break," in which the basic 4/4 beat ceases and a soloist goes off on a flight of fancy which nevertheless comes back surprisingly and unerringly to encounter the beat precisely where it would have been if it had kept going.

Once the momentum is established, it can continue until—after an interval dictated by some such external factor as the conventional length of phonograph records or the endurance of dancers—it stops. ("No stopping," as the signs on the thruways and parkways have it, "except for repairs.") And as if to guard against any Aristotelian misconceptions about an end, it is likely to stop on an unresolved chord, so that harmonically, as well as rhythmically, everything is left up in the air. Even the various coda-like devices employed by jazz performers at dances, such as the corny old "without a shirt" phrase of blessed memory, are often harmonically unresolved. They are merely conventional ways of saying "we quit," not, like Beethoven's insistent codas, ways of saying, "There now; that ties off all the loose ends; I'm going to stop now; done; finished; concluded; signed, sealed, delivered."

We think of jazz as a twentieth-century phenomenon, and it is true that it did not emerge as a national music until after the First World War. But there are close (and unexplored) analogies between jazz and other forms of popular arts which have deep roots in our national life. One is the nineteenth-century minstrel show. Constance Rourke gives a vivid description of it in her classic work on *American Humor:*

> Endmen and interlocutors spun out their talk with an air of improvisation. . . . In the dancing a strong individualism appeared, and the single dancer might perform his feats on a peck measure, and dancers might be matched against each other with high careerings which belonged to each one alone; but these excursions were caught within the broad effect. Beneath them all ran the deep insurgence of the Negro choruses . . . and the choral dancing of the walk-around made a resonant primitive groundwork.

Here we have several analogies with the structure of jazz—especially the improvisatory manner and the individual flights of fancy and fantasy held together by a rhythmic groundwork (the 4/4 beat of the walk-around). And there are other ways in which jazz is related to the minstrel show. The minstrel characters—Jim Crow, Zip Coon, Dan Tucker —were blackface creations, and many jazz musicians, both white and Negro, perpetuate the atmosphere of burnt-cork masquerade.

Related to these analogies are those between the form of jazz and the form of the humorous monologue, the dominant form in the tradition of American humor, from Seba Smith's Mayor Jack Downing to Mark Twain and Mr. Dooley and on down to the TV and night-club entertainers of our own time. In these humorous monologues the apparent "subject" is of little importance as is the tune from which a jazz performance takes off. It is the "talking around" the subject without hitting it, the digressing and ramifying, which matters.

TWAIN AND WHITMAN

Since Mark Twain is the acknowledged master of the humorous monologue in our literature, let us look at an example of his work. His writing was, of course, very largely the product of oral influences. He was a born storyteller, and he always insisted that the oral form of the humorous story was high art. Its essential tool (or weapon), he said, is the pause—which is to say, timing. "If the pause is too long the impressive point is passed," he wrote, "and the audience have had time to divine that a surprise is intended—and then you can't surprise them, of course." In other words, he saw the pause as a device for upsetting expectations, like the jazz "break."

Mark, as you know, was by no means a formal perfectionist. In fact he took delight in being irreverent about literary form. Take, for example, his account of the way *Pudd'nhead Wilson* came into being. It started out to be a story called "Those Extraordinary Twins," about a youthful freak consisting, he said, of a "combination consisting of two heads and four arms joined to a single body and a single pair of legs—and I thought I would write an extravagantly fantastic little story with this freak of nature for hero—or heroes—a silly young Miss [named Rowena] for heroine, and two old ladies and two boys for the minor parts."

But as he got writing the tale, it kept spreading along and other people began intruding themselves—among them Pudd'nhead, and a woman named Roxana, and a young fellow named Tom Driscoll, who before the book was half finished had taken things almost entirely into their own hands and were "working the whole tale as a private venture of their own."

From this point, I want to quote Mark directly, because in the process of making fun of fiction's formal conventions he employs a technique which is the verbal equivalent of the jazz "break"—a technique of which he was a master.

When the book was finished and I came to look round to see what had become of the team I had originally started out with— Aunt Patsy Cooper, Aunt Betsy Hale, the two boys, and Rowena the light-weight heroine—they were nowhere to be seen; they had disappeared from the story some time or other. I hunted about and found them—found them stranded, idle, forgotten, and permanently useless. It was very awkward. It was awkward all around, but more particularly in the case of Rowena, because there was a love match on, between her and one of the twins that constituted the freak, and I had worked it up to a blistering heat and thrown in a quite dramatic love quarrel, [now watch Mark take off like a jazz trumpeter flying off on his own in a fantastic break] wherein Rowena scathingly denounced her betrothed for getting drunk, and scoffed at his explanation of how it had happened, and wouldn't listen to it, and had driven him from her in the usual "forever" way; and now here she sat crying and broken-hearted; for she had found that he had spoken only the truth; that it was not he, but the other half of the freak that had drunk the liquor that made him drunk; that her half was a prohibitionist and had never drunk a drop in his life, and although tight as a brick three days in the week, was wholly innocent of blame; and indeed, when sober, was constantly doing all he could to reform his brother, the other half, who never got any satisfaction out of drinking, anyway, because liquor never affected him. [Now he's going to get back on the basic beat again.] Yes, here she was, stranded with that deep injustice of hers torturing her poor torn heart.

Mark didn't know what to do with her. He couldn't just leave her there, of course, after making such a to-do over her; he'd have to account to the reader for her somehow. So he finally decided that all he could do was "give her the grand bounce." It grieved him, because he'd come to like her after a fashion, "notwithstanding she was such an ass and said such stupid, irritating things and was so nauseatingly sentimental"; but it had to be done. So he started Chapter Seventeen with: "Rowena went out in the back yard after supper to see the fireworks and fell down the well and got drowned."

> It seemed abrupt [Mark went on], but I thought maybe the reader wouldn't notice it, because I changed the subject right away to something else. Anyway it loosened up Rowena from where she was stuck and got her out of the way, and that was the main thing. It seemed a prompt good way of weeding out people that had got stalled, and a plenty good enough way for those others; so I hunted up the two boys and said "they went out back one night to stone the cat and fell down the well and got drowned." Next I searched around and found old Aunt Patsy Cooper and Aunt Betsy Hale where they were aground, and said "they went out back one night to visit the sick and fell down the well and got drowned." I was going to drown some of the others, but I gave up the idea, partly because I believed that if I kept that up it would arouse attention, . . . and partly because it was not a large well and would not hold any more anyway.

That was a long excursion—but it makes the point: that Mark didn't have much reverence for conventional story structure. Even his greatest book, which is perhaps also the greatest book written on this continent —*Huckleberry Finn*—is troublesome. One can scarcely find a criticism of the book which does not object, for instance, to the final episodes, in which Tom rejoins Huck and they go through that burlesque business of "freeing" the old Negro Jim—who is, it turns out, already free. But, as T. S. Eliot was, I think, the first to observe, the real structure of *Huck Finn* has nothing to do with the traditional form of the novel—with exposition, climax, and resolution. Its structure is like that of the great river itself—without beginning and without end. Its structural units, or "cages," are the episodes of which it is composed. Its momentum is that of the tension between the river's steady flow and the eccentric superimposed rhythms of Huck's flights from, and near recapture by, the restricting forces of routine and convention.

It is not a novel of escape; if it were, it would be Jim's novel, not Huck's. Huck is free at the start, and still free at the end. Looked at in this way, it is clear that *Huckleberry Finn* has as little need of a "conclusion" as has a skyscraper or a jazz performance. Questions of proportion and symmetry are as irrelevant to its structure as they are to the total effect of the New York skyline.

There is not room here for more than brief reference to the other "literary" items on our list: Whitman's *Leaves of Grass*, comic strips, and soap opera. Perhaps it is enough to remind you that *Leaves of Grass* has discomfited many a critic by its lack of symmetry and proportion, and that Whitman himself insisted: "I round and finish little, if anything; and could not, consistently with my scheme." As for the words of true poems, Whitman said in the "Song of the Answerer"—

> They bring none to his or her terminus or to be
>   content and full,
> Whom they take they take into space to behold the
>   birth of stars, to learn one of the meanings,
> To launch off with absolute faith, to sweep through
>   the ceaseless rings and never be quiet again.

Although this is not the place for a detailed analysis of Whitman's verse techniques, it is worth noting in passing how the rhythm of these lines reinforces their logical meaning. The basic rhythmical unit, throughout, is a three-beat phrase of which there are two in the first line (accents falling on *none, his,* and *term . . . be, tent,* and *full*), three in the second (*take, take,* and *space . . . hold, birth, stars . . . learn, one, mean*), and three in the third (*launch, ab, faith . . . sweep, cease, rings . . . nev, qui, gain*).

Superimposed upon the basic three-beat measure there is a flexible, non-metrical rhythm of colloquial phrasing. That rhythm is controlled in part by the visual effect of the arrangement in long lines, to each of which the reader tends to give equal duration, and in part by the punctuation within the lines. For example, the comma pause after the second three-beat measure in line two (after *stars*) tends, since the first line consisted of two such measures, to establish an expectation of rest which is upset by the line's continuing for another measure. Then, in the final line, the placement of the comma pause reverses the pattern, requiring a rest after the first measure and doubling up the remaining two.

It is the tension between the flexible, superimposed rhythm of the rhetorical patterns and the basic three-beat measure of the underlying framework which unites with the imagery and the logical meaning of the words to give the passage its restless, sweeping movement. It is this tension and other analogous aspects of the structure of *Leaves of Grass* which give to the book that "vista" Whitman himself claimed for it.

If I may apply to it T. S. Eliot's idea about *Huckleberry Finn*, the structure of the *Leaves* is open at the end. Its key poem may well be the "Song of the Open Road," as D. H. Lawrence believed. "Toward no goal," Lawrence wrote. "Always the open road. Having no direction even. . . . This was Whitman. And the true rhythm of the American continent speaking out in him."

As for the comics and soap opera, they too—on their own frequently humdrum level—have devised structures which provide for no ultimate climax, which come to no end demanded by symmetry or proportion. In them both there is a shift in interest away from the "How does it come out?" of traditional storytelling to "How are things going?" In a typical installment of Harold Gray's *Little Orphan Annie*, the final panel shows Annie walking purposefully down a path with her dog, Sandy, saying: "But if we're goin', why horse around? It's a fine night for walkin' . . . C'mon, Sandy . . . Let's go . . ." (It doesn't even end with a period, or full stop, but with the conventional three dots or suspension points, to indicate incompletion.) So too, in the soap operas, *Portia Faces Life*, in one form or another, day after day, over and over again. And the operative word is the verb "faces." It is the process of facing that matters.

AMERICA IS PROCESS

Here, I think, we are approaching the central quality which all the diverse items on our list have in common. That quality I would define as a concern with process rather than product—or, to re-use Mark Twain's words, a concern with the manner of handling experience or materials rather than with the experience or materials themselves. Emerson, a century ago, was fascinated by the way "becoming somewhat else is the perpetual game of nature." The universe, he said, "exists only in transit," and man is great "not in his goals but in his transitions."

This preoccupation with process is, of course, basic to modern science. "Matter" itself is no longer to be thought of as something fixed, but fluid and ever-changing. The modern sciences, as Veblen observed forty years ago, cluster about the "notion of process," the notion of "a sequence, or complex, of consecutive change." Similarly, modern economic theory has abandoned the "static equilibrium" analysis of the neo-classic economists, and in philosophy John Dewey's instrumentalism abandoned the classic philosophical interest in final causes for a scientific interest in the "mechanism of occurrences"—that is, process.

It is obvious, I think, that the American system of industrial mass production reflects this same focus of interest in its concern with production rather than products. And it is the mass-production system, *not* machinery, which has been America's contribution to industry.

In that system there is an emphasis different from that characteristic of handicraft production or even of machine manufacture. In both of these there was an almost total disregard of the means of production. The aristocratic ideal inevitably relegated interest in the means exclusively to anonymous peasants and slaves; what mattered to those who controlled and administered production was, quite simply, the finished product. In a mass-production system, on the other hand, it is the process of production itself which becomes the center of interest, rather than the product.

If we are aware of this fact, we usually regard it as a misfortune. We hear a lot, for instance, of the notion that our system "dehumanizes" the worker, turning him into a machine and depriving him of the satisfactions of finishing anything, since he performs only some repetitive operation. It is true that the unit of work in mass production is not a product but an operation. But the development of the system, in contrast with Charlie Chaplin's wonderful but wild fantasy of the assembly line, has shown the intermediacy of the stage in which the worker is doomed to frustrating boredom. Merely repetitive work, in the logic of mass production, can and must be done by machine. It is unskilled work which is doomed by it, not the worker. More and more skilled workers are needed to design products, analyze jobs, cut patterns, attend complicated machines, and coordinate the processes which comprise the productive system.

The skills required for these jobs are different, of course, from those required to make handmade boots or to carve stone ornament, but they are not in themselves less interesting or less human. Operating a crane in a steel mill, or a turret lathe, is an infinitely more varied and stimulating job than shaping boots day after day by hand. A recent study of a group of workers on an automobile assembly line makes it clear that many of the men object, for a variety of reasons, to those monotonous, repetitive jobs which (as we have already noted) should be—but in many cases are not yet—done by machine; but those who *like* such jobs like them because they enjoy the process. As one of them said: "Repeating the same thing you can catch up and keep ahead of yourself . . . you can get in the swing of it." The report of members of a team of British workers who visited twenty American steel foundries in 1949 includes this description of the technique of "snatching" a steel casting with a magnet, maneuvered by a gantry crane running on overhead rails:

> In its operation, the crane approaches a pile of castings at high speed with the magnet hanging fairly near floor level. The crane comes to a stop somewhere short of the castings, while the magnet swings forward over the pile, is dropped on to it, current switched on, and the hoist begun, at the same moment as the crane starts on its return journey. [And then, in words which might equally be applied to a jazz musician, the report adds:] The whole operation requires timing of a high order, and the impression gained is that the crane drivers derive a good deal of satisfaction from the swinging rhythm of the process.

This fascination with process has possessed Americans ever since Oliver Evans in 1785 created the first wholly automatic factory: a flour mill in Delaware in which mechanical conveyors—belt conveyors, bucket conveyors, screw conveyors—are interlinked with machines in a continuous process of production. But even if there were no other visible sign of the national preoccupation with process, it would be enough to point out that it was an American who invented chewing gum (in 1869) and that it is the Americans who have spread it—in all senses of the verb—throughout the world. A non-consumable confection, its sole appeal is the process of chewing it.

The apprehensions which many people feel about a civilization absorbed with process—about its mobility and wastefulness as well as about the "dehumanizing" effects of its jobs—derive, I suppose, from old habit and the persistence of values and tastes which were indigenous to a very different social and economic system. Whitman pointed out in *Democratic Vistas* ninety years ago that America was a stranger in her own house, that many of our social institutions, like our theories of literature and art, had been taken over almost without change from a culture which was not, as ours is, the product of political democracy and the machine. Those institutions and theories, and the values implicit in them, are still around, though some (like collegiate gothic, of both the architectural and intellectual variety) are less widely admired than formerly.

Change, or the process of consecutive occurrences, is, we tend to feel, a bewildering and confusing and lonely thing. All of us, in some moods, feel the "preference for the stable over the precarious and uncompleted" which, as John Dewey recognized, tempts philosophers to posit their absolutes. We talk fondly of the need for roots—as if man were a vegetable, not an animal with legs whose distinction it is that he can move and "get on with it." We would do well to make ourselves more familiar with the idea that the process of development is universal, that it is "the form and order of nature." As Lancelot Law Whyte has said, in *The Next Development in Man:*

> Man shares the special form of the universal formative process which is common to all organisms, and herein lies the root of his unity with the rest of organic nature. While life is maintained, the component processes in man never attain the relative isolation and static perfection of inorganic processes . . . The individual may seek, or believe that he seeks, independence, permanence, or perfection, but that is only through his failure to recognize and accept his actual situation.

As an "organic system" man cannot, of course, expect to achieve stability or permanent harmony, though he can create (and in the great arts of the past, has created) the illusion of them. What he can achieve is a continuing development in response to his environment. The factor which gives vitality to all the component processes in the individual and in society is "not permanence but development."

To say this is not to deny the past. It is simply to recognize that for a variety of reasons people living in America have, on the whole, been better able to relish process than those who have lived under the imposing shadow of the arts and institutions which Western man created in his tragic search for permanence and perfection—for a "closed system." They find it easy to understand what that very American philosopher William James meant when he told his sister that his house in Chocorua, New Hampshire, was "the most delightful house you ever saw; it has fourteen doors, all opening outwards." They are used to living in grid-patterned cities and towns whose streets, as Jean-Paul Sartre observed, are not, like those of European cities, "closed at both ends." As Sartre says in his essay on New York, the long straight streets and avenues of a gridiron city do not permit the buildings to "cluster like sheep" and protect one against the sense of space. "They are not sober little walks closed in between houses, but national highways. The moment you set foot on one of them, you understand that it has to go on to Boston or Chicago."

So, too, the past of those who live in the United States, like their future, is open-ended. It does not, like the past of most other people, extend downward into the soil out of which their immediate community or neighborhood has grown. It extends laterally backward across the plains, the mountains, or the sea to somewhere else, just as their future may at any moment lead them down the open road, the endless-vistaed street.

Our history is the process of motion into and out of cities; of westering and the counter-process of return; of motion up and down the social ladder—a long, complex, and sometimes terrifyingly rapid sequence of consecutive change. And it is this sequence, and the attitudes and habits and forms which it has bred, to which the term "America" really refers.

"America" is not a synonym for the United States. It is not an artifact. It is not a fixed and immutable ideal toward which citizens of this nation strive. It has not order or proportion, but neither is it chaos except as that is chaotic whose components no single mind can comprehend or control. America is process. And in so far as Americans have been "American"—as distinguished from being (as most of us, in at least some of our activities, have been) mere carriers of transplanted cultural traditions—the concern with process has been reflected in the work of their heads and hearts and hands.

Toward Dialogue

Kouwenhoven's argument is, in places, a trifle farfetched. For example, Twain and Whitman may be prototypical American authors. But Hemingway and Frost are just as representative of what appeals to the American reader, and neither of them could be characterized as "process" writers, spinning yarns or developing characters or shaping ideas without an ending in mind, for telling's own sake.

And there is the question of that standard artifact of Americana: baseball. Is baseball more process- than product-oriented? True, it runs on for nine innings, but cricket, an English game, runs to an indefinite number of innings, and is therefore more eligible as an instance of "infinite extendibility." And, although baseball is extendible in time, is it more popular or more representative of American tastes than spectator sports controlled by the clock such as football and basketball?

However Kouwenhoven might answer these questions, his is still a thesis worth thinking about. If a people become enraptured with the processes of experience, is it not likely that they will gradually lose interest in their destiny as a people, in their mission in the world, in their ultimate reason for living as they do? And if this point be reached, is it a heaven or a hell?

Further Readings

Feigl, H., and May Brodbeck, eds. *Readings in the Philosophy of Science.* New York: Appleton-Century-Crofts, 1953.

Fletcher, Joseph. *Situation Ethics.* Philadelphia: Westminster Press, 1966.

James, William. *Pragmatism.* Cleveland: World Publishing Company, 1955; originally published in 1907.

Reichenbach, H. *The Rise of Scientific Philosophy.* Berkeley: University of California Press, 1951.

Toulmin, S. E. *The Philosophy of Science.* London: Hutchinson's University Library, 1953.

Whitehead, A. N. *Science and the Modern World.* New York: Macmillan Company, 1946; originally published in 1925.

Scientific Philosophy in Education

If the philosophies of science have told us anything, it is that scientists know how to know. The practicing scientific investigator has worked out a successful method of arriving at workable, usable knowledge. Scientific thinkers have customarily been dogmatic about this achievement. For instance, William Heard Kilpatrick, a generation ago, wrote:

> . . . we can say that knowledge in the realm of the physical and allied sciences is now more extensive, more accurate, and more usable than had ever before been thought possible.
>
> Epistemology, the study of how knowledge is possible, is a term often used in connections like this. For the experimentalist, the practical question of epistemology is *solvitur ambulando* [resolved by going at it]. So far as concerns finding experimentally-determined knowledge, it is a fact. This method does it; it does furnish usable knowledge. The experimental method furnishes an ever increasing amount of ever more usable knowledge. No alternative plan or proposal is, in comparison, worthy of consideration. If anything attempted by man has established itself, this has.[1]

If we now know how to know and if the act of learning is a special instance of the act of knowing, then we can say that the methods of knowing employed by the scientist can be put to work in the classroom as methods of learning. In this sense, epistemology as the study of knowing is to learning what physiology is to the practice of medicine. The physician needs to understand the functioning of the human body before he can apply his skill to any particular symptom of his patient. Likewise, the educator needs a general theory of human knowing before he can assist any individual to come to know, i.e., to learn.

This passage from epistemology to classroom practice, from a theory of knowing to a theory of teaching, reveals the impact of science on educational thinking. The method of science, variously called "reflective thinking," "critical intelligence," "controlled inquiry," or the "Complete Act of Thought" (see John Dewey's explanation of the "C.A.T.," pages 33–40) is now recommended as the paradigm method of learning. Put the child in the role of investigator or inquirer, mobilize his energies around his own curiosities or interests, help him organize his learning activities into problem solving projects, and assist him in acquiring the information and knowledge relevant to his undertaking. In the act of solving his problem or satisfying his curiosity, he will simultaneously learn important subject matter and the art of learning itself. This art will eventually become more important to him than the specific subject matter learned, for it is the art of learning—inquiry and investi-

[1] *Philosophies of Education*, N. B. Henry, ed., Part I. Forty-first Yearbook of the National Society for the Study of Education (Chicago: The Society, 1942), p. 43.

gation—which is the mark of an educated person. When formal schooling ends after 12 or 16 years, it is better for the youngster to have acquired a method of managing experience than to have been furnished with a large, organized body of subject matter much of which is irrelevant to meaningful living in today's world.

Scientifically oriented educators make one other important claim, namely, that their method not only guides learning and knowing but also directs the process of making moral judgments and justifying values and attitudes. If the consequences of experience determine what is true, the consequences of experience also determine what is right and good. Moral judgments, when acted upon, lead to empirical results in human affairs; these results tell us whether the moral judgment in question is sound or unsound. Hence, boys and girls may go to school not only for knowledge but also for values and moral attitudes.

In the selections to follow, John Childs, veteran advocate of the Dewey tradition at Teachers College, Columbia University, explains how the empirical method can be used to nurture the young, develop patterns of thought, test values, and socialize inquiry. Donald O. Hebb, a psychologist, explains how the higher vertebrates and man depend upon new experiences and a constant supply of problems for psychological survival. The scientific method, in short, may be not merely a useful method of knowing, but also a response to a basic need in man.

An idea can best be understood sometimes by seeing what foolishness it can lead to. In "The Barometer Story," Alexander Calandra pokes fun at the science-oriented educator's insistence on learning through problem-solving. Finally, a paper of my own offers a capsule version of education conducted under the aegis of scientific inquiry.

JOHN L. CHILDS

The Morality of Inquiry

. . . the deepest moral issue in education is whether we shall treat each child as an end in himself, or whether his growth is to be subordinated to the maintenance of some pre-established system. We have also emphasized that the characteristic of a democratic program of education which distinguishes it from all authoritarian programs, is the fact that

---

From *Education and Morals* by John L. Childs. Copyright 1950, by Appleton-Century-Crofts, Inc. Reprinted by permission of Appleton-Century-Crofts, Division of Meredith Corporation.

it seeks to make the growth of each child the supreme objective. In the morality of democracy growth is the ultimate criterion because a democracy recognizes no good other than the good of individual human beings. It is this opposition to the sacrifice of the potentialities of the child to the requirements of any absolute system that gives significant moral meaning to the maxim that "growth is its own end."

GROUP NURTURE AND INDIVIDUAL GROWTH

But to say that "growth is its own end" is not to say that "growth" defines itself, or that the child should be left to develop in his own way. Nor is this *moral* individualism to be confused with the individualism of an atomistic social system in which each individual is a law unto himself. The good life is a community affair and its ways are learned, not inborn. As we have emphasized throughout this book, adults organize and maintain schools because they are convinced that the immature human being needs help in his efforts to attain the means of his own development. The most basic of all these adult contributions to the growth of the child is the provision of the conditions that will help him achieve a mind of his own. By growth of mind is meant growth of the capacity of the individual to have ideas, to form reasonable expectations, to make good judgments, and to take responsibility for the consequences of his deeds. Without this capacity for reflective behavior, a human being is less than a complete person. All authoritarian systems of education at some point or in some manner seek to curb this full intellectual development of the young. Insofar as a program of education molds the child so that he is deprived of his ability to inquire into a particular sphere of human experience, it confiscates some of the potentialities of his personhood.

We have also emphasized that the capacity to make good judgments —the capacity for reflection—is not an original endowment. Apart from the nurture of culture, human creatures do not acquire the meanings that enable them to share in the life of reason. Any program of education, therefore, that is committed to the development of the intellectual potentialities of the young must provide for the transmission of race experience. Democratic societies should, of course, strive to transmit their values in such a manner as to provide for their further development, but this does not make the rôle of transmission in a program of democratic education any the less important. Without the transmission of meaning there can be no significant nurture of mind, and we misconstrue the whole nature of the process of human development when we assume that freedom and individuality can be intelligibly opposed to social nurture and the communication of that which the group has achieved.

Experience also clearly shows that the immature acquire meanings —scientific, aesthetic and moral—as a result of their participation in group activities as well as by their study of printed materials. Indeed, learning from books attains its maximum possibilities only when it is associated with opportunity for direct experience in human affairs. We educate for intelligence—the capacity to make valid judgments—not by insistence on the mechanical rote learning of that which others have discovered and organized into systems of life and thought, but by providing varied means for the child to grow as a result of his own first-hand experience with the affairs of his physical and social surroundings. It is by virtue of this direct participation in the world of persons and things that each human being achieves the structure of habits, meanings, and appreciations that is required to provide him with a basis for his own individualized responses to the practices of his society.

A mature mind cannot be developed by a program devoted solely to the instruction of the child in meanings derived from the experiences of others—a program that excludes all opportunity for criticism and for learning from direct observation and experience. Books can do much to broaden and deepen the perspective from which we interpret our own life circumstances, but they do not constitute a substitute for direct experience. Knowledge of what the intellectual and moral leaders of mankind have thought can nourish imagination and help free us from provincialism and parochialism, but it cannot in and of itself provide the core of personhood. Background is background, and to become a mature mind one must have done more than accumulate a stock of verbal generalizations; he must also have had experience with those primary events from which all generalizations or principles have been developed, and within whose context all principles must be applied, tested, revised and expanded. Apart from perception of their connection with conditions of primary experience, scientific principles and moral generalizations are not apt to function as tools of understanding; they are likely to become a non-functional, verbal possession or burden.

In brief, to become persons, we must own our ideas and not be enslaved by them. We grasp the significance of meanings that others have discovered and formulated only as we master their functional value in our own experience. Hence, education for the growth of persons must be a process in which acquiring and inquiring—the study of human records and participation in life affairs—are so interrelated in the experience of the developing child that the knowledge he acquires about the world becomes a real part of his ability to function in that world.

To hold that primary experience is essential to the development of mind is also to hold that empirical or experimental procedures should constitute the basic method of the school in a democratic society. Now the selection of the method by which the young are to be educated is one of the most crucial decisions in the organization of a school. No single factor has greater influence on the development of the basic intellectual and emotional dispositions of the young than the pattern of the method which permeates and regulates their mode of experiencing and interpreting their surroundings. In the course of their experience, human groups have developed rival and conflicting methods of responding to life conditions and of interpreting the significance of human events. Each of these modes of behavior, analysis, and interpretation has its basic intellectual and moral presuppositions; each inescapably has its definite consequences in the life practices, attitudes, and allegiances of those who are nurtured under it. The choice of an educational method therefore involves more than a choice among rival pedagogical devices; it is literally a choice among basic life alternatives and it is attended by far-reaching moral consequences. If educators are concerned to keep faith with parents, they will not try to conceal the intellectual and moral consequences of the method, or methods, that the school uses in the nurture of their children. In this chapter, we shall seek to make explicit some of the moral factors involved in the consistent reliance upon empirical procedures in the education of the young.

EMPIRICAL METHOD AND THE NURTURE OF THE YOUNG

Man lives in a world in which he has to act. And the aim of any program of education governed by respect for human personality is to help each child make his own actions more meaningful and more effective. All parents want their children to grow in their ability to form "reasonable expectations," to behave responsibly, and to take a creative rôle in the activities of their society. They also want them to develop competency in some particular sphere of human activity. They recognize that direct participation in life activities is required if their children are to achieve these abilities and attitudes. To this extent, at least, the choice of an empirical method for the education of the young is not an arbitrary choice; it is in line with that which experience shows is essential to the welfare of man.

As a matter of fact, all schools, regardless of their formal theories about educational method, necessarily give considerable place to empirical and experimental procedures. Experimental attitudes and methods have become so dominant in certain areas of human experience that reliance on alternative modes of gaining knowledge and control has all but disappeared. This shift in life outlook and method in so many different fields is now exerting profound influence on our view of the way in which children should be educated in these fields.

For example, if a school is to teach the children to garden, it will make every effort—irrespective of whether the school is private or public, religious or secular—to provide for an actual experience in gardening. The young will be given experience in marking the field into garden plots, in the preparation of the soil for planting, in the selection of seeds and plants, in the cultivation of the soil to keep it soft and to prevent the growth of weeds, in the use of fertilizers, in the control of the various means of irrigation, in the use of sprays and powders to destroy parasites and insects, in the protection of the plants against animals, in the pruning and the staking of plants, as well as in the gathering and caring for the fruits and vegetables as they mature. Manuals that outline the general principles of gardening, along with special tracts that give details about the cultivation of particular plants will be used, and these may well lead eventually into more systematic studies and lectures on plant life, the chemistry of the soil, and similar technical or scientific topics. Training may also be given in the use and the care of the different materials and tools that are involved. These special instructions—printed and oral—are indispensable for the nurture of the young in the knowledge and techniques of gardening, but their use in the introduction of the young to the art of gardening does not signify a blind reliance on tradition or external authority. All of this information has been accumulated from experience and experiment, and it has functional bearing and sensed significance for the children because it is taught in connection with an activity in which they are directly engaged. The young, moreover, have opportunity to put the directions they receive from lectures and printed materials to the test of action. In connection with their own gardening activities, they are encouraged to observe and to evaluate what happens, when under specified conditions, certain definite operations are performed.

In sum, in the sphere of gardening it is universally recognized that all controlling principles are developed from within the matrix of the activity itself, and that the young can achieve the ability to care for growing things only as they have first-hand experience with them. The children learn to garden with skill, understanding, and responsibility by direct sharing in the process; they grow in their capacity to form "reasonable expectations" by participating in the how and the what of the art of gardening. Through this participation—informed and broadened by what others have previously discovered—the children develop their own ability to order concrete means to accomplish significant outcomes.

This growth through experimental inquiry may be contrasted with learning from sheer trial and error, with slavish adherence to tradition and precedent, with reliance on external authority, with random activity, with all forms of wishful thinking, as well as with memoriter processes in which learning is construed as a passive acquiring for the purpose of the mere re-citing of prescribed lessons. The empirical principles and methods that are utilized in teaching the young the art of gardening are now recognized by most schools to hold for learning in many other fields. Few schools, for instance, would seek to nurture the young in the various sciences without opportunity for observation and first-hand experience through field trips and experimental work in the laboratory. The laboratory is now considered an essential part of the equipment of the ordinary high school, just as workrooms and playgrounds are also coming to be considered indispensable in providing opportunity for primary experience during the earlier years.

No school would attempt to teach children to play basketball, tennis, or any other game, by simply having them read books or listen to lectures by experts. Nor would we expect children to learn how to behave in their relations with other human beings apart from immediate experience with them. Knowledge of people may be greatly enriched by the study of anthropology, history, biography, novels, and dramas, but all that is acquired from these literary sources is necessarily sifted, interpreted, and evaluated by the young in terms of that which they have experienced and learned as a result of their own intercourse with their fellow human beings. The principles that hold for learning how to garden, to play games, to develop understanding in the various natural sciences, and to coöperate in group affairs, are now also accepted without question by both religious and secular schools in the education of the young in domestic science, in the various skilled crafts, in the operation of tools and machines in industry, in the interrelated fields of nursing, dentistry, and medicine, in various community undertakings, and in the different fine arts. In all of these areas we recognize that creative acts require acquaintance with conditions, materials, and tools, and that knowledge, standards, and regulative principles must be evolved from the actual field of practice. As one field of human experience after another thus becomes autonomous, it inevitably becomes permeated by experimental practices and outlooks, and the manner in which the subject-matters of these different fields are conceived and communicated to the young are modified accordingly.

EXPERIMENTAL INQUIRY AND PATTERNS OF THOUGHT

Parents and teachers miss the deeper significance of this empirical trend both in life and in education, if they do not perceive that it involves more than the mere increase of bodies of knowledge to be transmitted to the young and the development of new techniques in which the young must be trained if they are to be at home in the affairs of their society. Actually, this shift to experimental procedure and authority denotes a transformation in human experience that is breeding a new human mentality. It is because these new life attitudes are becoming established in the practices of the community that they are beginning to pervade the deliberate education of the young. The child who is learning by his own participation in experimental practices is not only acquiring new techniques, skills, and items of information, he is also acquiring an altered view of man and of the relation of man to his world. In fine, he is acquiring a new human outlook, for the outlook that is molded by a life practice that has become experimental in nature has its very definite characteristics.

It has in the first place a more vivid recognition of both the necessity and the possibility of human control. It is time that all who desire the young to grow in this capacity to understand and to control, come to realize that the experimental practices which the schools must use in order to nurture these abilities have deeper implications. The child, for example, who is learning to grow plants in order to help assure a human food supply is also learning that nature is so constituted that it will not take care of him apart from intelligent effort. In other words, he is learning, contrary to certain traditional views, that nature is not one, it is many; and that evil is not an illusion or a mere appearance, but a real trait of existence. So far as gardening is concerned, nature is a collective name for a variety of conditions, some favorable and some unfavorable to human interests. From the standpoint of the child's purpose to have a productive garden, these natural conditions have to be discriminated and dealt with, not in a wholesale, but in a piecemeal fashion. Seeds, soil, water, sunlight, and fertilizers are all natural things and they can be used as means to help further the life purposes of the gardener, but weeds, parasites, pests, killing frosts, droughts, and cyclones are equally natural, and they are the kind of natural forces that can destroy crops and frustrate human purposes. Through his daily experiences the child is learning that control is a function of an intelligent, discriminatory response to this plurality of conditions—friendly and hostile—we call "nature." Nor do the facts of man's experience show that this struggle for control is unreal, because affairs are so arranged that essential outcomes are assured regardless of the effort human beings put forth. Apparently the processes of nature that operated to bring human life into existence, also operated to produce many conditions antithetical to human existence. Man can survive and attain a satisfactory experience only as he learns to master these conditions. Implicit in the effort to achieve control through empirical means is the recognition that man lives not by passive trust in nature, but by the creative use of the conditions of nature for his own purposes.

Few teachers nowadays in either religious or secular schools will permit a child to substitute magical practices for the use of natural cause and effect relationships in the care of his garden plot. Few will permit him to rely on supernatural powers to water his garden; they expect him to get this result through empirical or natural means. Nor will the manifestation of a humble and contrite spirit in the life of the child be accepted as an adequate substitute for the exercise of intelligence and industry on his part. In the project of gardening teachers will not accept as satisfactory any alternatives of this type. The child is required to work and to try to get desired outcomes by the intelligent control of concrete, objective conditions. Society, having reached the conclusion that gardening involves mastery over definite empirical conditions and procedures, demands that its teachers nurture the young in the knowledge and the practices that are essential to this mastery.

But parents should recognize that as the school daily relies on procedures of this sort, it necessarily breeds in the minds of the young the experimental outlook inherent in these practices. This experimental outlook rejects the wholesale optimism that assumes nature is so biased in favor of human interests, that intelligent effort on man's part is not continuously required. It also rejects the wholesale pessimism or fatalism that assumes natural conditions are so stacked against human interests, that man is doomed to fail in spite of all his efforts to achieve a control that makes a humane existence possible. The experimental practice leads instead to the recognition that we live in the kind of world in which success is contingent. From the standpoint of human interests our world is a mixture of resources and obstacles; it must be accepted for what it is, an affair of affairs. In this plural world existence is precarious, and human well-being depends upon our ability to comprehend these diverse affairs and to learn how to use them on behalf of human interests. This recognition of the necessity of control is an attribute of the mind nurtured in experimental practices.

THE SEAT OF INTELLECTUAL AUTHORITY

The mind that has been molded by experimental inquiry has, in the second place, a definite conception of the meaning of truth. Truth denotes truths, and truths are not properties of existences, they are rather properties of human ideas about the nature of existences. As we emphasized in the previous chapter, an idea or a meaning is operational in character. An idea is significant if it defines (1) an action definite enough to be performed, and (2) an occurrence or an experience that will take place when the idea is put to the test of action, or experiment. It is by these operational criteria that the truth of an idea is tested. For an idea to be true, it must be valid in both of these aspects; it must define an act that can be carried out, and it must also define a condition that actually will come into existence when the prescribed action is carried out. In brief, ideas, or assertions, are warranted—they have the property of truth—if they verify when they are tested by experiment. Truth denotes accurate prediction. We have knowledge in any given field when we can predict how things in that field will behave under certain specified conditions.

This means that the mind nurtured by experimental procedures places the seat of intellectual authority within, not outside, the empirical procedures by which ideas are developed and tested. To return to the situation of the child learning to garden; a valid idea about gardening is not measured by the aesthetic appeal the idea makes to the mind of the child; nor is it measured by how fast his heart pounds and how hot his blood becomes when he contemplates the majesty of his vision, or intuition—the validity of the idea is not measured by any of these subjective feelings, but rather by what the idea actually leads to in the world of objective action. Unless an idea is responsibly defined as an operation to be performed—as a means adapted to some specified end—it will be dismissed as of no intellectual worth by those who are concerned with the practice that is gardening. Daily in our schools children are being taught in many different areas to think in terms of action, and to test their ideas by their consequences in action.

Similarly, no matter how exalted the person, the institution, the tradition, or the book from which an idea is derived, if the idea when put to the test of actual practice in the garden—to the crucial test of experiment—fails to produce the conditions or the consequences that it as idea predicts, it will be held invalid. On the other hand, no matter how lowly the source from which an idea comes, if the idea can make good in actual practice, it has worth and validity. For the mind habituated to empirical procedures both the meaning and the truth of an idea are internal, not external, they are internal to the operations by which they are subjected to the test of existence.

Experimentally established principles, to be sure, may be revised or even discarded by subsequent inquiries. All "truths" are subject to this correction by later developments and investigations, but this does not lead the experimental mind to retreat to external authority, or to seek refuge in the attitude of wholesale skepticism. The primary faith and security of the experimental inquirer is not lodged in this or that particular scientific finding or principle, but rather in the empirical method by which all beliefs are developed and tested. When the views of Newton are amended by the verified insights of an Einstein, the new situation in physics is readily accepted; it is viewed as a further triumph, not a defeat, for the procedures of experimental inquiry. In a world in which change is real, it marks a great human advance to have achieved a method of confirming beliefs that escapes alike the dogmatism of absolute, fixed truth, and the paralyzing skepticism that holds all views are equally worthy, or unworthy, because all alike are mere human opinions and all may be modified by the findings of later investigators. The experimental mind is the mature mind in the sense that it can operate on the basis of probability; it retains its confidence in the worth of intelligence in a world that makes knowledge a human necessity, and yet denies absolute finality to any particular human conclusion. For the empirical thinker many ideas and ideals have earned the right to our firm adherence, as they have been confirmed by a long experience, but none can be exempt from further scrutiny if developments call them into question.

EXPERIENCE AND MORAL STANDARDS

The experimental mind, in the third place, believes that values evolve within the course of ordinary experience. They have a natural basis and origin because man is a creature of interests, and he has to react selectively to his surroundings in order to maintain these life interests. Men become intelligent about values as they become intelligent about their actions—about the conditions upon which they depend, about the consequences to which they lead. As Dewey has emphasized, not all of the things that are immediately liked are likeable, nor are all of the things that men desire really desirable.[1] The difference between

[1] John Dewey, *Quest for Certainty* (New York, Minton, Balch & Company, 1929), pp. 260–261.

the merely "desired" and that which is counted "desirable" is the difference between organic impulsive acts, and those acts whose conditions and consequences have been inspected, evaluated, and judged to be good. The latter activities are considered desirable or valuable not simply because of their immediately prized qualities, but because they are judged to harmonize with other valued interests and to "lead-on" in such a way as to expand, not contract, the totality of significant experience, meaning and activity.

For the mind nurtured in experimental practices, morals and values do not constitute a separate realm and subject-matter. Since consequences cannot be separated from conditions, judgments about values cannot be divorced from judgments about facts. A human being can make an intelligent manifestation of preference only as he has knowledge of the concrete conditions that are involved in his various activities. The child who is learning through empirical procedures to discriminate the better from the worse in the different mundane spheres of human activity is, at the same time, growing in capacity for moral judgment. It is in and through these varied and interrelated life activities that the real occasions for moral decision arise, and the child grows in his capacity to function as a responsible moral agent as he grows in his ability to make judgments of the good and the bad in terms of concrete consequences. Moral behavior is thus a function of the entire experience of the child, and all education is inescapably a form of character education.

This capacity to judge life practices by their concrete consequences is what is meant by a reflective or experimental morality. It may be distinguished, on the one side, from a customary morality which automatically accepts the standards that happen to be current in the practices of a society as the norms for human conduct, and, on the other, from an authoritarian system of morality which holds that ordinary human beings are not qualified to develop their own governing principles, and therefore must rely on a supernatural source or other external authority to provide these controlling standards. An experimental morality is also to be distinguished from the formal and myopic morality that bids men to cling to such abstract and absolute principles as "right for right's sake," and "duty for duty's sake," without regard for actual consequences. The difficulty with an abstract morality of this sort is that it ignores the fact that men never act in a vacuum, but always in a definite life context, and that he who follows "right" and "duty" without empirical analysis and evaluation of consequences is most likely permitting others who know what their concrete interests are to determine the actual meaning of "duty" and the specific content of the "right." Finally, a reflective morality is to be distinguished from that of the cult of spontaneous self-expression— that is, from the practices of the group which identifies self-expression with impulsive activity that is not regulated by a regard for conditions and consequences. A reflective morality recognizes that the good life is a life within a human community, and that the desires of the individual must not only be reconciled with one another, but also with those of his fellows who share a common experience.

The young, nurtured today in empirical, experimental procedures that foster the disposition to judge all actions by their consequences, naturally find it difficult to turn to mystical and authoritarian modes of making value judgments. Intuitive and authoritarian modes of behavior simply do not harmonize with the life habits and attitudes of those who have been led by their own primary experiences to the conviction that in order to be moral you have to be intelligent, and that in order to be intelligent you have to take critical account of actual life alternatives.

EMPIRICAL METHOD AND THE SEARCH FOR CAUSES

Finally, and possibly most fundamental of all, the mind nurtured by experimental procedures develops a mode of response that has no place for unconditioned events. The experimental theory of knowledge is grounded in the empirical, operational test of meaning. It assumes that ordinary events are so involved in one another that certain conditions or phenomena may be reliably taken as the evidence of other conditions and developments. It also assumes that even the most *extraordinary* events are *ordinary* events, in the sense that we must seek to explain and understand them in terms of their operations—that is, in terms of the empirical conditions from which they arise, and of the empirical consequences to which they lead. In other words, the basic postulate of experimental method is that we get meanings—knowledge—by the process of referring consequences to conditions and conditions to consequences, and by no other method whatsoever. Without this resolute determination to seek for causes, meanings, and means of control within, and not outside, the course of observable occurrences, the expanding body of organized knowledge by which we increasingly regulate our activities would be deprived of its methodological foundation. It is this emphasis on unity of procedure in all realms of experience that is the distinctive mark of the experimental method. Its successes have been won by its steadfast refusal to turn the search for causes and explanations into a mystery by the introduction of non-identifiable and non-describable, and hence non-controllable, agencies.

Consider, for instance, the effort to discover the nature and the cure of cancer. It would be simple of course to declare that cancer is an evil that is due to the invasion of the body by an army of "demons," but science refuses to resort to this kind of explanation. Its interest is in knowledge that gives power to control, and that kind of knowledge about cancer comes only as we succeed in locating and describing the actual empirical conditions and processes that result in the definite developments in the human organism that we call cancer. No matter how difficult and costly the search, science continues to seek for causes that can be subjected to this sort of experimental description and prescription.

Should it abandon its effort to refer "effects" back to determinate conditions and operations, it would abandon the process by which "reasonable expectations" are developed and powers of control are extended. Such an abandonment of empirical method would signify a retreat from the ways of reason, it would mean the betrayal of the procedures that are mind. This faith in methodological continuity—in a method that can operate in all realms of human experience—is implicit in all educational efforts to get the young to become responsible, mature minds through reliance on empirical, experimental procedures. The commitment to the methods of experimental inquiry involves commitment to this empirical outlook. As one of our foremost students of the logic of scientific method states:

> It is frequently asserted that the principle of scientific method cannot rule out in advance the possibility of any fact, no matter how strange or miraculous. This is true to the extent that science as a method of extending our knowledge must not let accepted views prevent us from discovering new facts that may seem to contradict our previous views. Actually, however, certain types of explanation cannot be admitted within the body of scientific knowledge. Any attempt, for instance, to explain physical phenomenon as directly due to providence or disembodied spirits, is incompatible with the principle of rational determinism. For the nature of these entities is not sufficiently determinate to enable us to deduce definite experimental consequences from them. The Will of Providence, for instance, will explain everything whether it happens one way or another. Hence, no experiment can possibly overthrow it. An hypothesis, however, which we cannot possibly refute cannot possibly be experimentally verified.
>
> In thus ruling out ghostly, magical, and other supernatural influences, it would seem that scientific method impoverishes our view of the world. It is well, however, to remember that a world where no possibility is excluded is a world of chaos, about which no definite assertion can be made. Any world containing some order necessarily involves the elimination of certain abstract or ungrounded possibilities such as fill the minds of the insane.[2]

Thus experimental method not only postulates universal causation, it also has definite criteria by which it defines the characteristics that a thing must possess if it is to be accepted as a causal factor or agency. The compulsions, the efficacies, the correlations, and the sequential bonds that we associate with the principle of causality are held to be within, not outside, the course of natural events. The determination not to try to explain either physical or human phenomena by resort to extra-empirical agencies such as demons, angels, fairies, witches, and ghosts marks not merely a great change in our methods of seeking "practical" control; it also is associated with the dawn of a new human mentality. Not all areas of human experience have been penetrated by this empirical outlook, and there are groups who still contend that the moral and spiritual in-

    [2] Morris R. Cohen, *Reason and Nature* (New York: Harcourt, Brace and Co., 1931), pp. 158–59.

terests of the human race depend upon our refusing to permit the experimental method and outlook to achieve universal dominion. Before teachers and parents will be equipped to evaluate these so-called "moral" and "spiritual" claims, it will be necessary for them to perceive that experimental inquiry is not only a method of "practical" control, it is also a pattern of moral behavior. The morality of experimental practice marks a new approach to the problem of discovering, testing and reconstructing the principles by which men live.

MORALITY AND THE SOCIALIZATION OF INQUIRY

Undoubtedly much of the prestige of scientific inquiry derives from the success it has achieved in expanding the power of human control in so many different areas of human interest and need. But the claims of the method of experimental inquiry rest on *moral* as well as on *practical* grounds. Man is a creature of belief, and his operating beliefs about existence and values constitute the very core of his personhood. Human beings have often shown by their deeds that they are the kind of creatures who are willing to sacrifice life itself for that which they believe and value. As current conditions tragically demonstrate, differences of belief and value both within the same nation and between different nations frequently result in antagonisms that make coöperation for common ends difficult, if not impossible.

To the extent that beliefs are acquired automatically and are held dogmatically, they tend to foster stubborn, aggressive, and even fanatical behavior. Scientific inquiry signifies an effort to reduce the rôle of fanaticism in human affairs by removing arbitrariness and dogmatism from the processes by which beliefs are acquired, tested, revised, held, and communicated. Experimental procedures tend to result in this more rational behavior because of the extent to which they have socialized the process by which beliefs about questions of fact and value are developed. These socialized procedures of experimental science contain significant moral implications. They are frequently subjected to attack by moralists whose own methods are actually morally inferior to the very experimental procedures they attack—inferior because they are less socialized and hence more subjective, intuitive, and arbitrary. One of the most impressive tendencies of our period, has been the growing readiness of peoples in all parts of the world to adopt the empirical methods and the socialized attitudes of experimental inquiry. The moral characteristics of a method that has been able to evoke this universal human response in a period marked by intensified national rivalry, and by a growing conflict of cultural values, are worthy of serious consideration. Experimental procedure is grounded in the perception that the attainment of knowledge is a process from which the human factor cannot be eliminated. Recognizing the inescapable rôle of fallible human agents in all efforts to get knowledge, experimental inquiry seeks to get rid of an arbitrary individualism by the deliberate and the coöperative control of the process by which men reach conclusions and establish beliefs. One of the ways by which it gets this result is to open the process of inquiry to all who have competence in the field, irrespective of nationality, cultural tradition, race, sex, class status, religious affiliation, or geographical location. In other words, experimental inquiry seeks objectivity through universality, and it seeks universality through reliance on procedures which are equally available to all who are concerned to conduct investigations in a given area. It is opposed to all attempts to make a private monopoly out of the procedures by which knowledge is gained.

In a world marked by rival and infallible systems of supernatural revelation, by conflicting group folkways and mores, by alternative sets of "first principles," by competing institutional authorities, by divergent intellectual and moral intuitions, as well as by rival deliverances from what is known as "common sense," experimental method undertakes a new approach to the problem of developing and testing beliefs. It recognizes at the outset that the fallibility of human experience cannot be overcome by refusing to admit its existence through the assumption that we have privileged, transcendental roads to knowledge, or by any kind of procedure that makes the source or the parentage of an idea or a belief the test of its validity or authority. It lodges the authority of a principle, a value, or a belief not in the nature of its originating source—be it supernatural revelation, hallowed institution, mystical experience, the so-called laws of the mind, the intuitions of the heart, necessary axioms, or "common sense"—but rather in its actual working, that is, in its observable outcome or consequence.

When the priests of a fanatical order, during the Boxer trouble, told the Chinese leader, General Yuan Shih-kai, that his men need have no fear of foreign guns and bullets, because their magical rites had taken all potency from these foreign weapons, Yuan ruthlessly disposed of the dispute by lining the priests against a wall and subjecting their claims of magical control to the actual trial of bullets fired at them from the alleged impotent foreign guns. Most operational tests are not so cruel, simple and final as this, but they, nevertheless, have an authority against which the dogmas and the intuitions rooted in the mere superiority of origin or source are not able to stand. The fact that everybody knew by "common sense" that the earth was flat, was not sufficient to make that belief prevail when men demonstrated the world was round by sailing around it. The public deed settled the private and subjective doubts.

It should be noted that this shift from first principles and sources to ultimate consequences does not eliminate the human factor from the process by which we discover and test beliefs. Experimental method gains its control over the personal human factor by socializing and in a sense democratizing the manner in which that factor plays its rôle in the process of inquiry. Human beings have no part in determining the cultural groups and traditions into which they are born, but irrespective of these factors of group birth and membership, scientific inquiry invites all to join the community of those who verify beliefs by the observation of their workings and the evaluation of their consequences. Beliefs from any source are welcome, provided their sponsors are willing to have their credentials put to the test of operational procedure. On the other hand, no belief is its own warrant, no matter how exalted its source. In this crucial respect all beliefs stand on the same footing—all must be subjected to the test of an experience that is experimentally directed.

This is not to say that those untrained in particular fields can directly check the diagnosis, the operations, and the results of the experimental work of experts in those fields. But the growing tendency of the lay public to commit itself to the procedures of the expert is not a blind faith in authority. A farmer may not know how the hybrid seed corn is produced, but he can nevertheless judge the results when it is substituted for the earlier seed corn. A patient is frequently unable to observe and interpret the data on which the surgeon relies in his diagnosis, but he trusts the surgeon with his life because he has come to trust the empirical and public methods and controls under which the surgeon serves. The increasing demand among medical leaders for universal autopsy is further evidence of this tendency to bring the work of specialists under the control of competent observers. The authority of the expert is an authority that rests, in the last analysis, on the empirical and public character of the methods by which he works and produces his results.

Experimental method also seeks to promote the ends of objectivity by the exclusive reliance on data and procedures that can be identified and observed by all concerned to work in a particular field. Thus the opposition of empirical method to private, esoteric data and processes is not an arbitrary thing. It is a function of the demand for a public procedure that seeks to eliminate the subjective and the arbitrary by opening the avenues of inquiry to all interested investigators. The same concern for objectivity lies back of the demand for a full and accurate public record of each experiment. This record with its description of the factors involved in the problem, of the definite actions undertaken, and of the concrete results attained by the experiment, supplies an account of the undertaking that makes it possible for others to check on both the procedures and the findings. The unwillingness of the experimental worker to "cook" his data, or to over-extend the generalizations he draws from the data of his experiment are also aspects of the morality implicit in a public, coöperative method of conducting inquiries. The fact that all scientific findings are regarded as tentative because they may be corrected by the work of later investigators is further recognition that the principle of socialization should be extended to include not only the inquiries of our time but those of generations yet unborn.

At no point does the morality of experimental inquiry make more exacting demands than in its mode of treating doubt. It seeks security of belief not by suppressing doubt, but by making a constructive use of it.

Minds habituated to the principles of experimental activity do not seek to minimize or to override the objecting case, or factor. On the contrary, they cherish those elements that resist the existing explanatory principle or law, because these objecting factors can be made into *objects* for further observation and inquiry and may become the means of new knowledge.

Thus experimental method demands of its adherents the intellectual and emotional maturity to recognize that our most cherished beliefs are not absolute—they may be revised, reconstructed, or even discarded, by the results of further study. For the experimental mind security of belief is not sought by clinging tenaciously to tradition and precedent, by asserting that whatever is in line with our preferences must be true, nor by holding to dogmas in spite of evidence; it is rather gained by eliminating doubt through the resolute pursuit of inquiry until that inquiry culminates in conclusions that are indubitable—indubitable because they cannot be doubted significantly by any responsible inquirer. In a world in which change is real, intellectual and moral security is attained, in the first instance, by putting our confidence in public experimental methods of testing existing beliefs, and, secondly, by giving our allegiance to those beliefs that demonstrate they are trustworthy because they have gained a real consensus in and through the process of open and untrammeled inquiry.

But the tentative attitude of experimental inquiry is not to be confused with an attitude of indifference or of wholesale skepticism. Faith in the process of "winnowing and sifting" is actually faith in the possibility of attaining knowledge. The open mind of experimental inquiry does not denote the empty mind. As the history of modern research science indicates, the self-correcting procedures of experimental inquiry are the best means known to man of furnishing the mind with beliefs worthy to organize and direct human experience.

Experimental inquiry reaches unity of belief, not by reliance on external authority and suppression of difference, not by persuasion through propaganda, not by the individualistic process of inner intuition, but by universalizing the community of inquirers, by confronting and utilizing doubt to test and expand beliefs, and by employing empirical and public data and methods that foster uncoerced coöperation in the search for knowledge and standards. Through the use of these procedures, experimental inquiry has socialized the process by which man comes to know. The morality implicit in this socialized method of attaining belief defines a primary objective in any program of education concerned to treat human beings not as mere means, but as ends in themselves.

Toward Dialogue

An advocate always chooses his examples carefully. Childs rests a large segment of his argument on the illustration of "gardening" in the curriculum, and it would be hard to fault his analysis and treatment of this kind of learning.

Many of us would like to know, however, just how typical is "gardening" as a prototype component of schooling. Certainly the child should encounter many "gardening"-type, or "how to" learning experiences in the school, and it may be true that the empirical, problem-solving method of learning is most appropriate in these cases. But how would one acquaint the learner with his historical heritage, with the meaning of the French or American Revolution, or with the bloody issue that divided our people during the Civil War? How teach the great literature of Shakespeare or Cervantes or the art of the ages, from Rubens and Bach to Klee and Copland? Would the method of inquiry fit these kinds of circumstances?

There is a great deal of mumbo-jumbo in educational literature about the behavioral base of all learning. It is claimed that education is defined as the changing of behavior and that if there is no overt, empirically observable change in the learner's behavior, then no learning has occurred. This thesis is implicit in Childs' essay. But sometimes human beings grow not through their behavior—what they say or what they do —but through their insights and feelings. They see relationships which are not always vocalized and articulated in their daily lives; they arrive at understandings of self and others which lie below the threshold of empirical observations by the polltaker, the social scientist or, for that matter, the educational psychologist studying learning curves in the classroom. It appears that, to the science-oriented educator, these phenomena do not really count as acts of learning. And the question nips at the edges of our thought: Is a scientific empiricism really large enough to comprehend all that can occur in the education of a human being?

DONALD O. HEBB

Problem-Solving and Survival

We have already seen that the nonspecific projection system of the brain stem, whose activity constitutes arousal, is excited by downstream paths from the cortex as well as by afferent paths. If we assume that arousal constitutes a general drive state (with or without qualitative variations . . .), we might expect to find cases in which arousal, and therefore drive, depend not on the presence of primitive need but on the complex cue functions of the cortex. Such cases in fact appear to make up an important part of the higher animal's motivations. Though they are not at all well understood it is essential not to overlook them.

When the mammal's primitive needs are reasonably well satisfied, when he is not under the control of stimuli directly associated with such needs, certain other motivations appear. In the primate these may be as compelling as noxious stimulation; they are less strong, but still clearly evident, in lower mammals. One example in the primate is the irrational fears of certain strange objects, which do not arise by association with prior injury but from a conflict of perceptions; another is the exploratory tendency which is so ubiquitous in vertebrates that it has frequently been treated as a special drive. Motivations of the kind that we are discussing now involve both approach and avoidance, and the great riddle that they present is in the fact that the *same* object or event can attract and repel. Which happens, apparently, depends on the strength of the disturbance produced, a weak disturbance attracting and a strong one repelling.

Placed in familiar surroundings, but with access provided to an unfamiliar region, the animal orients toward the latter. If he is in his home cage with the door open, he moves cautiously toward the dangerous outer world; he acts as though moving toward a point of balance between the strength of the exploratory motivation, on the one hand, and fear of the strange on the other, any sudden noise producing prompt retreat. Each exploration of course reduces strangeness, so the territory covered increases with time, and evidence of fear may vanish; but the significant point here is the earlier stage when the strange part of the environment excites both approach and avoidance.

Again, the chimpanzee that was exposed to the sight of a model head might be so disturbed that he ran screaming out of sight; but others, definitely frightened, retreated to a safe distance and then seemed un-

---

From **A Textbook of Psychology** by Donald O. Hebb. (Philadelphia: W. B. Saunders Company, 1958), pp. 170–176.

able to take their eyes off the object of fear. They were both repelled and attracted. Man in this society is definitely repelled emotionally by the dead body, flowing blood and gross bodily injury, and yet avidly reads or listens to accounts of traffic accidents or axe murders (a good axe murder is definitely more attractive than a poisoning, and a poisoning better than natural death).

A different example of this kind of ambivalence is the attraction of dangerous sports; here the human subject acts just like the rat venturing from home ground onto strange territory, very cautious at first but becoming increasingly venturesome as familiarity (and skill) increase. This sort of behavior has usually been explained by supposing that it is a search for prestige—in other words, it is in itself unpleasant, done only for extrinsic social rewards. This seems clearly untrue. The fact that people will pay money to get on a roller coaster, where no prestige is involved, makes it at least a doubtful explanation; and the further fact that animals behave in exactly the same way, in circumstances in which there is definitely no extrinsic reward, makes the explanation untenable. The "thrill" of danger in certain circumstances is sought for its own sake, as is the thrill of ghost stories and accounts of disasters.

A comparable ambivalence is found in the fact that man, who is undoubtedly opposed to work in many forms and especially when there is too much of it, promptly becomes unhappy when there is too little: here too, in other words, he seeks an optimum level. The statement includes mental as well as physical work, and may be misunderstood if the term "work" is interpreted in too narrow a way. Playing golf, physiologically, is work just as much as carrying another man's golf clubs. A game of chess is work, psychologically, and may be harder work than writing business letters. *Play*, in other words, may be defined for psychological purposes as work that is done for its own sake, without extrinsic reward. The frequency with which games have been invented that make intellectual demands as well as physical is a most important piece of evidence concerning the nature of human motivation. As with the dangerous sports, the explanation cannot be found in the search for social prestige; for there are forms of self-imposed problem-solving in which no prestige is gained (for example, playing solitaire, one form of which is widely known as Idiot's Delight), and here too the subhuman animals show the behavior when prestige does not enter into the question. For example:

Monkeys will work for hours at solving simple mechanical problems. Chimpanzees on occasion will work at learning tasks, if the tasks "interest" them, while leaving the food reward untouched. The rat that is offered a short direct route to food, and a longer route that involves passing through a simple maze problem, will frequently take the more difficult route (from 10 to 80 per cent of runs are indirect, depending on the difficulty of the problem and whether it is changed on every run: if it is unchanged it loses its excitation value and the rats revert to the direct route).

What these data tell us is that there are circumstances in which an animal will prefer to work rather than be idle, to do more work rather than less. The "principle of least effort" is extremely misleading as a general guide to understanding behavior in lower animals, and still more so in the primate. It may apply when behavior is motivated by a serious biological need, but not when such needs have been met: in the latter condition, it is clear, the principle is reversed and the organism's need is to expend energy. Moreover, the need is not merely for muscular activity, especially in the higher animal, for this could be achieved by monotonous physical exercises. There is, in effect, a need to exercise the brain as well.

This appears very clearly in the following experiment. College students were paid $20 a day to do nothing, lying 24 hours a day on a comfortable bed with eyes, ears and hands shielded to minimize perception of the environment. These conditions were relaxed only to allow the subject to eat or go to the toilet. Few could endure them for more than two or three days (the upper limit was six). Though the subjects were in need of money, they turned from this "job" to ones that paid much less but demanded much more of them in the way of physical and mental effort. They developed a need to be exposed to patterned stimulation of almost any kind, and this need to perceive and react to the environment eventually became overwhelming.

The experiment draws attention to what must be part of the explanation of the kind of motivation we are now discussing: the role of variety in maintaining arousal. With repetition, any one pattern of stimulation rapidly declines in arousal value. In the sleeping cat, for example, a series of unfamiliar sounds A-B-C produces arousal, waking the cat up. With a number of repetitions arousal decreases, and now the cat neither wakes nor shows the effect of arousal in the EEG. Next, the pattern is changed to C-B-A: the cat again wakes up, and the EEG shows the full arousal picture. When an animal, therefore, looks at a fully familiar object or scene the arousal effects must be small, and if no need-associated stimuli are present the probability of response is low. But if a strange object is introduced, or if familiar objects act in an unfamiliar way, producing arousal at the moment when the animal perceives the new element in the situation, the probability of response is high.

We may suppose further that there is an optimal level of arousal, as implied by the earlier discussion of drive reduction and drive enhancement as factors in learning. The subject will tend to repeat behavior that raises drive level from a low to a moderate level, and not to repeat behavior that raises it from a moderate to a high level. That is, he will seek conditions that produce a moderate level of arousal, and will tend to avoid monotony as well as pain.

It has already been said that this is a speculative line of theory. The statement can be reinforced by pointing out now a glaring defect: it makes no provision for sleep, a topic that psychologically and physiologically remains mostly mysterious. We know that there is a "waking center" which is part of the arousal system, and probably a "sleep center" as well; but how these achieve the 24-hour cycle is not known. External stimulation can postpone sleep, or lack of it can hasten it, but only to a certain degree. There appears to be in the brain stem a pacemaker, a physiological timing process, which is not very subject to sensory control. What it is we do not know; but in the meantime, the statements of the preceding paragraph need to be qualified by addition of the words, "during the waking state." An animal will seek a moderate level of arousal— until, as we say, he begins to "feel sleepy." Then he begins to seek conditions which minimize arousal.

THE GOALS OF THE HIGHER ANIMAL

This chapter may be concluded by asking, What are the mammal's goals, and especially, What are man's?

In the first place come the primitive biological needs involved in survival; when these are not met (particularly if the lack is chronic) the attempt to satisfy them generally becomes the dominant motive. Sexual needs, equally primitive biologically, become more complex and less directly compelling in the higher animal, but still remain a powerful motivating influence.

When such needs have been met, however, in the well-fed comfortable animal with adequate sexual opportunities, we find ourselves looking at a very different picture. Now we find the subject embarking on explorations even if these take him away from a safe and biologically adequate locus. We find him looking for or inventing problems to solve, and mild risks to be run, apparently for their own sake. In man, with his high intellectual capacity, these tendencies produce complex and expensive mechanical devices (e.g., racing dinghies, bathyspheres, roulette wheels) and endless verbal elaborations of soluble and insoluble problems (e.g., philosophy). The machinery of the nervous system, presumably enlarged under the influences of evolution as of value in seeking food and avoiding injury, has also developed certain intrinsic peculiarities which become very evident in an economically successful human society—a kind of Frankenstein's monster whose activities are not all undesirable.

Besides the seeking for excitement and the manipulation of the environment, just referred to, there are also the irrational fears and dislikes discussed earlier (which as we have seen are more marked in the higher animal). Some of these tendencies are of incalculable value: problem-solving for its own sake, for example, is the essence of science. Others, such as the tendency to fear (and so be hostile to) the stranger, the one whose beliefs and habits differ from ours, are potentially disastrous for the species. It is the problem of developmental and social psychology to learn how to handle these tendencies, to make the most of the valuable and minimize the dangerous ones. There is reason to believe that this can be done, but at present we know little of practical value about the problem. In view of man's present capacity to destroy himself as a species, this has become the most urgent of the problems of science.

SUMMARY

Motivation refers broadly (i.e., it is not a precise term) to the state or process which makes possible activity of the whole animal, as distinct from a local reflex activity. Motivation does not supply the energy of response—this comes from the animal's oxygen and food supply—but determines whether the energy will be available for response, or for a particular class of response. Emotion is even less precise as a scientific term; it seems to mean that there is something special going on in the organism, motivationally, but the nature of this "something special" in the case of one emotion (e.g., joy) has apparently little in common with that of another (e.g., anger or despair).

The conception of motivation adds nothing, has no explanatory value, in the understanding of reflex activity. The behavior is produced by a system which is connected in parallel and which is always ready for action unless fatigued or inhibited by some other system. Some of an animal's biological needs are supplied reflexively, and as long as this happens such needs do not influence the animal's motivation: reflexive breathing usually supplies oxygen and removes carbon dioxide, sweating or shivering controls temperature, and so on. But when a strong need is not satisfied reflexively, motivation becomes involved at once. The pattern of activity in higher centers changes, the behavior of the whole animal is directed toward meeting the need, and any competing behavior is suppressed.

Drive refers to a particular kind of hypothesis about motivation. It implies that there are separate processes in the CNS that determine the animal's level of behavioral activity, apart from the processes that guide this behavior. Roughly, this is like the distinction between the power system of an automobile and its steering system. We know that drive does not actually supply the power in behavior, the energy that cells use in being active; but it does seem needed to mobilize cellular energies in the CNS, to coordinate them so that they are available for behavior. There are differing ideas about drives and how they work; a hypothesis is discussed which relates drive to arousal, but no final answer to the problem is available at present.

Special motivations or drives may be acquired by learning. In some cases, however, as in the fear of strange animals, we are also dealing with maturation, and learning has a smaller role in causing the fears than it may seem to have. In some of these cases there is a species-predictable susceptibility, characteristic of the higher primates particularly. The nature of this susceptibility, however—the mechanism of response in these "irrational fears"—is not known, and it is possible that the essence of the process is some conflict of present sensory input with pre-established mediating processes.

Homeostatic processes are ones that keep the "internal environment" constant. They include breathing, sweating or shivering, eating and drinking, and the "artificial hungers" of addiction. Hunger and addiction are partly learned processes, in combination with basic physiological changes. The avoidance of pain may also be considered homeostatic (though less directly); like normal hunger, pain is a complex process and not an elementary sensation, and is far from being fully understood at present.

Sexual behavior is biologically primitive also, but cannot be considered homeostatic since it is not a regulator of the internal environment. It is closely related to the level of sex hormones in the blood stream, but in the male mammal and the higher primates particularly it is also profoundly influenced by learning and mediating processes.

A special feature of motivation in higher animals, one dependent on a well-developed cerebrum, is an ambivalent attitude toward threatening situations and ones calling for mental as well as physical work. When there is a biologically-primitive need or serious threat of need, this tends to dominate behavior; but when need is absent or at a low level the higher animal (and particularly man) seems to seek out the threat-producing or puzzle-making situation. He avoids a too-easy or monotonous environment, and this motivation can be very powerful indeed.

Toward Dialogue

What is one to make of Hebb's claim that "problem-solving for its own sake is the essence of science?" This assertion is one to which even the most thoroughly "scientized" philosophers might take strenuous exception. Science, they say, is the method of understanding and managing the environment; it is a methodology for bringing human thought to bear upon the conditions of human existence and, thus, advancing and improving those conditions. In this role, science cannot be considered an end-in-itself; it is a means to a more humane existence.

But listen to what Hebb is saying. His argument is that a truly humane, i.e., human, existence is not possible without a continuous resupply of problems and puzzles and curiosities; that if man runs out of interesting problems to work on, he will invent new ones. Indeed, civilization in its broadest sense might be viewed as the result of this impulse. Man builds cities, creates intricate societies and governments, concocts complex moral rules, invents automobiles and airplanes, and shoots himself to the moon because he is basically bored with nature. He wants more challenge from his existence than his own nature provides; he is literally bored to death with his natural condition, so he improves on nature by creating goals and ends which are not in his original endowment. And this is what makes him human.

Now, what would constitute a science-shaped education if the Hebb thesis is correct? Would it not mean that problem-solving in education, just like problem-solving in civilization, is an activity which is its own justification? And would we not say that a growing individual who had developed the ability to solve problems was an educated person—not because it made him more competent in life's affairs but because that skill, in and of itself, was the mark of being human?

Kouwenhoven (see pages 41–55) is making the same point as Hebb. There is something intrinsically fascinating about the experience of dealing with a problematic environment. Science is the method par excellence for this kind of operation. The American people, the most sophisticated in matters scientific, may have to recognize that their culture has no end beyond itself; perhaps its methodological, scientific, problem-solving character is a final recognition that man does not want to go anywhere, he just wants to go.

ALEXANDER CALANDRA

The Barometer Story—
A Problem in Teaching Critical Thinking

Some time ago, I received a call from a colleague who asked if I would be the referee on the grading of an examination question. It seemed that he was about to give a student a zero for his answer to a physics question, while the student claimed he should receive a perfect score and would do so if the system were not set up against the student. The instructor and the student agreed to submit this to an impartial arbiter, and I was selected.

THE BAROMETER PROBLEM

I went to my colleague's office and read the examination question, which was, "Show how it is possible to determine the height of a tall building with the aid of a barometer."

The student's answer was, "Take the barometer to the top of the building, attach a long rope to it, lower the barometer to the street, and then bring it up, measuring the length of the rope. The length of the rope is the height of the building."

From *Current Science* (Teacher's Edition), 44 (January 6–10, 1964), pp. 1–2. Special permission granted by *Current Science*, published by American Education Publications, Columbus, Ohio.

Now, this is a very interesting answer, but should the student get credit for it? I pointed out that the student really had a strong case for full credit, since he had answered the question completely and correctly. On the other hand, if full credit were given, it could well contribute to a high grade for the student in his physics course. A high grade is supposed to certify that the student knows some physics, but the answer to the question did not confirm this. With this in mind, I suggested that the student have another try at answering the question. I was not surprised that my colleague agreed to this, but I was surprised that the student did.

Acting in terms of the agreement, I gave the student six minutes to answer the question, with the warning that the answer should show some knowledge of physics. At the end of five minutes, he had not written anything. I asked if he wished to give up, since I had another class to take care of, but he said no, he was not giving up. He had many answers to this problem; he was just thinking of the best one. I excused myself for interrupting him, and asked him to please go on. In the next minute, he dashed off his answer, which was:

"Take the barometer to the top of the building and lean over the edge of the roof. Drop the barometer, timing its fall with a stopwatch. Then, using the formula $S = \frac{1}{2} at^2$, calculate the height of the building."

At this point, I asked my colleague if he would give up. He conceded and I gave the student almost full credit. In leaving my colleague's office, I recalled that the student had said he had other answers to the problem, so I asked him what they were. "Oh, yes," said the student. "There are many ways of getting the height of a tall building with the aid of a barometer. For example, you could take the barometer out on a sunny day and measure the height of the barometer, the length of its shadow, and the length of the shadow of the building, and by the use of simple proportion, determine the height of the building."

"Fine," I said. "And the others?"

"Yes," said the student. "There is a very basic measurement method that you will like. In this method, you take the barometer and begin to walk up the stairs. As you climb the stairs, you mark off the length of the barometer along the wall. You then count the number of marks, and this will give you the height of the building in barometer units. A very direct method.

"Of course, if you want a more sophisticated method, you can tie the barometer to the end of a string, swing it as a pendulum, and determine the value of 'g' at the street level and at the top of the building. From the difference between the two values of 'g,' the height of the building can, in principle, be calculated."

Finally he concluded, "If you don't limit me to physics solutions to this problem, there are many other answers, such as taking the barometer to the basement and knocking on the superintendent's door. When the superintendent answers, you speak to him as follows: 'Dear Mr. Superintendent, here I have a very fine barometer. If you will tell me the height of this building, I will give you this barometer.' "

At this point, I asked the student if he really didn't know the answer to the problem. He admitted that he did, but that he was so fed up with college instructors trying to teach him how to think and to use critical thinking, instead of showing him the structure of the subject matter, that he decided to take off on what he regarded mostly as a sham.

WHAT IS SCIENCE?

In acting as a consultant for various school systems, I am often called upon to give advice on how to teach critical thinking. There is usually so much confusion on this topic that I urge the teachers to look first at the meaning of science and the method of critical thinking.

The word *science* originally referred to the study of the physical environment, the study of the atmosphere, the soil, the ocean, plants, animals, the stars, the planets, etc. The emphasis was on the materials of science rather than on the method. During the 18th century, it became generally recognized that science was making great progress, and it was hoped that other subjects could make advances of a similar kind. Benjamin Franklin expressed this hope:

> The rapid progress true science now makes occasions my regretting sometimes that I was born too soon. It is impossible to imagine the heights to which may be carried, in a thousand years, the power of man over matter. O that moral science were in as fair a way of improvement, that men would cease to be wolves to one another, and that human beings would at length learn what they now improperly call humanity.

It was about the time of Franklin that many people began to think that progress in other subjects could be made simply by using the method of science—critical thinking. This idea is still with us, but it is quite unrealistic; for if you ask any scientist what step of critical thinking he is taking, he will probably not know what you are talking about, and if he does, he will think that you are very naive.

Most scientists operate in much the manner that P. W. Bridgeman described when he said that critical thinking was nothing more than doing one's best with one's mind. Although Bridgeman's definition of critical thinking was probably a reaction to pat formulas which appear in textbooks, it can also be justified on different grounds. Let us do this by examining the nature of critical thinking and its relation to the evolutionary origin of the human mind.

EVOLUTION AND CRITICAL THINKING

Critical thinking as outlined in textbooks usually appears as some variation of the pattern of observation, hypothesis, and verification.

Now, it must be obvious that man has used this method for many of his activities for a very long time—in fact, ever since he came into existence. For if in his search for food, shelter, and a mate, he had not observed, made hypotheses, and verified them by experiment, he would never have survived. Thus, critical thinking ability is part of man's mental equipment, and in one way or another it is as natural for him to think critically as it is for him to eat and breathe.

From this point of view, we conclude that the method of critical thinking is a natural result of the evolution of the nervous system and not an invention of scientists. Thus, teachers who excitedly labor critical thinking are often in much the same position as Polonius, who was thrilled to discover that he was speaking prose.

A reasonable question to ask in this connection is: "If critical thinking is so old, how does it happen that the disciplines of physics, chemistry, and biology did not develop long before this time?" Much of the answer to this is quite simple. In the growth of a subject there is a point, the discovery of key ideas which, when reached, makes for very rapid progress. In physics, much of this occurred with the formulation of the laws of motion in the 17th century; in chemistry it took place with the discovery of oxygen in the 18th century; and in biology, it was the development of the theory of evolution in the 19th century.

Thus we conclude that science, the study of our physical environment, develops much like the solving of a jigsaw puzzle. In the beginning, it is hard to get started, but after a number of key pieces have been found and fit into place, progress is quite rapid. In fact, the last piece falls into place by itself.

The moral of all this is that critical thinking is not the thing which is characteristic of science. The characteristic feature of the scientific enterprise is that it has found many of the key pieces required for putting together the puzzle of the physical environment. The reason why this happened first in science is that the study of the physical environment is much simpler than that of our social environment.

Unless this is made clear, the teaching of critical thinking as such is misleading. In fact, as students mature, they come to realize it, and lose respect for those who have suggested otherwise, as we found in the barometer story. It seems that in the elementary grades, the youngsters are fascinated by the idea of a scientific method, in high school they accept it as a part of the folklore of science teaching, in college they begin to be bored by it, and by the time students finish college, they have usually forgotten it or resent it.

SOME PRECAUTIONS

Now that the dangers of overemphasizing the method of critical thinking have been explored, let us ask the question: "Is there any advantage in showing the student some systematic ways of arriving at answers?" There is, provided that a number of precautions are taken. Here are some that seem reasonable to me:

1. Point out that the general pattern of observation, hypothesis, and verification is a method which is natural to the human mind, and is not peculiar to science except to the extent that it is easier to apply to the physical environment.

2. This pattern, used in a formal, systematic way, is more helpful in analyzing or talking about results than in obtaining them, for most discoveries are made with a great deal of trial and error, intuition, hunches, educated guesses, and repeated frustrations with results that do not agree with predictions.

3. The pattern as a systematic method of discovery is useful in the lower elementary grades (2 and 3), where the examples studied are very simple.[1]

4. Ideas about critical thinking, especially after grade 5, are best taught in connection with the systematic development of subject matter. If method is divorced from systematic study of subject matter, it runs into the same difficulties as those for which some education courses are criticized.

5. Make a real effort to practice those techniques, namely controlled experimentation and mathematical interpretation, which scientists have found very useful in many disciplines in science. (A good case can be made for considering mathematics as the method of modern science.)

6. Avoid implying that a scientist is a different kind of person from the rest of humanity. The idea that the scientist is basically more objective as a result of his work is not borne out by his behavior outside of science. If he is more objective or honest in his work, it is because work in science is such that (a) a scientist has to be objective to get results in his scientific work, or (b) dishonest work is readily discovered because the experiments that a scientist does can usually be repeated and checked.

7. Do not give students the idea that a scientist thinks while other people do not. Not only is this untrue, but it also tends to make insufferable intellectual snobs out of children who should be learning the humility associated with the most worthwhile efforts in science.

Toward Dialogue

Calandra's satire on the problem-solving technique of learning can teach us at least this much: there are ways to solve problems and then there are ways to solve problems. Every teacher is familiar with the in-

---

[1] Suggestions as to how this can be done appear in *Look, Guess, and Check: A Method of Learning,* by Alexander Calandra, Washington University Bookstore, Dept. 105, St. Louis, Missouri, price: $1.00.

ventive or simply impatient student who decides to go at his exercises in his own idiosyncratic way. Although we generally applaud creativity and inventiveness, there is also reason to wonder whether such an individual is really learning. An elementary school pupil may invent his own way of adding eight and nine on his fingers and, in an emergency, toes. But we would not consider his answer of 17 "correct" just because he somehow arrived at it. We want to know whether he can deal with symbolic abstractions as such, since the calculating efficiency of fingers and toes will not carry him very far.

Calandra's hypothetical physics student, however, presents a more sophisticated problem for the educator. This student indicated he was fed up with teachers trying to teach him how to think instead of showing him "the structure of the subject matter." The question which this attitude suggests is this: Does every subject matter have a "structure?" Is there a frame and form not only to physics and mathematics and chemistry, but also to literature, history, and art? It would be an understatement to say that in the educational community there is some doubt about this.

VAN CLEVE MORRIS

Progressive Education

Contrary to popular belief, John Dewey did not think up progressive education all by himself. He had help. His help came from two general sources, namely, American history and a remarkable philosophic "invention."

Historically, the American people have always shown an inordinate fascination for the future. Out of their colonial experience, their frontier westering, and, more recently, their mastery of technological processes, they have always been a little different from other people in their interest in what lies ahead, what remains to be done, in change, in progress. Intellectually, they have been people who believe that knowledge is not merely to be possessed but *used*, and that life's zest is to be found not merely in knowing the real world we live in but in redesigning the world through the use of human intelligence. Hence, even if John Dewey had never lived, the American people would have had to create him, or at least the outlook on life that he was able to articulate in their behalf. For he was not so much a speculative philosopher in the grand

From *Council for Basic Education Bulletin,* October 1960, pp. 2–6.

tradition of Plato or Hegel, but rather a synthesizing summarizer of what the American people had already produced as a theory of life.

The philosophical "invention" was the inspiration of a little known American philosopher of the latter 19th century, Charles Sanders Peirce, and his younger and more famous contemporary, William James. It turned about a technical point in logic, to wit: the meaning of an idea lies in its practical effects, that is to say, in the consequences that follow from acting on it. Earlier philosophies had always maintained that ideas originated outside the experience of man and that their true meanings could be apprehended through contemplative and rational operations of the human intellect. But to Peirce and James, ideas were only "plans of action" which required to be "cashed in" at the "bank" of experience before their meanings were understood or their truth known, much like a bank check must be cashed to see if it is negotiable. Turning this idea forward, Dewey then went on to say that, if ideas are tested in the consequences to which they lead in experience, then ideas may be thought of as tools or instruments by which desired consequences are to be brought into being. Thus, an *instrumental* logic was developed in philosophy which succeeded in showing that all thinking is prospective in function; that is, it always points forward into action. Thought is not contemplative, as the older philosophies had said, but instrumentally functional in the ordering of experience.

This philosophical invention, it is obvious, nicely fits the historical conclusion the American people had already come to independently, viz., that knowledge was to be used, not merely held. Taken together, the historical conclusion and the philosophic invention found a superb application in science; and since science came to have such a wide appeal in American life and was potentially applicable not only to the physical environment but to social and moral questions as well, Dewey suggested that education become the social agency for training the young to use this instrumental scientific logic in dealing with the problems of life.

Obviously, to organize education on this principle represents a revolution in educational thought. The school is asked to begin its work in the experiences of people rather than in the subject matter handed down from our predecessors. This does not mean that subject matter is repudiated or legislated out of existence; it means only that subject matter changes its function and role in life and education. Instead of being set out and mastered for its own sake, it is used to solve problems which are encountered in ordinary experience. And in the *using* of subject matter it is learned. The main point is this: subject matter, far from being lost, merely changes its place; it becomes instrumental to the main aim of education, namely, the development of trained intelligence in the use of the new logic.

Working on this principle, progressive education has turned away from a curriculum of inherited subject matter, nicely compartmented into bodies of knowledge, and moved in the direction of a curriculum drawn from the problematic experiences of the learners themselves. Latin and Ancient History have yielded to Language Arts and Problems of American Democracy. And since the range of problems to which subject matter can be applied is much broader than a mere catalogue of the major bodies of knowledge themselves, the curriculum of the progressive school has expanded to include any area in which society requires trained intelligence: auto mechanics, home economics, citizenship training, art, music, creative writing, journalism, drama, health and nutrition, business mathematics, typewriting, physical education, driver education, and many others. As a concession to the colleges, progressive schools have usually retained the standard academic subjects for their college-bound students, but even here—in mathematics, in history, in the foreign languages—the principle of "learning-through-use" is increasingly evident.

The methodology of the progressive teacher has shifted away from an expository, lecture-type, "telling" method in favor of a problem-solving method which shifts the responsibility for learning from teacher to learner and is carried out in class projects: the social studies class sitting as a Continental Congress to re-live colonial history; the language arts class writing and producing a play; the life science group learning their botany in the school's garden plot.

Since the problem-solving project method of teaching and learning requires more interplay between learners, the dynamics of group inter-action have come in for special study and control. Social adjustment and the development of inter-personal relations are elevated into primary educational aims, not because of a soft sentimentalism but because social skills are necessary to the effective use of the new logic in social life in the wider community. "Life Adjustment" education (possibly an unfortunate term) is not a call to the young to blend into the social landscape, an interpretation traditionalists insist on giving it because of their intellectual reliance upon a view of reality as a fixed and permanent order. It is a call to develop working relationships with others so as more effectively to mobilize collective human effort in the solving of social problems in a changing world.

There is no doubt that the progressive theory of education has done a great deal to humanize education, to make it less of a grind and a chore, and more of a genuine adventure which is, after all, what it ought to be. Progressivists point to the fact that first-graders generally like to go to school but twelfth-graders do not. Somewhere along the line, youngsters lose their love of the adventure of learning. According to progressivists, the dawn of this disenchantment occurs in the vicinity of the seventh and eighth grades when young people discern for the first time that they are no longer at the center of the educative process but are being displaced by a battery of subject matters which are to be given. priority in the years ahead.

This situation can be corrected, say the progressivists, by applying to secondary education the experience-centered learning which has already won wide acceptance in elementary schools. It is the prosecution of their argument at the secondary (and higher) level which is currently arousing so much controversy.

Progressive theory at the secondary level has, of course, served to expand the areas of educational interests beyond the academic, as noted above, and thus answer to a much wider range of needs in the young. In this office, therefore, progressive education has become the educational instrument for realizing the Jacksonian aim of equality of opportunity for all. Perhaps this is progressivism's greatest triumph: a democratic egalitarianism in the form of an education for all American youth.

There is no denying, however, that the purchase of this triumph has been made at a price. There is much waste motion in progressive education, at least in these early years of its application in American schools. Teachers who have been trained in ignorance of the basic theory or who, through thinness of perception, misconstrue it, have failed to distinguish for instance between what is significant and what is trivial in classroom projects. Children are set to work on activities of no consequence: on basket weaving, on play acting, or on committee work and group discussions which are without purpose. In teacher education, where the theory is more widely practiced than anywhere else in higher education, workshop participants foregather to fritter away valuable professional time "pooling ignorance" and solving minor pedagogical problems brought to the workshop by individual teachers. The mistake is made of thinking that problem-solving, as such, makes for effective learning, whereas only problem-solving *at and beyond* the sophistication of the participants leads to genuine growth.

This tendency of progressive theory (in the hands of ill-trained practitioners) to be content with the trivial has meant, among other things, that the theory has not enjoyed as much success with groups of high ability as with average and slower groups. Bright youngsters are bored with the prosaic problems of their classmates, and able, self-motivated teachers have nothing but scorn for the vacuity of some of their courses and workshops in university schools of education.

Whether these deficiencies represent incorrigible faults in the theory or merely tactical failures at the level of practice is a question that is perhaps not yet decided. Understandably, progressivists incline toward the latter view, believing that once the American teacher really understands the underlying logic and develops skill in the method at the appropriate level of challenge for each learner, he shall have developed a pedagogy splendidly suited to the genius of American civilization.

Toward Dialogue

Professor Morris seems rather too confident that experience-centered learning will spontaneously start up if you simply leave the learner free to explore his own curiosities in the classroom. The trouble with this argument is that it leaves out a prior ingredient, namely, curiosity-generating experience by the learner. How, for instance, is the youngster to be expected to have curiosities about mathematics or poetry or science if he has not been introduced to some of the interesting, thought-provoking, curiosity-awakening subject matter of those fields?

There is a great deal of sentimental double-talk in some of the professional literature about the wonders of a child's mind, the claim being made that there are more starting points for learning, more interests, more nerve-ends of inquisitiveness in the school pupil than all your educational philosophies ever dreamed of. And, the argument proceeds, if educators would just forget about their lesson plans and throw away the Board of Education's curriculum design, real learning could get started. Although this injunction may have some merit for some youngsters, it is hard to see how it could apply to all students. For the deadening, barren and lifeless backgrounds many children bring to school are hardly likely to encourage the kinds of questions and curiosities out of which genuine learning is made.

The main question for science-oriented progressive education to answer is not how to conduct learning once the problem-solving inquiry has been set in motion, but how to generate genuine problems in the first place. It is this first step in all teaching which the literature in progressive pedagogy so often ignores or overlooks. If a teacher can arouse a child's interest and make him inquisitive about something, his job is ninety per cent done; if this has been achieved, possibly any pedagogy would succeed.

Further Readings

Dewey, John. "Science in the Course of Study," Chapter 17 in *Democracy and Education*. New York: The Macmillan Company, 1916.

Jacobson, Nolan P. "The cultural role of scientific behavior," *Educational Theory*, 18 (Winter, 1968), 23–31.

Maccia, Elizabeth. "The scientific method and its implications for education," *Educational Theory*, 7 (October, 1957), 234–248.

Nagel, E. "The place of science in a liberal education," *Daedalus*, 88 (Winter, 1959), 56–74.

Scheffler, I. "Science, morals and educational policy," *Harvard Educational Review*, 26 (Winter, 1956), 1–16.

Stevenson, C. L. "The scientist's role and the aims of education," in *Philosophy and Education*, Israel Scheffler. Boston: Allyn and Bacon, Inc., 1958.

Modern Movements in Educational Philosophy

3

Philosophical Anthropology in Educational Thought

Philosophical Anthropology

To begin with, just what is "philosophical anthropology?"

Philosophy as a discipline has concerned itself, among other subjects, with value—the meaning of human existence and how man ought to live. In this undertaking, philosophical scholarship has customarily been directed to the search for the origin of values and ethical principles in some natural, supernatural, or in any case, universal, realm. Failing this, philosophers have turned to the criticism and validation of values and ethical norms through some logical or linguistic procedure, announcing at the close of their labors that some values are more "valuable" than others. Philosophers have thus shown a strange and stubborn unwillingness to study values where they actually function, i.e., in the lives of ordinary people for whom ethical decision-making is a daily task. By refusing to get down "into the street" where what they say might make a difference, by remaining insulated from values as they are used in life, philosophers enjoy the luxury of making pronouncements about values which are neither right nor wrong but merely irrelevant.

Why not study values where one finds them, where people live—in culture? Why not study actual historical answers to the question of what human life is all about and how we ought to live? Enter the anthropologist. I have, he says, developed methods that might be of help. I know how to study human societies to determine what values they actually hold and the ways they live out those values in their daily lives. When we get an idea of what they actually value, we can then proceed with the criticism and evaluation of those values, i.e., to see if these are good principles to live by.

Consider the subject from the vantage point of anthropology. Over the course of the last five or six decades, while anthropology was becoming a systematic discipline, there has been an ever-widening concern with the total "pattern" or configuration of a given culture. And when patterns differed, the anthropologist has become intrigued with the basic orientation of differing societies—what fundamental principles move and stir their peoples. He wonders why some cultures (like the United States) are essentially Promethean and activist in spirit, valuing the man of action who can conquer and manipulate the environment; why some others (like Polynesia or Southern California) are fun-loving, Dionysian pleasure domes extolling the seeking and finding of bodily delights; why still others are primarily meditative, inwardly reflective and Buddhistic in temperament (like Nepal or Tibet). And inevitably, when one ponders these different ways to live, he begins to wonder which is best and why. When he asks this, he is raising a philosophical question.

Thus, we come to the anthropological study of philosophy, or the philosophical study of anthropology. In either case, we are raising the types of questions which form the subject matter of philosophical anthropology. It is the study of man and of what man can become; what man is and what he ought to be—questions, obviously, in which educational theory has a vital stake.

In the selections to follow, Ernst Cassirer, one of the pioneer figures in this field, begins with some historical background. Then David Bidney explores the concept of culture from the standpoint of value and weighs the possibility of defining "the good society."

ERNST CASSIRER

The Definition of Man in Terms of Human Culture

It was a turning point in Greek culture and Greek thought when Plato interpreted the maxim "Know thyself" in an entirely new sense. This interpretation introduced a problem which was not only alien to

From Ernst Cassirer, *An Essay on Man*, Doubleday & Company edition, pp. 87–93. Copyright © 1944 by Yale University Press. Reprinted by permission of Yale University Press.

pre-Socratic thought but also went far beyond the limits of the Socratic method. In order to obey the demand of the Delphic god, in order to fulfill the religious duty of self-examination and self-knowledge, Socrates had approached the individual man. Plato recognized the limitations of the Socratic way of inquiry. In order to solve the problem, he declared, we must project it upon a larger plan. The phenomena we encounter in our individual experience are so various, so complicated and contradictory that we can scarcely disentangle them. Man is to be studied not in his individual life but in his political and social life. Human nature, according to Plato, is like a difficult text, the meaning of which has to be deciphered by philosophy. But in our personal experience this text is written in such small characters that it becomes illegible. The first labor of philosophy must be to enlarge these characters. Philosophy cannot give us a satisfactory theory of man until it has developed a theory of the state. The nature of man is written in capital letters in the nature of the state. Here the hidden meaning of the text suddenly emerges, and what seemed obscure and confused becomes clear and legible.

But political life is not the only form of a communal human existence. In the history of mankind the state, in its present form, is a late product of the civilizing process. Long before man had discovered this form of social organization he had made other attempts to organize his feelings, desires, and thoughts. Such organizations and systematizations are contained in language, in myth, in religion, and in art. We must accept this broader basis if we wish to develop a theory of man. The state, however important, is not all. It cannot express or absorb all the other activities of man. To be sure, these activities in their historical evolution are closely connected with the development of the state; in many respects they are dependent upon the forms of political life. But, while not possessing a separate historical existence, they have nevertheless a purport and value of their own.

In modern philosophy Comte was one of the first to approach this problem and to formulate it in a clear and systematic way. It is something of a paradox that in this respect we must regard the positivism of Comte as a modern parallel to the Platonic theory of man. Comte was of course never a Platonist. He could not accept the logical and metaphysical presuppositions upon which Plato's theory of ideas is based. Yet, on the other hand, he was strongly opposed to the views of the French ideologists. In his hierarchy of human knowledge two new sciences, the science of social ethics and that of social dynamics, occupy the highest rank. From this sociological viewpoint Comte attacks the psychologism of his age. One of the fundamental maxims of his philosophy is that our method of studying man must, indeed, be subjective, but that it cannot be individual. For the subject we wish to know is not the individual consciousness but the universal subject. If we refer to this subject by the term "humanity," then we must affirm that humanity is not to be explained by man, but man by humanity. The problem must be reformulated and re-examined; it must be put on a broader and sounder basis. Such a basis we have discovered in sociological and historical thought. "To know yourself," says Comte, "know history." Henceforth historical psychology supplements and supersedes all previous forms of individual psychology. "The so-called observations made on the mind, considered in itself and *a priori*," wrote Comte in a letter, "are pure illusions. All that we call *logic, metaphysics, ideology,* is an idle fancy and a dream when it is not an absurdity:"[1]

In Comte's *Cours de philosophie positive* we can trace step by step the nineteenth-century transition in methodological ideals. Comte began merely as a scientist, his interest being apparently wholly absorbed in mathematical, physical, and chemical problems. In his hierarchy of human knowledge the scale goes from astronomy through mathematics, physics, and chemistry to biology. Then comes what looks like a sudden reversal of this order. As we approach the human world the principles of mathematics or of the natural sciences do not become invalid, but they are no longer sufficient. Social phenomena are subject to the same rules as physical phenomena, yet they are of a different and much more complicated character. They are not to be described merely in terms of physics, chemistry, and biology. "In all social phenomena," says Comte, "we perceive the working of the physiological laws of the individual; and moreover something which modifies their effects, and which belongs to the influence of individuals over each other—singularly complicated in the case of the human race by the influence of generations on their successors. Thus it is clear that our social science must issue from that which relates to the life of the individual. On the other hand, there is no occasion to suppose, as some eminent physiologists have done, that Social Physics is only an appendage to Physiology. The phenomena of the two are not identical, though they are homogeneous; and it is of high importance to hold the two sciences separate. As social conditions modify the operation of physiological laws, Social Physics must have a set of observations of its own."[2]

The disciples and followers of Comte were not, however, inclined to accept this distinction. They denied the difference between physiology and sociology because they feared that acknowledging it would lead back to a metaphysical dualism. Their ambition was to establish a purely naturalistic theory of the social and cultural world. To this end they found it necessary to negate and destroy all those barriers which seem to separate the human from the animal world. The theory of evolution had evidently effaced all these differences. Even before Darwin the progress of natural history had frustrated all attempts at such differentiation. In the earlier stages of empirical observation it was still possible for the

---

[1] Comte, *Lettres à Valat*, p. 89; cited from L. Lévy-Bruhl, *La philosophie d'Auguste Comte*. For further details see Lévy-Bruhl, *op. cit.* English trans., *The Philosophy of Comte* (New York and London, 1903), pp. 247 ff.

[2] Comte, *Cours de philosophie positive. English trans.* by Harriet Martineau, *Positive Philosophy* (New York, 1855), Intro., chap. ii, 45 f.

scientist to cherish the hope of finding eventually an anatomical character reserved for man. As late as the eighteenth century it was still a generally accepted theory that there is a marked difference, in some respects a sharp contrast, between the anatomical structure of man and that of other animals. It was one of Goethe's great merits in the field of comparative anatomy that he vigorously combated this theory. The same homogeneity, not merely in the anatomical and physiological but also in the mental structure of man, remained to be demonstrated. For this purpose all the attacks on the older way of thinking had to be concentrated upon one point. The thing to be proved was that what we call the intelligence is by no means a self-dependent, original faculty. Proponents of the naturalistic theories could appeal for proof to the principles of psychology established by the older schools of sensationalism. Taine developed the psychological basis for his general theory of human culture in a work on the intelligence of man.[3] According to Taine, what we call "intelligent behavior" is not a special principle or privilege of human nature; it is only a more refined and complicated play of the same associative mechanism and automatism which we find in all animal reactions. If we accept this explanation the difference between intelligence and instinct becomes negligible; it is a mere difference of degree, not of quality. Intelligence itself becomes a useless and scientifically meaningless term.

The most surprising and paradoxical feature of the theories of this type is the striking contrast between what they promise and what they actually give us. The thinkers who built up these theories were very severe with respect to their methodological principles. They were not content to speak of human nature in terms of our common experience, for they were striving after a much higher ideal, an ideal of absolute scientific exactness. But if we compare their results with this standard we cannot help being greatly disappointed. "Instinct" is a very vague term. It may have a certain descriptive value but it has obviously no explanatory value. By reducing some classes of organic or human phenomena to certain fundamental instincts, we have not alleged a new cause; we have only introduced a new name. We have put a question, not answered one. The term "instinct" gives us at best an *idem per idem*, and in most cases it is an *obscurum per obscurius*. Even in the description of animal behavior most modern biologists and psycho-biologists have become very cautious about using it. They warn us against the fallacies which appear to be inextricably connected with it. They try rather to avoid or to abandon "the error-freighted concept of instinct and the oversimple concept of intelligence." In one of his most recent publications Robert M. Yerkes declares that the terms "instinct" and "intelligence" are outmoded and that the concepts for which they stand are sadly in need of redefining.[4] But in the field of anthropological philosophy we are still,

3 *De l'intelligence* (Paris, 1870), 2 vols.
4 *Chimpanzees*, p. 110.

apparently, far from any such redefinition. Here these terms are very often accepted quite naïvely without critical analysis. When used in this way the concept of instinct becomes an example of that typical methodological error which was described by William James as the psychologist's fallacy. The word "instinct," which may be useful for the description of animal or human behavior, is hypostatized into a sort of natural power. Curiously enough this error was often committed by thinkers who, in all other respects, felt secure against relapses into scholastic realism or "faculty-psychology." A very clear and impressive criticism of this mode of thinking is contained in John Dewey's *Human Nature and Conduct.* "It is unscientific," writes Dewey, "to try to restrict original activities to a definite number of sharply demarcated classes of instincts. And the practical result of this attempt is injurious. To classify is, indeed, as useful as it is natural. The indefinite multitude of particular and changing events is met by the mind with acts of defining, inventorying, and listing, reducing to common heads and tying up in bunches. . . . But when we assume that our lists and bunches represent fixed separations and collections *in rerum natura,* we obstruct rather than aid our transactions with things. We are guilty of a presumption which nature promptly punishes. We are rendered incompetent to deal effectively with the delicacies and novelties of nature and life. . . . The tendency to forget the office of distinctions and classifications, and to take them as marking things in themselves is the current fallacy of scientific specialism. . . . This attitude which once flourished in physical science now governs theorizing about human nature. Man has been resolved into a definite collection of primary instincts which may be numbered, catalogued and exhaustively described one by one. Theorists differ only or chiefly as to their number and ranking. Some say one, self-love; some two, egoism and altruism; some three, greed, fear and glory; while today writers of a more empirical turn run the number up to fifty and sixty. But in fact there are as many specific reactions to differing stimulating conditions as there is time for, and our lists are only classifications for a purpose."[5]

After this brief survey of the different methods that have hitherto been employed in answering the question: What is man? we now come to our central issue. Are these methods sufficient and exhaustive? Or is there still another approach to an anthropological philosophy? Is any other way left open besides that of psychological introspection, biological observation and experiment, and of historical investigation? I have endeavored to discover such an alternative approach in my *Philosophy of Symbolic Forms.*[6] The method of this work is by no means a radical innovation. It is not designed to abrogate but to complement former views. The philosophy of symbolic forms starts from the presupposition that, if

[5] John Dewey, *Human Nature and Conduct* (New York, Holt & Co., 1922), Pt. II, sec. 5, p. 131.
[6] *Philosophie der symbolischen Formen.* Vol. I, *Die Sprache* (1923); Vol. II, *Das mythische Denken* (1925); Vol. III, *Phaenomenologie der Erkenntnis* (1929).

there is any definition of the nature or "essence" of man, this definition can only be understood as a functional one, not a substantial one. We cannot define man by any inherent principle which constitutes his metaphysical essence—nor can we define him by any inborn faculty or instinct that may be ascertained by empirical observation. Man's outstanding characteristic, his distinguishing mark, is not his metaphysical or physical nature—but his work. It is this work, it is the system of human activities, which defines and determines the circle of "humanity." Language, myth, religion, art, science, history are the constituents, the various sectors of this circle. A "philosophy of man" would therefore be a philosophy which would give us insight into the fundamental structure of each of these human activities, and which at the same time would enable us to understand them as an organic whole. Language, art, myth, religion are no isolated, random creations. They are held together by a common bond. But this bond is not a *vinculum substantiale*, as it was conceived and described in scholastic thought; it is rather a *vinculum functionale*. It is the basic function of speech, of myth, of art, of religion that we must seek far behind their innumerable shapes and utterances, and that in the last analysis we must attempt to trace back to a common origin.

Toward Dialogue

The foregoing, an admittedly murky section from Ernst Cassirer's *An Essay on Man*, might be paraphrased and summarized as follows:

When Socrates uttered his famous dictum, "Know thyself," he meant it literally: understand your own being by means of your own private experience. Plato, however, chose to interpret this dictum more broadly: know thyself as a member of a class, a representative instance of the Idea or Form of Man. We want to know not what you or I might be but what Man is, and the definition of man is to be found not in your private experience or mine but in the manifest human qualities exhibited by all men.

The nineteenth-century French philosopher, Auguste Comte, was the first to approach this problem in a systematic way. To know Man, he said, know history, i.e., what man has done. Forget your metaphysics and ideologies; these are illusions. Instead, study man in society through empirical observation, what we might call Social Physics, a new discipline rather similar to Natural Physics but requiring its own set of observations.

Comte's followers made the mistake of not keeping the two sciences separate, and continued to believe that the study of man-in-society was a purely naturalistic undertaking governed by the same rules as those of physics or biology, rather like studying cells in a living organism or molecules in a chemical reaction. Man, they argued (with Darwin's help), is physiologically not very different from the remainder of the animal kingdom. Even his so-called "intelligence" is not a special principle or privilege of human nature but simply a more refined version of the reaction mechanism we find in all animal behavior.

Such naturalistic theories, however, fail to deliver all that they promise. In striving for scientific exactness, for example, the naturalistic sociologists tried to identify human instincts. But the term "instinct" doesn't explain anything; it is merely an arbitrary class name for some phenomena which the investigator wishes to bunch together. Using a vague, pseudo-classificatory term like "instinct," you can run the list of instincts to fifty or sixty items, or as far as you want or have time for. But what, in the end, does this tell you?

So, after this survey of methods which have been used to answer the question, What is Man? we must ask: Do these methods help? Do they do us any good? Or is there another approach to anthropological philosophy?

Yes, there is. We can call it the Philosophy of Symbolic Forms. This philosophy begins with the assumption that if there is any definition of man's nature or "essence," it can be understood only in a functional sense. "Man's outstanding characteristic, his distinguishing mark, is not his metaphysical or physical nature—but his work. It is this work, it is the system of human activities, which defines and determines the circle of 'humanity.' "

This final paragraph of paraphrase is philosophical anthropology "in a nutshell." Cassirer means that we must understand man by what he makes and uses. Of course, we know that man makes things—tools, vehicles, cities. But more important, perhaps, are his symbolic forms— language, myth, religion, art, science, and history.

But what else ought we to include in the "circle of humanity?" How about man's institutions, his customs, his morals, his prejudices? If man is to be defined by culture, what must be included in our definition of the word 'culture'?

DAVID BIDNEY

Normative Culture and the Categories of Value

In considering what constitutes the unity of a culture it seems scarcely sufficient to point out that the elements of a culture are functionally interdependent, since the significant question concerns how the culture is unified and how it differs from other culture systems? Psychologically, it is understandable that wholeness, or unity, should be valued highly in an age which is characterized by fractionalism and social crises and that the concept of integration should appear to be a magic formula, so to speak, for resolving our sociocultural dilemmas. Upon critical analysis, however, it soon becomes apparent that integration apart from its relation to some dominant end, or objective, has no cultural significance. In evaluating any given culture the essential problems are how it is integrated and for what it is integrated, not is it integrated? The quest for wholeness and unity is not intelligible apart from some specification of the value of a given form of unity in relation to other forms.

THE CATEGORIES OF VALUE AND THE TYPES OF CULTURE

Since the meaning of a culture is to be understood teleofunctionally by reference to the end, or final objective, which its adherents strive to realize individually and collectively, we must next consider the basic types of value which it is possible for man to pursue. Ever since the time of Plato, philosophers have recognized that there are three fundamental categories of value, namely, truth, goodness, and beauty. Truth may be defined as an attribute of thought by virtue of which the mind conceives the real nature of things. The good may be understood as a property of things and acts considered desirable. Beauty may be defined as an attribute of the forms of things which renders them attractive. I think it may be demonstrated that actual historical cultures have been oriented so as to manifest the dominance of one or the other of these categories of value.

The problem of values as applied to culture may be considered from two distinct points of view. On the one hand, one may investigate the category of value which serves as a focus of integration for any given culture. On the other hand, one may inquire whether culture itself, that is, the concept of culture may not be conceived as essentially a value expression. Thus, the question as to whether a given culture is to be understood as primarily aesthetic, moral, or factual is to be differentiated

From *Theoretical Anthropology* by David Bidney (New York: Columbia University Press, 1953), pp. 400–432.

from the question whether the concept of culture is to be conceived in similar terms. I think it may be shown that the concept of culture has been interpreted as if it referred primarily to aesthetic, moral, or factual-scientific phenomena. This may explain why definitions of culture in the literature of the humanities, as well as in ethnology, have been so numerous and diverse. Similarly, the ethnological perspective and evaluation of cultural phenomena will in turn depend upon the concept of culture which is utilized implicitly or explicitly. Thus, if culture be understood as essentially an aesthetic phenomenon, the student of culture will be concerned with the aesthetic aspects of the cultures he is investigating and will tend to neglect other aspects of culture. Similarly, a moralistic conception of culture will predetermine one to orient his studies with reference to moral interests to the neglect of the aesthetic and the noetic. In order to illustrate this thesis I shall begin with a brief historical survey of the philosophical and ethnological literature which treats of culture as an aesthetic norm.

CULTURE AS AN AESTHETIC NORM

We owe to the Greek Sophists and to Protagoras in particular the insight that "man is the measure of all things" and that man as a creator of culture is an artist molding himself in conformity with his beliefs and ideals. So conceived, human culture in general may be understood as "the art of living," or as the general art which comprises all the special arts of human society. Like any special artistic expression, the culture of a particular society may be contemplated as an aesthetic configuration manifested in the static artifacts of a culture, as well as in the actual modes of life and thought. In this sense aesthetic style is the final distinctive measure of man, taken individually and collectively.

Historically, this view of culture is best known to us in the West from a study of classic Greek culture, although Chinese culture also developed it to a high degree. In fact "form" and "face-saving" have much greater significance in the East than in the West—a point modern ethnologists who have participated in both types of culture have noted. In classic Greek culture the important role of music, literature, drama, the choral dance, and gymnastics, as well as the mathematical sciences, bears witness to its aesthetic orientation. Even Plato's attempt, under Socratic influence, to reorient Greek culture toward moral interests succeeded only in reaffirming the primacy of the aesthetic values, since it was the mathematical forms which served to define his Idea of the Good.

From a sociological standpoint Plato's aesthetic conception of culture may be best understood against the background of the Athenian society of his time. Greek culture was actually a culture of the leisure class made possible by the utilization of slave labor for all the menial, utilitarian tasks of social life. Thus, when Plato and Aristotle discoursed upon education and culture, they had in mind the free-born Athenian citizen and gentleman who had the social opportunity and leisure to cultivate the liberal arts and sciences. This partly explains why the natural sciences, such as physics, were scarcely developed except in a speculative way, since technology and science seemed to Greek educators antithetical. By contrast, the conceptual or theoretical sciences, such as mathematics and astronomy, reached a high stage of development in the Platonic academy.[1]

This liberal tradition of a cultural aristocracy was transmitted to the Romans, but under Stoic influence it became transformed into a universal human ideal, the ideal of *humanitas*, considered as the mark of all that is distinctively and normatively human.[2] This Roman tradition was carried on throughout the Middle Ages as the study of the "humanities," comprising the *trivium* (grammar, rhetoric, and logic) and the *quadrivium* (arithmetic, music, geometry, and astronomy). This program of education also set the pattern for the modern liberal arts and the study of the humanities.

So it has come about that culture, which for the Greeks comprised all the liberal arts and sciences as integrated in an over-all aesthetic pattern, has for the educated people of the West come to mean popularly a refinement of taste manifested in literary, emotional, and intuitive appreciation of the fine arts, such as music and painting, together with a knowledge of classical literature and contemporary letters. Our aesthetic culture has become divorced from our daily life as an added refinement, not necessarily bearing any connection in practice to social conditions. Aesthetic culture, far from being a total vision of life, a "testament of beauty," as Robert Bridges phrased it, has become an ornament, or luxury, which enables a select few to escape from the vulgarities of daily experience. In brief, the major paradox of our contemporary democratic culture is the fact that our educational system is based upon abstract, aristocratic cultural values, whereas our social system is organized on democratic lines, and our scientific technology is geared to material wealth and national power. The incompatibility of our cultural ideals and practices is demonstrated daily by the social esteem in which our educational system is held and the distrust of the educated man in practical affairs.

In modern times Alfred North Whitehead seems to have recaptured this Greek mathematical-aesthetic vision of culture by recognizing that mathematics as the generalized study of pattern is a prerequisite of understanding good and beauty in all forms of culture. According to Whitehead:

> The notion of pattern is as old as civilization. Every art is founded on the study of pattern. Also the cohesion of social systems depends on the maintenance of patterns of behaviour; and advances in civili-

[1] Farrington, *Greek Science*, Vol. I, ch. ix.
[2] Bidney, "The Philosophical Anthropology of Ernst Cassirer," in *The Philosophy of Ernst Cassirer*, pp. 478–84.

zation depend on the fortunate modification of such behaviour patterns. Thus the infusion of pattern into natural occurrences, and the stability of such patterns, and the modification of such patterns, is the necessary condition for the realization of the Good. Mathematics is the most powerful technique for the understanding of pattern, and for the analysis of the relationships of patterns. Here we reach the fundamental justification for the topic of Plato's lecture. . . . The essence of this generalized mathematics is the study of the most observable examples of the relevant patterns; and applied mathematics is the transference of this study to other examples of the realization of these patterns.[3]

Thus, for Whitehead, as for Plato, the real world is good when it is beautiful.

It is important to bear in mind that one may arrive at an aesthetic philosophy of culture and life by either of two logical approaches. One may, as in the case of Plato and Whitehead, base his philosophy of culture upon a comprehensive metaphysical and scientific foundation and come to believe in the primacy of the aesthetic category. Or else, one may come to a similar conclusion by the impressionistic method of denying any metaphysical truths and by accepting the immediate aesthetic impressions of experience. According to this relativistic perspective, one philosophy and mode of life is as good and true as another, and the criterion of choice is simply the preference of the individual. In Somerset Maugham's classic story *Of Human Bondage* the author summarizes his conclusions on the meaning of life.

As the weaver elaborated his pattern for no end but the pleasure of his aesthetic sense, so might a man live his life, or if one was forced to believe that his actions were outside his choosing, so might a man look at his life, that it made a pattern. . . . Out of the manifold events of his life, his deeds, his feelings, his thoughts, he might make a design, regular, elaborate, complicated, or beautiful; and though it might be no more than an illusion that he had the power of selection, though it might be no more than a fantastic legerdemain in which appearances were interwoven with moonbeams, that did not matter; it seemed, and so to him it was. In the vast warp of life, (a river arising from no spring and flowing endlessly to no sea,) with the background of his fancies that there was no meaning and that nothing was important, a man might get a personal satisfaction in selecting the various strands that worked out the pattern. There was one pattern, the most obvious, perfect and beautiful, in which a man was born, grew to manhood, married, produced children, toiled for his bread and died; but there were others, intricate and wonderful, in which happiness did not enter and in which success was not attempted; and in them might be discovered a more troubling grace.[4]

There is obviously a vast difference between Maugham's empirical, impressionistic view of life patterns divorced from all considerations

[3] Whitehead, "Mathematics and the Good," in *The Philosophy of Alfred North Whitehead*, ed. by P. A. Schilpp, pp. 677–78.
[4] Maugham, *Of Human Bondage*, p. 590.

of truth and finality and the metaphysically oriented intellectual vision of Plato and Whitehead. For Maugham each pattern of life, whether it be rational or irrational, has a romantic beauty of its own, simply because it is an expression of life capable of yielding satisfaction to someone. For Whitehead, a pattern of life to be significant must be grounded in the eternal harmony of nature.

Among modern philosophers, Nietzsche was one of the first to consider the problem of a philosophy of culture and to classify cultures according to their dominant value-orientation. According to Nietzsche, all culture is a delusion of the will to life, and he distinguishes three such "planes of illusion." In *The Birth of Tragedy* he writes:

> One is chained by the Socratic love of knowledge and the delusion of being able thereby to heal the eternal wound of existence; another is ensnared by art's seductive veil of beauty fluttering before his eyes; still another by the metaphysical comfort that beneath the flux of phenomena eternal life flows on indestructibly: to say nothing of the more ordinary and almost more powerful illusions which the will has always at hand. These three planes of illusion are on the whole designed only for the more nobly formed natures, who in general feel profoundly the weight and burden of existence, and must be deluded by exquisite stimulants into forgetfulness of their sorrow. All that we call culture is made up of these stimulants; and, according to the proportion of the ingredients, we have either a dominantly *Socratic* or *artistic* or *tragic* culture; or, if historical exemplifications are wanted, there is either an Alexandrian or a Hellenic or a Buddhistic culture.[5]

When we substitute for Nietzsche's tragic type the moralistic type, then his classification corresponds to the three basic value categories.

Nietzsche prophetically rejected a predominantly theoretical, or scientific, culture of the Socratic, Alexandrian type, because, notwithstanding its inherent optimism and delusion of limitless power, it gradually "drifts towards a dreadful destruction" when the barbaric slave class comes to regard their mode of existence as an intolerable injustice. So, too, artistic, or Hellenic, culture is unsatisfactory because its underlying attitude toward existence is unrealistic and negative; it seeks to escape from the struggle and pain of existence by contemplating aesthetic forms rather than by grappling with life's problems. The only acceptable alternative for Nietzsche is tragic culture (also called Dionysian culture in his *Ecce Homo*), which expresses an affirmative, realistic attitude toward the intrinsic tragedy of existence. Tragic culture is said to symbolize a Dionysian wisdom (which takes the place of science) as to the inherent evil of life through Apollonian art media. This Dionysian-Apollonian vision gives one the courage to live resolutely and without the "effeminate" scruples of the traditional Christian ethos. Nietzsche may be thought of as accepting an ethically oriented culture expressed in Apollonian individualistic art forms and as rejecting either a positivistic type

[5] *The Philosophy of Nietzsche*, pp. 287–88.

of culture, which encourages the development of technological civilization, or an artistic type which, as in Schopenhauer, seeks escape into the dream world of art forms.

It is important to note that for Nietzsche, Apollonian and Dionysian art forms are polar opposites in a metaphysical and also in an empirical sense. Apollonian culture expresses not only measured restraint but also the principle of individuation (*principium individuationis*) as exemplified in the forms of the dream world, as well as in sculpture and the plastic arts. Dionysian culture symbolizes the "drunkenness" of spirit, the emotion of ecstacy, which enables the individual to lose self-consciousness and to experience a mystic feeling of oneness—the primordial unity—with his fellowmen and nature. This experience of unity was attained in Greek music and the Bacchic choruses. Apparently for Nietzsche the main significance of these Greek art forms lies in their deeper metaphysical and cosmic meanings, the characteristics of measured restraint and ecstatic frenzy being only the psychological concomitants. Through Apollonian culture media one gives expression to the principle of individuation, to finitude, or limitation of form; through Dionysian culture media, such as music and the dance, one attains the feeling of the infinite, of the undifferentiated unity of man and nature. These fundamental metaphysical principles were synthesized in Plato's *Timaeus* as the union of geometrical Forms or Ideas with the Receptacle or undifferentiated material ground principle, which gives rise to the empirical world of changing nature.

Ruth Benedict's *Patterns of Culture* is significant historically as an attempt by a contemporary ethnologist to apply the concept of Dionysian and Apollonian culture types, which she derived from her study of Nietzsche, to native tribal cultures. As interpreted by her, the Dionysian type of man is imbued with the desire to achieve excess in personal experience in order to attain "the illumination of frenzy." The Apollonian type of man is said to be guided in all his activities by a certain measure and norm. Benedict finds that the Zuñi Indians of the Southwest reveal an Apollonian pattern in their culture, whereas the Plains Indians, with their ecstatic visions, manifest a Dionysian mentality. The terms "Dionysian" and "Apollonian" do not represent fixed constellations of traits identical in every culture, but rather certain types or patterns compatible with diversity of empirical content.

With reference to our analysis of Nietzsche's views, it is difficult for me to understand how Benedict could have arrived at the conclusion that "Greece did not carry out, as the Pueblos have, the distrust of individualism that the Apollonian way of life implies, but which in Greece was scanted because of forces with which it came in conflict. Zuñi ideals and institutions, on the other hand, are rigorous on this point."[6] As I understand Nietzsche, the essence of Apollonian culture is precisely its

[6] Benedict, *Patterns of Culture*, p. 73.

emphasis upon the principle of individuation—a factor which in practice made for extreme individualism among the Greeks, as Thucydides testifies in his history of the Peloponnesian War. By contrast, the cultural function of the Dionysian festivals and mysteries was to foster a feeling of sympathy and ecstasy which transcended individual consciousness. Thus, Dionysian art forms, far from fostering extreme individualism, actually served to merge individual differences in a transcendental feeling of cosmic unity.

In abstracting the notions of measured restraint and ecstatic community of feeling from their context in Greek culture, Benedict has retained only a nominal similarity to the original ontological meaning of the terms "Apollonian" and "Dionysian" and has in fact perverted the philosophical values intended by Nietzsche. In seeking individual supernatural visions, and in trying to shame their rivals, the Plains Indians and the Kwakiutl Indians of the Northwest coast endeavored to emphasize their individual differences. Their so-called "Dionysian excesses" are the antithesis of the Greek Dionysian rituals whose object it was to achieve ecstatic self-forgetfulness. Similarly, the so-called "Apollonian rituals" of the Indians of the Southwest tend functionally to promote a sense of the harmony of man and nature and to suppress individual competition—an attitude which is the antithesis of the Greek Apollonian. One must differentiate, therefore, between Apollonian and Dionysian "excess" so as to determine whether the excess leads to accentuation or elimination of individual differences. To attribute all excess to the Dionysian mentality and all restraint to the Apollonian mentality is not to conform to the true meaning of the concepts as employed by Nietzsche. By emptying the terms "Apollonian" and "Dionysian" of all ontological meaning, Benedict has failed to see that "excess" and "restraint" are relative terms whose ontological import varies with the objective which the adherents of a given culture seek to achieve.

CULTURE AS A MORAL NORM

Moralistic culture is culture lived and organized according to some dominant idea of the good for a given society. It is culture regarded as a "way of life" and prescribing an ideal of how one ought to live to become an acceptable member of society. As an absolute normative ideal, the concept of *humanitas*, or humanity, is to be understood as the way of life peculiar to man and involving the development of those ethical characteristics which differentiate man from the beasts. Absolute moral culture tends to become identified with "civilization," as when we speak of civilization versus barbarism and ask rhetorically, "Are we civilized?" By contrast, relativistic moral culture, as described by anthropologists and sociologists, is only the way of life characteristic of a given people and does not involve any evaluation of its validity for all mankind.

In a moralistic conception of culture, emphasis is placed on the functional significance of traits and institutions for the life of the individual and his society. This, it appears, is the reason for the basic difference between the aesthetic approach to culture of Kroeber and Benedict, on the one hand, and the functionalistic approach of Malinowski and Radcliffe-Brown, on the other. Through his insistence that "culture must be understood as a means to an end, that is, instrumentally or functionally,"[7] Malinowski has implicitly adopted a moralistic approach to ethnology in general. Thus, for the functionalist the unit of culture is the social institution which fulfills basic biosocial requirements, whereas for those who adopt an aesthetic approach, as does Benedict, the unit of culture is the pattern or configuration. The reason underlying this disparity of culture units is, I suggest, that each party tends to conceive culture in general under a different value category.

Psychologically, the most significant characteristic of moral culture is the fact that those who share it entertain a tragic and more or less ascetic way of life. Metaphysically, the mores are thought to have intrinsic connections with the processes of nature and to receive divine sanction and support. It becomes, therefore, a matter of life and death for the individual, as well as his society, that these mores be adhered to strictly. This, it appears, is the ontological basis of many primitive taboos and renders intelligible the severe trials which many native peoples impose upon their numbers in the critical "rites of passage" marking the human life cycle from birth to death.[8] These ordeals and rituals provide meaning and dignity to native life by associating their culture with cosmic processes and offering social recognition of the individual's acquired status and role. Contrary to the novelistic fiction that natives lead care-free lives, ethnologists have demonstrated that native peoples have a predominantly tragic outlook upon life, since they imagine nature as an organic whole in which all forces and events interact so as to promote or hinder human welfare.[9] This explains why *primitive religion must be understood as the integrative factor in primitive culture*, binding together all its institutions and pervading all its manifold rites and customs. It is because religion is "an everpresent dimension of experience" that native peoples fail to designate by a special term.[10]

All the Hebrew-Christian-Muslim scriptures may be described as authoritative historic revelations of the knowledge of good and evil which, it is believed, the Deity revealed to mankind for their salvation. Although Genesis relates that man was originally forbidden to partake of the tree of knowledge of good and evil, the Deity subsequently became reconciled to this perverse human curiosity and arranged to sup-

[7] Malinowski, *A Scientific Theory of Culture*, pp. 67–68.
[8] Tozzer, *Social Origins and Social Continuities*, ch. iii.
[9] Radin, *Primitive Man as a Philosopher*, ch. xi; Lévy-Bruhl, *Primitives and the Supernatural*; Thompson and Joseph, *The Hopi Way*.
[10] Lee, *Religious Perspectives in Anthropology*, p. 8.

plement human reason and experience by divine revelation and example. Henceforth this way of life became, as Hebrew and Christian theologians testify, the prime objective of human interest and a matter of vital concern calling for crucial decision and acts of faith.[11] By comparison, the detached, disengaged attitude of theoretical speculation and the leisurely enjoyment of aesthetic forms and patterns seemed to rest on a tragic misconception of human values and human destiny. Human life on earth was regarded as a series of tragic moral crises brought about by man's willful disobedience and transgression of natural and divine law.

From a philosophical perspective the culture of the West may be said to be indebted to Aristotle for its moralistic outlook, just as it is obligated to Plato to some extent for its aesthetic orientation. For it was Aristotle who was responsible for the teleological approach to the study of nature and culture and for the subsequent philosophical emphasis upon ends, or final causes. In the field of politics and ethics his naturalistic analysis of human virtue and social organization still retains much of its validity for us, since it is in accord with the biological orientation of modern thought.

Historically, it is noteworthy that the Greek term *ethos* draws attention to the process of habituation with reference to a given ideal. The Latin term *mores* tends to divert attention from habit to custom, or convention (the Greek *nomos*), and thus sharpens the contrast between nature and art which the Greek term *ethos* harmonized. By indicating that ethics is natural and yet not given by nature, that we are adapted by nature for virtue, but require training and habituation to achieve it, Aristotle[12] kept in mind what I have called the polarity of nature and culture. The idea of the good was for Aristotle a practical and rational human ideal, not an impersonal, transcendental form of reality and thought, as in Plato, to be contemplated for its aesthetic value.

In the great medieval synthesis of Greek philosophy and Christian religion, moral-religious culture was intensified and integrated to a degree hitherto unknown. The *Summa theologica* of St. Thomas Aquinas and the *Divine Comedy* of Dante gave classic theoretical and poetic expression of the ideals of this culture. The essence of this way of life is the view "that this is a moral world and that sin and virtue not merely have a practical issue but an eternal significance; they not only matter but they matter eternally."[13]

The ideal man of medieval Christian culture was not, as among the Greeks, the wise man or philosopher in quest of rational wisdom, but rather the saint, the righteous man, dedicated to a life of ascetic holiness and imbued with faith in divine grace and love.[14] Life on earth was

---

[11] Kierkegaard, *Either/Or*; also *Concluding Unscientific Postscript*.
[12] Aristotle, *Nicomachean Ethics*, 1103a.
[13] Mumford, *The Condition of Man*, p. 146.
[14] Turner, *The Great Cultural Traditions*, II, 1144, 1161.

conceived as a "pilgrim's progress," as a way fraught with temptation and moral crises in which the individual prepared himself for the Day of Judgment and life after death. The whole process of living from birth to death became the direct concern of the Church, since the Church alone was the spokesman of God on earth.

Metaphysically, the final synthesis achieved by St. Thomas was the doctrine that God was to be conceived as the highest and universal good and the end which man was destined to seek. The human soul was said to achieve its consummate happiness through the beatific vision of the Divine Good, thereby transcending itself and participating in the infinite source of its being. Unlike Aristotle, St. Thomas maintains that the specific object of moral value is God, the supreme good from whom all beings derive their goodness. The Platonic Idea of the Good, which Aristotle found so unintelligible and for which he could provide no place in his naturalistic ethics, became, when combined with the notion of the personal God of the Hebrew-Christian tradition, the very cornerstone of the whole medieval cultural synthesis.[15] It is this latent Platonism, concealed in the Aristotelian terminology, which accounts, in my opinion, for the final Thomistic identification of theoretical and practical virtue.[16]

With the growing secularization of thought during the seventeenth and eighteenth centuries, ethical and political theories were separated largely from theology, but the essential moralistic orientation of Western culture remained. The rationalists of the period utilized the Stoic ideal of *humanitas* as a postulate of their political theory and regarded the state as a historical institution organized to serve the common interests of its component citizens. In conjunction with the doctrine of natural rights, sanctioned partly by the Christian belief in the intrinsic value of the individual soul, the universal ideal of a common humanity served as a powerful revolutionary instrument of political and social reform in the struggle against arbitrary government and outmoded institutions. This moralistic perspective was embodied later in the Constitution of the United States of America, which set forth the doctrine of the inalienable rights of the individual as against the state. Whatever discrepancies may still exist between the ideals of the Constitution and actual social and political practices, the fact remains that the ideal culture of the United States has been primarily a moral one, guided by fixed principles of right and wrong. There is, in my opinion, a necessary, logical connection between the moral orientation of American culture and the fact that the United States has intervened in two world struggles and given generously of its resources without expecting to gain dominion over others.

States organized on an amoral basis, such as Germany, Italy, and Japan in the period between the First World War and the Second World War, have always regarded themselves as "beyond good and

15 A. E. Taylor, *Plato; the Man and His Work*, pp. 288–89.
16 Gilson, *The Spirit of Mediaeval Philosophy*.

evil" and as not bound by moral conventions of right and wrong. Such states have always underestimated the dynamic power of moral ideals, even when they are imperfectly adhered to, and in their cynical adherence to *realpolitik* they have failed to reckon with the real efficacy of the ideal as a determining cultural force. In the moral state and society might is joined with right, and power is not deliberately sought as an end in itself irrespective of the human costs. The organization of the United Nations is a profession of faith in the ideal of a common humanity, and its validity as an ideal is not impaired by the fact that the world is still divided into two blocks whose aims and methods are antithetical. In proclaiming anew the doctrine of the universal rights of man and in outlawing genocide, the peoples of the world are seeking to reintroduce a moral perspective into the government of men and are laying the foundations for an emergent world culture.

CULTURE AS AN IDEOLOGICAL NORM

Culture may also be viewed from an intellectual perspective as essentially an ideology, or system of ideas. Thus, some modern ethnologists have defined culture as "communicable intelligence," as "conventional understandings," and as "communicated ideas." The distinguishing characteristic of all such ideational views of culture is their identification of culture with a given tradition of ideas. Whereas the aesthetic approach to culture looks at culture from the perspective of feeling and intuition, and the moral approach views culture in terms of human will and effort, the ideational view of culture regards the intellect as the primary source of cultural experience. According to this ideational view of culture, the unit of culture may be said to be the symbolic form, idea, or meaning, rather than the aesthetic pattern, or the institution.

Politically, the enthronement of the intellect may lead to the dictatorship of the "philosopher-king," as in Plato's *Republic.* If all virtue and culture are based upon scientific knowledge, it appears foolish to leave the government of the state in hands other than those of the scientist, who should know the absolute truth concerning man and society.

It is significant that in the nineteenth century another philosopher-scientist, Auguste Comte, also sought to establish a "positive polity," with a hierarchy of scientist-priests who were to impose their scientific political and social culture upon their society. Notwithstanding Comte's opposition to theological authoritarianism and to any metaphysical absolutes, he reintroduced the very political dictatorship which he opposed in others in the name of positivism.

Historically, too, when the doctrine of positivism was tried out in practice in Latin America, it served as a justification of dictatorship. As Leopold Zea has shown in his instructive survey "Positivism and Porfirism in Latin America,"[17] the dictatorship of Porfirio Diaz in Mexico

---

[17] Zea, "Positivism and Porfirism in Latin America," in *Ideological Differences and World Order,* ed. by Northrop, pp. 166–91.

(1884–1911) received the active support of educators, who consciously adhered either to the "sociocracy" and "religion of humanity" of Comte or to the bourgeois liberalism of John Stuart Mill and Herbert Spencer. The only liberty allowed by the Diaz government was economic liberty; political liberty, it was assumed, would automatically be attained with the diffusion of scientific education. As Zea concludes, "Positivism had become another instrument serving the desire of power and dominion that had distinguished Spanish Americans at all times. Scientific absolutism had superseded religious absolutism."[18]

Similarly, it is not an accident of history that modern Communism, with its doctrine of the "dictatorship of the proletariat," should claim absolute scientific validity. Instead of the political positivists, we now have the Communist state, which arrogates to itself in the name of Marxism the right to determine the truth of scientific theories.[19] Political dictatorship is justified in the name of dialectical and historical materialism, just as formerly it had been proclaimed in the name of positive science.

Among contemporary American philosophers, Whitehead and Northrop have attempted to reinterpret the basic vision of Greek scientific and philosophical thought for modern life. Whitehead, we have noted, recaptured the Greek mathematical-aesthetic perspective of Plato by maintaining that mathematics provides the basis for an understanding of the good and the beautiful in a normative culture. The ultimate good is thought of as an aesthetic pattern conceived through mathematical insight. Northrop, on the other hand, seeks to achieve a synthesis of modern science and art by combining the ontological principles of finite form and the infinite, undifferentiated aesthetic continuum, as suggested in Plato's *Timaeus*. The forms are conceptual postulates indispensable for an understanding of modern science; the undifferentiated aesthetic continuum is known by immediate intuition. Thus, whereas Whitehead derives the concept of the beautiful directly from mathematical pattern, Northrop derives the experience of beauty from a distinct metaphysical and epistemological source. By identifying intellectual concepts by postulation as the distinctive contribution of Western culture and aesthetic concepts by intuition as the contribution of Oriental culture, Northrop neatly divides world culture into two opposite and complementary segments, which require only mutual appreciation to bring about an integrated, normative world culture.[20]

The important point to note in this connection is that the theory of the scientific-aesthetic integration of culture tends to reduce the category of the good to the category of the true. Northrop, in particular, has restated this Platonic thesis most explicitly:

> The good is neither a fact nor a meaning; it is a set of philosophical presuppositions. These presuppositions have nothing to do with

18 *Ibid.*, p. 189.
19 Huxley, *Heredity, East and West.*
20 Northrop, *The Meeting of East and West.*

ethics, since empirically and intellectually speaking, there is no such thing as ethics. There are no purely ethical facts as there are no purely ethical meanings. There is only the nature of things and one's basic theory concerning what is. One's philosophical presuppositions designate this basic theory. "Good" is merely a single word for this basic theory. It is one's philosophy rather than, as modern ethical teachers suppose, an item, either naturalistic or idealistic, within that philosophy.[21]

In other words, the word "good" is but a name for the deductively formulatable system of empirically verified basic common denominator concepts of natural science, when these concepts are considered not with respect to their truth as tested by natural science against nature but with respect to their implication for the fulfillment of the true nature of man when applied to an act of human behavior and to human relations. In short, ethics is not a science yet to be created; ethics is an art, the art which takes the basic common denominator concepts as determined and verified by natural science and applies them to personal behavior and social relations.[22]

According to Northrop, a knowledge of scientific facts of nature together with their philosophical presuppositions as defined in a philosophy of science is sufficient to identify the good and to provide a norm for human conduct. By identifying philosophical scientific truth with "the good" and denying any purely ethical facts or meanings, he has explained away any specifically moral problems. This position is the antithesis of the Aristotelian and Kantian positions, which specify a distinct moral good and practical reason other than scientific theory of nature and theoretical reason. Northrop's categorical position appears to be the opposite of that of the Neo-Kantians, who would reduce the category of the true to that of the good. That is, whereas Neo-Kantians, such as W. M. Urban,[23] argue that "what ought to be" is the criterion of "what is" taken as factually true, Northrop holds that "what is" ontologically, as defined by a given philosophy of science, is the criterion of "what ought to be" in cultural life. The entire Kantian theory of the autonomy of ethics is dismissed as an "error," and "the assumption of British philosophy of both the Cambridge realistic and the Oxford idealistic version that ethics is moral science" is said to be "similarly misguided."[24]

FACTS AND CULTURAL VALUES

What is particularly significant about modern empirical science is its methodical exclusion of the values, such as the good and the beauti-

[21] Northrop, "Philosophy and World Peace," in *Approaches to World Peace*, p. 644.

[22] Northrop, "Ethics and the Integration of Natural Knowledge," in *The Nature of Concepts, Their Inter-relation and Role in Social Structure*, p. 124.

[23] Urban, *The Intelligible World*; see also Bidney, "The Philosophical Anthropology of Ernst Cassirer," in *The Philosophy of Ernst Cassirer*, ed. by Schilpp, p. 501.

[24] Northrop, "Ethics and the Integration of Natural Knowledge," in *op. cit.*, p. 124.

ful, in its pursuit of scientific truth. For scientific purposes the world is viewed as an order of natural forces subject to mathematical measurement and manifesting universal invariant uniformities, or laws. The function of the scientist is to discover the efficient causes of natural phenomena, how things work and the principles which explain why they function as they do. The scientist is interested only in ascertaining the facts of nature; his theories are but the pragmatic instruments which he has devised to render intelligible the interrelation of the phenomena he has observed. The scientist is not concerned to praise or to blame, but to understand the invariant order of nature.

At this point is is important to indicate the inherent ambiguity of the term "fact." Facts are usually contrasted with values. Facts are said to be the data which the scientist observes in nature; they are what he discovers in nature. Hence, facts are thought to be "objective" and independent of the preferences of the observer. By comparison, values are "subjective" preferences and without any basis in the order of nature. In this way, the more man extends his scientific knowledge of nature, the less significant nature becomes to him, since his values seem to have no objective basis in nature. In brief, modern science appears to lead to value-nihilism, to the doctrine that there is no objective basis in nature for moral and aesthetic values.

As against this thesis, I maintain that the dichotomy of scientific facts and cultural values is not valid. So-called facts are really truth values, human evaluations as to the truth of one's ideas concerning the order of nature and cultural experiences. "Facts" are judgments as to what is the case and may change with one's beliefs and interpretations. This is demonstrated particularly in the constant revaluations to which historical "facts" are subjected in the course of time.[25] What the scientific method of investigation has demonstrated is the relative autonomy of truth values and their comparative independence of moral and aesthetic values in the sphere of nature. In contrast to the prescientific practice of arguing a priori from the moral or aesthetic properties of a thing to its actual existence, the critical scientist maintains that the goodness and beauty of an object are irrelevant to the truth of its existence. A priori arguments, he maintains, are contentious, provoking emotional conflicts, but not increasing our effective knowledge and power.

But this does not mean that truth values and moral and aesthetic values have nothing to do with one another. There are such things as a "true good" and a "true beauty" in contrast to a false, or apparent, good and beauty. A scientific demonstration may be "beautiful" to those who are impressed by its clarity, and the beauty of a noble deed may shine brightly notwithstanding failure to accomplish a given objective. Of the three categories of value, truth values are primary, since they underlie all other judgments of value. But each category of value

[25] Trevelyan, "Bias in History," in his *An Autobiography and Other Essays.*

has a certain relative autonomy and is not to be reduced to the others. The concepts of the true, the good, and the beautiful are phenomenologically distinct and have to be conceived independently of one another. Yet, they are also mutually related in nature and culture.

If, then, by science we mean the discipline which is concerned with the establishment of truth values by empirical methods, then obviously science is very much concerned with values. Besides, cultural values are "facts" to the social scientist who investigates them; they are observable factors effective in the cultural experience of a society. In the sphere of human culture and society the scientific observer cannot avoid studying value phenomena as such and he must apply himself to the task in the same spirit as does the natural scientist.

THE CONCEPT OF A NORMATIVE SCIENCE OF CULTURE

If it be granted that there may be a science of cultural values, then the way is prepared for the recognition of a possible normative science of human culture. By the concept of a normative science of culture I mean a science of culture concerned with the formulation of cultural ideals as possible means and ends of sociocultural life. Hitherto it has been thought that science deals only with facts, with what is the case, and cannot therefore deal with values, with what ought to be. Hence the notion of a normative science was regarded as a contradiction in terms. If, however, it be granted that the antithesis of facts and values is false, then it seems that the concept of a normative science is not at all self-contradictory.

The function of a normative science, as distinguished from a positive science, is to investigate and suggest new modes of human conduct which may serve as norms for cultural experience and experimentation. As contrasted with the old positivistic thesis that an empirical, comparative study of "social facts" will reveal moral laws comparable to the laws of physics, a normative anthropology would concern itself not only with what is the case actually and historically but also with what may be and ought to be, with possible alternative ideals suggested by the facts of cultural experience and natural science, but not given actually in any cultural system. The objective of such a normative anthropology is not to discover "laws" of cultural development, but rather to discover new cultural possibilities and potentialities which may be of practical significance in cultural invention and innovation.

The position here suggested is an attempt to avoid the extremes of either a theory which completely separates the natural sciences from the social sciences or one which reduces the social sciences to natural sciences. If the first alternative were to be adopted, as the Neo-Kantian philosophers and historians have done, then one would set up a sphere of *Geisteswissenschaften* with objects and methods of their own. In practice this division has led to a complete separation between cultural ends, or values, and scientific means, thereby reintroducing the same duality of value-free natural science and subjective values which earlier thinkers had anticipated. Even realistic philosophers, such as Bertrand Russell, tend to perpetuate the antithesis of "science" and "values" by maintaining that moral values are ultimately matters of choice and are not derived from scientific knowledge.[26] On this premise cultural ideologies are left without a basis in scientific fact, and the way is left open for the supremacy of the myth of the state.

On the other hand, if one were to adopt the second alternative and reduce the human sciences to natural sciences, then he would fail to allow for the element of human will for the realization of ideal values not given in cultural experience. Furthermore, by the identification of the ideal and the actual in culture the way is prepared for political dictatorship, since no scope is afforded for the realization of ideal, alternative values not prescribed by positive science. Thus, in practice we have a meeting of extremes. Cultural and political dictatorship may be brought about in the name of positive science, as well as in the name of ethnocentric myth. Communistic "dictatorship of the proletariat" is a modern instance of a state which is validated in the name of positive natural science; the Nazi state of Hitler justified sociocultural dictatorship by reference to "the myth of the twentieth century" of Alfred Rosenberg. The Nazi doctrine lacked universal appeal because it involved the notion of a chosen people whose destiny it was to rule all others. The Communist gospel, however, since it appeals to science and the universal values of the common man, has a certain idealistic attraction and has been successful in winning converts, particularly among the more idealistic self-sacrificing individuals who were influenced by its messianic message. In practice, however, modern Communist states tend to value political solidarity and "integration" above scientific, objective integrity.

Only by recognizing the validity of a normative science of man do we avoid the dangers of both of these extremes. According to our thesis, man is envisaged as part of the order of nature subject to natural laws, but at the same time recognition is given to the factors of cultural creativity and self-determination, as well as to the role of ideals in furthering cultural enterprise.

THE DISPARITY OF THE IDEAL AND THE ACTUAL

The concept of a normative science involves the principle of the disparity of ideal and actual truth. This principle was first clearly formulated by Plato. As Cassirer has stated,

> It is one of the first principles of Plato's theory of knowledge to insist upon the radical distinction between empirical and ideal truth. What experience gives is, at best, a right opinion about things; it is

[26] Russell, "The Science to Save Us from Science," *New York Times* Magazine, Sunday, March 19, 1950, p. 33.

not real knowledge. The difference between these two types, between *doxa* and *episteme*, is ineffaceable. Facts are variable and accidental; truth is necessary and immutable.[27]

The ideal is never given in experience, but may be suggested by it. With reference to the sphere of the natural sciences, this ideal truth represents the limit of the metaphysical knowledge of nature. In the sphere of the social sciences and human studies, this ideal truth represents a norm, or goal, of human endeavor, a possibility compatible with human potentialities, but does not correspond to any actual, historical cultural situation. Here, too, cultural ideals are "social facts," but they are facts of a different order from the empirical facts of a given culture. The ideal truths of science and philosophy are products of cultural experience; yet they transcend the empirical limits of actual cultural experience. They are timeless, atemporal ideals, suggested by experience, but pointing to a metacultural reality which surpasses anything given in the context of historical experience.

Ultimately, the issue involved is a metaphysical, or metacultural, one. If the only reality is a cultural reality and relative to the experience of an organism, as cultural and sociological relativists maintain,[28] then the concept of an ideal truth other than given cultural experience becomes meaningless. As against this position, I maintain that the postulate of objective reality, independent of the observer, is a fruitful one, since it serves as a normative guide to research and presents an intelligible goal for the scientist to approximate. Our conceptual and empirical knowledge of reality varies with our interests and experiences, but reality as an ontological existent independent of man is an absolute object to which our ideas progressively conform in the course of our pursuit of knowledge by scientific methods. Similarly, moral and aesthetic values are real attributes of objects, although for purposes of physical science the former may be disregarded. Moral and aesthetic values may be said to be real and objective in the sense of having a basis in nature, human and cosmic.

With this perspective one can understand the fallacy involved in asserting that virtue is knowledge or that culture is a communicated system of ideas. In either instance the ineradicable difference between the ideal and the actual is not recognized. To identify culture with a knowledge of "social facts" is to exclude all those cultural ideals which are presupposed in any historical culture and serve as regulative norms without being consistently practiced. The positivistic fallacy, as it may be called, consists in the identification of the ideal with the actual, of the "ought" with the "is" of cultural experience. My point is that attempts to derive cultural ideals from actual empirical facts and in general to identify the category of truth with that of the good are bound to lead to the positivistic fallacy, regardless of whether the "is" of fact

[27] Cassirer, *The Myth of the State*, p. 69.
[28] Lundberg, *Foundations of Sociology*, ch. i; Znaniecki, *Cultural Sciences; Their Origin and Development.*

is conceived in purely phenomenal terms or is understood in conceptual, ontological terms. The converse fallacy, the normativistic fallacy, is the reduction of the "is" of scientific fact to the "ought" of moral judgment and practical reason. The latter fallacy is best exemplified in the Neo-Kantian axiological approach. In either instance an attempt is made to explain away the ineradicable disparity of the normative ideal and actual facts.

The history of human thought demonstrates clearly the temptation to reduce ideal to factual truth. In the case of Plato himself this is shown by his *Republic*, which is a theory of the ideal state, as well as of the best state.[29] As an ideal state, the republic can admit of no compromise and must therefore exclude the poets and artists, who by definition are not concerned with the pursuit of truth and reality. As the best state under the circumstances, the republic compromises by utilizing the cultural heritage at its disposal. In the best state Plato is prepared to include the poets and myth-makers, since he admits the necessity of "noble fictions" to inspire the young with the proper moral ideals. I find that the idealistic philosopher and the practical statesman in Plato were never quite reconciled, although in his later work, such as the *Laws*, one can discern a tendency toward conservatism and practical idealism. The danger in Plato's utopia, as in all subsequent utopias, is that by making his ideal state concrete the utopian idealist inevitably tends to introduce some of the historical culture of his day, with all its local and temporal limitations. There is also danger of engaging in wishful, impractical thinking insofar as the utopian idealist fails to reckon with the facts of human nature, by imagining men as disembodied intellects interested in ideal truths and disregarding the irrational impulses and cultural limitations of actual men. In brief, since the ideal truths of culture and society transcend our immediate experience, they cannot be visualized in concrete form without serious falsification. The culture of the "world of tomorrow" is always partially beyond our grasp. To claim that the ideal has been realized, whether in the name of science or of religion, is to set up a false absolute, which by claiming perfection automatically halts and restricts cultural progress.

In historical experience the price of identifying the ideal with the actual of culture is intolerance, born of a false absolute. Once it is asserted that a given cultural system embodies all the ideal values, then the way is prepared for a justification of intolerance toward all who deviate from this absolute norm. No one is more ruthless and intolerant than a utopian idealist who believes that his particular vision provides the only means of salvation for mankind. This explains why in the sphere of religion we are confronted with the historical spectacle of an Inquisition which engaged in mass persecution in the name of a

29 See Bidney, "The Philosophical Anthropology of Ernst Cassirer," in *The Philosophy of Ernst Cassirer*, ed. by Schilpp.

religion of love. In philosophy, we have the example of the Hegelian philosophy, which identified the real with the rational and sought to justify the Prussian state of its day as the embodiment of absolute values. Similarly, Marxism, which is an inverted Hegelianism, involves the worship of history as manifested through the processes of dialectical and historical materialism. In conformity with the utopian myth of Marxism, only the Communist state embodies all the social virtues and only the proletarian class is fit to represent mankind.

In the autobiographical accounts compiled in *The God That Failed*[30] we are given an intimate view of the experiences of some ex-Communists and Communist sympathizers. At first they regarded the Communist state of Soviet Russia as the realization of the kingdom of God on earth, until, through a slow process of disillusionment, each discovered in turn the gap between his own vision of the ideal good and the actual practice of the Communist party and state. According to the logic of the emotions, it was assumed that because contemporary capitalistic society was deficient in moral values, therefore the Communist state represented the realization of social idealism. It was a case of prior faith seeking rationalization and justification. All incompatible facts and experiences were explained away as minor imperfections which in no way impaired one's faith in the infallibility of the party and in the dialectical course of history. By this mode of reasoning, young idealists and scientists were led to betray their countries in order to serve mankind and to help realize the utopian state and world order of the future.

What is particularly noteworthy in the case of the "Soviet myth" is that here, for the first time in history, the identification of the absolute ideal with political real was undertaken in the name of a particular party and state, as well as in the so-called interests of mankind as a whole. Henceforth, it is held, all who adhere to this ideal of society and are prepared to support the policies of this state are scientific, progressive, and the friends of mankind; all who are opposed are deluded reactionaries and the enemies of mankind. Mankind is divided into two camps, the enlightened and the saved by the grace of Marxism and the deluded and the damned by the sin of capitalism and idealism. There is no more tragic example in the whole of human history than this mythological identification of the absolute ideal and the historically real—a myth which has split the world asunder into hostile camps.

There is also the complementary danger of setting up "Democracy" as an antithetical absolute and justifying the *status quo of* our culture as the fulfillment of the ideal. To some liberal, pragmatic apologists "Democracy" has become "the religion of religions," and cultural pluralism the world's panacea.[31] By contrast, the thesis I wish to maintain is that no historical social system is free from some defects and limita-

---

[30] *The God That Failed*, ed. by R. Crossman.
[31] Kallen, *The Education of Free Men*, ch. xvii.

tions of one kind or another and that to identify the ideal and the historically given is bound to lead to a falsification of the ideal absolute. On this assumption, constructive criticism is always in order, since one may point out the disparity between professed ideals and actual accomplishments with a view to bringing them into closer accord. Otherwise, if one were complacently to accept the *status quo* of a given culture, one would be led to indulge in rationalization and mythical propaganda as the only means of reconciling the ideal and the actual, what ought to be with what actually prevails.

Criticism of any sociocultural system must consider two distinct types of deficiency in a given cultural situation: first, deficiencies inherent in the given ethos; secondly, deficiencies owing to the disparity between valid ideals and actual social practices. Among those who now abjure "the God that failed" disillusion is frequently the result of a consciousness of the disparity of ideals and practices, but the cultural idol itself is still worshiped. Complete conversion would require rejection of the ideals, as well as the practices.

A false absolutism may be effected in various ways. Historically, relative ethnocentric absolutism is the most common. This is a naïve absolutism in which it is assumed that one's own culture system and values are superior to all others. Secondly, there is classical absolutism, the notion that a particular cultural epoch marked the summit of human achievement. On this assumption, all one can do is attempt to recapture this bygone vision, whether it be "the glory that was Greece" or the great synthesis of medieval European culture in the thirteenth century. Thirdly, there is historical absolutism, which involves the belief that whatever is, is best for the time being. This is a serial absolute which the nineteenth-century doctrine of evolutionary progress rendered plausible. As Niebuhr has remarked, "the dominant note in modern culture is not so much confidence in reason as faith in history."[32] Time and history have become self-explanatory and the source of intelligibility of all cultural processes. This has led to a false optimism as regards the growth of human freedom and to tragic disillusionment when events failed to justify this mythological belief.

In contemporary ethnological theory culture has become the new absolute and self-explanatory reality, the measure of man and his works. This new cultural absolute is no longer used to justify cultural progress, but rather to justify cultural relativism. While culture is said to be the measure of all things, all historical value systems are treated as equally valid. Having set up culture as the new historical absolute and principle of intelligibility, contemporary American anthropologists have tended to deny the former faith of the nineteenth-century ethnologists in laws of cultural evolution, as well as in the validity of any absolute ideal of cultural progress.

[32] Niebuhr, *Faith and History*, p. 3.

CULTURAL REALITY AND CULTURAL RELATIVISM

Among contemporary cultural anthropologists, Herskovits in particular has articulated the thesis of cultural relativism in its most uncompromising form. In *Man and His Works* he has devoted an entire chapter to "The Problem of Cultural Relativism," and I shall, therefore, examine his main arguments in order to indicate his basic presuppositions.

Philosophically it is extremely interesting that Herskovits adopts the thesis of historical idealism and quotes Cassirer with approval to corroborate his view that "experience is culturally defined."[33] According to Herskovits, "Even the facts of the physical world are discerned through the enculturative screen so that the perception of time, distance, weight, size and other 'realities' is mediated by the conventions of any given group."[34] Thus, having adopted the thesis of cultural idealism, Herskovits finds that there is literally no other reality than cultural reality, and hence he concludes logically that the only values which are acceptable to the individual are those which are relatively valid for his culture at a given time.

Herskovits distinguishes between cultural absolutes and cultural universals. There are said to be cultural universals in the formal sense that there are universal types of institution, and morality in general is an example of such a universal, since it is a characteristic of all cultures. But the actual forms of morality are functions of given historical experiences of the societies that manifest them. That is why there can be no absolutes in the sense of fixed standards which admit of no historical variations.

Thus, we are asked to transcend our ethnocentrism in the name of cultural relativism. "Cultural relativism" is used as a value-charged term denoting a positive, praiseworthy attitude, while "ethnocentrism" connotes a negative value incompatible with an unbiased, objective approach. Herskovits does not explain how it is theoretically possible to have cultural relativism without ethnocentrism, in view of the fact that cultural conditioning necessarily leads the members of any given society to prefer their own value system above all others. What he apparently has in mind is a culture system which inculcates the relative validity of its own values for its own adherents, together with recognition of the equal value of other systems. He implies, therefore, an ideal cultural relativism totally different from the real cultural relativism of historic cultures, which recognize the absolute validity of their own values and deny equal recognition to other systems. A major source of confusion in Herskovits's thesis is that he fails to differentiate clearly between this implicit ideal cultural relativism which he advocates and

[33] Herskovits, *Man and His Works*, p. 27.
[34] *Ibid.*, p. 64.

the real, historic relativism which he posits to account for the variety of actual systems.

There are, apparently, two kinds of ethnocentrism—a vicious and a benign kind. The vicious kind of ethnocentrism involves belief in objective absolute values and hence intolerance of other codes. The benign kind involves preference for one's own value system, as well as mutual respect for those of other societies. How it is possible to transcend ethnocentrism of the intolerant variety, if there is no objective standard of comparison, is not explained. Furthermore, it is not at all clear why one should prefer his own system of cultural values rather than some other system, provided the cultural blinkers which have been imposed on him do not prevent him from envisaging some other system. It may be expedient to adhere to a given social code at a special time and place, but it is difficult to see why one should adhere to it exclusively or exercise moral restraint in the presence of other culture systems. The fact of cultural variations in historic cultures does not imply the absolute value of cultural differences and the obligation to respect them. The "is" of cultural relativism does not imply the "ought," that is, the obligation to respect other people's codes and norms. To derive the "ought" from the "is" of culture is to commit what I have termed "the positivistic fallacy."

As an axiological position, the doctrine of cultural relativism involves "the transvaluation of values." The absolute values of truth, goodness, and beauty which men profess are said to have only a limited historical validity for a given society and culture. All so-called "absolute" values are really "relative absolutes" whose validity is recognized only within the context of a given culture. We must distinguish, however, sociological relativism from cultural relativism. According to sociological relativism, cultural values are functions of social organization and vary with its modes. That is, the sociological relativist explains the origin of a particular value system by reference to the society and the class interests which it fosters. Thus, Nietzsche evaluated moral values by reference to two social classes, the masters and the slaves, engaged in a conflict of wills to power, and Marx evaluated moral values as reflecting the economic interests of classes, such as capitalists and workers. By contrast, the cultural relativist does not explain the origin of social values, but accepts them as given. Philosophically, contemporary ethnologists find historical idealism most congenial and postulate cultural reality as a reality *sui generis* which renders all the phenomena of experience intelligible. At most, we are informed that cultural relativism is a fact of ethnographic experience and a necessary product of cultural conditioning. Values are said to be conditioned by culture, but culture itself must be taken for granted as self-explanatory. This is what is meant by the assertion that culture is a "closed system."

The issue as interpreted by the cultural relativists apparently turns on two alternatives: one must either accept a doctrine of fixed absolute values or deny objective norms in favor of historic relativity and the relative validity of values. I do not think, however, that we are necessarily limited to these two alternatives. In the sphere of natural science there is a cumulative advance in man's knowledge of nature notwithstanding the continuous reevaluation of beliefs and postulates. The scientist does not argue that because some former truth values have been rejected because of new, objective evidence, therefore there is no objective criterion of truth. On the contrary, it is because of his faith in an objective order of nature amenable to gradual human discovery that he is prepared constantly to question his assumptions and generalizations and to alter them in accordance with his available empirical evidence. The natural scientist does not use objective evidence to discredit objective truth values. Similarly, in the sphere of moral truths it is not logical to reject objective moral norms simply because some alleged objective moral norms are seen to have a purely subjective validity within a given cultural context. There is no reason on principle why there may not be a cumulative increment in our knowledge and achievement of moral ideals comparable to our advance in the attainment of knowledge in the natural sciences. Murder and incest, for example, are even now instances of negative moral values which are concrete ethnological universals, even though there is considerable disparity in the range of their application in different cultures.

The social and cultural relativists maintain that society determines the ideological perspective of its members and hence can see no common measure in cultural values. For them there are only historic "relative absolutes," since each culture system is asserted to be absolutely valid. What is overlooked by the relativists is the important consideration to which Kant drew attention in his essay "Idea for a Universal History with Cosmopolitan Intent," namely, that "in man (as the only rational creature on earth) those natural faculties which aim at the use of reason shall be fully developed in the species, not in the individual."[35] That is, man has a capacity for reason which is developed in the history of human society, but not in the experience of the individual, since the life of the individual is far too short to achieve complete rationality. Mankind has the potentiality for developing rationality to its fullest extent, and rationality is, therefore, a universally valid ideal. Thus, if society, through its culture, is responsible for warping the perspective of the individual through its relative absolutes, it is also the only means for achieving in time the maximum degree of objectivity and universality of thought which man is capable of attaining. Similarly, if the perspective of the individual is a product of his culture, it is also true that individuals may in turn affect the cultural perspective of their society in the direction of greater rationality and objectivity.

Finally, the cultural relativists fail to see that cultural ideologies are effective precisely because they are believed and acknowledged to have absolute value by their adherents for all mankind, not only for

[35] *The Philosophy of Kant*, ed. by Friedrich, p. 118.

their adherents. If a given value system were not accepted as objectively valid, it would soon lose its effectiveness as a motivation for conduct. Social and cultural relativists tend to assume that men would continue to adhere to and respect their cultural values, even after they were convinced by the sophisticated ethnologists that their so-called absolute and universal values were but subjective delusions. Modern states, however, are not so impractical and have instituted rigid systems of thought control and censorship to prevent their subjects from acquiring a critical comparative judgment. They have preferred to follow the counsel of pragmatic sociologists, such as Sorel and Pareto, and regard social myths as indispensable for social action. What is important is that the myth should be believed and serve as an inspiration for heroic action.

The practical, effective alternatives are not cultural absolutism versus cultural relativism, as contemporary ethnologists are inclined to maintain, but rather rational norms with a potentiality for universal acceptance and realization versus mythological absolutes destined to lead to perpetual crises and conflicting political policies. Far from resolving our international problems, cultural relativism leads to conflicting political and social mythologies. The only effective alternative to a mythical relative absolute is a better, more rational and more objective ideal of conduct and belief capable of overcoming the limitations of the former.

In their anxiety to obviate the evils of national ethnocentrism, especially when allied with the quest for power and domination over weaker peoples, contemporary anthropologists have unwittingly tended to substitute serial ethnocentrism for the static ethnocentrism which they abhor. By "serial ethnocentrism" I mean the attitude of viewing each culture from its own perspective only, as if that were the primary virtue of the objective anthropologist. So timid and wary has the modern anthropologist become, lest he commit the fallacies of the evolutionary ethnologist of the nineteenth century, that the very thought of "the comparative method" strikes him with terror. Thus comparative studies are viewed as unscientific adventures reminiscent of an outmoded era in cultural anthropology.

As long as anthropology remains at the descriptive stage, anthropologists may rest content with cultural pluralism and relativism on the ground that they do not wish to overstep the bounds of scientific fact. But if anthropology is to attain the stage of making significant generalizations concerning the conditions of the cultural process and the values of civilization, then comparative studies of cultures and their values must be made in order to demonstrate universal principles of cultural dynamics and concrete rational norms capable of universal realization. Hitherto the task of suggesting and prescribing normative ideals and goals has been left chiefly to utopian philosophers and theologians. I suggest that it is high time for anthropology to come of age and for anthropologists to show their respect for human reason and science by cooperating with other social scientists and scholars so as to envisage practical, progressive, rational norms worthy of winning a measure of universal recognition in the future.

For the positivists and pragmatists in philosophy and social science, this distinction between the absolute ideal and the varying historical cultural norms does not appear valid. Since the former maintain that the real is that which is given in immediate experience, or is similar to such empirical data, there can be for them no significant difference between the goal and the going, between the end and the means. Hence, to the positivist and the pragmatist "the best" and the "absolute ideal" are arbitrary terms. "It represents the preference of a person, not the perfection of a thing." [36] Ideals as they are known in experience are subject to historical change, and the concept of a timeless absolute ideal which transcends cultural experience is thought to be an invalid abstraction.

According to the position here maintained, the concept of an absolute value is a significant regulative norm. It is a fact of experience no less than the empirical data of the positivist, but it is a "fact" of a different order; it is a fact created by and as a result of experience. The absolute norm is real insofar as it is conceived as an ideal possibility whose validity is independent of its actual realization in cultural experience. Hence, the absolute ideal may serve as a goal of cultural endeavor which is radically different from the process, the going, whereby it is approximated. The concept of the best is not merely a preference of a given historical society; the normative best is a metacultural ideal which transcends the actually given of historical experience and yet as a regulative norm is a significant factor in molding experience. The concept of an absolute ideal truth, good, or beauty connotes an ideal which to some extent transcends empirical experience and yet serves to bring about a closer conformity of cultural facts and ideals. As a regulative norm and ideal possibility, it is a product of cultural experience and yet not quite a part of it; it functions within the historical process and is not subject to the historical process itself. The moment this absolute norm is given expression within the context of a given culture, it becomes in part falsified. That is why every attempt to identify the ideal with the actually existent is a delusion, a myth which sets up a false idol and hinders cultural progress. The ideal absolute is compatible with cultural freedom and diversity, since it does not dictate categorically the particular form which historical cultures must assume, but serves only as a regulative norm and measure by which to evaluate diverse cultural approaches. There may be more than one cultural way to the heaven of the ideal truth, goodness, and beauty.

[36] Kallen, *The Education of Free Men*, p. 304.

THE FUNCTION OF SCIENCE IN MODERN CULTURE

The problem of normative culture and relative values may be discussed profitably by reference to the function and role of science in modern culture. There are two main approaches to the problem of the nature and function of science. On the one hand, science has been regarded as a body of authoritatively established truths based on verification by empirical evidence. On the other hand, there is the pragmatic view that science is essentially a method for pursuing truth which yields practical results and enables man to adjust successfully to his environment. The "quest for certainty" and the knowledge of an ultimate reality independent of the knower are held to be delusions, since there is no absolute certainty and no knowledge of a reality independent of the knower. The only constant is said to be the scientific method; there is no body of scientific "truth" which is fixed and established once and for all. The first, positivistic view tends to regard science as an absolute achievement, a more or less closed system, to which details may be added, but which is not subject to basic revision. According to the second, pragmatic view, nothing at all is fixed except the method, or road; the results are subject to constant revision in the light of experience and practice.

Recently, however, there have been attempts to reconcile these two antithetical views in the interests of cultural integration. Science, it is realized, is not merely an instrument for gaining mastery over the forces of nature; it has also a normative, humanizing function in determining one's entire cultural perspective. Science is not merely an instrument of technology, but also an end in itself, a humanity which determines the spirit of a culture. As the progressive quest for truth concerning nature and human culture, science must serve the interests of humanity as a whole. It is the spirit of science, at once rational, progressive, and self-corrective, which may serve as an absolute norm for culture as a whole, irrespective of its factual and technological achievements. As the rational and empirical pursuit of truth, science is an absolute value and a moral good. The use of scientific method for irrational purposes, such as the communication of irrational myths, superstitions, and prejudices, is a perversion of the spirit of science. In normative science ends and means are in harmony, since normative science involves the use of rational means to communicate verified knowledge.

It is because of this separation of ends and means in the utilization of scientific method that science has been decried as an evil which has exiled man from the Garden of Eden, in which he might otherwise dwell. There must be a will to truth, a willingness to acknowledge the absolute value of scientific truth and to utilize it for rational moral and aesthetic ends, if science is to serve to humanize mankind and in the development of a normative civilization. Science, taken in abstraction from moral and aesthetic values, tends to be abused and perverted in the service of ends incompatible with scientific pursuits. A science which is used for irrational ends is the agent of its own destruction; a science of means apart from a science of ends is self-defeating.

Thus, the proposition frequently put forth in the name of science by eminent scientists and philosophers, that science has nothing to do with moral values and aesthetic feelings, while it appears plausible in the sphere of technology, is only a half-truth concealing a great illusion. The scientific pursuit of knowledge is itself a moral good, and the scientist has his own ideal code of professional ethics to obey. Furthermore, the scientist requires a social and cultural environment suitable for the pursuit of his vocation, namely, one which permits him complete freedom of thought and experiment in the pursuit of scientific truth and cultural knowledge. That is why the scientist as scientist must be actively concerned with the preservation of the basic cultural freedoms lest he jeopardize his own enterprise. The unethical pursuit of science leads to ultimate self-destruction, as does the unscientific pursuit of ethics and aesthetics.

As against the extreme antithetical views that science is either a method without content or else a method yielding a fixed body of necessary truths, the position taken here is that normative science is a progressive, cumulative, self-critical discipline and comprises a cumulative fund of verified truths. Science is normative in the sense that it offers a criterion whereby myth and superstition may be differentiated from rational and empirical knowledge. Normative science is a cumulative process which establishes a fund of authentic knowledge, while revising some of its tentatively accepted theories. It is neither absolutely fixed nor in constant flux; it is partly fixed and partly changing. Normative science is an approximation to the ideal absolute truth and involves the postulation of a metaphysical reality which transcends our limited experience. As a historical cultural process, science is subject to constant revision; yet scientific knowledge puts man in touch with a metacultural reality which transcends the cultural limitations of any particular space-time culture. In this sense normative science makes for substantial progress.

Edmund W. Sinnott has presented a vigorous argument against the extremes of intolerant absolutism and tolerant indifference. In his essay "Ten Million Scientists" he writes:

> Science is by no means completely tolerant. Its goal is to seek out the truth, and its history has been one of steady progress toward this end. If truth could not be disentangled from error, science would have no meaning. So long as a particular element of truth has not been discovered or is only imperfectly known, the seeker's mind must be completely open to help from other quarters; but once a portion of the truth has been found, has been separated from error and become a part of the intellectual capital of mankind, then the conception of tolerance to ideas incompatible with it quite loses its meaning. Tolerance of what has been proved to be untrue is mani-

festly absurd. Thus, science builds an ever-growing body of certainty, of assured and proved truth.[37]

Thus, normative science combines freedom and tolerance in the pursuit of truth with intolerance of falsity when it has attained convictions. As Sinnott has stated, "the spirit of science, if it truly takes possession of a man, can carry him along the middle way which leads both to that freedom and tolerance so necessary for the democratic way of life, and to the convictions and enthusiasms that keep life from growing flabby and stale."

The spirit of normative science is a cultural universal which is applicable to any cultural discipline, regardless of its subject matter. But normative science is more than a disembodied spirit; it is also a body of knowledge carrying conviction through empirical evidence and rational demonstration. Normative science does make for absolute standards and is also compatible with freedom of inquiry and cultural progress. The belief that the application of tolerance to cultural pluralism regardless of common values will in time lead to harmonious integration and "orchestration" of world cultures is but a pious, aesthetic delusion. Unless science can provide potentially universal cultural values capable of winning ardent adherents, other methods will be found to fill this need, such as the mythological appeal to race, class, or nationality. The choice is between "contentious knowledge" of conflicting mythological ideologies and normative scientific, rational truths capable of producing a rational consensus among the peoples of the world.[38] Only a cultural unity based upon a common core of rational values and brought into being by voluntary deliberate consent can endure indefinitely.

Toward Dialogue

On page 117, Bidney asserts that anthropology needs to graduate out of a positive, descriptive science into what he calls "a normative science." That is, anthropology now can tell us how men actually live; but it ought to go on to examine "possible alternative ideals suggested by the facts of cultural experience and natural science, but not given actually in any cultural system."

One of the "facts of cultural experience" is that every society has something very seriously wrong with it, even our own beloved "democracy." As Bidney says, "no historical social system is free from some defects and limitations . . ."

Working from these two general propositions, Bidney implicitly invites us to suggest changes and modifications, "alternative ideals," for

[37] Sinnott, "Ten Million Scientists," *Science*, CXI (1950), 123–29.
[38] Bidney, "The Concept of Value in Modern Anthropology," in *Anthropology Today*, edited by A. V. Kroeber, pp. 682–99.

the American style of living. If such an invitation were proffered in earnest, what might we have to recommend?

For example, consider this: The cultural relativist claims that there is no such thing as a "good" or a "bad" culture, that there are simply different cultures and different life patterns. Anyone who claims otherwise, he insists, is simply thinking ethnocentrically, from the value base of his own culture. Many years ago, Lyman Bryson of Columbia University used to analyze this thesis in his lectures and always came away from the argument somehow dissatisfied. Isn't there, he wondered, some criterion for a good society that is not a product of any particular social or cultural value system? To answer his own question, he would first consider a sampling of criteria which had been advanced over the years by other philosophers and anthropologists, eventually disqualifying each of them as unsatisfactory for one reason or another. Then he would cautiously advance his own criterion: A society is good in the degree to which the mass of its citizens are capable of realizing the primary values of the society. In short, the larger the proportion of its citizens who can and do realize the values of a society, the better that society is.

Now, let us apply this criterion to life in the United States. Take but one prime American value: success. A major goal in our pursuit of the good life is personal success in our various undertakings—education, career, or social encounters. Success, by definition, is mathematically limited to a very small proportion of the population; and it is therefore inevitable that a great many individuals will be unable to realize it. What are we to make, then, of the vaunted virtue of the "American Way of Life?" Or consider the high value we place on money, social position, good looks, and popularity. Are not these the kinds of values which the American culture summons us to aspire to? And are they not of the same general sort—exclusive and excluding? It would appear that Americans have a genius for identifying and attaching themselves to goals which, in the very nature of things, only a relative few can hope to attain.

If we were able to reverse this pattern and to select "alternative ideals" for our own system capable of satisfying the Bryson criterion, what would they be? Would a more passionate commitment to 'life, liberty, and the pursuit of happiness" engender a culture that could meet his terms?

Further Readings

Dewey, John. *Freedom and Culture.* New York: G. P. Putnam's Sons, 1939.

Dewey, John. "Philosophy," in *Encyclopedia of the Social Sciences,* Vol. XII, pp. 118–128.

Lippman, W. *An Inquiry into the Principles of the Good Society.* Boston: Little, Brown, 1937.

Marcuse, Herbert. *Eros and Civilization.* Boston: Beacon Press, 1966.

Opler, Marvin K. *Culture, Psychiatry and Human Values.* Springfield, Ill.: Charles C Thomas, 1956.

Sorokin, P. A. *Social Philosophies in an Age of Crisis.* Boston: Beacon Press, 1950.

White, Leslie. *The Science of Culture.* New York: Farrar, Straus and Cudahy, 1949.

Philosophical Anthropology in Education

Anthropology is not interested in individuals. As a social science, an institutionalized mode of inquiry into man's ways, it deals only with groups. When anthropology becomes philosophical, as we have seen in the preceding section, its interests are the cultural values and life styles of these groups—how they live, what they stand for, what they regard as the mode of being which all men should adopt. Philosophical anthropology, unlike the scientific philosophies, does not therefore imply or impose a specific pedagogy, for its concerns are not with the way human beings know and learn but with what they ought to believe and work for. It is ideological in character rather than epistemological and psychological. Hence, when we consider the impact of philosophical anthropology on educational thought, we encounter ideas more relevant to the general ends of the educational establishment in a society than to the internal procedures used by educators in their work.

In choosing among ends, the educational establishment confronts a variety of strategic decisions. Three in particular are worth considering here. First, one of the chief jobs of any school system is to induct the young into the mores, customs, and dispositions of the wider adult community. Going to school is the modern form of "cultural apprenticeship," i.e., formal induction into the tribe. This means that the school must reflect the attitudes and beliefs of the wider community in bringing the young into full social membership. But just how complete and faithful should this reflection be? Is the school obligated to pass on everything the culture believes in or practices? Does not the educator exercise a critical function as well, trying to encourage the best in the culture, the noblest ideals, and to discourage the destructive and pernicious elements in the culture, the mean and harmful practices extant in the community? Is it not to be expected that the school will encourage egalitarian attitudes and discourage racism and prejudice in its pupils? If the answer is Yes, then the school is editing the beliefs and attitudes of the culture before transmitting them to the young. If this is a legitimate function—and most of us would agree that it is—to just what degree is it legitimate? That is, how far may the school properly go—how far must it morally go—in criticizing the established order?

Second, and closely related to this question, is the problem of the educator's relationship to social change. As we all know, we live in a time of rapid cultural transition; there are, indeed, signs of incipient revolution for the 1970's. Now, when the culture is in quasi-upheaval, when the established order is being rocked by militant and violent dissidents, where does the school stand? Does it side with the Establishment and continue to plead for law, order and reason? Or does it awaken the young to the problems of a society in agony and begin to prepare them for active participation in bringing about the necessary changes in the system? Does it, to put the issue another way, merely describe and interpret the social order to the young or does it actively seek to reconstruct the social order along a new and more humane design?

Third, the school has customarily been an agent for the transmission of knowledge, and only incidentally an agent for the awakening of feelings and emotions. In the language of the psychologist, it has been principally a cognitive and only passingly an affective social institution. But is education really all head and no heart? Is it all intellect, intelligence, reason, and knowing and only incidentally feeling, sharing, loving, and wanting? The psychotherapeutic revolution of American psychology, from Freud to Fromm, suggests a gradual awakening of the "feeling" side of man. And it is now being asked if the educator does not have something vital to contribute to this aspect of human development. Is not the cultivation of personality, in the widest sense of the term, now coming to be coordinate with the cultivation of mind as the proper end and purpose of a society's educational resources?

In a very loose, editorial sense, the three selections which follow explore and expand upon these three strategic questions. The well-known opening chapter of John Dewey's Democracy and Education casts the argument into a culturological setting by showing how society develops through a process of transmission and communication. Abraham Edel reviews the points of contact between philosophical anthropology and education, and then examines the problem of social change and cultural reform as a philosophical issue in educational theory. Finally, Theodore Brameld coins a new term, "anthropotherapy," and shows how it might be used in the better comprehension of the anthropological study of educational aims.

JOHN DEWEY

Education as a Necessity of Life

RENEWAL OF LIFE BY TRANSMISSION

The most notable distinction between living and inanimate things is that the former maintain themselves by renewal. A stone when struck resists. If its resistance is greater than the force of the blow struck, it

Reprinted with permission of The Macmillan Company from **Democracy and Education** by John Dewey. Copyright 1916 by The Macmillan Company, renewed 1944.

remains outwardly unchanged. Otherwise, it is shattered into smaller bits. Never does the stone attempt to react in such a way that it may maintain itself against the blow, much less so as to render the blow a contributing factor to its own continued action. While the living thing may easily be crushed by superior force, it none the less tries to turn the energies which act upon it into means of its own further existence. If it cannot do so, it does not just split into smaller pieces (at least in the higher forms of life), but loses its identity as a living thing.

As long as it endures, it struggles to use surrounding energies in its own behalf. It uses light, air, moisture, and the material of soil. To say that it uses them is to say that it turns them into means of its own conservation. As long as it is growing, the energy it expends in thus turning the environment to account is more than compensated for by the return it gets: it grows. Understanding the word "control" in this sense, it may be said that a living being is one that subjugates and controls for its own continued activity the energies that would otherwise use it up. Life is a self-renewing process through action upon the environment.

In all the higher forms this process cannot be kept up indefinitely. After a while they succumb; they die. The creature is not equal to the task of indefinite self-renewal. But continuity of the life process is not dependent upon the prolongation of the existence of any one individual. Reproduction of other forms of life goes on in continuous sequence. And though, as the geological record shows, not merely individuals but also species die out, the life process continues in increasingly complex forms. As some species die out, forms better adapted to utilize the obstacles against which they struggled in vain come into being. Continuity of life means continual readaptation of the environment to the needs of living organisms.

We have been speaking of life in its lowest terms—as a physical thing. But we use the word "life" to denote the whole range of experience, individual and racial. When we see a book called the *Life of Lincoln* we do not expect to find within its covers a treatise on physiology. We look for an account of social antecedents; a description of early surroundings, of the conditions and occupation of the family; of the chief episodes in the development of character; of signal struggles and achievements; of the individual's hopes, tastes, joys and sufferings. In precisely similar fashion we speak of the life of a savage tribe, of the Athenian people, of the American nation. "Life" covers customs, institutions, beliefs, victories and defeats, recreations and occupations.

We employ the word "experience" in the same pregnant sense. And to it, as well as to life in the bare physiological sense, the principle of continuity through renewal applies. With the renewal of physical existence goes, in the case of human beings, the re-creation of beliefs, ideals, hopes, happiness, misery, and practices. The continuity of any experience, through renewing of the social group, is a literal fact. Education, in its broadest sense, is the means of this social continuity of life. Every one of the constituent elements of a social group, in a modern city as in a savage tribe, is born immature, helpless, without language, beliefs, ideas, or social standards. Each individual, each unit who is the carrier of the life-experience of his group, in time passes away. Yet the life of the group goes on.

The primary ineluctable facts of the birth and death of each one of the constituent members in a social group determine the necessity of education. On one hand, there is the contrast between the immaturity of the new-born members of the group—its future sole representatives —and the maturity of the adult members who possess the knowledge and customs of the group. On the other hand, there is the necessity that these immature members be not merely physically preserved in adequate numbers, but that they be initiated into the interests, purposes, information, skill, and practices of the mature members: otherwise the group will cease its characteristic life. Even in a savage tribe, the achievements of adults are far beyond what the immature members would be capable of if left to themselves. With the growth of civilization, the gap between the original capacities of the immature and the standards and customs of the elders increases. Mere physical growing up, mere mastery of the bare necessities of subsistence will not suffice to reproduce the life of the group. Deliberate effort and the taking of thoughtful pains are required. Beings who are born not only unaware of, but quite indifferent to, the aims and habits of the social group have to be rendered cognizant of them and actively interested. Education, and education alone, spans the gap.

Society exists through a process of transmission quite as much as biological life. This transmission occurs by means of communication of habits of doing, thinking, and feeling from the older to the younger. Without this communication of ideals, hopes, expectations, standards, opinions, from those members of society who are passing out of the group life to those who are coming into it, social life could not survive. If the members who compose a society lived on continuously, they might educate the new-born members, but it would be a task directed by personal interest rather than social need. Now it is a work of necessity.

If a plague carried off the members of a society all at once, it is obvious that the group would be permanently done for. Yet the death of each of its constituent members is as certain as if an epidemic took them all at once. But the graded difference in age, the fact that some are born as some die, makes possible through transmission of ideas and practices the constant reweaving of the social fabric. Yet this renewal is not automatic. Unless pains are taken to see that genuine and thorough transmission takes place, the most civilized group will relapse into barbarism and then into savagery. In fact, the human young are so immature that if they were left to themselves without the guidance and succor of others, they could not acquire the rudimentary abilities necessary for physical existence. The young of human beings compare so poorly in original efficiency with the young of many of the lower animals, that even the powers needed for physical sustentation have to be acquired under tuition. How much more, then, is this the case with respect to all the technological, artistic, scientific, and moral achievements of humanity!

EDUCATION AND COMMUNICATION

So obvious, indeed, is the necessity of teaching and learning for the continued existence of a society that we may seem to be dwelling unduly on a truism. But justification is found in the fact that such emphasis is a means of getting us away from an unduly scholastic and formal notion of education. Schools are, indeed, one important method of the transmission which forms the dispositions of the immature; but it is only one means, and, compared with other agencies, a relatively superficial means. Only as we have grasped the necessity of more fundamental and persistent modes of tuition can we make sure of placing the scholastic methods in their true context.

Society not only continues to exist *by* transmission, *by* communication, but it may fairly be said to exist *in* transmission, *in* communication. There is more than a verbal tie between the words common, community, and communication. Men live in a community in virtue of the things which they have in common; and communication is the way in which they come to possess things in common. What they must have in common in order to form a community or society are aims, beliefs, aspirations, knowledge—a common understanding—like-mindedness as the sociologists say. Such things cannot be passed physically from one to another, like bricks; they cannot be shared as persons would share a pie by dividing it into physical pieces. The communication which insures participation in a common understanding is one which secures similar emotional and intellectual dispositions—like ways of responding to expectations and requirements.

Persons do not become a society by living in physical proximity, any more than a man ceases to be socially influenced by being so many feet or miles removed from others. A book or a letter may institute a more intimate association between human beings separated thousands of miles from each other than exists between dwellers under the same roof. Individuals do not even compose a social group because they all work for a common end. The parts of a machine work with a maximum of coöperativeness for a common result, but they do not form a community. If, however, they were all cognizant of the common end and all interested in it so that they regulated their specific activity in view of it, then they would form a community. But this would involve communication. Each would have to know what the other was about and would have to have some way of keeping the other informed as to his own purpose and progress. Consensus demands communication.

We are thus compelled to recognize that within even the most social group there are many relations which are not as yet social. A large number of human relationships in any social group are still upon the machine-like plane. Individuals use one another so as to get desired results, without reference to the emotional and intellectual disposition and consent of those used. Such uses express physical superiority, or superiority of position, skill, technical ability, and command of tools, mechanical or fiscal. So far as the relations of parent and child, teacher and pupil, employer and employee, governor and governed, remain upon this level, they form no true social group, no matter how closely their respective activities touch one another. Giving and taking of orders modifies action and results, but does not of itself effect a sharing of purposes, a communication of interests.

Not only is social life identical with communication, but all communication (and hence all genuine social life) is educative. To be a recipient of a communication is to have an enlarged and changed experience. One shares in what another has thought and felt and in so far, meagerly or amply, has his own attitude modified. Nor is the one who communicates left unaffected. Try the experiment of communicating, with fullness and accuracy, some experience to another, especially if it be somewhat complicated, and you will find your own attitude toward your experience changing; otherwise you resort to expletives and ejaculations. The experience has to be formulated in order to be communicated. To formulate requires getting outside of it, seeing it as another would see it, considering what points of contact it has with the life of another so that it may be got into such form that he can appreciate its meaning. Except in dealing with commonplaces and catch phrases one has to assimilate, imaginatively, something of another's experience in order to tell him intelligently of one's own experience. All communication is like art. It may fairly be said, therefore, that any social arrangement that remains vitally social, or vitally shared, is educative to those who participate in it. Only when it becomes cast in a mold and runs in a routine way does it lose its educative power.

In final account, then, not only does social life demand teaching and learning for its own permanence, but the very process of living together educates. It enlarges and enlightens experience; it stimulates and enriches imagination; it creates responsibility for accuracy and vividness of statement and thought. A man really living alone (alone mentally as well as physically) would have little or no occasion to reflect upon his past experience to extract its net meaning. The inequality of achievement between the mature and the immature not only necessitates teaching the young, but the necessity of this teaching gives an immense stimulus to reducing experience to that order and form which will render it most easily communicable and hence most usable.

THE PLACE OF FORMAL EDUCATION

There is, accordingly, a marked difference between the education which every one gets from living with others, as long as he really lives instead of just continuing to subsist, and the deliberate educating of the young. In the former case the education is incidental; it is natural and important, but it is not the express reason of the association. While it may be said, without exaggeration, that the measure of the worth of any social institution, economic, domestic, political, legal, religious, is its effect in enlarging and improving experience; yet this effect is not a part of its original motive, which is limited and more immediately practical. Religious associations began, for example, in the desire to secure the favor of overruling powers and to ward off evil influences; family life in the desire to gratify appetites and secure family perpetuity; systematic labor, for the most part, because of enslavement to others, etc. Only gradually was the by-product of the institution, its effect upon the quality and extent of conscious life, noted, and only more gradually still was this effect considered as a directive factor in the conduct of the institution. Even today, in our industrial life, apart from certain values of industriousness and thrift, the intellectual and emotional reaction of the forms of human association under which the world's work is carried on receives little attention as compared with physical output.

But in dealing with the young, the fact of association itself as an immediate human fact, gains in importance. While it is easy to ignore in our contact with them the effect of our acts upon their disposition, or to subordinate that educative effect to some external and tangible result, it is not so easy as in dealing with adults. The need of training is too evident; the pressure to accomplish a change in their attitude and habits is too urgent to leave these consequences wholly out of account. Since our chief business with them is to enable them to share in a common life we cannot help considering whether or not we are forming the powers which will secure this ability. If humanity has made some headway in realizing that the ultimate value of every institution is its distinctively human effect—its effect upon conscious experience—we may well believe that this lesson has been learned largely through dealings with the young.

We are thus led to distinguish, within the broad educational process which we have been so far considering, a more formal kind of education—that of direct tuition or schooling. In undeveloped social groups, we find very little formal teaching and training. Savage groups mainly rely for instilling needed dispositions into the young upon the same sort of association which keeps adults loyal to their group. They have no special devices, material, or institutions for teaching save in connection with initiation ceremonies by which the youth are inducted into full social membership. For the most part, they depend upon children learn-

ing the customs of the adults, acquiring their emotional set and stock
of ideas, by sharing in what the elders are doing. In part, this sharing
is direct, taking part in the occupations of adults and thus serving an
apprenticeship; in part, it is indirect, through the dramatic plays in
which children reproduce the actions of grown-ups and thus learn to
know what they are like. To savages it would seem preposterous to seek
out a place where nothing but learning was going on in order that one
might learn.

But as civilization advances, the gap between the capacities of the
young and the concerns of adults widens. Learning by direct sharing in
the pursuits of grown-ups becomes increasingly difficult except in the
case of the less advanced occupations. Much of what adults do is so
remote in space and in meaning that playful imitation is less and less
adequate to reproduce its spirit. Ability to share effectively in adult
activities thus depends upon a prior training given with this end in
view. Intentional agencies—schools—and explicit material—studies—are
devised. The task of teaching certain things is delegated to a special
group of persons.

Without such formal education, it is not possible to transmit all
the resources and achievements of a complex society. It also opens a way
to a kind of experience which would not be accessible to the young, if
they were left to pick up their training in informal association with
others, since books and the symbols of knowledge are mastered.

But there are conspicuous dangers attendant upon the transition
from indirect to formal education. Sharing in actual pursuit, whether
directly or vicariously in play, is at least personal and vital. These qualities compensate, in some measure, for the narrowness of available opportunities. Formal instruction, on the contrary, easily becomes remote
and dead—abstract and bookish, to use the ordinary words of deprecia-
tion. What accumulated knowledge exists in low grade societies is at
least put into practice; it is transmuted into character; it exists with the
depth of meaning that attaches to its coming within urgent daily interests.

But in an advanced culture much which has to be learned is stored
in symbols. It is far from translation into familiar acts and objects. Such
material is relatively technical and superficial. Taking the ordinary
standard of reality as a measure, it is artificial. For this measure is connection with practical concerns. Such material exists in a world by itself, unassimilated to ordinary customs of thought and expression. There
is the standing danger that the material of formal instruction will be
merely the subject matter of the schools, isolated from the subject
matter of life-experience. The permanent social interests are likely to
be lost from view. Those which have not been carried over into the
structure of social life, but which remain largely matters of technical
information expressed in symbols, are made conspicuous in schools.
Thus we reach the ordinary notion of education: the notion which ignores its social necessity and its identity with all human association that

affects conscious life, and which identifies it with imparting information about remote matters and the conveying of learning through verbal signs: the acquisition of literacy.

Hence one of the weightiest problems with which the philosophy of education has to cope is the method of keeping a proper balance between the informal and the formal, the incidental and the intentional, modes of education. When the acquiring of information and of technical intellectual skill do not influence the formation of a social disposition, ordinary vital experience fails to gain in meaning, while schooling, in so far, creates only "sharps" in learning—that is, egoistic specialists. To avoid a split between what men consciously know because they are aware of having learned it by a specific job of learning, and what they unconsciously know because they have absorbed it in the formation of their characters by intercourse with others, becomes an increasingly delicate task with every development of special schooling.

SUMMARY

It is the very nature of life to strive to continue in being. Since this continuance can be secured only by constant renewals, life is a self-renewing process. What nutrition and reproduction are to physiological life, education is to social life. This education consists primarily in transmission through communication. Communication is a process of sharing experience till it becomes a common possession. It modifies the disposition of both the parties who partake in it. That the ulterior significance of every mode of human association lies in the contribution which it makes to the improvement of the quality of experience is a fact most easily recognized in dealing with the immature. That is to say, while every social arrangement is educative in effect, the educative effect first becomes an important part of the purpose of the association in connection with the association of the older with the younger. As societies become more complex in structure and resources, the need of formal or intentional teaching and learning increases. As formal teaching and training grow in extent, there is the danger of creating an undesirable split between the experience gained in more direct associations and what is acquired in school. This danger was never greater than at the present time, on account of the rapid growth in the last few centuries of knowledge and technical modes of skill.

Toward Dialogue

We have associated the idea of education with schools for so long that it is sometimes difficult to appreciate the full magnitude of what Dewey is driving at. He says ". . . all communication (and hence all genuine social life) is educative." What this must mean is that whenever one is in contact with other people he is in the process of learning. And this, in turn, must mean that most of our learning is unintentional, since we are in contact with other people most of our waking hours. And if school learning is really only a very small and inconsequential part of all learning, perhaps the educator should pay less attention to the technical aspects of his own formal teaching—lesson plans, programmed learning, intelligence testing, and all the rest—and more attention to what happens to the child outside the school doors. It is there, apparently, that most of the child's total structure is put together.

Dewey accents this idea with the further remark that, "not only does social life demand teaching and learning for its own permanence, but the very process of living together educates." And when these instances of "living together" are formalized and regularized into what the anthropologist calls "social institutions," the educative effect is correspondingly heightened. The family, the neighborhood gang, the school clique, the church, the labor union, the office crowd, the corporation, the crime syndicate, the Black Power Movement, the Republican Party—all are educational institutions, and without really intending to be so. But deliberately or not, they teach; and the question any educator must raise is whether these educational institutions should somehow be made more accountable to the general polity for the educational effect they have on people. For their work is very often at odds with what the formal educational apparatus of the community is trying to accomplish.

ABRAHAM EDEL

The Contribution of Philosophical Anthropology to Educational Development

THE TASKS BEFORE US

Philosophy in general contributes to educational development by making educational theory self-conscious about its aims and limitations, about its methods and principles of selection, about its presuppositions concerning the nature of man and society and of the human predicament and human development. To stimulate such systematic self-consciousness is the age-old task of philosophizing since Socrates and the

From *Philosophy and Educational Development* ed. George Barnett (Boston: Houghton Mifflin, and London: George G. Harrap and Company, 1966), pp. 69–91.

venerable Protagoras first exchanged words on whether virtue, like knowledge, was teachable.

How does philosophical anthropology in particular make its contribution to educational development? Unfortunately, the term "philosophical anthropology" has come to be used for many and diverse inquiries. Some use it for a specific branch of anthropology—the world-outlooks of primitive peoples—just as in economic anthropology the economic practices of primitive peoples are studied. Some philosophers take philosophical anthropology to be the systematic critique of the anthropologist's methods of inquiry, such as digging out his metaphysical presuppositions about culture—for example, whether he is a monist in treating each culture as an organic unity or an extreme pluralist in seeing it as an aggregate of isolable and separably replaceable traits. Some philosophers have recently begun to use the term "philosophical anthropology" in a rather unusual way for what has more frequently been called philosophical psychology—an analytic consideration of concepts about man's actions, such as concepts of agent, act, choice, responsibility, and so on. A more traditional use of the term, since Cassirer at any rate, is for that philosophical speculation which seeks a definition of "man" and lines up such candidates as man the tool-user, man the symbol-maker, and so forth. No doubt all of these inquiries have educational implications. For example, if in the last sense I offered a definition of man as the kind of animal that is capable of asking " What is man?" and instead of answering, questioning the meaning of his question, I would have shifted the "essence" of man and I could look for a consequent shift in the "essence" of education—probably to an objective of sharpening the mind by cultivating criticism. I might then go on to trace far-reaching changes in the junior-high-school curriculum, since that is a time when sensitive youngsters wake up to broader issues. I forego the temptation to trace the effects on the bureaucratic structure of educational administration!

I shall deal with philosophical anthropology in none of the special senses I have indicated, but in a more general way. I mean by it the direct utilization of the materials and modes of inquiry developed in modern anthropological work to achieve the philosophical task of developing systematic self-consciousness—in this case, in educational theory. The resultant picture is pretty familiar by this late date in contemporary thought, at least in abstract terms. First, we are liberated from a narrowing ethnocentrism in which we think of our own ways as the fixed order of nature. Second, we come to expect in every phase of life that there has been and can be a wide range of differences. Third, we see differences not simply as varying items but as shaping up into varied systematic patterns. Fourth, in spite of discovered variety—perhaps even because of it—we are better able to discern what kinds of common or invariant elements, what sort of basic unity, there has been in mankind. Fifth, we come to understand the different ways in which human beings have tried to do similar jobs, and are prompted to develop criteria for effectiveness in doing these jobs. Sixth, as a result of such inquiries, we develop the habit of looking for the relations of particular human ways and practices to the general cultural setting; we anticipate the complexity of differing subpatterns and the interinfluence of groups with different ways; we become conscious of persistent changes and the deeply socio-historical character of human life. And seventh, we gain a sensitive awareness of the forms of expression that the human spirit has taken, and come to realize its creative character. On the practical side, this means that men are always choosing among possibilities in hammering out their next historical steps. On the intellectual side, it means articulating a comparative approach which not merely gives different results but—and this is increasingly central in philosophy today—restructures the questions asked.

All this adds up to a philosophical view of man, not just a few lively items suggested by anthropology. And I need scarcely add that it is a philosophical inquiry, whether carried on by philosophers, or anthropologists, or educators. In principle, of course, this growth of consciousness need not have required anthropological derivation. It might have come directly from sensitive reflection, by observing small differences and extending them in thought, by studying historical changes in a single culture, and so on. In the ancient world, differences in men's ways were closer at hand. The tremendous growth of Western civilization in its uniform aspects has tended to obscure them. It has been the achievement of modern anthropology to exhibit extreme differences, to furnish a larger variety of patterns, and to render comparison analytic and self-conscious. If all mankind spoke a single language which remained basically unchanged, we might never have conceived of alternative languages. It is much easier to develop a science of linguistics when there are thousands of languages. But this is a necessary, not a sufficient condition for self-consciousness. That there are thousands of religions and thousands of moralities has not yet been sufficiently exploited for theoretical understanding. What about the theory of education?

At the heart of any view of educational development lies some concept of education itself. Our traditional concept has been that of schooling—and a static one at that. Here are the materials to be learned, waiting eternally to be imparted. Here are the (more or less recalcitrant) learners-to-be, and here, the teachers trained in the eternally valid modes of transmission. The input is tearful children torn from the bosom of the family. The plant consists in separate buildings shut off from the community. The machine process is what goes on within those sacred precincts. The output is shining faces in caps and gowns, equipped with skills, character, and knowledge. I leave it to students of the history of education to decide whether this really has been a prevalent concept, or is a man of straw for the convenience of educational philosophers.

The broadened view furnished by anthropological materials poses basic questions for such a concept. In his survey of North American primitive education, Pettitt says,

> . . . in primitive society, which had no school system, we find a fairly complete picture of what a people must do to insure the transmittal of its traditions, beliefs, ideals, and aspirations to the younger generation. Through study of such school-free efforts we may obtain a clearer conception of the manifold ramifications of the process of conditioning children and of safeguarding a culture pattern. With such a conception in mind we are then in a better position to judge whether schools and professional teachers, either in justice to themselves or to the public, should be expected to assume the whole responsibility at so much per month.[1]

Philosophical anthropology utilizes the comparative material to elicit two points in our consciousness of what education is doing. The first is a clarified distinction between *schooling* as a narrower concept and *enculturation* as the wider idea of the total transmission in one mode or another of the ways of the culture from generation to generation. It involves a discovery of the full range of types of ways transmitted and modes of transmission, and a recognition of the selective character of schooling. And so it poses the question of the principles, explicit or tacit, operative in that selection. The second point, once the full range is before us, is the discovery that schooling itself is always doing much more than we are inclined to credit it with. That we recognize this fact is shown in the familiar adage that the personality of the teacher counts almost as much as his knowledge of the subject; but we narrow the view by saying that some types of personality are better able to transmit the subject than others. A full anthropological treatment of schooling startles us by its findings.

My first task here is to exhibit the contributions of philosophical anthropology on these points. But when this is done, we will have merely the raw material on which a theory of educational development can operate, not the principles of selection for the educational focus of the schools. The second task, therefore, is to consider what light anthropological methods can shed on the functional relations of schooling to culture and society as a whole. The outcome of such inquiry is a consciousness of the unavoidably normative character of educational theory. It is commonly recognized that such theory is normative for educational institutions, but the significant point in an anthropological perspective is the ways in which it is normative for the culture as a whole. Hence, my third task will be to raise the question of the value base of normative social decision in our age, and whether it furnishes grounds for a special or central focus in educational development.

---

[1] George A. Pettitt, *Primitive Education in North America*, University of California Publications in American Archaeology and Ethnology, Vol. 43, No. 1 (1946), p. 3.

WHAT DOES THE LEARNER LEARN?

No general reference can do justice to the full range of dimensions that come into view when the narrower concept of schooling is enriched by the anthropological concept of enculturation. We require at least a brief itemization.

What strikes us first about the schools, of course, is content—whether we are examining skills such as reading, writing, and French, or subject-matter such as chemistry, mathematics, or Shakespeare. Often we have trouble distinguishing between a skill and a bit of knowledge, and with Shakespeare we may hedge a bit on what we are teaching as we shift from memorization and plot detail to a sense of language or an exuberant outlook. Few theoretical implications might at first seem to follow from the fact that the content of our curriculum has changed over the centuries, nor from the comparative fact that, say, the Aztec priesthood schools included fasting and self-torture. The basic reason why we often take for granted a changing subject-matter of teaching is itself a cultural acquisition. We have stabilized the ideal of a *growing* body of knowledge, and it is this central phenomenon of modern society which is taken to give substance to schooling.

The schools take it for granted that beyond conveying knowledge and skills they are building character. Anthropological impact on the theory of character and attitude development has been quite far-reaching. The lining up of contrasts is overwhelming: for example, the contrast of Zuni modesty and reserve with Kwakiutl ostentation and arrogance; of the typical, matter-of-course generosity found in many American Indian cultures, with our own dominant self-regard; of the male stoicism of the Plains Indians with the gentle tenderness of the Arapesh males; and so on in almost endless contrasts.[2] These striking differences enter into the very organization of concepts as, for example, a particular Chiga character term will apply both to stealing and to inhospitality as if they were one in essence, just as our own term "shiftless" may fuse "lazy," "dirty," and "poor," even though these characteristics are only empirically related under special social conditions. Even more penetrating is the recognition that not only the content of moral attitudes—which acts rouse feelings of guilt—is culturally variable, but the actual type and quality of "conscience" itself, that is, whether one feels guilty or ashamed or disgusted or some other emotional configuration.[3] Also, the ways of expressing feeling are quite different, as can be seen in the impassivity of the Bali, the emotional outpouring of south Europeans, and the

[2] See Ruth Benedict, *Patterns of Culture* (Boston: Houghton Mifflin Company, 1934), and Margaret Mead, *Sex and Temperament in Three Primitive Societies* (New York: William Morrow & Co., Inc., 1935).

[3] See Margaret Mead, "Social Change and Cultural Surrogates," *The Journal of Educational Sociology*, Vol. XIV (October, 1940), pp. 92–109; also, Ruth Benedict, *The Chrysanthemum and the Sword* (Boston: Houghton Mifflin Company, 1946).

familiar British reserve. There are even widely varying attitudes toward such a physiologically common phenomenon as pain—feeling it typically as simply something to be gotten rid of or primarily as a threat because it is a symptom of something wrong in the body.[4] Many of our assumptions about unavoidable attitudes give way in comparisons: for example, the assumed inevitability of stresses and strains in adolescence, which Margaret Mead challenged in her early *Coming of Age in Samoa*. Or the inevitability of childhood anthropomorphism, which she found absent in the early realism of the Manus child. Or the attitudes toward privacy, which she posed in the striking contrast between the Samoan girl who might say that she slept with a boy but would never tell whether she loved him, and the typical American girl who might openly confess she loved a boy but never tell whether she slept with him![5]

Much of what I have said about character and attitude holds equally for social principles. It has taken a long time to realize that our democratic school system has not merely harbored but actively imparted non-equalitarian attitudes. We still do not realize that we are teaching bureaucratic attitudes through the example of the bureaucratic structure of our large educational system. An anthropological survey of our goings-on cannot miss this.

The subtlety of what we are imparting to the young does not end with content and skills, character and attitudes and social principles. Hallowell and Redfield and the Kluckhohns have shown how every culture provides orientations of a basic sort for its individuals—modes of reference for their very selves, orientations to space and time and direction.[6] For example, time sweeps from the unseen back to the visible past in front, for the people of one culture, while in another we march forward into the future ahead. (Think how startled we would be if we were told we had a great future behind us!) One people may feel themselves a part of nature, while another feel themselves outside of nature, not cooperating with it but dominating it. In mechanistic fashion, we think of our bodies as machines with almost replaceable parts; primitive societies more often stress a conception of organic unity of self and world. One society lives in the present, another turns its young, as ours does—and the school embodies this stress—to working for the future,

[4] See Mark Zborowski's contrast of Italian and Jewish patients in "Cultural Components in Responses to Pain," *Journal of Social Issues*, Vol. VIII (1952), pp. 16–30.

[5] Margaret Mead, *Coming of Age in Samoa* (New York: William Morrow & Co., Inc., 1928), and *Growing Up in New Guinea* (New York: William Morrow & Co., Inc., 1930).

[6] A. Irving Hallowell, *Culture and Experience* (Philadelphia: University of Pennsylvania Press, 1955), especially Chapter 4; Robert Redfield, *The Primitive World and Its Transformations* (Ithaca, N.Y.: Cornell University Press, 1953); Clyde Kluckhohn and others, "Values and Value-Orientation in the Theory of Action" in *Toward a General Theory of Action*, ed. Talcott Parsons and Edward A. Shils (Cambridge, Mass.: Harvard University Press, 1951); Florence Kluckhohn and Fred L. Strodtbeck, *Variations in Value Orientations* (Evanston, Ill.: Row, Peterson & Company, 1961).

postponing gratification, even robbing the present of its non-future meaning. (Recent study has shown this to be a middle-class pattern, which is one reason why middle-class teachers often quite fail to understand the ways of their lower-class pupils.) Often the school imparts overt attitudes to restraint and control. In recent decades we have talked a great deal about leeway for self-expression. The Ashanti sound much more like our conservative critics of progressive education when they say, "When your child dances badly, tell him saying, 'Your dancing is not good,' and do not say to him '[Little] soul, just dance as you want to.' "[7] Beneath overt attitudes to expressiveness or control lie patterns of cultural character that vary both in the modern and primitive worlds.

Again, in learning itself, the mode in which one is taught produces a second-order learning, what Bateson has aptly called "deutero-learning."[8] It is at this point that concepts of method, of authority, of how to go about things and how to fuse thought and experience are inculcated. Wylie's description of the mode of teaching in a French village school is a good example of this:

> In teaching morals, grammar, arithmetic, and science the teacher always follows the same method. She first introduces a principle or rule that each pupil is supposed to memorize so thoroughly that it can be repeated on any occasion without a slightest faltering. Then a concrete illustration or problem is presented and studied or solved in the light of the principle. More problems or examples are given until the children can recognize the abstract principle implicit in the concrete circumstances and the set of circumstances implicit in the principle. When this relationship is sufficiently established in the minds of the children, the teacher moves on to another principle and set of related facts.
>
> The principle itself is not questioned and is hardly discussed. Children are not encouraged to formulate principles independently on the basis of an examination of concrete cases. They are given the impression that principles exist autonomously. They are always there: immutable and constant.[9]

A philosopher reading this will be tempted to interpret it as the deutero-learning of a Cartesian rationalism. Contrast it with Anthony Leeds' anthropological description of the way of many American educators:

> . . . the *process* of learning itself is crucial and content secondary, if not actually unimportant, since it will be learned by virtue of ingesting the process itself, a process labelled "experiencing" and conceptually derived from a systematic distortion of the scrolls writ by their culture hero, John Dewey. The neonate is to be put through "experiences" about which he subsequently "intellectualizes." This

---

[7] R. S. Rattray, *Ashanti Proverbs*, 344, as quoted in J. S. Slotkin, *Social Anthropology* (New York: The Macmillan Co., 1950), p. 526.

[8] Gregory Bateson, "Social Planning and the Concept of 'Deutero-Learning,' " Conference on Science, Philosophy, and Religion, New York, 1942.

[9] Laurence Wylie, *Village in the Vaucluse* (New York: Harper & Brothers, 1957), p. 73.

process apparently prepares him, intellectually or in "life-adjustment," as one of the favourite phrases of American educators goes, for any future exigency in learning.[10]

Space forbids a detailed treatment of other phases here, but I cannot forbear running through their variety. To take the question of who teaches: in primitive societies often the whole community serves as teachers, sometimes specialized priests or elders, while among us teachers are a specially trained group. Yet how much among us that is vocational should be learned on the job? Or what part of the learning is of a kind for which at its earlier levels a neighborhood parental group could be enlisted? Again, who is taught? In early China, Linton reminds us,[11] only nobles attended higher schools, and they learned the six liberal arts of ceremonies, music, architecture, charioteering, mathematics, and writing. The ideal of universal education is so recent that its partial achievement calls for reassessing the whole character of our schools. Are we still teaching a kind of charioteering and ceremonies? Again, what are the contexts of learning? We think primarily of a classroom, and even in considering only the college level, have difficulty in thinking of a library as a learning context rather than a preparation for class—to say nothing of the college breakfast table, where students teach each other some of the things they have been learning in class! Primitive societies exhibit more clearly the parental context, the apprenticeship context, learning on the job, the teaching role of striking ceremonials such as initiation rites, the teaching role of designated relatives such as mother's brother or grandparents. Lining all this up poses more consciously the question of who should teach what, where, rather than dumping every critical learning need onto the schools. (Where *should* a child learn how to drive a car, how to repair an electric switch, how to dance, and the facts and norms of sexual life?) And what of the techniques of teaching? Primitive societies use not only talk, but music, folklore, and dance to teach: Driberg points out that animal dances are used to portray the characteristics of animals and how to hunt them,[12] and much teaching is done through myths, folk stories[13] (how late we have come to teaching through comic books!), and dramatized ceremonies such as the Hopi use of kachinas (elaborately masked impersonators of ancestral spirits). In all these comparisons there is implicit the obvious lesson that learning is a multiple

[10] Anthony Leeds, "Cultural Factors in Education: India, Brazil, the United States, the Soviet Union: Some Problems of Applied Anthropology," in *Contemporary India*, ed. Baidya Nath Varma (New York: Asia Publishing House, 1964), pp. 291–292.

[11] Ralph Linton, *The Tree of Culture* (New York: Alfred A. Knopf, Inc., 1955), pp. 541–542.

[12] J. H. Driberg, *At Home with the Savage* (London: Routledge & Kegan Paul, 1932), p. 242.

[13] Walter Goldschmidt points out that educational requirements may be seen to influence primitive folk-tales in the fact that juveniles are utilized as leading characters. See his *Exploring the Ways of Mankind* (New York: Holt, Rinehart & Winston, Inc., 1960), p. 217.

business, achievable in many ways, and that specialized modes require analysis and evaluation. Plato knew this; do we require philosophical anthropology to convey the lesson?

And what of the prime issue of sanctions in learning? The coercive aspect is often dominant in our educational systems: how many of us still remember the school principal's flat strap for which we were expected to hold out our hand, bravely if not willingly—itself a learning experience? And the truant officer is still much with us. Pettitt concludes that among primitive societies corporal punishment is rare, not because of the innate kindliness of these people but because it is contrary to developing the type of individual personality they set up as the ideal.[14] He finds ridicule, praise, and reward more common. Yet shame can work in different ways. Consider the aggressive shaming of pupils that Wylie describes in a French village school:

> "What is seven times nine, Marie?"
> "I don't know, Madame."
> "Ah! She doesn't know seven times nine. Everyone in this class
> knows that. Class, what is seven times nine?"
> The class roared the answer.[15]

Compare this with the Pueblo school, in which no child will give the answer till everyone has it, for you must not shame anyone! Of course, in the long run, theory recognizes, the sheer desire to learn would be the very best sanction. (St. Augustine, in the first book of his *Confessions*, looking back on his early sin in preferring Virgil to eternal mathematics, says: "No doubt then, that a free curiosity has more force in our learning these things than a frightful enforcement.") Margaret Mead points out that the shift from learning what everyone agrees everyone would *want* to know, to teaching what some think others *should* know is a differentiating mark between most primitive education and modern complex schooling.[16] Whatever the source of such distinction, once there is this complex, separately existing system maintaining compulsory attendance, the problem of incentives and the discrimination between more and less desirable ones is unavoidable for educational theory.

Let these considerations suffice for exhibiting the impact of the wider concept of enculturation on the narrower concept of schooling. Note, however, that the wide range of dimensions and the breadth of

---

[14] George A. Pettitt, *op. cit.*, p. 161.

[15] Laurence Wylie, *op. cit.*, pp. 84–85.

[16] Margaret Mead, "Our Educational Emphases in Primitive Perspective," *The American Journal of Sociology*, Vol. XLVIII, No. 6 (May, 1943), p. 634. Mead traces interesting comparisons with religions proselytizing on the assumption of infallible superiority. She also points to causal factors such as possibilities of changing status and education as a mechanism of change, political factors such as maintaining national loyalty through inculcating a system of ideas, and so on. For consideration of a wide variety of learning modes seen in the general framework of cultural communications, see Mead's *Continuities in Cultural Evolution* (New Haven, Conn.: Yale University Press, 1964), Chapters 4–6.

different possibilities within each only throws open—it certainly does not solve—the problem of choice in educational theory. One cannot, for example, simply cull a set of attractive attitudes and character-traits, set them into a beautiful mosaic, and hold them up as a shining model for school systems. We should have, instead, to study the psychological, cultural, and historical depth of our own particular character-formation before making recommendations for reconstruction. Anthropology itself quickly passed beyond merely descriptive items of difference to a grounding or difference in the needs, problems, cultural patterning, and historical development of the particular peoples studied. A school system, then, once it has emerged as a separate institutional form—similar to the state or a legal system—is not seen as endowed with an "essence" of its own. At most it has a shifting essence. It has crystallized and temporarily stabilized some aims, methods, techniques, and so on, within which and with which it operates. But it remains bound by a thousand ties to the matrix of needs and causes and informal processes of the body from which it emerged. Its existence and its values reflect the fuller matrix on which it rests; its assessment and its policies can never be self-enclosed and divorced from this reference to its functions. And so we turn to our second task—to consider the contributions of philosophical anthropology to our understanding of the functional relations of schooling to culture and society.

WHAT DOES SCHOOLING DO IN SOCIETY?

The concept of function is, of course, a familiar one in anthropological and sociological theory. The study of functions—latent as well as manifest—reveals men's aims, both through discovering intended consequences and noting social reaction to unintended consequences. For example, anthropologists have noted how the women of a community may feel dissatisfied when the village well is replaced by water piped into individual dwellings. Their labor has been eased and their families' health probably improved, but their daily social life has been ruined; they now have to go out of their way to learn the latest gossip. Now in the village in which I spend my summers we go for drinking water to a spring just outside the village. Occasionally I exchange words with a local inhabitant bent on the same errand. But often a number of cars will line up—usually with out-of-state licenses—and each person will wait, shut off in his car, till his turn comes. Obviously the latent functions of the village well have changed since the days of Isaac and Rebecca. So, too, the manifest functions of Latin have been transformed in our educational systems, and tradition desperately looks for latent functions to support itself against change.

Anthropology obviously was not needed to reveal the fact that men have aims and that their social practices embody them. But precisely because it studied bits of social practice in the context of fuller cultural patterning it was able to stimulate the *systematic* investigation of functions. When this is done in education, it often reveals unexpected aspects and may quite restructure the mode of evaluation. For example, on questions of discipline—to take a psychological function—Plains Indians are horrified by the idea of our striking a child. When they found it necessary to check a very young child's crying to prevent their camp being located by the enemy at night, they dashed water in its face, and conditioning appears to have taken place effectively. But this was necessity, not cruelty. Other people elsewhere—e.g., the Tikopia in Polynesia —may strike a child occasionally in anger, but not in cold retribution.[17] From an outside observer's view, our modes of corporal punishment are clearly seen as aggressive and incompatible with the dignity of the child.

Again, looking to social functions, I am reminded of Thorstein Veblen's analysis of the latent functions of classical education as an embellishment, with a manifest insistence on its lack of utility, but with a consequent enhancement of repute precisely because it constitutes conspicuous waste.[18] At a later time, in some cities at least, the non-vocational character of liberal arts education, especially for girls, obscured the fact that it was largely preparation for teaching as a career. The role of the contemporary educational system in assisting upward social mobility for lower-middle-class groups and for second-generation immigrant groups is well recognized. So too is its provision of a trained personnel for industry and business. Anthropological concern with total patterning sometimes makes it possible to elicit the functional profile of a whole educational system. Leeds[19] suggests, for example, that the Brazilian school system "is thoroughly tied to the class system and is, in fact, latently intended to support and reproduce its present form. Brazilian education is meant to conserve privilege for the privileged, and to create a manipulable lower class for exploitation by the privileged classes." He supports this opinion by reference both to the multiple types of specific schools for different classes, and to the general ideology of the school system.

Functions become self-conscious when they begin to serve as bases for justification or critique. For example, pure research, as long as it has little manifest social function, is justified in the individual terms of the speculative intellect and its intrinsic value, often with theological components. When its social functions become clear, it becomes "basic research" and is integrated within our university educational system. The

---

[17] Raymond Firth, *We, the Tikopia* (Boston: Beacon Press, 1963), p. 141. See also the interesting suggestions concerning modes of corporal punishment (e.g., use of the kitchen spoon or of the hairbrush) and parts of the body focused on, in Martha Wolfenstein, "Some Variants in Moral Training of Children," in *The Psychoanalytic Study of the Child*, Vol. V, ed. Ruth S. Eissler, *et al.* (New York: International Universities Press, 1950), pp. 310–328.

[18] Thorstein Veblen, "The Higher Learning as an Expression of the Pecuniary Culture," Chapter XIV in *The Theory of the Leisure Class* (New York: The Macmillan Co., 1908).

[19] Anthony Leeds, *op. cit.*, p. 298.

contemporary social role of social science is currently a matter of wide controversy. We may leave to historians to delineate the changing functions of intellectual theory in the past few centuries—for example, the impact of the dismal economic science or the succession of political philosophies. For an interesting, out-of-the-way functional suggestion, see Michael Oakeshott's treatment of Machiavelli and Locke as furnishing cribs for princes and classes that had not been born to power but came to it in ignorance; this observation is itself cast within a defense of conservatism.[20]

Again, as functions emerge, even out of differences, there is often a growing awareness of common human aims. Take, for instance, such an apparently remote phenomenon as witchcraft, remembering that spells and ceremonials and the use of herbs constitute a quite sizable part of some primitive education. Careful comparative analysis soon causes the shedding of any treatment of the subject as meaningless superstition and leads one to look for the functions of medicinal endeavor, psychological assuagement, substitute satisfaction, social techniques of control, especially in interpersonal conflict, and so on.[21] Thus quite different practices may be seen as ways of dealing with aims that are common. This tends to stimulate the development of criteria for more or less effective achievement. It is a strange dialectic of inquiry by which the search for differences, pressing on into the grounding of those differences, becomes a most helpful way of discovering common aims in human life generally, as well as in education.

On the other hand, the study of education in functional relation to the community does not always yield simple harmonious congruence. There is not merely complexity, but also discrepancy, conflict, and change, especially in a period of socio-historical transformation. These phenomena take innumerable forms. There is often a simple contradiction between educational lessons and social practices. (Wylie, listening to a lesson in which French children repeat and learn by heart, "Let us be the friends and protectors of the little birds," observes, "In a region where a favorite dish is roasted little birds, where a husky man boasts of consuming fifty or sixty warblers at a sitting, there is little likelihood that this lesson will have effect."[22]) There is often a gap between the culture developed in the schools and that of the parent generation that is obvious in immigrant groups but present also in subtler form in native-born groups, because of the rapidity of social change. There is the impact of class differences in aim and mode of life, often focusing sharply in the schools; Lloyd Warner points out that school boards are 94 per cent upper-middle class or higher; teachers, 94 per cent middle-

[20] Michael Oakeshott, *Rationalism in Politics* (New York: Basic Books, 1962), pp. 24–26.
[21] For a particular study of this subject, see J. D. Krige, "The Social Function of Witchcraft," *Theoria*, Vol. I (1947), pp. 8–21.
[22] Laurence Wylie, *op. cit.*, p. 65.

class; and students, 60 per cent lower-class and 30 per cent lower-middle class.[23] And underlying the whole process are the obvious vast changes in technology, industry, economic life, and the social forms of the twentieth century.

The most extreme conflicts arise in cases in which the educational system is set against the dominant culture, not simply against that of a particular immigrant group. Anthropological studies of acculturation in the modern world amply illustrate such processes. Take, for example, the treatment of education in Absolom Vilikazi's recent *Zulu Trans-formations, A Study of the Dynamics of Social Change*. The conflict is not something that the investigator need take pains to discover: the people themselves are quite conscious of what is going on. Professor Vilikazi points out that the Zulu distinguish socialization (*imfundiso* or *inkuliso*) from education (*imfundo*). The former equips the child with the values, knowledge, and skills of the culture, and is essentially informal. The latter

> . . . is education in the western sense of the word and is designed to pass on to the child book learning and Christianity and all the things that are characteristic of western civilization. Its aim is and always was to civilize or westernize. It is a new form of upbringing for a new world whose value systems are diametrically opposed to those of the traditional Zulu world. It now dominates the life of the child during all the years of childhood and carries its influence over the childhood years into adulthood.[24]

The consequences of the educational system are quite concrete. The child, not the parent, is able to read a letter or count money. The old culture tells the child not to be disrespectful in talking to an old person by looking directly into his face or eyes; the school teaches that to look away is a sign of shiftiness or dishonesty.[25] The old culture stresses family, kinship, tribal group; the school points to individualism and its education, to economic power and independence. And so on over a wide area of conflicts in belief and attitude.

The changed conception of education we have been considering, imposes a clear mandate on a theory of educational development. The properties of schooling—whether aim, process, or outcome—are to be understood as a function of wider social relations. In societies in which there are internal conflicts, diverse, complex sub-patterns, or basic transformations in process, schooling reflects these variations and conflicts, and educational theory inevitably takes sides or proposes fresh paths. Hence, a theory of educational development is committed to a fuller understanding of causality and qualitative dependence, and it in-

---

[23] W. Lloyd Warner, *American Life: Dream and Reality*, rev. ed. (Chicago: University of Chicago Press, 1962), p. 212.

[24] Absolom Vilikazi, *Zulu Transformations* (Pietermaritzburg, South Africa: University of Natal Press, 1962), p. 122.

[25] *Ibid.*, p. 132.

volves normative choices. It is in principle based on a theory of desirable social development and desirable cultural configuration. If it is based on anything less, it is either partially blind or unconsciously reactive. It is to this normative aspect that I now turn.

SOCIAL VECTORS AND EDUCATIONAL DIRECTIONS

If it is the task of educational development to chart the course for the schools, then, as I have suggested, the third major contribution of philosophical anthropology is to bring about the realization that the work of educational development is irretrievably normative, not merely for the schools but for the whole culture.

Take so simple and essential an objective as universal literacy. Professor Leeds suggests that mass literacy accompanies largescale shifts from a primarily agrarian base to a commercial-manufacturing and commercial-industrial base,[26] and that it is also tied to certain dissolutions in social stratification and the appearance of egalitarian ideals. Hence to move toward universal literacy in India, still only 16.6 per cent literate in 1955, is to effect an overwhelming economic and social transformation.

Or take even the theoretical concepts of an educational theory. We often speak of education as transmitting the culture from generation to generation. But why transmit? Why not change? Is there a conservative potential in the very definition of education? In her article on "Our Educational Emphases in Primitive Perspective" Margaret Mead proposes that "instead of attempting to bind and limit the future and to compromise the inhabitants of the next century by a long process of indoctrination which will make them unable to follow any path but that which we have laid down . . . we [should] devise and practice a system of education which sets the future free."[27] The future will set its own goals.

Now even to set forth such an educational ideal is to offer a critique of our culture, a proposal for its reorientation. Yet this proposal is not wholly divorced from our cultural needs and development, for it expresses the ideal of a fully self-reliant, democratic culture under conditions of extremely rapid social change in which the rate of acceleration of change can be anticipated to rise sharply.

Some educators have at times seemed to thrust upon educational theory the burden of total social change—for example, George Counts in his *Dare the School Build a New Social Order?* in the 1930's. On the whole, an analysis of our society and its culture does not support such a prospect. For one thing, it falls too readily into our cultural habit of piling every problem on the schools and then ignoring the problem elsewhere—forgetting even to increase the school budget! In many respects the schools have followed rather than led in social development:

---

26 Anthony Leeds, *op. cit.*, pp. 304–305.
27 *The American Journal of Sociology, op. cit.*, p. 639.

they are under strong traditional controls, they respond to social causes and necessities belatedly instead of exercising whatever leadership they may be capable of, and teachers on the whole have themselves tended to be conservative. Beyond this there is always the risk that when the schools rush in to make changes, a foreshortened analysis of aims, geared to some temporary emergency, may create a situation in which havoc results and the structure that creates the problem is reinforced instead of transcended. The clearest case in recent times was the near-sighted national attempt in the 1950's to gear the schools to national policy in the cold war, rather than to pursue the long-range goal of global peace.[28]

For its full articulation, a theory of educational development that looks for lights by which to steer its course cannot rest content with merely upholding general ideals, however attractive, any more than it can with merely solidifying even the best traditions of the schools of the past. To take the currently discussed examples, it can turn neither to the concept of the self-development of the individual of progressive education nor the emphasis on basic subject-learning of the tradition-alists. If the analysis I have offered is to point the way, nothing less than a full-scale valuational base which recognizes the complexity of schools in the contemporary world and their roots in our developing historical situation can begin to do the job. Such an inquiry falls into two parts. The first is the determination of the basis for judgment, which is a wider task than education alone, since it is fixing the operative value-determinants for a contemporary outlook in all social endeavor. The second is specifically educational, in applying the base in the light of the means and techniques of the schools in the present period. I will offer a few final remarks on each of these tasks.

I have dealt at length elsewhere with what seem to me to be the constituents of a complex valuational base adequate to value-determination in the contemporary world.[29] I mean the types of constituents that enter, for the content is a still further problem. There will be *perennial values*, such as advancing the body of knowledge. There will be *universal needs*, such as health, attitudes that enable one to cope with reality, sound interpersonal relations. There will be *pervasive goals*, such as possessing special skills or having a job or raising a family. There will be the *great instrumentalities* or central necessary conditions for pursuit of the good life in our historical epoch, such as the industrialization of the globe. And finally, there will be *highly critical contingent factors*, such as the need for peace or the removal of racial discrimination. How

---

[28] For a study of the impact of these events on one field of education, see Paul F. Lazarsfeld and Wagner Thielens, Jr., *The Academic Mind: Social Scientists in a Time of Crisis* (Glencoe, Ill.: The Free Press, 1958).

[29] Abraham Edel, *Ethical Judgment: The Use of Science in Ethics* (Glencoe, Ill.: The Free Press, 1955), Chapter 9. For some application to education, see "Education and the Quest for Values," *The Philosophical Forum* (Boston University), Vol. XX (1962–63).

to distinguish the genuine from the spurious is a vast problem in itself, involving the cooperation of ethics and all the sciences of man. It means doing a job for ethics in full realization of the kinds of lessons I have suggested for education throughout this essay. But with nothing less than this can we show why love without knowledge is blind, or why knowledge without love is empty, or how to distinguish love itself from its inauthentic shadows. And with nothing less will we be able to show what numerous ways there are for fantasy to replace reality in social relations; how to distinguish the kind of automation by which the machine becomes an extension of man from the kind by which man becomes an extension of the machine; why the attempt to remove racial discrimination in America is an authentic ideal, whereas the attempt to achieve racial separation in South Africa is inauthentic; why the attempt to transcend the capitalist-communist conflict by the growth of abundance is authentic, whereas the attempt to stamp out communism all over the globe is inauthentic. And so on. These are long and arduous tasks. There is no royal road to basic ethical judgment or the determination of social policy. I am suggesting that nothing less than a rounded valuational base worked out in concrete depth will do.

The second inquiry focuses on the schools, what they have to work with and what they can become. Here the task is one of appropriate selection from what the first inquiry has established. It involves discriminating emphases within the host of multiple undertakings. Just as there are desirable courses of conduct which one would not dream of turning over to legal enforcement, so there are desirable social practices whose cultivation may have no place in the school. (For example, it has been increasingly recognized that religion has no place in the public schools; we may ask comparably whether patriotism in the traditional sense does not also belong in the family, in civic, political and other such institutions rather than in the schools.) Again, just as administrative law grew up under the complex social need for regulation in societies having large-scale industry, so all kinds of educational institutions may arise that are not directly connected with the schools. (Already we have research institutes, at one extreme, and technological rehabilitation centers for displaced workers, at the other. And general adult education has woven its way in and out of the schools, as has educational TV and a kind of "do-it-yourself" education through the use of machines.) We are in for an age of educational experiment—in teaching methods, in content-selection, in setting, and in all of the other aspects of learning indicated above. And this is right and proper, for educational development, though centrally geared at present to the schools, must be society-wide in its vision.

These, then, are the theoretical contributions of philosophical anthropology to educational development: (1) the stimulation of a full, systematic consciousness of the culturally specific character of our historically developed school system; (2) the understanding of variety along all relevant dimensions and the view of alternative possibilities; (3) the search for functional relations and underlying aims; (4) the awareness of the normative character of educational policy for the culture as a whole; and (5) the full relation of educational development to a valuational base that fuses knowledge and value in the given age. Stated abstractly, these contributions may sound bare and truistic, but examined concretely with comparative cultural detail and in philosophical depth, they can revolutionize our thinking and, if applied, transform our schools.

In conclusion, I should like to ask whether there is a central stress for the schools which one might be tempted to suggest. I think there is, if it will not be turned from a general thread into a monistic aim. I offer it separately here, because it would have to be independently established, and disagreement with it would not in any way affect the theoretical conclusions I have presented up to this point.

I suggest that we think in terms of making our schools *bastions of criticism.* I think the implementation of this recommendation will meet a pervasive need in all areas. Concepts are cracking in scientific work, and new ones are being demanded. Traditional media and standards of taste in humanistic fields are being transformed. Political schemata, ideologies, and neat oppositions are breaking down. The mass transformations of life in the past half century are reaching the point where they have burst into consciousness as the central phenomenon of mankind. Repression, however widespread, has shown its hollowness, whether in the communist world or the Western world. In spite of rightist outbursts, there is a wider intellectual recognition of the need for independent thought than there has been since John Stuart Mill wrote his *Liberty* a century ago. The word "conformist" is fast becoming a term of disparagement. Most recently, we have witnessed the upsurge of the younger generation in a movement whose character—despite its turbulence, impatience, and sharp breaks with many established attitudes—is described by responsible observers as profoundly moral. In the field of foreign policy, we are observing the "uprising" of the professors, who are making the unheard-of demand for wedding more accurate knowledge and greater moral sensitivity with our foreign relations. And most basic of all is the changing social position of education itself, from a requisite for sober work and occasional professions to the necessary prerequisite for the actual running of a machine-automated economy.

But in spite of all these objective conditions for rapid changes and all this flaring of consciousness, I do not think the schools will lead the way. There is, however, a fighting chance that, given their new social role, they can be extricated sufficiently from their traditional servitude. If they can become permanent bastions of criticism, with this commitment as a recognized cultural role, this will add genuine substance to our cultural slogan of freedom.

Toward Dialogue

By far the most interesting "contribution of philosophical anthropology to educational development" is Edel's Item (4) on page 158; "the awareness of the normative character of educational policy for the culture as a whole." Indeed, it seems as if Edel considers this the main thesis of his argument, since he closes his essay with the summation that the schools should become "bastions of criticism."

Edel realizes of course that he is not the first individual to suggest this. Indeed, it has been a sweet, earnest melody vocalized by many energetic educational liberals over the last few decades. We are reminded of the active debate set off in the Thirties by George S. Counts' manifesto on the school's role in reshaping the social order. And Theodore Brameld, author of the next selection, has made virtually an entire career out of urgent advocacy of a Reconstructionist philosophy of education.

Much of this debate, however, seems to have missed the point, or at least to have ignored a vital variable: Can the school do it? Let alone whether the school dare build a new social order or even whether it should, is the school by its very design and structure capable of becoming an agent of reform and reconstruction? Isn't there something to be learned from the fact that of all the social institutions in American life, the school has historically been among the most conservative? Perhaps the church surpasses it in downright stolidity and commitment to the way things are; but among all of the other major American social institutions—family, political parties, the business community, the mass media, government and the courts, the entertainment industry, even middle-class society itself—the public school has shown itself to be the most conservative, literally "conservationist" in outlook, and the slowest to adjust to cultural changes. As long as the local school superintendent and his board of education are more exercised by the length of skirts or haircuts than by solutions to public problems, there is reason to think that "change" is somehow intrinsically unnatural to the institution of the school as we have created it in this country. At any rate, the American people seem hopelessly unready to accept the idea that the public school is going to become the "Mr. Clean" of the 1970's and lead the way in helping us to set things right. It is an argument that contradicts history and boggles even the most imaginative of minds.

THEODORE BRAMELD

Anthropotherapy—Toward Theory and Practice

It was the American philosopher, Charles Peirce, who first persuasively contended that concepts have the power to remake reality by discharging into meanings that were not hitherto available to some parts of man's experience—concepts that enable man thereby to reinterpret and often to control that experience so that no longer does it mean what it meant before.

Every such explosive concept is, of course, the end-product of a long chain of earlier ones. In the behavioral sciences, as in the physical sciences, no meaning is ever totally new. At moments, nevertheless, a concept is invented and symbolized in a way that manages to crystallize and integrate a number of previously diffused and sometimes even contradictory meanings into a newly convergent formulation.

"Anthropotherapy," I shall argue, could prove to be this kind of concept. I emphasize "*could* prove," however, for two reasons. In the first place, a good deal of theoretical elaboration is demanded beyond the bare outline to be presented here. In the second place, and surely crucial in terms of the Peircian philosophy of science, the worth of the concept will depend upon prolonged experimental application in a variety of research situations. As an introduction to both obligations, I shall regard my presentation as merely a theoretical prolegomenon.

I

Although I have been unable to discover in the literature any explicit reference to or development of the term, anthropotherapy, it is of course anticipated in dozens of important works. "Social psychiatry," which Marvin Opler especially has done so much to promote[1] is one such anticipation. George Spindler, whose anthropological interest in education overlaps with mine, mentions the term "cultural therapy," although in a narrower sense than I would intend.[2] More widely, many suggestions are to be found in *Human Organization*, the journal of the Society for Applied Anthropology, and occasionally in the *American Anthropologist*. Certainly some of the most important recent theory

[1] Marvin K. Opler, *Culture, Psychiatry and Human Values*, Thomas, Springfield, Ill., 1956.
[2] George D. Spindler (ed.), *Education and Culture*, Holt, New York, 1963, pp. 168–171.

From *Human Organization,* 24 (Winter 1965), pp. 288–293.

both in psychiatry and anthropology, as well as in other behavioral sciences, points toward the target of meaning I intend.

If, nevertheless, these contributions provide at best a direction only, surely one obvious but yet important reason for insufficient conceptualization centers in the infancy, or at most the adolescence, of the whole "culture and personality" field. True, the pioneering studies of anthropologists such as Margaret Mead, Ruth Benedict, and Bronislaw Malinowski radiate with psychocultural significance. Yet it is helpful to recall that one of the first invitations ever extended by anthropologists to psychologists to consider possible intermeshings was published under the sponsorship of the Viking Fund but fifteen years ago; that Géza Róheim and Edward Sapir were just beginning to open the field theoretically in very different ways during the decade or two preceding this conference; that Ralph Linton and Abram Kardiner formed virtually the first anthropologist-psychiatrist team in the 1940's; that the first extensive collection of writings was published under the editorship of another anthropologist and psychiatrist, Clyde Kluckhohn and Henry A. Murray, only in 1953; and that the first textbook on personality-and-culture was published just one year later by John J. Honigmann.[3]

The struggles to achieve a mature formulation have been made arduous by other factors than that of extreme youth. For one thing, the majority of specialists in both anthropology and psychology have continued their preoccupations with circumscribed research of more orthodox types that have kept them divided oftener than not. More fundamentally, a substantial theoretical literature has opposed any serious rapprochement. Thus, Leslie White[4] and his disciples have been militant in their opposition to all efforts to psychologize culture. Nor is it difficult to discover at least equally strong resistance to the anthropologizing of personality—a phenomenon painfully noticeable in professional schools for training teachers. Not only does anthropology remain a largely neglected discipline among them, but major stress continues to be placed upon psychologies of education that are conspicuous chiefly for their lack of sophisticated attention to the social and cultural dimensions of human learning and development. The average teacher in the average classroom of the average community in all countries is almost totally illiterate in the field of personality-and-culture.

Several further reasons may occur to you as to why we have not hitherto seemed ready for the conception of anthropotherapy, but I shall choose two only. One reason stems from a reluctance in conventional scientific thought to come to grips with the axiological aspects of either psychology or anthropology. This reluctance is not, of course, confined to these two disciplines—it extends to all sciences, physical and behav-

---

[3] For a useful bibliography of the above writers and others, cf. Bert Kaplan (ed.), *Studying Personality Cross-culturally*, Row, Peterson, Evanston, Ill., 1961.
[4] Leslie White, *The Science of Culture*, Farrar, Straus, and Cudahy, New York, 1949.

ioral alike. I need not belabor here the reasons why issues of value in science have so frequently been bypassed; they have been considered often. What is important is that these issues have only in recent years begun to receive the kind of attention that philosophers have always insisted they deserve. This attention, in turn, is of two kinds. To adopt the terminology of Ernest Nagel[5] a behavioral scientist may make "characterizing value judgments" that simply describe a condition in an animal or a group of people which he finds, let us say, diseased or otherwise suffering from some malfunction. But he may also make "appraising value judgments"—that is, judgments leading him to conclude that such a condition is undesirable and in need of curative treatment according to norms that he holds of animal or group health.

The kind of concern with issues of value that has achieved most respectability among behavioral scientists, when they are concerned at all, has been confined chiefly to characterizing rather than to appraising value judgments. Indeed, to a great extent the knotty questions involved in the latter even more than the former have not been adequately clarified at all. Until they are clarified further, attempts to move from the stage of descriptive or characterizing value judgments about personality-and-culture to the stage of prescriptive or appraisable value judgments will continue to be resisted.

The other reason that I am able to note here for the tardiness of adequate conceptualization emerges from the conflict and uncertainty that prevail within contemporary social institutions as to their own various and desirable roles in the wider culture. Again I shall not be able to examine here the reasons for this situation; they extend deep and far. The relevant fact rather is that these institutions are also uncertain as to how, should the possibility occur to them at all, such disciplines as psychology and anthropology could perform useful collaborative functions that might, in turn, lead to more adequate role performance by the institutions themselves.

Almost any major social institution—political, economic, religious, educational—illustrates my contention. The one with which I happen to be most familiar is as good as any, however. Most thoughtful critics of education will agree that the present period affords a sorry spectacle of cross-purposes, opportunism, vituperative accusations and counter-accusations about almost every phase of school theory and practice.

Yet, with few exceptions, two of the most valuable resources by which this unhappy and dangerous situation could be hopefully attacked are oftener than not ignored—the resources of philosophy and the sciences of man. True, psychology among all the behavioral sciences receives limited attention. Even granting, however, that at times it is studied effectively or that some school psychologists succeed in helping youngsters to cope with their personal troubles, where can one discover

5 Ernest Nagel, *The Structure of Science*, Harcourt, New York, 1961, pp. 482–495.

anywhere a single full-time school anthropologist? The contention that education is the central institutional agency of the reciprocal encultura- tive processes of transmission and innovation, and that it could function much more successfully were its roles as such an agency clarified and implemented through systematic, testable action research in the human sciences working in close conjunction, is a contention that has not so far as I know thus far been clearly recognized either in America or in any other country.

The chronic confusions of education—confusions which, I repeat, are by no means confined to this institution but are typical rather of most if not all other social institutions—are compounded again by the problems of values. That characterizing value judgments are constantly made concerning education is, of course, true. So, too, are appraising value judgments. In certain respects, accordingly, few if any educational theorists would care to deny either that the contents and processes of education *are* laden with values or that they *should* thus be laden. The trouble arises from the fact that neither kind of value judgment is clearly perceived or clearly differentiated in everyday educational experience. Rather, both characterizing and appraising value judgments are usually made haphazardly, impulsively, half-consciously if not unconsciously, and even contradictorily by teachers, administrators, parents, students, and citizens in general. They are made in these ways because no disci- pline in theory or practice is available by which they might be made in any better way. Education, by and large, is an axiological morass.

At the same time, it assuredly is not to be held wholly responsible for its own ineptitudes. After all, education is peculiarly the creation of culture as a whole—in its most comprehensive sense the central institu- tion through which every culture perpetuates and modifies the customs, habits, values, and other accretions of human evolution that *are* the stuff of culture. The weaknesses and strengths of any kind of education are inextricably bound to weaknesses and strengths of the wider human milieu. In contemporary American life, for example, its own professionals —the so-called educationists—are seldom taken seriously by other pro- fessionals, a fact supported by the relative rarity with which anthropolo- gists are eager to cooperate with educationists in the cultural laboratory of the school itself. If, indeed, it is true that the school is derelict in not drawing upon the resources of anthropology to vitalize its own roles, equally true is the fact that most experts in the field of personality-and- culture frequently ignore the school as too far removed from their own esteemed niche in the academic pecking order.

II

The principal purpose of the discussion thus far has been to clear the ground. The impression that I hope emerges is that the past thirty years mark a period of searching for rather than achieving a mature interdisciplinary conception of man-in-culture that is operable throughout institutional experience. The past decade has been devoted, in considerable part, to channeling, reshaping, and unifying the resources germane to this very large task. The progress that has been accomplished is well exemplified by Milton Singer's essay, "A Survey of Culture and Personality Theory and Research." That other behavioral sciences besides psychology and anthropology are indispensable to the field is indicated by Singer's inclusion of sociologists and social psychologists. He concludes that

> The culture and personality approach thus requires an alternating and almost simultaneous use of two different perspectives—that of culture and that of the individual person.

Moreover,

> If personality and culture theory does not depend for its derivation on a unique source of data but consists of a variety of constructions from similar bodies of data, then it is equally true that the validation of the theory does not depend on establishing correspondence with a single body of data.[6]

And just as the data and their validation are multiple, so too are the methodologies by which the data are interpreted and applied in action. One of the important virtues of the personality-and-culture movement is that it is anti-reductionist.

Let me turn now to a set of working propositions which, though by no means undebatable, are essential to the task of conceptual formulation. In stating them, it is necessary to be both selective and abbreviative. They are indebted to many more scholars than it is possible to mention. Nevertheless, I do wish to name those who have especially influenced this quest for convergence.

Among philosophers, John Dewey, George Herbert Mead, Ernst Cassirer, and Alfred North Whitehead will surely occur to you. Among psychologists I may mention Erich Fromm, Lawrence K. Frank, Kurt Lewin, Gardner Murphy, Hadley Cantril, Abraham Maslow, and Harry Stack Sullivan. Among anthropologists, besides those earlier named, I select only Alfred L. Kroeber, A. I. Hallowell, Dorothy Lee, Ashley Montagu, David Bidney, Morris Opler, Florence Kluckhohn, and Laura Thompson. All of these scholars, and several I have not mentioned, wonderfully exemplify not only concerned opposition to reductionism but to any tendency to splinter the image of man. Even more apropos, they are opposed to the exclusion of axiological considerations and they denounce every attempt to rigidify, absolutize, or reify our knowledge of culture.

III

1. Man and nature, and therefore man and culture, are engaged in *continuous transactions*—complementary sharings of experience—in

6 Milton Singer, in Bert Kaplan, *op. cit.*, pp. 65, 67 f.

which each is modified endlessly by the impact of the other. Bifocal vision is the corollary of these transactions.

2. Man, like most if not all other animals, engages in *both conflicting and cooperating experiences* throughout life. On the post-organic level of evolution, however, contrasted with both the pre-organic and organic levels, a mutation or series of mutations has occurred which enables *homo sapiens*, its indigenous species, to engage in the control and direction of his conflictive-cooperative life by consciously planned deliberations and actions. This is not to say, of course, that man invariably utilizes this capacity even in small part, or that when he does utilize it he is always successful. Failures are abundant. It is to say that to a degree far beyond that of any other animal man *has* the capacity and that occasionally he learns to utilize it quite efficiently. In short, he learns to recognize, to analyze, to reorganize, and to direct both the conflicts and the cooperations in which he is forever involved during the course of his evolution.

3. Conflict and cooperation are important instances—in various respects probably most important—of values that are as universal to man as evolution is universal. About both of them we constantly make *characterizing value judgments*. These in turn become *appraising value judgments* when we decide that a case of human conflict or of human cooperation is desirable or undesirable. When this occurs some added criterion of appraisal becomes necessary by means of which to judge the case in one way or the other.

4. The dominant criterion of value by which appraising judgments of such values or disvalues as conflict and cooperation are determined may be expressed by the term *social-self-realization*. Its meaning has been developed elsewhere.[7] In essence it symbolizes both the desire and the desirability of human beings to fulfill themselves individually and collectively to the maximum of their physical-emotional-intellectual powers, and to do so both as single personalities and in relation to other personalities living in many kinds of simple or complex social institutions. Social-self-realization, therefore, is both polaristic and organismic. Empirically, its expression ranges in time and place from strongly personalistic to strongly sociocultural behavior. Yet it is never purely one or the other: no human being is ever a self-contained being, and no social institution or cultural order is ever devoid of individuals who differ among themselves.

At the same time, social-self-realization is not a universal norm in any absolute or non-empirical sense. All that is contended is that increasing although still limited evidence from the sciences of man supports the contention that a very large proportion of our species aspires to its optimum attainment. This is true even when the behavior of some individuals and some groups mitigate against or even deny it, and even though the precise ways in which the aspiration is expressed vary widely

[7] Theodore Brameld, *Toward a Reconstructed Philosophy of Education*, Holt, New York, 1956, pp. 111–135.

both within and between the cultures of the world. In any case, those of us who join in this normative consensus are also joining in one of the most empirically universal of appraising value judgments.

5. While it is unnecessary for all behavioral scientists to guide their investigations by the value of social-self-realization or some symbolic equivalent, it is both necessary and desirable for some behavioral scientists to do so. These are, of course, scientists interested in the *active and practical application* of their knowledge to the quest of mankind for a fuller, richer life on the post-organic evolutionary plane. By the same token, they are scientists eager to attack the frustrations and alienations that impede and block such a life. Finally, they are scientists prepared to join not only with philosophers in axiological investigations that could help to clarify the place of values in personality-and-culture, but also with practitioners in social institutions—education for one—who are searching for normative goals commensurate with their obligations to the culture in which they function.

6. The empirical universals of *conflict and cooperation should now be judged in the normative context of social-self-realization.* In short, the appraising value judgments to be drawn from the characterizing value judgments that we make about either of these kinds of behavior depend upon whether they enhance or retard personal and cultural fulfillment. Conflict is a disvalue or negative value when it blocks development toward that goal and a positive value when it enhances such development. The same alternatives apply to cooperation. This is not to contend that conflict and cooperation are exclusively instrumental values; often the experience of engaging in one or the other produces its own intrinsic value or disvalue, although always in a continuum of means and ends. The crucial point is that, contrary to familiar usage, conflict is by no means always appraisable as an experience connoting something bad or wrong, nor is cooperation always appraisable as something good or right.

Education affords an illustration. On the side of personality, a student who generates some form of conflict either within himself or with a required course of study against which he rebels may simply be searching for a more mature and honest way of expressing his own integrity. Conversely, a teacher who evaluates a class in laudatory terms because every student "cooperates" with her may mean, in fact, that everyone is passively conforming to her own disciplinary rules. On the side of society, the need for appraising value judgments governed by a normative standard is similar. Conflict between groups—as in a union strike—not only may result in better wages for the workers involved but may provide enriching experiences in a common cause. Again conversely, cooperation within a group, although as in the example of union solidarity it does often carry its own positive value, may as in an army or assembly line produce more of the negative value of submission to authority or debilitating monotony. In every case, social-self-realization is the normative measuring-stick.

7. Anthropotherapy may now be defined in preliminary fashion as

the theory and practice of descriptive and prescriptive human roles. It provides analyses particularly of conflictive and cooperative situations and makes characterizing value judgments in the light of such analyses. It provides prognoses of these situations and makes appraising value judgments in the light of such prognoses. It operates within social institutions such as education; accordingly, it regards and utilizes enculturation as the inclusive human process not only for transmitting but for innovating both personal behavior and cultural patterns.

The prefix "anthropo-" is more connotative of the intended meaning than either "psycho-" or "culturo-": it synchronizes both of the latter meanings in the bifocal meaning of "man" as personality and culture in continuous transactional relationships.

8. The theory and practice of *psychotherapy* has much to contribute to the development of anthropotherapy. Particularly in neo-Freudian interpersonal psychiatry, not only does one note more and more sensitivity to the socio-cultural and ecological matrix, but also more and more explication of the normative character of this applied science. The patient is encouraged to explore without coercion the roots of his own large unconscious neurotic or psychotic troubles, but not without consciousness on the part of the therapist as to how they are neurotic or psychotic—that is, destructive—when gauged by the constructive criterion of personal-cultural fulfillment. Unlike some styles of earlier psychotherapy that tried quite unsuccessfully to rule out appraising value judgments, the styles to which I refer by no means rule them out.

Nor do they, as did some earlier styles, tend to assume that conflict is to be invariably judged as disvaluable and cooperation invariably as valuable. Once more, the converse view may in many cases lead to a correct diagnosis of the troubles of a patient: he may, for example, fear engaging in any kind of conflict—with an employer, say—and so he compensates for his fear by a kind of acquiescent cooperation that only drives his misery deeper. In many instances, therefore, "maladjustment" may prove paradoxically to be far more desirable as a therapeutic goal than the more comfortable one of "adjustment."

To take education again as an example, any competent school psychologist or counselor is committed, first of all, to performing the role that Fromm calls the "observant participant." He is the kind of psychotherapist who is "fully engaged with the patient" [student], who is "soaked with him, as it were, in this center-to-center relatedness."[8] A genuine transaction occurs between the two because both patient and counselor are changed by that kind of relatedness. Indeed, what is true of the school counselor extends ideally to every teacher—a term, incidentally, that Fromm himself applies to the effective analyst. And is this not understandable? The destructive and constructive conflicts and cooperations endemic to our age are matters both of acute anxiety and

---

[8] Erich Fromm, "Psychoanalysis and Zen Buddhism," in D. T. Suzuki, Erich Fromm, and Richard De Martino, *Zen Buddhism and Psychoanalysis*, Grove, New York, 1963, p. 12.

of great potential benefit not merely to children so ill as to need psychotherapy; they are now endemic to a larger and larger proportion of the human race. Certainly they are endemic to young people growing up in our kind of world—a world fraught with dread of thermonuclear annihilation, with political, economic, esthetic, and scientific revolutions, and above all with rapid deterioration of the kinds of moral anchorage provided by traditional customs and religions. In the sense of the term that I am inferring, the thoroughly effective teacher *is* a psychotherapist.

9. In another sense, however, psychotherapy remains much too constrictive a term, too loaded with dubious assumptions which tempt us to believe that virtually all we need to cure the ailments of our time is to attack them, as it were, from the inside out as though the objective world will become healthy and sound only when the subjective psyche has *first* become healthy and sound. This is the supreme psychotherapeutic fallacy. It is peculiarly dangerous in education because it offers moral sanction for aloofness from the most controversial issues of society and politics. Its bias is correctible only through *the unity of a discipline in which psychotherapy's own theory and practice are amalgamated with the theory and practice of planned sociocultural diagnosis and prognosis.*[9]

Probably the single most essential operating principle that has thus far emerged from the social sciences of planned change is correlative with Fromm's concept of observant participation in psychotherapy. To be effective in the long run, planned change cannot be manipulative or superimposed; rather, it requires genuine, pervasive involvement on the part of the applied social scientist in the affective-cognitive experiences of every community where conflict and/or cooperation may have generated any kind of problem in need of resolution. Here the cultural anthropologist contributes most to the required working principle: he has long known that the field experiences of participant observation are indispensable to fruitful results. Even so, the task of bringing about systematized change in any kind of community pattern is arduous indeed —no doubt even more arduous than bringing about change in the personality structure of an individual through psychotherapy. On this score, the hard-headed realism of deterministic anthropology is salutary: change in human beings, individually *or* socially, is never easy and sometimes it is apparently impossible.

Nevertheless, with Bidney, I contend that the inference of some anthropologists that culture is the sufficient cause of human change is to commit the "culturalistic fallacy"[10]—the counterpart of the psychotherapeutic fallacy at the other extreme. Planned improvement of human life could become much less difficult and much less impossible if, by means of the theory and practice of anthropotherapy, we came to accept not only the research axiom of sustained involvement in the life of any cul-

[9] Cf. Warren G. Bennis, Kenneth D. Benne, and Robert Chin (eds.), *The Planning of Change,* Holt, New York, 1962.

[10] David Bidney, *Theoretical Anthropology,* Columbia, New York, 1953, p. 51.

ture where personal and social change is contemplated, but the axiological principle that such change must be governed by empirically defensible human goals. Fromm's words apply here at least equally as well to anthropotherapy as to psychotherapy:

> the therapeutic aim cannot be achieved as long as it remains limited and does not become part of a wider, humanistic frame of reference[11]

—a frame of reference through which, in our language, social-self-realization is globally extended.

10. I conclude this theoretical outline by what may be termed several major precautionary propositions. The first is that the axiological unity of mankind is by no means as well demonstrated thus far as the *axiological diversity of mankind*. Florence Kluckhohn's work in variations among value orientations[12] cannot be appreciated too much as a safeguard against oversimplifications about the common denominators among cultural values. In radically different terms, May and Abraham Edel[13] urge a rapprochement between anthropology and axiological theory that again stresses the difficulties but by no means the impossibility of moving from pluralistic, descriptive comparisons of cultural values to inclusive normative generalizations about them.

If we regard social-self-realization as this kind of normative generalization, let us note in turn the following precautions that follow from it. The universal significance of social-self-realization is by no means completely grasped and probably never will be. It is itself subject to refinement in the light of knowledge that we do not yet possess. No culture can be expected to understand or explicate its meaning in identical terms. Many cultures are not even prepared to admit that they could benefit by experimentation in behalf of that meaning. Finally and perhaps most importantly, the distinction between characterizing value judgments based upon descriptive evidence and appraising value judgments resulting in prescriptive programs for testing should always be kept clear.

11. The second precautionary judgment relates to the first. Anthropotherapists engaged in action research must ever be on the alert to accept contingencies which they had not anticipated. Certainly *the methodology of participant observation will at all times encourage every personality and group involved to express as fully as possible their own values and other interests according to their own perceptions and not according to the anthropotherapist's*.[14] If cultural change does then re-

---

11 Erich Fromm, *op. cit.*, p. 137.

12 Florence Kluckhohn and Fred L. Strodtbeck, *Variations in Value Orientations*, Row, Peterson, Evanston, Ill., 1961.

13 May and Abraham Edel, "The Confrontation of Anthropology and Ethics," *The Monist*, XLVII, 489–505.

14 Cf. Severyn Bruyn, "The Methodology of Participant Observation," *Human Organization*, XXII, 224–235; *Communities in Action*, College and University Press, New Haven, 1963.

sult in achieving some expression of the encompassing normative goal, it occurs because the largest possible proportion of those directly involved wish it to occur. The supreme test of the anthropotherapist's own hypotheses concerning, for example, a destructive intracultural conflict is whether in the behavior of those involved it proves to reduce the anxieties, prejudices, or other disvalues characterizing that conflict and thereby achieves greater warrant for the appraising value judgment of social-self-realization that prevailed before.

12. The third precautionary proposition is that *anthropotherapy is not merely the science but the art of planned human evolution.* I do not mean this merely in the trite sense that rarely can human behavior, individually or socially, be reduced to mathematical equations. Nor do I mean it in the sense only that, as in the case of psychotherapy, the importance of feeling, intuition, insight—above all, the unconscious—are critically important. Both of these senses are germane, but I would add a third. Anthropotherapy is an art because it is an experience in the *re-creation* of personality-and-culture. Just as the psychotherapist may, in one sense, be compared with an artist whose canvas is the patient, so the anthropotherapist is, in another sense, one who aims to reshape not merely personalities as the efficient cause of culture but cultures themselves. The pragmatic test again is relevant: to the extent that a community discovers for example, the unconscious sources of particular negative values and then proceeds therapeutically to change itself enculturatively in the direction of positive values—to that extent has the community performed a work of re-creation upon and with itself. It has, as it were, drawn closer to its own "ideal superego."

13. As a last precautionary proposition, anthropotherapy, as and if it proves to be the kind of crystallizing concept which I anticipate, requires precise and manifold operations in the clinical laboratories of real communities. The point I wish to underscore, however, is not merely this necessity but also that of *extending limited clinical experience to the wider problems of mankind as a whole.* Microcosmic studies should be extended both across particular cultures and toward a macrocosmic vision of man and his encompassing goals. As Laura Thompson puts it,

> A unified science of mankind is emerging . . . on the basis of new perspectives . . . in the life sciences . . . Such a science [of mankind] could not be born until social scientists, seeking solutions to urgent human problems, began to question anachronistic models and to alter their working hypotheses in keeping with the conceptual revolution.[15]

Anthropotherapy, I contend, is clairvoyant of this revolution.

[15] Laura Thompson, *Toward a Science of Mankind,* McGraw-Hill, New York, 1961, p. 236.

Toward Dialogue

When Brameld defines anthropotherapy as "the theory and practice of descriptive and prescriptive human roles," he introduces a troubling ambiguity into the term. On the one hand, it seems that anthropotherapy is therapy, that is, a form of treatment that we can arrange for people to help them achieve what he calls "social self-realization." On the other hand, the wording of the definition, together with what Brameld says in the essay, gives the impression that anthropotherapy is a new branch of knowledge, a discipline which offers its own subject matter to be studied by a special band of inquirers. Perhaps he intends the term to cover both meanings.

At any rate, if we stick to the former connotation of the term, that of a form of treatment, we must ask how and under what circumstances "descriptive and prescriptive human roles" are made to assume a therapeutic form. For example, Brameld asserts in item 8 on page 168 that "the thoroughly effective teacher is a psychotherapist." Now we may know what this means for the pupil, but we also ought to wonder what it means for the teacher. What kind of "social self-realization" is made possible by a teacher assuming the descriptive, or more likely prescriptive, role of psychotherapist? That is to say, if anthropotherapist Brameld believes that teaching, to be effective, must contain elements of psychotherapy, and if this aspect becomes one of the prescriptions of the role of teacher, what "social self-realization" is achieved by the teacher who happens not to identify with this kind of role but who, instead, interprets the role of teacher as "information transmitter" or "trainer of cognitive processes" and prefers not to get involved in personality development? What happens to the teacher, in short, who sees the prescriptive role of teacher in a different light?

Further Readings

Brameld, Theodore. "Philosophical Anthropology: The educational significance of Ernst Cassirer," *Harvard Educational Review*, 26 (1956), pp. 207–232.

Brameld, Theodore. *The Remaking of a Culture—Life and Education in Puerto Rico.* New York: Harper and Brothers, 1959.

Brameld, Theodore. *Toward a Reconstructed Philosophy of Education.* New York: Holt, 1956.

Counts, George S. *Dare the School Build a New Social Order?* New York: John Day, 1932.

Counts, George S. *Education and American Civilization.* New York: Columbia Teachers College Bureau of Publications, 1952.

Frankel, Charles. *The Democratic Prospect.* New York: Harper and Row, 1962.

Mannheim, K. "Education as groundwork," Chapter 10 in *Freedom, Power and Democratic Planning.* London: Routledge and Kegan Paul, 1951.

4

Analytic
Philosophy
in
Educational
Thought

Analytic Philosophy

What we might call "the analytic movement" has caused one of the most remarkable revolutions in the history of philosophy. It has descended on the academic community in both Europe and the United States, advertised as a deliverance from the errors of the past. As a new mode of philosophizing, virtually a redefinition of philosophy itself, it calls into question almost everything that philosophy has been talking about for the last 2500 years. Analytic philosophy is therefore difficult to be neutral about. People used to remark a generation ago that the amusing irony of Pragmatism was that it exerted a strange, religious effect on those who studied it; as a point of view, it somehow commanded an emotional as well as an intellectual loyalty. For philosophical analysis, the irony—and the amusement—is heightened: the analysts, secular and doggedly empirical as they are, brandish a form of dogmatism all their own.

Their argument runs something like this: The scientific philosophies (see pages 15–56) are essentially correct. When it comes to acquiring dependable and usable knowledge, science has developed the method par excellence—we must put our beliefs to the test of experience to see if they are really believable or, to put it another way, worth believing. If an idea cannot be put to an empirical, scientific test, it is not worth our trouble. Now it so happens that all ideas must be expressed in sentences, or what the philosopher calls "propositions." And it is not always easy to tell, just by looking, whether a given proposition is couched in the kind of language which would make it scientifically testable. It has to be analyzed. Hence, before scientific inquiry can really begin, we have to inquire into how we put our ideas in propositional form, i.e., how we talk.

Our talk, unfortunately, is more complicated than it sounds. In expressing our ideas, we sometimes don't even speak in sentences. And when we do, the sentences or propositions are of many different kinds. One is called the analytic proposition, such as, "All men are mortal," or "Two things equal to the same thing are equal to each other." In these instances, we declare the propositions meaningful by virtue of the fact that the predicates are analyzed out of or are mere restatements of some of the meanings contained in the subject. It is not necessary to put these statements to the test of experience; they are true as they stand. Another kind of proposition is the synthetic. When we assert that "All men are Republicans," or "The annual rainfall in Dubuque is X inches," we set forth a hypothesis which requires the synthesizing, the artificial putting together, of the subject and predicate. The propositions are neither true nor false as they stand. But we know how to go about deciding whether they are true or false: by gathering the evidence. It is this synthetic type of proposition which makes up the bulk of scientific language, and the gathering of evidence in support or refutation of such propositions is what the scientist calls putting these statements to the test of experience.

The analysts, with varying degrees of certitude, have decided that only these two kinds of propositions are allowable in philosophical discourse, for the reason that no other types of sentences make any cognitive sense. All other propositions are literally nonsense or are, for one reason or another, useless in the quest for knowledge which is, after all, the chief business of philosophy. This rules out such metaphysical statements as, "All men are created equal," "God's in his heaven; all's right with the world," and "Man's destiny is freedom." These kinds of propositions are neither analytic nor synthetic. They are certainly not true as they stand; nor are they verifiable—we wouldn't know how to go about gathering evidence to support or refute them.

The analyst's position also rules out all normative propositions, i.e., those expressing "oughts" or "shoulds," or those assigning value: "Thou shalt not covet thy neighbor's wife," "One ought not tell lies," "Beethoven's Ninth is the greatest piece of music ever written," or "Picasso is either faking or pulling my leg." These propositions also are neither analytic nor synthetic. Indeed, it is not even relevant to ask whether they are "true" or "false." Rather one should ask if they are "right" or "wrong." But since there is no evidence that reveals clearly what is right or wrong, all we can do with these kinds of propositions is to ask various people how they feel about them.

In any case, the analytic philosopher insists that until we sharpen and "clean up" our language, the quest for knowledge will continue to be the haphazard and imprecise activity it has always been. Philosophy's main business, therefore, is to clarify our concepts and set rules for how we are to talk about them. In the selections which follow, Abraham Kaplan first shows the manner in which linguistic analysis has been a natural outgrowth of Pragmatism and the scientific outlook; he labels this "semantic empiricism." Then A. J. Ayer explains the central idea of analytic philosophy, "the criterion of verifiability," and with one blast from his shotgun, eliminates all metaphysics. Finally, John Wilson explores the way in which this kind of thinking changes our attitude toward truth and how we go about achieving it.

ABRAHAM KAPLAN

Concepts

THE EMPIRICAL BASIS

If science is to tell us anything about the world, if it is to be of any use in our dealings with the world, it must somewhere contain empirical elements (or, like mathematics, be used in conjunction with such elements). For it is by experience alone that information about the world is received. We can continue to process the information when the channels are closed, but we must have something to work on. Perception is fundamental to all science. Just what the channels are need not, and indeed, cannot be prejudged. Whether there are extrasensory perceptions, or whether logic states and the like have any cognitive worth, are questions which can be answered only on an empirical basis. The limits of possible experience cannot be drawn, for as Wittgenstein pointed out, we would have to stand outside experience to see on both sides of such limits; we can point to them only from within.

It is in the empirical component that science is differentiated from fantasy. An inner coherence, even strict self-consistency, may mark a delusional system as well as a scientific one. Paraphrasing Archimedes we may each of us declare, "Give me a premise to stand on and I will deduce a world!" But it will be a fantasy world except in so far as the premise gives it a measure of reality. And it is experience alone that gives us realistic premises. "Some fool has put the head of this nail on

---

From *The Conduct of Inquiry: Methodology for Behavioral Science* by Abraham Kaplan, published by Chandler Publishing Company, San Francisco. Copyright © 1964 by Chandler Publishing Company. Reprinted by permission.

the wrong end." "You idiot, it's for the opposite wall!" To be sure, if the space of physical objects allowed motions of translation only, and not also rotations. That space has such a geometry is a fantasy; experience shows otherwise. It is only experience that makes this complaint and the rejoinder a dialogue of madmen.

What knowledge requires of experience, and what experience provides, is an independence of our mere think-so. The pleasure principle governing the life of the infant gives way to the reality principle as wishes encounter obstacles to their fulfillment. The word "object," it has been said, can be understood as referring to that which objects. That is objective which insists on its own rights regardless of *our* wishes, and only experience can transmit its claims to us. Experience is ultimate because it confronts us with a continuous ultimatum. For a man to by-pass experience in the pursuit of truth is to make himself God, for only He can say, "Let there be!" and there is. The subjectivist lives in a fool's paradise; in truth, he is damned.

Now a fool's paradise is good—but only while it lasts. Inevitably our wishes urge us on from subjective fantasies to the objective world which is the locus of their fulfillment. A hungry man may dream of food but he wakes to the reality that he cannot feed on dreams. However selfless the love of truth for its own sake may be, the self, to satisfy its needs, needs knowledge of what to do. And appropriate action on things depends on experience of them: only empirical knowledge provides a basis for successful action.

Moreover, human beings interact, and act jointly; the locus of social action is a shared world which each individual must make his own in order to play his part effectively. Now it is experience through which private perspectives open out onto public objects. Subjectivity is held in check with the question, "Do *you* see what *I* see?" Many philosophers, to be sure, have conceived of experience as ineluctably private and of an "external world" as problematic. But the solipsism to which such an epistemology is inevitably impelled is, for methodology at any rate, a reduction to an absurdity. Science itself is a social enterprise, in which data are shared, ideas exchanged, and experiments replicated. It is precisely the cumulation of empirical evidence which shapes a welter of diverse opinions into scientific knowledge common to many minds.

Semantic and Epistemic Empiricism

What has been stated so far is an *epistemic empiricism*: we cannot know without depending somewhere on experience. This is the position taken by epistemologists from Locke through Kant. In the last hundred years or so a further doctrine has merged: that not only knowledge but even meaning is dependent on experience. We may call this *semantic empiricism*. It is the view that to be meaningful at all a proposition must be capable of being brought into relation with experience as a test of its truth. Its meaning, indeed, can be construed only in terms of just such experiences as provide a test. That semantic empiricism entails the epistemic is clear, but not the converse. For semantic empiricism asserts that what cannot be known by experience cannot be said either, or more accurately, that there *is* nothing more to be said. Epistemic empiricism, as in Kant, may allow for truths which cannot be known because they transcend experience, but which may somehow be acknowledged by faith. But semantic empiricism does not deny these truths; rather, it denies meaning to the statements that allege them.

Three main variants of semantic empiricism have been influential on the contemporary scene: logical positivism, operationism, and pragmatism.

Logical Positivism

The logical positivist position is embodied in what has come to be called "the verifiability theory of meaning." As its proponents have often pointed out, it is better construed, not as a theory, but as a rule or methodological norm. Loosely, it prescribes that a statement is to be taken as meaningful only if it is capable of empirical verification, and its meaning *is* the mode of its verification. The problems encountered in the search of a strict and generally acceptable formulation have been traced by Hempel and others. A few problems may be noted here.

To start with, falsification rather than verification is also sufficient for meaningfullness. Of course, a proposition which is manifestly false is often colloquially dismissed as "nonsense." But such a proposition is only the negation of a truism (we should call it a "falsism"); and if a proposition is meaningful, so also is its negation. Popper, indeed, has urged that falsification is the basic process. The important scientific propositions have the form of universals, and a universal can be falsified by a single counterinstance, while no number of supporting instances correspondingly establishes it. Scientific laws may always be taken as denying the existence of something: the second law of thermodynamics states in effect that there are no perpetual-motion machines, and Michels' "iron law of oligarchy" states that there are no persistently democratic organizations. Experience is of particulars only. We might some time be in a position to say, "No, *here* is a black swan!" but never can we say, "Quite right, all swans *are* white!"

But in both cases the possibility of being mistaken still remains. The supposed counterinstance may only look like one. On the other hand, we may have very good reason indeed to believe that there really are none, if we have looked carefully where they would be found if there were any. ("Not known to be subversive" means one thing in a smear sheet and quite another in the report of an intensive security clearance.) Verification and falsification, in short, must be replaced by some process admitting of gradations. Carnap speaks here of "degree of confirmation," and Reichenbach of the "weight" which can be assigned to a proposition. A proposition is meaningful if experience can give it some weight or other, whether low or high.

But what does it mean to say that we "can" assign a weight to a proposition? It is a matter of whether it is possible to carry out a process of confirmation, and several kinds of possibility are involved. Reichenbach distinguishes three: "technical," "physical," and "logical" possibility. It is technically possible if as a matter of fact, given the circumstances and the state of technology, we are able to do it. It is physically possible if no laws of nature would be violated by the process of confirmation called for, and logically possible if the laws of logic at any rate would not be violated. (Note that the possibility applies to the process of confirmation, not to the fact alleged in the proposition being confirmed.) We can confirm statements about the behavior of Siamese twins by observing them. A confirmation that calls for joining the nervous systems of two distinct organisms is only physically and not technically possible. On the other hand, a wholly disembodied mind is not even a physical possibility, though (we may suppose) it involves no logical contradictions.

Each of these kinds of possibility determines a corresponding domain of meaning. Science needs all three. We must be able to entertain a hypothesis before we have a way of checking it, even before we know whether the laws of nature would permit a way, for it is sometimes by such inquiry that we determine what the laws of nature are (the theory of relativity is usually cited in this connection). Our conception of what is possible, even of what is logically possible, grows with the growth of knowledge. As a result, the situation is not that we first establish what propositions are meaningful, then determine which of them are true. Truth and meaning move forward hand in hand.

Historically, the verifiability theory of meaning was employed primarily as a "criterion of demarcation," to use Popper's phrase. Its significance lay in the distinction it proposed to draw between scientific and unscientific statements, not on the basis that the latter were false, but on the basis that they said nothing at all. In the main, however, attention was focused on philosophical issues, and only derivatively on the scientific ones. The criterion was a needle with which to prick metaphysical pretensions in science, or, in a more robust metaphor, a cathartic for purging science of metaphysical wastes like vitalism and holism in biology or like dualism and epiphenomenalism in psychology.

The scientist himself, however, cannot do much with a criterion for demarcating the scientific from the unscientific. For him the problem is not so much to set aside metaphysical nonsense as it is to identify and clarify scientific meaning. How are we to understand and use concepts like "unconscious motivation," "social structure," and "the utility of money"? These are not characteristically metaphysical notions, but what meaning have they?

The verifiability theory of meaning in fact has two parts, of which only the first is a criterion of demarcation, defining the class of meaningful propositions, while the second proposes a procedure for specifying *what* the meaning is.

Consider Reichenbach's formulation of this second one. Roughly, two propositions have the same meaning if they are given the same weight by all observations, and the meaning they have is nothing other than the class of all the propositions which have the same meaning they do. The appearance of circularity in this definition is only an appearance; it is formally unobjectionable, and is known as "definition by abstraction." Compare the following sort of definition of mass: Two objects have the same mass if they balance one another (on a suitably constructed scale); their mass is specified by the set of all equally massive objects, for to assign to something a mass of, say, one thousand grams, is to say that it balances *this* object (the standard kilogram) and any other object like it in mass.

Some difficulties remain, however. Whether two propositions *are* equi-significant (apart from trivial verbal equivalences) is not always easy to determine. How shall we find out just how much weight a particular observation gives to each of them, and not knowing how much, can we nevertheless know that it must be the same weight for both? In practice, the confirmation of any particular proposition is likely to involve the whole theory of which it is a part, so that connecting two concepts at work in different theories is a subtle and complex task. In any case, the relationship between the concept and the observations is seldom simple and direct, and even straightforwardly descriptive terms have a penumbra of vagueness.

Operationism

The form of semantic empiricism that has been most influential on behavioral science is operationism. A few decades ago the cry for "operational definitions," especially in psychology, rose almost to a clamour. It was felt that here at last was the way to give our concepts of human behavior a solid scientific basis. By now those early extravagant claims and hopes (for which, it must be said, Bridgman himself was not responsible) have been considerably moderated or even abandoned altogether, in a way that parallels the history of the verifiability theory of meaning.

The basic idea of operationism was attractively simple. The application of concepts to the materials of experience calls for the performance of physical operations on the objects of experience. Quantitative concepts like "length" and "mass" depend on appropriate measurements; and even qualitative concepts depend for their application on laboratory manipulations (like those of the chemist), or at least, on operations on the instruments of observation (as in astronomy) with which we make the appropriate discriminations. To each concept there corresponds a set of operations involved in its scientific use. To know these operations is to understand the concept as fully as science requires; without knowing them, we do not know what the scientific meaning of the concept is, nor even whether it has a scientific meaning. Thus operationism provides, not just a criterion of meaningfulness, but a way of discovering or declaring *what* meaning a particular concept has: we need only specify the operations that determine its application. Intelligence, in the famous dictum, is what is measured by intelligence tests.

Difficulties begin to arise almost at once. One common line of objection to operationism is, I think, misdirected, and may be set aside. It is expressed in the question why one set of operations is selected rather than another, why *that* particular concept is given an operational definition. If intelligence is defined only by the tests, how shall we explain why the tests were constructed in just that way, or even why they were constructed at all? The question is indeed an important one, but that operationism itself provides no answer is no shortcoming of operationism. For the same question can be directed to *any* principle of specifying meanings. The task of such a principle is only to show how concepts can be analyzed and understood. Why they are selected for service in the scientific enterprise is a matter, not of their meaning (provided only it be clear), but of their validity or truth. We need not suppose that intelligence tests are designed to measure something whose meaning is already known. The meaning is defined by certain operations, and the intelligence test constructed as it is, in the expectation that the decision to select *those* operations will be useful for the formulation of psychological laws and theories. Operationism displays no fault in not making clear the logical ground for such an expectation. Its task is only to make clear what the expectation is about.

Other difficulties, however, cannot be sidestepped. We speak of "the" operations for applying a particular concept; but specifically what constitutes the identity of an operation? There is a proverb that when two say the same, it is not the same; how is it when two do the same? What justifies the assumption that the operation I perform is the same as the one you carry out? The operationist principle is that different operations define different concepts. Without the assumption, therefore, no two scientists could ever understand any scientific idea in the same way, and mutual criticism or corroboration would become impossible. The difficulty arises even for a single scientist: each performance of the operations is different in some respects from any other. Unless these differences are dismissed as irrelevant, it is impossible to replicate even one's own experiments. As Gustav Bergmann has pointed out, an extreme operationist would presumably refuse "to 'generalize' from one instance of an experiment to the next if the apparatus had in the meantime been moved to another corner of the room. Yet there is no a priori rule to distinguish relevant from irrelevant variables." Constancy of meaning would depend on empirical constancies which cannot always be anticipated.

It will not do to reply, "We simply stipulate which variables are to be taken as irrelevant, and finding we have not made a wise choice does not imply that we have not clearly specified the meaning of the concept, but only that the concept is not as useful as we had hoped." The reason why this reply will not do is that science must allow for the possibility of the same concept being measured or applied on the basis of totally different operations, that is, operations differing precisely in the relevant variables. Present estimates of what is misleadingly called "the age of the universe" are of the order of six billion years or so; what makes this figure of scientific interest is that about a dozen different lines of inference from correspondingly different observational data lead to substantially the same magnitude. Operationally we should have to say that twelve different "ages" are in question. Even though in these terms it would remain of scientific interest that they all have approximately the same numerical value, the significance of this fact would be obscured. We should like to be able to say that it is because they all measure the same thing, and this statement is precisely what operationism must deny. But the objection is far from conclusive.

There is also a difficulty of quite another sort. Most scientific concepts, especially the theoretical ones, relate to experience only indirectly. Their empirical meaning depends on their relations to other concepts as fixed by their place in the theory, and it is only these others that have a sufficiently direct application to experience to allow for specifying operations. We do not measure how high is the morale of a group or how deep is the repression of a memory by the manipulation of physical objects in any way at all comparable to the manipulation involved in measuring the temperature of a gas or the hardness of a mineral (both of which are also "intensive" magnitudes like the first two). Operations are used, but the interpretation of their outcome depends on the meanings of an open set of other terms. The attempt has been made to meet this difficulty by speaking of "symbolic operations" as those involved in tracing the connections among theoretical terms, or between these and more directly observational ones. But criteria for the scientific usefulness or even admissibility of such operations are virtually impossible to formulate. Once "symbolic operations" are included, the operationist principle is so watered down that it no longer provides methodological nourishment. To find what a scientific concept means, examine how you apply it, or how you apply other concepts related to it. But what else has any one ever done? Indeed, what else *is* there to do?

Pragmatism

Both logical positivism and operationism ask essentially the same question about any statement whose meaning is in doubt: Is it possible to establish the truth of the statement, and if so, how do we go about doing it? The pragmatist version of semantic empiricism takes another tack. It asks instead, what difference would it make to us if the statement were true? The meaning of the statement lies in these implications, and, as William James put it, a difference which makes no difference is no difference. The test of meaningfulness, the criterion of demarcation, is simply whether we can make something of a statement, whether it could conceivably matter to us, in a word, whether it signifies. And a statement's meaning lies in the difference it makes. Classic epistemic empiricism was retrospective: it traced the origin of ideas in sensation, then analyzed meaning in terms of the experiences from which the idea emerged. The pragmatic approach is prospective; what counts is not origins but outcomes, not the connections with experience antecedently given but those which are yet to be instituted.

The positivist and operationist are quite right to insist that meaning is inseparable from the capacity for truth, even more, for truth which can be known. But knowledge is not a reflection of its object, not the contemplation of reality reflected in the mirror of the mind. Knowing is not one thing that we do among others, but a quality of any of our doings: its logical grammar is that of the adverb, not the verb. To say that we know is to say that we do rightly in the light of our purposes, and that our purposes are thereby fulfilled is not merely the sign of knowledge, but its very substance. Meaning is purpose abstracted and generalized so as to fit any occasion. Every meaningful statement, Peirce suggested, may be regarded as determining a correlation between desire and action. The statement that such-and-such is the case means that if we want a we are to do x, if we want b we are to do y, if we want c we are to do something else again, and so on. We understand a statement only in so far as we know clearly what we would do, if we believed it, in any conceivable circumstance. The meaning is nothing other than this plan of action.

In spite of the fact that this pragmatic approach is the oldest of the three versions of semantic empiricism I am considering (Peirce first formulated the pragmatic maxim in 1878), it is in some ways the most modern in spirit. It invites reformulation in the contemporary idiom of the theory of games, of rational decision making, and the like. A statement is meaningful if it can enter into the making of a decision, and its meaning is analyzable in terms of the difference it makes to the decision taken. To get at the meaning of a statement the logical positivist asks, "What would the world be like if it were true?" The operationist asks, "What would we have had to do to come to believe it?" For the pragmatist the question is, "What would we do if we *did* believe it?" To believe a proposition is not to lay hold of an abstract entity called "truth" with a correspondingly abstract "mind"; it is to make a choice among alternative sets of strategies of action.

Pragmatists have been persistently and widely misunderstood (they themselves may be partly responsible) by reason of the impossibly narrow sense given to the key word "action." There is a vulgar pragmatism in which "action" is opposed to "contemplation," "practice" to "theory," and "expediency" to "principle." It goes without saying (that is, I am afraid I must say it and apologize for doing so) that this vulgar doctrine is almost the direct antithesis of pragmatism, which aims precisely at dissolving all such dualities. The "action" that is relevant to the pragmatic analysis of meaning must be construed in the broadest possible sense, so as to comprise not only the deeds that make up the great world of affairs, but also those that constitute the scientific enterprise, whether it be as "practical" as performing an experiment or as "contemplative" as formulating a theory. The "usefulness" that pragmatism associates with truth is as much at home in the laboratory and study as in the shop and factory, if not more so. If we are to continue to speak with William James of the "cash value" of an idea, we must be careful to have in mind a universally negotiable currency, and especially one that circulates freely in the world of science itself.

There is another difficulty, however, that cannot so readily be dismissed as merely a misunderstanding. We are concerned, not with what difference believing a proposition would make in fact, but with the difference it *should* make, that is, the difference it would make if the believer were affected only by the logical content of the proposition. For first, our actions are often affected by differences in the mere form of a statement even if these do not correspond to differences in content. Bavelas has shown, for instance, that groups in identical communication nets perform differently if they are given geometrically different but topologically equivalent representations of the net. Second, we react to extralogical contents (so-called "connotations" and the like) even if these are not part of what is strictly meant: a map in which the oceans were pink and the continents blue would be disturbing. And third, meaning depends on the action that would be taken under any "conceivable" circumstance, but what a man can conceive depends as much on him as on the proposition he is entertaining. In short, pragmatism faces the problem of marking out the core of logical meaning within a psychological matrix.

Though the difficulty is a genuine one, I believe that it is unduly magnified by the reconstructed logic which draws too sharp a distinction between so-called "cognitive meaning" and "emotive meaning." Often what passes for "emotive" has a cognitive content, in the sense that it could enter into cognitions if the context were such as to make them appropriate. The same is true of "mere" differences of form. The difference in meaning between "A is larger than B" and "B is smaller than A" is a real one, and could very well be important: the first puts A at the focus of attention and the second B. Though identity is symmetrical, nevertheless, if I were Caesar I would be a Roman, whereas if Caesar were I, he would be an American. And as for "mere" connotations, William Empson and an increasing number of other students of poetic discourse are directing attention to the referential basis of the "emotive" quality of language. A girl with "raven tresses" does not just have long black hair, but some of the other attributes of a character in a romantic ballad or something worse. What appears to be a merely psychological effect of a statement may well be a part of its logical content when it is properly analyzed. Nevertheless I believe that the pragmatic approach encounters problems here just as do those of logical positivism and operationism.

The distinctive contribution to methodology of the pragmatic version of semantic empiricism lies, it seems to me, in this: If meanings are to be analyzed in terms of action, they must make reference sooner or later to the ordinary objects and situations which provide the locus for action. Some empiricists have held that all scientific propositions can be interpreted, "in the last analysis," as being "about" sensations—subscribing to the phenomenalism of the older positivists like Ernst Mach and Karl Pearson. Others take the physicalist position that every statement "ultimately" says something about electrons or the like, since this is all there is for the statement to be about. Now both the phenomenalist and the physicalist reconstructions may well be possible, though both have encountered enormous difficulties in detail. But for methodology, neither of them begins to compare in usefulness with the pragmatist reference to the sorts of discriminations on which everyday action depends. Eddington's famous pointer-readings are neither merely patches of black on white nor merely the eye and hand movements of a strict operationism; they are the results obtained by a properly trained observer from scientific instruments of determinate character and calibration. Otherwise put: Every scientific language, however technical, is learned and used by way of the common language of everyday life; it is that everyday language to which we inevitably turn for the clarification of scientific meanings.

For some decades English-speaking philosophers, especially under the influence of the British schools, have been emphasizing the basic role of "ordinary language." Though the label, I suppose, would be anathema to many, the position taken is in my opinion essentially that of pragmatism. What is insisted on is that language is an instrument, and that to use language is to perform an action. The analysis of meanings must therefore focus on the particular contexts in which the action is performed, and on the purposes which the action as a whole is meant [sic] to achieve. This prescription incorporates, I believe, the methodological import of semantic empiricism. What more that doctrine implies in one or another more exact formulation is primarily a matter of philosophic rather than scientific interest.

Toward Dialogue

What Kaplan calls "semantic empiricism" is a more precise name for the tendency of scientific philosophy to search for meaning before searching for truth. That is, our sentences must carry meaning before we place them against the evidence of experience to decide whether to believe them or not.

One of the continuing problems of the semantic empiricists indirectly alluded to on page 183, is whether the idea of meaning can be further analyzed into "cognitive meaning" and "emotive meaning." The problem centers about the latter term: is it possible for emotive statements to have meaning in the same sense that cognitive statements have meaning? When we utter the cognitive statement, "Evanston is a residential community," we understand the meaning of the statement even if we don't know whether it is true or not. But when we say, "Evanston is a loving community," we are in a different situation. We are not quite sure just what would count as evidence for the truth or falsity of this emotive statement. The meaning of the statement is hazy.

So, then, we must ask whether emotive statements—those expressing feeling, value or judgment—are really susceptible to being labeled either meaningful or meaningless. Do they perhaps belong in a different class altogether from meaningful-meaningless propositions? If so, what quality do they share analogous to the quality of meaningfulness which cognitive propositions share?

A. J. AYER

The Elimination of Metaphysics

The traditional disputes of philosophers are, for the most part, as unwarranted as they are unfruitful. The surest way to end them is to establish beyond question what should be the purpose and method of a philosophical enquiry. And this is by no means so difficult a task as the history of philosophy would lead one to suppose. For if there are any questions which science leaves it to philosophy to answer, a straightforward process of elimination must lead to their discovery.

We may begin by criticising the metaphysical thesis that philosophy affords us knowledge of a reality transcending the world of science and common sense. Later on, when we come to define metaphysics and account for its existence, we shall find that it is possible to be a metaphysician without believing in a transcendent reality; for we shall see that many metaphysical utterances are due to the commission of logical errors, rather than to a conscious desire on the part of their authors to go be-

From *Language, Truth and Logic*, 2nd ed., by A. J. Ayer (London: Victor Gollancz Ltd., 1949), pp. 33–45.

yond the limits of experience. But it is convenient for us to take the case of those who believe that it is possible to have knowledge of a transcendent reality as a starting-point for our discussion. The arguments which we use to refute them will subsequently be found to apply to the whole of metaphysics.

One way of attacking a metaphysician who claimed to have knowledge of a reality which transcended the phenomenal world would be to enquire from what premises his propositions were deduced. Must he not begin, as other men do, with the evidence of his senses? And if so, what valid process of reasoning can possibly lead him to the conception of a transcendent reality? Surely from empirical premises nothing whatsoever concerning the properties, or even the existence, of anything superempirical can legitimately be inferred. But this objection would be met by a denial on the part of the metaphysician that his assertions were ultimately based on the evidence of his senses. He would say that he was endowed with a faculty of intellectual intuition which enabled him to know facts that could not be known through sense-experience. And even if it could be shown that he was relying on empirical premises, and that his venture into a nonempirical world was therefore logically unjustified, it would not follow that the assertions which he made concerning this nonempirical world could not be true. For the fact that a conclusion does not follow from its putative premise is not sufficient to show that it is false. Consequently one cannot overthrow a system of transcendent metaphysics merely by criticising the way in which it comes into being. What is required is rather a criticism of the nature of the actual statements which comprise it. And this is the line of argument which we shall, in fact, pursue. For we shall maintain that no statement which refers to a "reality" transcending the limits of all possible sense-experience can possibly have any literal significance; from which it must follow that the labours of those who have striven to describe such a reality have all been devoted to the production of nonsense.

It may be suggested that this is a proposition which has already been proved by Kant. But although Kant also condemned transcendent metaphysics, he did so on different grounds. For he said that the human understanding was so constituted that it lost itself in contradictions when it ventured out beyond the limits of possible experience and attempted to deal with things in themselves. And thus he made the impossibility of a transcendent metaphysic not, as we do, a matter of logic, but a matter of fact. He asserted, not that our minds could not conceivably have had the power of penetrating beyond the phenomenal world, but merely that they were in fact devoid of it. And this leads the critic to ask how, if it is possible to know only what lies within the bounds of sense-experience, the author can be justified in asserting that real things do exist beyond, and how he can tell what are the boundaries beyond which the human understanding may not venture, unless he succeeds in passing them himself. As Wittgenstein says, "in order to draw a limit to thinking, we should have to think both sides of this limit,"[1] a truth to which Bradley gives a special twist in maintaining that the man who is ready to prove that metaphysics is impossible is a brother metaphysician with a rival theory of his own.[2]

Whatever force these objections may have against the Kantian doctrine, they have none whatsoever against the thesis that I am about to set forth. It cannot here be said that the author is himself overstepping the barrier he maintains to be impassable. For the fruitlessness of attempting to transcend the limits of possible sense-experience will be deduced, not from a psychological hypothesis concerning the actual constitution of the human mind, but from the rule which determines the literal significance of language. Our charge against the metaphysician is not that he attempts to employ the understanding in a field where it cannot profitably venture, but that he produces sentences which fail to conform to the conditions under which alone a sentence can be literally significant. Nor are we ourselves obliged to talk nonsense in order to show that all sentences of a certain type are necessarily devoid of literal significance. We need only formulate the criterion which enables us to test whether a sentence expresses a genuine proposition about a matter of fact, and then point out that the sentences under consideration fail to satisfy it. And this we shall now proceed to do. We shall first of all formulate the criterion in somewhat vague terms, and then give the explanations which are necessary to render it precise.

The criterion which we use to test the genuineness of apparent statements of fact is the criterion of verifiability. We say that a sentence is factually significant to any given person, if, and only if, he knows how to verify the proposition which it purports to express—that is, if he knows what observations would lead him, under certain conditions, to accept the proposition as being true, or reject it as being false. If, on the other hand, the putative proposition is of such a character that the assumption of its truth, or falsehood, is consistent with any assumption whatsoever concerning the nature of his future experience, then, as far as he is concerned, it is, if not a tautology, a mere pseudo-proposition. The sentence expressing it may be emotionally significant to him; but it is not literally significant. And with regard to questions the procedure is the same. We enquire in every case what observations would lead us to answer the question, one way or the other; and, if none can be discovered, we must conclude that the sentence under consideration does not, as far as we are concerned, express a genuine question, however strongly its grammatical appearance may suggest that it does.

As the adoption of this procedure is an essential factor in the argument of this book, it needs to be examined in detail.

In the first place, it is necessary to draw a distinction between practical verifiability, and verifiability in principle. Plainly we all understand,

---

1 *Tractatus Logico-Philosophicus*, Preface.
2 Bradley, *Appearance and Reality*, 2nd ed., p. 1.

in many cases believe, propositions which we have not in fact taken steps to verify. Many of these are propositions which we could verify if we took enough trouble. But there remain a number of significant propositions, concerning matters of fact, which we could not verify even if we chose; simply because we lack the practical means of placing ourselves in the situation where the relevant observations could be made. A simple and familiar example of such a proposition is the proposition that there are mountains on the farther side of the moon.[3] No rocket has yet been invented which would enable me to go and look at the farther side of the moon, so that I am unable to decide the matter by actual observation. But I do know what observations would decide it for me, if, as is theoretically conceivable, I were once in a position to make them. And therefore I say that the proposition is verifiable in principle, if not in practice, and is accordingly significant. On the other hand, such a metaphysical pseudo-proposition as "the Absolute enters into, but is itself incapable of, evolution and progress,"[4] is not even in principle verifiable. For one cannot conceive of an observation which would enable one to determine whether the Absolute did, or did not, enter into evolution and progress. Of course it is possible that the author of such a remark is using English words in a way in which they are not commonly used by English-speaking people, and that he does, in fact, intend to assert something which could be empirically verified. But until he makes us understand how the proposition that he wishes to express would be verified, he fails to communicate anything to us. And if he admits, as I think the author of the remark in question would have admitted, that his words were not intended to express either a tautology or a proposition which was capable, at least in principle, of being verified, then it follows that he has made an utterance which has no literal significance even for himself.

A further distinction which we must make is the distinction between the "strong" and the "weak" sense of the term "verifiable." A proposition is said to be verifiable, in the strong sense of the term, if, and only if, its truth could be conclusively established in experience. But it is verifiable, in the weak sense, if it is possible for experience to render it probable. In which sense are we using the term when we say that a putative proposition is genuine only if it is verifiable?

It seems to me that if we adopt conclusive verifiability as our criterion of significance, as some positivists have proposed,[5] our argument will prove too much. Consider, for example, the case of general propositions of law—such propositions, namely, as "arsenic is poisonous"; "all men are mortal"; "a body tends to expand when it is heated." It is of the

---

[3] This example has been used by Professor Schlick to illustrate the same point.

[4] A remark taken at random from *Appearance and Reality*, by F. H. Bradley.

[5] e.g. M. Schlick, "Positivismus und Realismus," *Erkenntnis*, Vol. I, 1930. F. Waismann, "Logische Analyse des Warscheinlichkeitsbegriffs," *Erkenntnis*, Vol. I, 1930.

very nature of these propositions that their truth cannot be established with certainty by any finite series of observations. But if it is recognised that such general propositions of law are designed to cover an infinite number of cases, then it must be admitted that they cannot, even in principle, be verified conclusively. And then, if we adopt conclusive verifiability as our criterion of significance, we are logically obliged to treat these general propositions of law in the same fashion as we treat the statements of the metaphysician.

In face of this difficulty, some positivists[6] have adopted the heroic course of saying that these general propositions are indeed pieces of non-sense, albeit an essentially important type of nonsense. But here the introduction of the term "important" is simply an attempt to hedge. It serves only to mark the authors' recognition that their view is somewhat too paradoxical, without in any way removing the paradox. Besides, the difficulty is not confined to the case of general propositions of law, though it is there revealed most plainly. It is hardly less obvious in the case of propositions about the remote past. For it must surely be admitted that, however strong the evidence in favour of historical statements may be, their truth can never become more than highly probable. And to maintain that they also constituted an important, or unimportant, type of nonsense would be unplausible, to say the very least. Indeed, it will be our contention that no proposition, other than a tautology, can possibly be anything more than a probable hypothesis. And if this is correct, the principle that a sentence can be factually significant only if it expresses what is conclusively verifiable is self-stultifying as a criterion of significance. For it leads to the conclusion that it is impossible to make a significant statement of fact at all.

Nor can we accept the suggestion that a sentence should be allowed to be factually significant if, and only if, it expresses something which is definitely confutable by experience.[7] Those who adopt this course assume that, although no finite series of observations is ever sufficient to establish the truth of a hypothesis beyond all possibility of doubt, there are crucial cases in which a single observation, or series of observations, can definitely confute it. But, as we shall show later on, this assumption is false. A hypothesis cannot be conclusively confuted any more than it can be conclusively verified. For when we take the occurrence of certain observations as proof that a given hypothesis is false, we presuppose the existence of certain conditions. And though, in any given case, it may be extremely improbable that this assumption is false, it is not logically impossible. We shall see that there need be no self-contradiction in holding that some of the relevant circumstances are other than we have taken them to be, and consequently that the hypothesis has not really broken down. And if it is not the case that any hypothesis can be

---

[6] e.g. M. Schlick, "Die Kausalität in der gegenwärtigen Physik," *Naturwissenschaft*, Vol. 19, 1931.

[7] This has been proposed by Karl Popper in his *Logik der Forschung*.

definitely confuted, we cannot hold that the genuineness of a proposition depends on the possibility of its definite confutation.

Accordingly, we fall back on the weaker sense of verification. We say that the question that must be asked about any putative statement of fact is not, Would any observations make its truth or falsehood logically certain? but simply, Would any observations be relevant to the determination of its truth or falsehood? And it is only if a negative answer is given to this second question that we conclude that the statement under consideration is nonsensical.

To make our position clearer, we may formulate it in another way. Let us call a proposition which records an actual or possible observation an experiential proposition. Then we may say that it is the mark of a genuine factual proposition, not that it should be equivalent to an experiential proposition, or any finite number of experiential propositions, but simply that some experiential propositions can be deduced from it in conjunction with certain other premises without being deducible from those other premises alone.*

This criterion seems liberal enough. In contrast to the principle of conclusive verifiability, it clearly does not deny significance to general propositions or to propositions about the past. Let us see what kinds of assertion it rules out.

A good example of the kind of utterance that is condemned by our criterion as being not even false but nonsensical would be the assertion that the world of sense-experience was altogether unreal. It must, of course, be admitted that our senses do sometimes deceive us. We may, as the result of having certain sensations, expect certain other sensations to be obtainable which are, in fact, not obtainable. But, in all such cases, it is further sense-experience that informs us of the mistakes that arise out of sense-experience. We say that the senses sometimes deceive us, just because the expectations to which our sense-experiences give rise do not always accord with what we subsequently experience. That is, we rely on our senses to substantiate or confute the judgements which are based on our sensations. And therefore the fact that our perceptual judgements are sometimes found to be erroneous has not the slightest tendency to show that the world of sense-experience is unreal. And, indeed, it is plain that no conceivable observation, or series of observations, could have any tendency to show that the world revealed to us by sense-experience was unreal. Consequently, anyone who condemns the sensible world as a world of mere appearance, as opposed to reality, is saying something which, according to our criterion of significance, is literally nonsensical.

An example of a controversy which the application of our criterion obliges us to condemn as fictitious is provided by those who dispute concerning the number of substances that there are in the world. For it

* Professor Ayer explains this passage more fully in the Introduction to the book from which this selection was taken. Ed.

is admitted both by monists, who maintain that reality is one substance, and by pluralists, who maintain that reality is many, that it is impossible to imagine any empirical situation which would be relevant to the solution of their dispute. But if we are told that no possible observation could give any probability either to the assertion that reality was one substance or to the assertion that it was many, then we must conclude that neither assertion is significant. We shall see later on that there are genuine logical and empirical questions involved in the dispute between monists and pluralists. But the metaphysical question concerning "substance" is ruled out by our criterion as spurious.

A similar treatment must be accorded to the controversy between realists and idealists, in its metaphysical aspect. A simple illustration, which I have made use of in a similar argument elsewhere,[8] will help to demonstrate this. Let us suppose that a picture is discovered and the suggestion made that it was painted by Goya. There is a definite procedure for dealing with such a question. The experts examine the picture to see in what way it resembles the accredited works of Goya, and to see if it bears any marks which are characteristic of a forgery; they look up contemporary records for evidence of the existence of such a picture, and so on. In the end, they may still disagree, but each one knows what empirical evidence would go to confirm or discredit his opinion. Suppose, now, that these men have studied philosophy, and some of them proceed to maintain that this picture is a set of ideas in the perceiver's mind, or in God's mind, others that it is objectively real. What possible experience could any of them have which would be relevant to the solution of this dispute one way or the other? In the ordinary sense of the term "real," in which it is opposed to "illusory," the reality of the picture is not in doubt. The disputants have satisfied themselves that the picture is real, in this sense, by obtaining a correlated series of sensations of sight and sensations of touch. Is there any similar process by which they could discover whether the picture was real, in the sense in which the term "real" is opposed to "ideal"? Clearly there is none. But, if that is so, the problem is fictitious according to our criterion. This does not mean that the realist-idealist controversy may be dismissed without further ado. For it can legitimately be regarded as a dispute concerning the analysis of existential propositions, and so as involving a logical problem which, as we shall see, can be definitively solved. What we have just shown is that the question at issue between idealists and realists becomes fictitious when, as is often the case, it is given a metaphysical interpretation.

There is no need for us to give further examples of the operation of our criterion of significance. For our object is merely to show that philosophy, as a genuine branch of knowledge, must be distinguished from metaphysics. We are not now concerned with the historical ques-

[8] Vide "Demonstration of the Impossibility of Metaphysics," *Mind*, 1934, p. 339.

tion how much of what has traditionally passed for philosophy is actually metaphysical. We shall, however, point out later on that the majority of the "great philosophers" of the past were not essentially metaphysicians, and thus reassure those who would otherwise be prevented from adopting our criterion by considerations of piety.

As to the validity of the verification principle, in the form in which we have stated it, a demonstration will be given in the course of this book. For it will be shown that all propositions which have factual content are empirical hypotheses; and that the function of an empirical hypothesis is to provide a rule for the anticipation of experience. And this means that every empirical hypothesis must be relevant to some actual, or possible, experience, so that a statement which is not relevant to any experience is not an empirical hypothesis, and accordingly has no factual content. But this is precisely what the principle of verifiability asserts.

It should be mentioned here that the fact that the utterances of the metaphysician are nonsensical does not follow simply from the fact that they are devoid of factual content. It follows from that fact, together with the fact that they are not *a priori* propositions. And in assuming that they are not *a priori* propositions, we are once again anticipating the conclusions of a later chapter in this book. For it will be shown there that *a priori* propositions, which have always been attractive to philosophers on account of their certainty, owe this certainty to the fact that they are tautologies. We may accordingly define a metaphysical sentence as a sentence which purports to express a genuine proposition, but does, in fact, express neither a tautology nor an empirical hypothesis. And as tautologies and empirical hypotheses form the entire class of significant propositions, we are justified in concluding that all metaphysical assertions are nonsensical. Our next task is to show how they come to be made.

The use of the term "substance," to which we have already referred, provides us with a good example of the way in which metaphysics mostly comes to be written. It happens to be the case that we cannot, in our language, refer to the sensible properties of a thing without introducing a word or phrase which appears to stand for the thing itself as opposed to anything which may be said about it. And, as a result of this, those who are infected by the primitive superstition that to every name a single real entity must correspond assume that it is necessary to distinguish logically between the thing itself and any, or all, of its sensible properties. And so they employ the term "substance" to refer to the thing itself. But from the fact that we happen to employ a single word to refer to a thing, and make that word the grammatical subject of the sentences in which we refer to the sensible appearances of the thing, it does not by any means follow that the thing itself is a "simple entity," or that it cannot be defined in terms of the totality of its appearances. It is true that in talking of "its" appearances we appear to distinguish the thing from the appearances, but that is simply an accident of linguistic usage. Logical analysis shows that what makes these "appearances" the "appearances of" the same thing is not their relationship to an entity other than themselves, but their relationship to one another. The metaphysician fails to see this because he is misled by a superficial grammatical feature of his language.

A simpler and clearer instance of the way in which a consideration of grammar leads to metaphysics is the case of the metaphysical concept of Being. The origin of our temptation to raise questions about Being, which no conceivable experience would enable us to answer, lies in the fact that, in our language, sentences which express existential propositions and sentences which express attributive propositions may be of the same grammatical form. For instance, the sentences "Martyrs exist" and "Martyrs suffer" both consist of a noun followed by an intransitive verb, and the fact that they have grammatically the same appearance leads one to assume that they are of the same logical type. It is seen that in the proposition "Martyrs suffer," the members of a certain species are credited with a certain attribute, and it is sometimes assumed that the same thing is true of such a proposition as "Martyrs exist." If this were actually the case, it would, indeed, be as legitimate to speculate about the Being of martyrs as it is to speculate about their suffering. But, as Kant pointed out,[9] existence is not an attribute. For, when we ascribe an attribute to a thing, we covertly assert that it exists: so that if existence were itself an attribute, it would follow that all positive existential propositions were tautologies, and all negative existential propositions self-contradictory; and this is not the case.[10] So that those who raise questions about Being which are based on the assumption that existence is an attribute are guilty of following grammar beyond the boundaries of sense.

A similar mistake has been made in connection with such propositions as "Unicorns are fictitious." Here again the fact that there is a superficial grammatical resemblance between the English sentences "Dogs are faithful" and "Unicorns are fictitious," and between the corresponding sentences in other languages, creates the assumption that they are of the same logical type. Dogs must exist in order to have the property of being faithful, and so it is held that unless unicorns in some way existed they could not have the property of being fictitious. But, as it is plainly self-contradictory to say that fictitious objects exist, the device is adopted of saying that they are real in some non-empirical sense —that they have a mode of real being which is different from the mode of being of existent things. But since there is no way of testing whether an object is real in this sense, as there is for testing whether it is real in

9 Vide *The Critique of Pure Reason*, "Transcendental Dialectic," Book II, Chapter iii, section 4.
10 This argument is well stated by John Wisdom, *Interpretation and Analysis*, pp. 62, 63.

the ordinary sense, the assertion that fictitious objects have a special non-empirical mode of real being is devoid of all literal significance. It comes to be made as a result of the assumption that being fictitious is an attribute. And this is a fallacy of the same order as the fallacy of supposing that existence is an attribute, and it can be exposed in the same way.

In general, the postulation of real non-existent entities results from the superstition, just now referred to, that, to every word or phrase that can be the grammatical subject of a sentence, there must somewhere be a real entity corresponding. For as there is no place in the empirical world for many of these "entities," a special non-empirical world is invoked to house them. To this error must be attributed, not only the utterances of a Heidegger, who bases his metaphysics on the assumption that "Nothing" is a name which is used to denote something peculiarly mysterious,[11] but also the prevalence of such problems as those concerning the reality of propositions and universals whose senselessness, though less obvious, is no less complete.

These few examples afford a sufficient indication of the way in which most metaphysical assertions come to be formulated. They show how easy it is to write sentences which are literally nonsensical without seeing that they are nonsensical. And thus we see that the view that a number of the traditional "problems of philosophy" are metaphysical, and consequently fictitious, does not involve any incredible assumptions about the psychology of philosophers.

Among those who recognise that if philosophy is to be accounted a genuine branch of knowledge it must be defined in such a way as to distinguish it from metaphysics, it is fashionable to speak of the metaphysician as a kind of misplaced poet. As his statements have no literal meaning, they are not subject to any criteria of truth or falsehood: but they may still serve to express, or arouse, emotion, and thus be subject to ethical or æsthetic standards. And it is suggested that they may have considerable value, as means of moral inspiration, or even as works of art. In this way, an attempt is made to compensate the metaphysician for his extrusion from philosophy.[12]

I am afraid that this compensation is hardly in accordance with his deserts. The view that the metaphysician is to be reckoned among the poets appears to rest on the assumption that both talk nonsense. But this assumption is false. In the vast majority of cases the sentences which are produced by poets do have literal meaning. The difference between the man who uses language scientifically and the man who uses it emotively is not that the one produces sentences which are incapable of arousing emotion, and the other sentences which have no sense, but

[11] Vide *Was ist Metaphysik*, by Heidegger: criticised by Rudolf Carnap in his "Überwindung der Metaphysik durch logische Analyse der Sprache," *Erkenntnis*, Vol. II, 1932.

[12] For a discussion of this point, see also C. A. Mace, "Representation and Expression," *Analysis*, Vol. I, No. 3; and "Metaphysics and Emotive Language," *Analysis*, Vol. II, Nos. 1 and 2.

that the one is primarily concerned with the expression of true propositions, the other with the creation of a work of art. Thus, if a work of science contains true and important propositions, its value as a work of science will hardly be diminished by the fact that they are inelegantly expressed. And similarly, a work of art is not necessarily the worse for the fact that all the propositions comprising it are literally false. But to say that many literary works are largely composed of falsehoods, is not to say that they are composed of pseudo-propositions. It is, in fact, very rare for a literary artist to produce sentences which have no literal meaning. And where this does occur, the sentences are carefully chosen for their rhythm and balance. If the author writes nonsense, it is because he considers it most suitable for bringing about the effects for which his writing is designed.

The metaphysician, on the other hand, does not intend to write nonsense. He lapses into it through being deceived by grammar, or through committing errors of reasoning, such as that which leads to the view that the sensible world is unreal. But it is not the mark of a poet simply to make mistakes of this sort. There are some, indeed, who would see in the fact that the metaphysician's utterances are senseless a reason against the view that they have æsthetic value. And, without going so far as this, we may safely say that it does not constitute a reason for it.

It is true, however, that although the greater part of metaphysics is merely the embodiment of humdrum errors, there remain a number of metaphysical passages which are the work of genuine mystical feeling; and they may more plausibly be held to have moral or æsthetic value. But, as far as we are concerned, the distinction between the kind of metaphysics that is produced by a philosopher who has been duped by grammar, and the kind that is produced by a mystic who is trying to express the inexpressible, is of no great importance: what is important to us is to realise that even the utterances of the metaphysician who is attempting to expound a vision are literally senseless; so that henceforth we may pursue our philosophical researches with as little regard for them as for the more inglorious kind of metaphysics which comes from a failure to understand the workings of our language.

Toward Dialogue

In the foregoing passages, A. J. Ayer—who is regarded by many people as "Mr. Analytic Philosophy" himself—offers perhaps the most economical and astringent brief ever written on behalf of the "criterion of verifiability." It is this criterion, carefully applied, which makes possible the dissociation of metaphysics, once and for all, from philosophy.

In a kind of self-canceling argument, however, we may investigate the status of the criterion itself if put to its own test. Is the criterion of verifiability *itself admissible to philosophy as being, as Ayer puts it, "factually significant"? Well, let's take a look.* On page 187 he puts the criterion as follows: "*. . . a sentence is factually significant to any given person, if, and only if, he knows how to verify the proposition which it purports to express—that is, if he knows what observations would lead him, under certain conditions, to accept the proposition as being true, or reject it as being false.*" Now what kind of proposition is this?

On the one hand, it appears to resemble a definition such as one might find in a dictionary. In this case, it would seem to be a tautology in which the predicate is simply an enlargement on the meanings contained in the subject. But if, as is likely, Ayer would object to this classification, we need to test other possibilities. Is the statement factually significant? That is, do we know what observations would lead us to accept the verifiability criterion as true? This line of thinking gets us nowhere, since no observations are really relevant to it.

We are left with the unsettling thought that the verifiability criterion is either nonsensical, as in the case of Bradley's quoted remark about "the Absolute," or that it is merely a personal opinion, in which Ayer is saying not much more than "I myself think that a sentence is factually significant if, and only if, . . ."

JOHN WILSON

Truth

We shall now try to answer some of the questions raised at the end of the last chapter, and see how our different statements stand in relation to truth. Let us first, however, as befits cautious students of language, investigate the notion of truth itself.

THE CONDITIONS OF TRUTH

Truth is always supposed to be something very important and useful: and it is plain enough how advantageous it is for us to know when things are true. We express much the same point when we talk of the importance of 'knowledge', and of men's desire for 'certainty'. Some people want truth and knowledge for its own sake: others, rightly believing that knowledge is power, want it for the advantages it brings.

From *Language and the Pursuit of Truth* by John Wilson (Cambridge: Cambridge University Press, 1958), pp. 75–105.

Yet it is doubtful whether many people are properly aware of the uses of the words 'truth', 'knowledge' and 'certainty', together with many other words which express the same meaning.

If these things are as important as we think then it is a matter of prior importance to know what they are, and how to get them. We know enough by now to dismiss the superficial view that they are 'things' which we can find by a sort of mental or spiritual search, rather as we might find a lost ball or a lost umbrella. We shall rather try to answer the question: What does it mean to say that something is 'true', or that one 'knows' or 'is certain of' something? What counts as being 'true', or 'knowing', or 'being certain of'?

Let us confine our attentions for the present to 'true'. In almost all uses of the word, it is applied to statements or beliefs. We say 'That's true', referring to a statement just made by someone else: or else we say 'It's true that . . .'. Sometimes, as when we say 'Christianity is true' or 'The theory of relativity is true', we are referring to a number of beliefs for which we use the shorthand words 'Christianity' and the phrase 'the theory of relativity'. Beliefs, if they are to be expressed at all, must be expressed in statements; and so we can safely say that truth is something which has to do with statements. The supreme importance of the study of language is at once obvious: for if 'being true' is a property of statements, we shall plainly need to know a great deal about the different types of statements, and about how we can tell when they have this property. We have already covered some of this ground in the last chapter.

If I am to be able to say correctly that a statement is true, I must necessarily be able to do three things first:

(i) Know what the statement means.

(ii) Know the right way to verify it.

(iii) Have good evidence for believing it.

Unless these three conditions are satisfied, it would be ridiculous to say that the statement is true. If I say 'It is true that the earth is round' but add either 'I don't know what that statement means', or 'I don't know how one could verify that statement', or 'I have no good evidence for that statement', any of these additions makes my original statement absurd. To say that something is true, therefore, implies all these three conditions.

The same analysis can be applied to the phrases 'I know that . . .' and 'I am certain that . . .', with the minor exception that it may just be possible that the third condition does not apply to 'I am certain that . . .'. I *can* say without too much absurdity 'I am certain that the earth is round, but I have no good evidence for thinking so', rather as one might say 'I am certain that Hyperion will win the Derby, but I have no good evidence for it'. But even this is rather curious. Apart from this exception, the conditions for truth are the same as those for knowledge and certainty: I shall not waste time by repeating the analysis.

I have stated the three conditions in order of logical importance. Obviously we must find the meaning and method of verification for a statement before we can collect evidence for its truth; otherwise, we should not know what we were collecting evidence *for*, or the way to set about collecting it. As students of language, we shall be almost wholly concerned with these first two conditions: that is why in the last chapter we spent so much time classifying statements and observing their verification-methods. For the actual collection of evidence is a different matter altogether: a matter of ordinary or scientific observation. Thus if we take the statement 'The earth is round', it is our business to see that everyone knows the meaning of it, and the right way to verify it: but it is the scientists' business actually to make the observations and find the concrete evidence.

None of these three conditions is more important than another, for they are all essential. But we can note as a matter of historical fact that when the first two are satisfied, satisfying the third is largely a matter of hard work and patient research. This can be exemplified by comparing our progress in discovering truth in various fields. It is commonly and rightly said that man's scientific knowledge has far outstripped his knowledge in the fields of morals, politics, and religion. This is because we are agreed about the meaning and verification of the sort of statements scientists make, and have been so agreed for a long time; for their meaning has been made clear by their use in scientific hypotheses. No logical problems arise in connection with most of them, though some are vague enough to warrant analysis. Consequently, we have been able to get down to the job of making actual observations which we know to be relevant to proving their truth. Because we know the right *method* of verification, we can collect evidence: for we know the sort of evidence we want.

As we may already have seen from the last chapter, this is not the case with morals, politics or religion. Statements concerned with these topics are usually value statements or metaphysical statements, whose verification is doubtful, together with a number of other types of statements thrown in to add to the confusion. Few people are clear about the meaning and method of verification of such statements: and not many people can even distinguish one type from another. Little wonder, then, that we have not reached much agreement about what is true in these matters: for we have not reached agreement on the first two conditions —what the statements mean, and what is to count as evidence for them. This, perhaps, is why so many people place more faith in science and scientists than they do in moralists, philosophers, politicians or men of religion. The scientists produce results. The others do not.

Let us now run through the list of different types of statements once more, and see how we stand:

1. Imperatives and attitude-statements.
2. Empirical statements.
3. Analytic statements.

4. Value statements.

5. Metaphysical statements.

We can notice at once that the first three of these present no problems as regards truth. (1) Imperatives and attitude-statements are not used to convey truth at all: they are simply not the kind of statements which we would ever wish to call 'true' or 'false'. (2) Empirical statements already satisfy the first two conditions for truth, since we know quite well what they mean, and how to verify them: namely, by means of our sense-experience. We are also agreed about what kinds of sense-experience are relevant to determining the truth of various empirical statements. Thus, certain experiences are relevant for determining or verifying whether it is raining, certain other experiences for verifying whether the earth is round, and so on. We need only to collect the evidence—itself to have the experiences—in order to prove them true or false. (3) Analytic statements also satisfy the first two conditions for truth, since we know what they mean and how they are used, and we also know their method of verification: namely, by deducing them if they are true, or showing them to be self-contradictory if they are false, in accordance with the rules of logic or language. We also know what sort of rules will be used in such deduction, though we may not know how the deduction can be made. Thus, for an analytic statement like '$32 + 99 = 131$', we know that we must use the rules governing the addition of integers; for 'A puppy is a young dog', the definitions of the words given in a reputable dictionary; for 'The sum of the three angles of a triangle is 180 degrees', to the axioms and definitions of Euclid, and the rules of logic by means of which the statement necessarily follows from those axioms and definitions.

But there are important problems connected with value statements and metaphysical statements; and in this chapter we shall try to make some progress towards clarifying their status in reference to the conditions of truth. It is worth observing how this difference between the first three types of statements in our list and the last two affects our discovery of truth and the progress of knowledge. We usually classify our knowledge under various headings, such as 'history', 'chemistry', 'psychology', 'mathematics' and 'languages'. The reason why these departments of knowledge flourish and produce useful results is partly because they use empirical and analytic statements, and hence the conditions of truth can be satisfied. 'History', 'languages' and the various branches of 'science' all spend their time stating or explaining empirical facts: facts about the past doings of people, facts about various languages, facts about the natural world. Pure mathematics is developed by means of a complex system of analytic statements, which enable us to make useful deductions from one set of facts to another.

But as we have already noticed, certain 'branches of knowledge' (or what is supposed to be knowledge) do not seem to flourish in the same way. There are some, of course, like psychology, which are still in their infancy: but this is because they have not yet quite succeeded in establishing their own status. Thus, we do in fact find in the writings of those who call themselves psychologists all kinds of statements: statements of fact, analytic statements, statements of value, and even metaphysical statements and imperatives. But it would be agreed by most reputable psychologists that the job of psychology is to produce laws which explain matters of fact. In other words, psychology is (or should be) a science, which will help us to know more about the minds of men and how they behave, and which should be able to make successful predictions like any other science. I think we all know, at least, what to expect of psychology. If it cannot yet flourish as it ought, it is not because of any logical difficulties of meaning or verification: more probably it is because psychologists have not yet collected enough evidence to be able to give us much information.

The 'branches of knowledge' which should worry us much more are those which deal in value and metaphysical statements. It is precisely in these fields that no progress seems to have been made. Great sages and philosophers, saints and mystics, heroes and moralists have appeared from time to time and tried to tell us the truth about what we ought to do, what God is like, what lies beyond the boundaries of the visible world, and so forth; but though each has many enthusiastic followers, mankind as a whole seems to be no nearer the truth. There has been no united advance on this front. Here, unlike other 'branches of knowledge', no statements are put forward which everyone thinks to be obviously true. The words generally used for those 'branches of knowledge' in which we notice this disturbing lack of progress are 'ethics' and 'metaphysics'. 'Ethics' is the word commonly used to refer to our ideas and discussions about value, and about moral value in particular. Questions about what actions are right, what sort of people and societies are good, and what we ought to do in our dealings with our fellow-men are all 'ethical' questions. 'Metaphysics' is usually employed to refer to our study of truths which are supposed to be supernatural, or in some way divorced from the immediately observable world of nature. Both words refer to 'branches of knowledge' or fields of study. For our purposes, however, we shall be concerned not with a mysterious 'branch of knowledge' called ethics, but with value statements: nor with another 'branch' called metaphysics, but with metaphysical statements. These two types of statements have already been sufficiently defined in the last chapter.

Everybody holds ethical and metaphysical views, and makes value and metaphysical statements. Nearly all our ideas on moral, political or religious questions are expressed in such statements: and these are the very ideas about which we feel the most strongly, and ought to want to learn the most. Unfortunately these are precisely the statements where the most difficulty about meaning and verification arises, as we have already noticed. Questions like 'Is there a God?', 'Ought we to obey the Ten Commandments?', 'Are the doctrines of Communism true?' and 'Is it right ever to fight wars?' are all questions in whose answers we are vitally interested. As we often put it: we want very much to 'get at the truth' of such matters.

I have said before (and shall say again and again, because most people do not seem to have grasped this essential point at all) that our difficulties with these statements arise because they do not satisfy the first two conditions of truth. Since this is so, our next task will be to investigate the nature of these two conditions more thoroughly—to look closely into the nature of meaning and verification, which have served us so well in the case of other statements.

THE BASIS OF MEANING AND VERIFICATION

It was pointed out that our use of signs in general, and language in particular, was based on the conventional agreement about how they should be used. We considered the example of a red stoplight, and saw how agreement about the use of a red light led to our ability to use it with a specific meaning, 'Stop!' We can now see that precisely the same applies to our established methods of verification: this is what we should expect, since verification and meaning are closely bound up with each other. We are agreed about how to verify empirical and analytic statements: the rapid advance of science and mathematics bears witness to this agreement. For the former uses empirical statements, and the latter analytic: and since there are no logical difficulties about verifying or understanding these statements, there are no barriers to progress. Our agreement about empirical statements is particularly well-marked: if it did not exist, we could not ever make true every-day remarks to each other like 'It's raining' or 'The fishmonger has fresh fish today'. Our successful communication depends on our common understanding of the meaning and verification of such remarks.

We must now observe that this agreement is of a special kind. It would be quite misleading to suggest that everyone who can communicate successfully had at some time met together, and decided what the meanings and verification-methods of words and statements were to be. In saying that there is an agreement, we do not mean that men have met together and consciously agreed to use words in a certain way. That would be untrue in point of fact. We mean only that everyone does in fact use words in accordance with a uniform and established set of rules. Of course, we do not often learn these rules consciously, in the case of our own language. We pick up our mother-tongue by imitation and practice. We have not had to face problems of meaning and verification by ourselves. The 'agreement' has grown up by trial and error, in a haphazard way which nevertheless works efficiently in respect of those statements where the agreement holds good.

There are a number of cases, however, where the agreement is genuine, in the sense that it has been consciously arrived at, not merely acquired unconsciously. This usually occurs in the sciences, where it has been found necessary to delimit certain concepts strictly, and to define the words which express them without ambiguity. In chemistry, for instance, there is a clear and unambiguous distinction between what is meant by a 'mixture' and what is meant by a 'compound'; in physics and mechanics the distinction between 'weight' and 'mass', and the meanings of words like 'force', 'work', 'wave' and 'frequency' are all clearly fixed. The student of these sciences has to learn to use their terminology accurately; and the clarity which results is partly the cause of the great advances which have been made by such sciences. Our agreement about this terminology has only been reached after a long process of trial and error; but we know that we ourselves could not grasp the meaning of scientific words by mere practice and imitation, as we pick up the meaning of non-technical words when we are children, simply by listening to our elders talk. We have to do it deliberately and consciously.

It follows, then, that if we are to reach agreement about meaning and verification for value and metaphysical statements, we shall have to reach it consciously: for after thousands of years of human history, during which practically everyone has made such statements, there is no indication that we are coming to such an agreement by practice, or trial and error. This offers the only hope of achieving truth in metaphysics and ethics, for without the agreement there can be no truth. There is no apparent reason why we should not succeed. Changes in our agreement about meaning and verification occur, and can continue to occur: we saw from the statement 'The earth is round', and the way in which its verification altered after Galileo's time, that such changes are possible. Another example is the phrase 'unconscious desires'. This would have been thought nonsense before the time of Freud: but the new data provided by modern psychologists from Freud onwards have enabled us to agree to give it a definite meaning.

These two examples give us the clue to discovering the basis for our agreement about meaning and verification. This basis is twofold. On the one hand, we agree because we have similar experiences. It seems that everyone except those who are colour-blind wishes to make distinctions between their experiences on seeing a poppy, a summer sky, snow, and ripe corn. Because of this similarity of experience, we can agree to use verbal signs for these occasions and many others which seem to be similar also; and in fact we have chosen the signs 'red', 'blue', 'white' and 'yellow'. Galileo's verification was accepted because it was possible for everyone to have the experiences which he had on looking through his telescope at the planets, and to make deductions from them. The meaning of 'unconscious desires' was agreed because the psychologists convinced us that certain observable facts of human behaviour required a new explanation: and the phrase was used to form part of that explanation. On the other hand, we agree because we find such agreement useful or advantageous. We distinguish our experiences primarily for reasons of utility. We find it useful to distinguish sugar from salt, pennies from counters, and chairs from gorsebushes. We have constructed our conventions of meaning and verification in order to give each other useful information. Galileo's verification was accepted for the same reason that any scientific theory is accepted: because it enables us to predict more accurately, and is more useful to us than the verification used previously. The phrase 'unconscious desires' is accepted because it is useful in explaining psychological illness and in curing it.

Advanced scientific concepts, indeed, are all accepted as meaningful and verifiable primarily because they are useful; and they are useful primarily because they enable us to predict. Prediction is one of the hall-marks of a science, and its usefulness is obvious enough. We depend continually on the reliability of scientific prediction. We are told that if we mix lemon juice with milk the milk will curdle, that if we connect one wire with another our electric lighting will be repaired, that if we use a block and tackle we shall be able to lift a weight much more easily, and so forth. Scientists can predict these things for us from their knowledge of the laws which govern the behaviour of natural phenomena. Most people do not know these laws, and may have little idea of how to verify them for themselves; but they accept that they are verifiable, because they work. It is true, of course, that scientific hypotheses are ultimately verifiable by sense-experience. If we took the trouble, we could have the same sense-experience as expert scientists have: for instance, we could look through telescopes, conduct chemical experiments and so on. But we trust scientific experts, not only because we know that we could have similar experiences to theirs if we wished, but also because their statements usually turn out to be reliable. They produce results. In science also, therefore, our agreement about meaning and verification arises partly from the similarity (or potential similarity) of our experiences, and partly from the obvious usefulness of such agreement.

This view is confirmed from many sources, not least from our observation of young children who are just beginning to talk. They learn first the words that are most useful to them—words like 'Mama' and 'Dadda': and it is evident that their experiences are similar to those of other children, for they are well able to understand each other's use of the signs. Sometimes, indeed, children will actually invent words to refer to their experiences. One boy of sixteen months' age invented the word 'go-go', which he used accurately and consistently to mean any object which he could carry, which had a handle, and which had a lid that would open and shut. He invented this word, because this was the type of object in which he was most interested at the time. Consequently the most *useful* word for him was 'go-go'. He knew what it meant, and how to verify what was a 'go-go' and what was not. Two other children shared a common language consisting of at least two words: 'ee-ee' which meant 'look, something unusual is happening' and 'aw-aw', which meant 'come on, let's swap toys'. Their experiences of unusual things happening, and swapping toys, were the same for both. Hence they agreed to use a common language, and a common standard of verification.

Our problem in dealing with value and metaphysical statements, then, is to see whether we do actually share experiences of a kind which would make it useful for us to agree upon an established meaning and verification for at least some of such statements. Here it is evident that we must begin to distinguish different *types* of experience. Empirical statements are verified, in the last analysis, by sense-experience. Analytic statements are verified by our experience and knowledge of the rules of logic. Can we find different types of experience which can be usefully employed to help us build up a framework of communication for value and metaphysical statements? Let us take them in turn.

VALUE STATEMENTS

In the last chapter, we discussed the verification of value statements, and observed that it depended ultimately on our criteria of value, which led us to commend things that had certain descriptive qualities. Thus when we commend a knife as 'good', we have at the back of our minds a set of criteria for judging what is to count as a 'good' or commendable knife—one that cuts well, does not break easily, and so on. We also observed that different people had different sets of criteria for making value statements; and that in some cases we could range sets of criteria in ascending order of importance, using a higher set to justify a lower set, and so on until we arrived at our ultimate criteria of value.

Let us be quite clear about the logical status of these ultimate criteria. Suppose *A*'s ultimate principles for judging whether a state of affairs is good or bad consist of seeing whether there is happiness, life and love: and suppose that *B*'s criteria are precisely the opposite, and consist of the existence of misery, death and hate. Neither *A* nor *B* supports any values or moral standards higher than these. In such a case, it looks as if neither can convince the other. For the question between them is 'Is this set of criteria better than that one?' This is a question of value, and its answer could only be a value statement. But this statement would be unverifiable: for it would require a higher set of criteria to verify it, and there cannot logically be a higher set of criteria than the ultimate set. Neither *A* nor *B* can offer any criteria to judge their ultimate criteria. They have run out of ammunition.

Our only hope, therefore, as we suggested in the last section, is that they may be able in some way to share the same set of criteria. There is no *logical* way of compelling either of them to abandon his set, and adopt the other's, as there is in the case of empirical statements. But there may be other ways. This is not too hard to imagine, if we remember that our adoption of an agreed meaning and verification even for empirical statements depends ultimately on our common experience and desires. We can logically compel someone to admit that what passes the verification-tests for being 'red' is actually red: but we cannot logically compel him to agree to accept the verification-tests themselves. He usually does accept them, because he has the same experiences and desires as other men. In other words, there may be psychological reasons why he should be a party to the agreement, even though there are no logical reasons.

Even though we obviously do not always share the same criteria or verification-tests for value statements, therefore, there is hope that we may be able to do so. This hope is augmented when we consider the numerous cases where we do share them. We are agreed about the goodness of things which are useful to us, such as knives, horses, motor-cars, houses and many other things. We are also—and this is perhaps more significant—agreed to a great extent about the goodness of works of art, music and literature. Thus, it is generally accepted, at least within European society, that Beethoven and Bach are good composers, that Shakespeare and Goethe are good writers, that Michelangelo and Velasquez are good painters. We share a common set of criteria in judging their value.

We agree about such criteria of value as these for two chief reasons —because we have had sufficient experience and knowledge of the objects concerned, and because we are not usually subject to violent prejudices or emotional bias for or against them. This is particularly obvious in the judgments we make about works of art and literature. In order to reach agreement about these works, we require time to appreciate them and to learn about them, and the ability to consider their merit without prejudice or bias. That is why we are better able to agree about great artists who lived in the distant past than about modern artists: for with the latter, we have had insufficient time to experience their works, and are more subject to prejudice. The same is also true of our agreement about useful objects like knives and motor-cars. By knowing how they work, and not being prejudiced about them, we are able to agree which are to be called good and which bad. To put it briefly, we know what we *want* them to be like.

Where we do not share criteria, it is because either we do not yet possess enough factual knowledge, or we are prejudiced. This is sufficiently obvious if we consider the actual cases of disagreement about values. They nearly all concern the goodness or badness of *men*, and the actions, motives and political institutions of men. Even here, we are usually agreed on at least some points. Thus, we agree that taking another's legal property is bad, because it does not require very much experience for us to see that we do not want this kind of action. Even an observer who had no interest in supporting any kind of morality or religion would find it inconvenient to commend such behaviour. But where we disagree, we usually find both lack of knowledge and prejudice. Criteria of what counts as good sexual behaviour, for example, vary greatly from society to society and age to age. This is because very little is known of the results of different kinds of sexual behaviour on the people and society concerned; and also because people are liable to react strongly to any behaviour which does not accord with their own set of criteria. Hence few people are in a position to consider what criteria are the best without prejudice. Again, the value of one sort of society as against another—democracy versus totalitarianism, for instance—is not agreed, because few people ever have the experience of living under both systems, and few people are without prejudice.

We disagree about the criteria for human values, because we do not know much about human beings, and because we do not admit our ignorance, preferring prejudice instead. The sciences which are supposed to give us the information we require are, of course, psychology, sociology (which amounts to mass psychology), anthropology, and history. Of these sciences, none have yet reached the stage of advanced development where they can give unerring and useful information, and the first three are still in their infancy. Even so, they have already done much to bring the agreement on questions of value which we seek closer to us: psychology in particular has persuaded many people to change their criteria of value. As for our prejudice, we need only observe the way in which most people, even today, feel hostile towards these very sciences, and the strong and sometimes violent disapproval which those who believe themselves to be 'moral' display to those who hold other criteria.

The importance of science and the methods of science in this respect can hardly be overemphasised, for only a scientific approach to our problems of value can help to solve them. By 'a scientific approach' I mean, in the first place, that absence of prejudice and open-mindedness which characterises the work of a good scientist: and secondly, the operation of the scientific method of observation, experiment and hypothesis. Perhaps an example will help to make this clear. Until quite recently in our history the rightness of capital punishment for murder was almost universally accepted. It was considered right and just that a man who had killed should himself be killed. This seemed so obvious that nobody took the trouble to find out whether the death penalty acted as an effective deterrent to murder. It would have been wiser to doubt the obviousness of this principle at least to the extent of discovering the sociological results of the death penalty. A good scientist, I think, would have suspended judgment on the matter until he had been able to collect evidence by observation and experiment. Today many people are in serious doubt about the wisdom of capital punishment, and are well aware of the importance of the sociological sciences, particularly perhaps of statistics, in giving them enough facts to form a considered and unprejudiced opinion. Such statistics as are available, for instance, do not by any means prove the contention that capital punishment is a uniquely effective deterrent; and this fact is plainly of great importance to anybody who wishes to judge the matter rightly.

The reason why the sociological sciences are still in their infancy is that most people, even today, find it abhorrent to adopt a scientific approach to problems which involve the behaviour—particularly the moral behaviour—of human beings. Thus in the not too distant past it was taken for granted that criminals should be treated harshly, that children should be brought up strictly and beaten whenever they did not know their Latin grammar, and that certain types of sexual behaviour were dangerous and wicked. These are all things about which people have strong views, and towards which they adopt emotionally-conditioned attitudes. To allow scientists to investigate such matters seems to them unnecessary, for their minds are already made up; indeed, such investigation would represent a threat to their prejudices. Yet questions like 'What sort of treatment best reforms criminals, and what sort most effectively deters potential evildoers?', or 'What effect does prolonged physical punishment have on the minds of children?', are plainly important questions, and can only be answered by careful and patient scientific research. On the other hand, although the sociological sciences may still be weak, we owe their very existence partly to the great successes achieved by their elder brothers. It is partly because we have learned to rely upon the established sciences that we are today prepared, to some extent at least, to accept the use and importance of scientific method in dealing with human problems.

The advance of the relevant sciences must, of course, be left to the scientists concerned; and I shall say something about overcoming prejudice in a later section. Here we must note only that if we can gain the one, and conquer the other, we have every hope that our criteria will gradually come to be uniformly accepted throughout mankind. More knowledge and experience, on the one hand, of the things and people to which we assign or deny value, and less prejudice, on the other, will bring the agreement which we seek. Of course this cannot be proved: we shall have to wait and see, and in the meantime we must admit to doubt and ignorance. But since in all other cases where knowledge and lack of prejudice have been at work we have reached such agreement, it is very likely that this process will continue (or can continue) so as to cover cases in which we now disagree.

If that happens, we shall all hold the same set of criteria for all values: and this is to say that we shall have agreed about the meaning and verification-method for all value statements. Then we shall be in a position to say what is true and what is not true in ethics with certainty: for our three conditions of truth (see p. 197) will be able to be fulfilled. It will, of course, still be open to us to change our verification-method if we choose to do so: but that is not to the point. We can, and do, change our verification-method for empirical statements also. Provided that we all change together, we can still say what is true: for all that is necessary for discovering truth is that we should all be agreed about what method is appropriate.

METAPHYSICAL STATEMENTS

In the last chapter we defined metaphysical statements as statements whose meaning and verification were not agreed. Our business here is to see if there is any method by which we might come to agree.

We must admit at once that many metaphysical statements, as we have already seen in the section quoted, must be classified as attitude-statements. In the former case the question of truth does not arise, for attitude-statements are not intended to convey truth; and in the latter, we can deal with them as we have already dealt with other value statements in the last section. What we are interested in is the type of metaphysical statement which we may be able to treat as conveying special information of its own: a type, therefore, analogous to empirical statements.

In considering value statements, we saw that lack of experience and the existence of prejudice had so far prevented us from reaching agreement about meaning and verification: and [later] we saw that the basis for reaching such agreement in general depended on similarity of experience, and the usefulness of expressing it by means of established frameworks of verification. These considerations apply equally to metaphysical statements. Just as our sense-impressions allowed us to build up a framework of verification for empirical statements, and our common experiences and desires enabled us to agree about our verification of value statements, so it may be possible to discover or notice experiences of a special kind which we might use as a basis for the verification of metaphysical statements.

There seems to be no doubt that these special experiences do exist. There is certainly no logical reason to deny their possibility. We have already established the existence of different kinds of experience. When we use our senses, we have one sort of experience: when we consider whether we want to commend this action or that, we have another sort: when we consider whether a work of art is good or not, we have yet another sort: when we appreciate the nature of logical and mathematical rules, we have another sort again. For each of these types of experience, we have different frameworks of meaning and verification: hence the different types of statements described in the last chapter. Moreover, the facts seem to point to the existence of a special type of 'metaphysical' experience. That which is felt by religious people when they pray and worship, by mystics when they contemplate, or even by ordinary people when they feel 'in tune with' the world, seem all to be instances of a type of experience which exists in its own right, and cannot be assimilated to any other type.

It is not strictly necessary for the acceptance of a universal method of verification that all people should actually have these special experiences. Our experiences of art and music are very limited: we accept what critics and other experts tell us, because we believe that if we had time and inclination, we too should have the experiences they have. Similarly, we accept the findings of scientists, not through personal experience of their methods, but because we believe that we could make the same observations as they do, and would make the same deductions from them as they make. All that is necessary is that we should agree that these special experiences are available, that they are the same or similar for all or most people, and that we want to describe them in the same way. If we reach that agreement, we shall be able to agree about the use of verbal signs to describe them, and a common method of verification and meaning for statements about them.

What is needed, then, is an intensive investigation of these experiences. From that investigation it may emerge—I personally believe that it will—that there are at least some experiences which we may all have which we should want to describe by statements that are now classified as metaphysical. For example, if we all had experiences of what I shall loosely call 'love' and 'power' which could not be accounted for by observation of the natural world, we might wish to describe the source of these experiences by the word 'God'. 'God exists' would then have a definite meaning and method of verification, just as 'That table exists' has. By discovering these similar experiences, and agreeing to use certain signs to describe them, we should be able to build up a secure language of metaphysics. The statements of that language would not be metaphysical, in our sense of having doubtful meaning and verification. We might perhaps classify them all as 'empirical': or we might prefer to say that empirical statements were verified by sense-impressions and sense-experience, whereas these statements were verified by experience which was not given us by our senses. In the latter case we should have to find a new name for them, or else use 'metaphysical' in a different sense to the sense in which we have hitherto been using it.

Such investigation, however, has never been undertaken; and just as prejudice stands in the way of the social sciences, so it stands in the way of the investigation of religious or metaphysical experience on an objective basis. Most supporters of religion or any other type of metaphysical beliefs think that they already have the truth. In fact, of course, they cannot logically be in this position, since the three conditions of truth (see pp. 196–201) have not been satisfied. But this does not prevent them from retaining their prejudice. I have dealt with this prejudice more fully in the next section.

I do not wish to commit myself on the question of which statements amongst those now classified as metaphysical will survive this investigation, and which will be found to be useless for purposes of truth and falsehood. I venture to believe that some, at least, can be removed from the 'metaphysical' class, and reclassified: that some, in other words, can be made to give genuine and true information, because people will agree to accept a definite meaning and verification for them. Others, as I have said, will remain metaphysical (and hence useless), or be absorbed into other statement-classes. But we must not allow prejudice either for or against any religion or metaphysic to prevent us from realising the true position. It cannot now be said with certainty of *any* metaphysical statement that it is true or false: it cannot even be said that it is meaningful or verifiable. But there is at least hope for the future.

PREJUDICE

The study of words, statements and language from a logical viewpoint is not merely an amusing game. Its purpose is to enlarge and clarify our knowledge and to discover truth: and this book will have failed if it does not enable its readers to do this more effectively. I have preferred throughout to appeal to reason, and not to use the persuasive tricks of honeyed words, skilful oratory, or emotional appeal to convince the reader. The latter would be self-stultifying: for it is part of my thesis that we have often to combat them as dangerous enemies. I have grouped them together under the title of 'prejudice': and we shall now see that it is perhaps this factor, more than any other, which stands between us and the truth.

For something to be true, we must remember, we have to be agreed about its meaning and its verification, and must have good evidence for it. One would have thought the importance of the first two of these conditions for attaining truth would have been sufficiently obvious to anyone at all interested in morals, politics or religion. But if they are obvious, at least no attempt is made to satisfy them. Moralists and ordinary people, governments and governed, clergy and laymen seem entirely unconcerned and unaware of the difficulties in giving their statements a definite meaning and method of verification. This looks very much like wilful ignorance, and does incalculable harm. Apparently it is not sufficient for our laws and educational system, to say nothing of uncontrolled propaganda, to impress upon adults and children the necessity of believing a large number of metaphysical and value statements, under pain either of social or religious disapproval, or physical punishment. Men are prepared to take more drastic action than that to enforce their unverifiable beliefs.

I need only quote two examples to show the damage that can be done by pretension to knowledge and truth, when even meaning and verifiability are not known. The mediaeval inquisitors tortured heretics and burnt them at the stake; and the Nazis in Germany, before and during the Second World War, persecuted and killed Jews. The alleged justification for these acts depended on statements which were entirely unverifiable, and possibly meaningless. The inquisitors argued: 'By burning the bodies of these heretics, we shall save their souls: the soul is more important than the body: therefore we ought to burn their bodies'. The Nazis argued: 'Jews are not of Aryan blood: all those not of Aryan blood are inferior: we can do what we like with those who are inferior: therefore we can do what we like with Jews'. One should object to these arguments, not because the statements they contain are not true; for there might be genuine differences of opinion about that, and if they were true we could not object to the conclusions. We should object because they lack definite meaning and verification; and to torture and kill people on the basis of meaningless and unverifiable statements seems to border on insanity.

We have no time to investigate the causes for the widespread and occasionally fanatical opposition to discovering meaning and verification, for our business concerns the logic of statements, not the psychology of those who make and hear them. But a few observations may be useful. First, many people have a vested interest in preserving their metaphysical statements intact. The government of Russia, for example, has every reason to insist that all its citizens believe the doctrines which Communism enjoins; for if they do, they can be governed more easily. Most religions, also, fear that too much questioning—especially searching queries about meaning and verification—will prove their houses to have been built upon logical sand, and not on rock. Second, the social and moral behaviour of the majority of people is based on religious or other metaphysical premises, and whilst they may not feel strongly that the premises are true, they are afraid to question them lest the behaviour of others (particularly their children) should become immoral and antisocial. Thus, a parent may not himself believe in the divine origin and absolute authority of the Ten Commandments: but he may think it useful to try to get his children to believe in this, so that they shall not steal, lie, murder, and so on. Third, men's desire for knowledge is more apparent than real. Their basic desire is for security: and questioning necessarily involves the insecurity of doubt. For one has to doubt to some extent whether a statement is true in order to approach it with an open mind: if one is already certain, one would not approach it at all. Most people find it more snug and warm to keep their minds closed. When they argue and declare their beliefs, they do not do so with the scientific and rational desire for knowledge, but in order to persuade others and to increase their own sense of certainty and security. The difficulty of getting anyone who makes metaphysical statements to give them meaning and verification is sufficient evidence of this. Finally, statements whose meaning and verification are obscure usually express beliefs on matters which are very close to our hearts. They concern morals, politics, and religion: and all these are subjects about which most of us have strong views. We are only too liable to react emotionally to anyone who wishes to investigate them by the use of pure reason.

Many people are aware of their weakness in this respect, and try to cover it by supporting curious theories about truth and knowledge which attempt to evade the necessity for a rational investigation of meaning and verification altogether. Since these theories are supposedly logical, we ought perhaps to observe their more obvious weaknesses. They usually take the form of an attack upon reason: sometimes in the name of 'faith', sometimes in the name of 'intuition', sometimes in some other name. They also usually speak of 'truth' as if it were something which was not gained by thinking, but by some special faculty, usually of a mystic or magical nature: and they apply this view also to knowledge.

Our analysis of 'true' in the last part should suffice as an answer to all such theories. It is simply not sense to say that you know that something is true if you do not know what it means, or how to verify it. You may have as many and as exciting mystic or magical experiences as you like: you may be more saintly than the saints, more moral than the moralists, or more passionately concerned for political welfare than the politicians: but if you claim certain beliefs and statements to be true, then our three conditions of truth must be satisfied. Moreover, though this is really a side-issue, the process of reasoning is necessarily involved in satisfying them all. By 'reasoning' we mean simply the necessity of having 'reasons' or evidence for our beliefs. We may rely upon 'intuition', but we should not normally do so unless we had evidence that our intuitions were reliable: and the same argument applies to the acceptance of 'conscience', or any other human or divine authority, as a guide in life.

If we wish to deal in truth, knowledge and certainty at all, we cannot avoid the use of reason in the study of language. This does not abolish or diminish the importance of 'intuition', 'conscience', 'emotion', 'faith' or anything else. We need faith, but we need to have reasons for it. Thus we have faith in the engine-driver, because we have good evidence that he will bring us to our destination safely. If we wish to 'have faith in God', we must be able to produce reasons for it. We need emotion, but we need our reason to ensure that it is rightly used. We may place our trust in anything which we have reason to trust in. Of course, there are plenty of activities which are not concerned with truth or knowledge. If we are writing a poem, painting a picture, swimming, eating, sun-bathing and so forth, questions of truth or knowledge do not play a great part. But that lies outside our province.

Insofar as the activities of moralists, politicians, teachers, and men of religion are not concerned with the discovery and exposition of truth, but rather with exhortation, indoctrination, propaganda and poetic communication generally, it is not our business to quarrel with them. But insofar as they concern truth, we feel bound to make some suggestions which might help to overcome the present barriers to truth which we have just noted. We have seen that it is necessary to apply the study of language, and perhaps in particular of meaning and verification, to all doubtful statements which purport to be true. But we shall not be able to apply it effectively unless certain conditions are fulfilled.

1. We need freedom from governmental control. It is, and should be, the government's job to persuade its citizens to act in accordance with the principles of social and political behaviour which the majority think good, to encourage what it thinks to be virtue and prevent what it thinks to be vice, and in particular to prevent one individual or group from harming others. But if this entails, as it need not, compelling its citizens to support unverifiable statements which are supposed to be true, by its control of the law or the educational system, then the price is nearly always too great. We may get a law-abiding and uniformly stable society, but unless people are allowed to challenge these metaphysical statements it will be a stagnant society and probably a dissatisfied one. Fortunately the Western democracies have realised this

vital point, unlike the totalitarian states. We are at least free from the more obvious forms of governmental control. Yet much still remains to be done. It can hardly be said that the authorities as a whole encourage children and adults to question the moral, political and religious beliefs of their society. Admittedly, such questioning can be highly dangerous, if it is not undertaken rationally; and it may be justifiable under certain circumstances for governments to prevent it. But without a good deal of questioning, we shall not be able to discover truth: and without discovering truth, there can be no real progress.

2. We need freedom from the control of religious and public convention. The force of public opinion on religious and moral questions can often be more compelling, and can quash more attempts to discover truth, than the direct control of any government. Again, we are fortunate in this country, in that there is no single body of religious or moral opinion that is overwhelmingly strong, and which can make us conform to its beliefs almost by its mere existence. This was true of the Church in the Middle Ages, and is true of Communism in Russia today; and it has usually been true of most societies. We ought to appreciate our uniquely lucky position. Nevertheless, there are still many people in our society whose opinions are shaped, not by rational enquiry or teaching, but by what I can only call the emotional shock-tactics of their immediate environment. At home and in school children are expected to hold certain metaphysical beliefs; and if they try to question them, they meet with the emotional disapproval of their elders. Perhaps this is to some extent inevitable; and it would not be dangerous, were it not that very few of these children ever get the chance of raising their doubts at a later stage. They mostly remain slaves to their environment: and under such circumstances one can hardly expect them to apply the study of language to beliefs which they have been forced to hold from an early age.

3. We need freedom from the control of our own emotions and fears. The two types of control mentioned above derive chiefly from the fear of doubt within the individual. We must recognise our own unwillingness to let go our hold upon cherished beliefs, even if they have hitherto formed the basis of our life, and take whatever steps we can to ensure that we do not pretend to knowledge that we do not possess. Most of our fears in this respect are empty ones. It is perfectly possible to lead a good life without giving assent to meaningless and unverifiable statements: indeed, it is difficult to see how giving assent to these statements can really benefit us at all. To recite a form of words which we do not understand may improve our self-confidence, but it can hardly improve our virtue. By all means let us indulge in poetic communication and ritualistic verbalism when we so desire: there are doubtless excellent psychological reasons why such indulgence should be desirable. But let us at least not base our lives upon ignorance.

Since this is not a book for politicians, moralists or clergymen only, but for ordinary people, we can suggest one remedy which might help us to overcome these barriers, and eventually to fulfil the above three conditions. It consists simply of getting as much practice as possible in applying the study of language to our beliefs. We can do this in the class-room, when we are thinking about our beliefs by ourselves, when we argue with others, read books, hear sermons and lectures, listen to speeches, and on all the thousand-and-one occasions when the truth of statements is in question. This is not difficult or specialist activity, to be labelled 'intellectual', 'highbrow', 'philosophical', and to be frightened of. It does not require outstanding intelligence: it requires only patience and the desire to learn. The results come with surprising speed. Let us at least try it, and see what happens.

Toward Dialogue

On pages 204–207, Wilson is working his way through the argument that statements of value might conceivably be verified, just like empirical statements, if we could decide what would count as evidence for them, that is, what experiences are both relevant to the problem and usefully advantageous to us. As Wilson puts it, "our problem in dealing with value and metaphysical statements, then, is to see whether we do actually share experiences of a kind which would make it useful for us to agree upon an established meaning and verification for at least some of such statements." Whereupon (page 206) he cites the illustration of capital punishment, saying that if we would only take the trouble to gather sociological evidence on the effect of capital punishment on future criminals or on society as a whole, we could then possibly decide on its rightness or wrongness.

There are many individuals, however, who believe that the effects of a moral position, the consequences of acting upon a certain moral principle, have nothing to do with whether the principle is right or wrong. What if capital punishment does not deter criminals! It makes no difference; the murderer should be put to death. It is simply right that he pay the price for what he has done.

What Wilson's argument comes down to is the hope that men will stop thinking one way and start thinking another way about moral and metaphysical propositions. In this connection, it is interesting to note the manner in which he wishes to restore metaphysical statements to legitimate discourse, whereas Ayer (pages 185–195) ran them out of town. We may stop to wonder just what Ayer would think of Wilson's valiant attempt to find some place for metaphysical experiences which are, he intimates, available to everybody. One can hear Ayer asking, "Are propositions which are generated by these experiences really significant, or are they nonsense like all the others?"

Further Readings

Austin, J. L. *How To Do Things with Words*. Cambridge: Harvard University Press, 1962.

Brown, R. W. *Words and Things*. Glencoe, Ill.: The Free Press, 1958.

Chappell, V. C., ed. *Ordinary Language*. Englewood Cliffs, N.J.: Prentice-Hall, 1964.

Hayakawa, S. I. *Language in Thought and Action*. New York: Harcourt, Brace and World, 1964.

Pap, A. *Semantic and Necessary Truth*. New Haven: Yale University Press, 1958.

Ryle, G. *Dilemmas*. Cambridge: Cambridge University Press, 1954.

Waissman, F. *The Principles of Linguistic Philosophy*, ed. R. Harre. New York: St. Martin's Press, 1965.

Warnock, G. J. *English Philosophy Since 1900*. London: Oxford University Press, 1958.

Man is a talking animal. He is a lot of other things too: a tool-maker, a problem-solver, a culture-builder, a value creator. But none of these bedrock definitions of man would amount to much were it not for the magic of symbolic communication, the power to recompose experience into an abstract code of sounds and markings by means of which we can share in each other's thoughts and lives.

We now know that language has become our "secondary environment," an environment of words which merely stand for the "real" world of sunlight and feeling. Indeed, the anthropologists have told us that man weaves his words so intricately that reality is sometimes obscured and edited into a form merely convenient to his own grammar. In English sentences, for example, subjects outrank verbs; our talk is about subjects, not predicates. Hence, we tend to think the world is made up of things behaving, rather than processes in which entities participate. The English language edits reality into a thing-bias orientation.

Language, then, is not merely a communication device nor, as the technical philosophers put it, an instrument for the ordering of experience; it is the order of experience itself. It is the world in which we live, in which we are trapped. It is the environment which, like the natural environment in an earlier epoch, we must learn to subdue, control, and turn to human account. To continue the metaphor, language like nature has its own hazards, its own puzzles and indeterminacies, even its own disasters and catastrophes analogous to nature's "acts of God." But language is too close, too much a part of us to see clearly. Like water to a fish, it is not only our environment, but a primary dimension of our existence. Hence, special effort is required to remove ourselves sufficiently to get a good look at it.

The analytic philosophers, more than anyone else, have urged us to make this adjustment. The world is full of disagreement and conflict, but most of it, they claim, is unnecessary; it is generated out of faulty use of those simple little sounds we learned at home before we went to school, words. If we can clean up our words—tighten the meanings we are trying to get them to express—most of our problems will go away.

Accordingly, over the last decade or two, analytic philosophy in education has undertaken the task of examining educational concepts and how they are put in verbal form. Four representative sons of this movement now explain how they work. Israel Scheffler examines the common terms 'knowing' and 'teaching,' and demonstrates that each has a number of meanings which must be sorted out before clarification can be achieved. Thomas Green offers a "topology of the teaching concept," a

mapping of the various terrains generally included in that vast country-
side called "teaching." Finally, Paul Komisar and James McClellan dis-
mantle a set of educational slogans to see what, if anything, they mean.

ISRAEL SCHEFFLER

Knowledge and Teaching

COGNITIVE AND EDUCATIONAL TERMS RELATED

How are the cognitive terms *knowing* and *believing* related to the
educational terms *learning* and *teaching?* The question is not as simple
as it may seem, and our consideration of it in this section will introduce
several points of relevance throughout our discussions.

We might, as a result of attending to certain simple cases, suppose
learning that to imply *knowing that*. If a student, for example, has
learned that Boston is the capital of Massachusetts, we should normally
say he has come to *know that* Boston is the capital of Massachusetts.
Yet we cannot generalize from such cases that whenever a person X
has learned that *Q*, he has come to know that *Q*.

Consider a student in some distant age or culture in which disease
has been attributed to the action of evil spirits. Such a student may well
have learned from his tutors that disease is caused by evil spirits, but
we should not be willing to describe him as having come to know that
disease is caused by evil spirits. *He* may, to be sure, have been perfectly
willing to say "I *know* that evil spirits cause disease," but nonetheless *we*
will not wish to describe him as having come to know that evil spirits
cause disease, for we should then ourselves be admitting that evil spirits
do cause disease. For us to say that some person knows that such and
such is the case is, in general, for us to commit ourselves to the embedded
substantive assertion that such and such *is* the case. Where such a commitment is repugnant to us, we will accordingly avoid attributing knowledge, though we may still attribute belief. In the present case, we will
deny that the student in question has come to know that evil spirits
cause disease, but we may safely describe him as having come to believe
that evil spirits cause disease, for our belief attribution does *not* commit us to the substantive assertion in question. In our earlier example,
by contrast, since we were perfectly willing to agree that Boston is the
capital of Massachusetts, the stronger attribution of knowledge to the

---

From *Conditions of Knowledge* (Chicago: Scott, Foresman, 1965), pp. 7–21.

student did not commit us to an embedded substantive claim we found repugnant.

We are thus led to contrast *learning that* and *knowing that* in the following way: To say that someone has come to know that Q, commits us generally to the substantive assertion represented by "Q." For example, if we say of a pupil that he has come to know that Cornwallis surrendered at Yorktown, we are ourselves committed to the substantive assertion, "Cornwallis surrendered at Yorktown." To say that someone has learned that Q, does not so commit us; we are, in general, limited only to the claim that he has come to believe that Q.[1]

There are, to be sure, certain uses of *learning that* which do, in fact, commit us substantively in the manner we have been discussing. Consider the following statement, for example: "Reporters, after extensive investigation, learned that secret negotiations had been in progress for three weeks before the agreement was announced publicly." The force of "learned that" in this statement approximates that of "found out that" or "discovered that," which do commit us substantively. We may label such a use of "learn that," a *discovery use,* and contrast it with the *tutorial use,* in which the expression refers (without committing us substantively) to what people come to believe in consequence of schooling. The existence of the tutorial use suffices to show that a *learn that* attribution does not, in general, commit us to the embedded substantive assertion. And as we saw earlier, this is sufficient to *block* the generalization that what X has learned he has come to know, permitting only the weaker generalization that what X has learned he has come to believe.

The weaker generalization, in other words, unlike the stronger one, frees us from commitment to repugnant substantive claims in all those cases where we attribute *learning that* tutorially but reject the content learned. The student mentioned earlier may well be admitted to have learned, and to have believed, that evil spirits cause disease, but he cannot well be admitted to have come to know this. Suppose, now, that we consider all and only those cases where (i) X has learned that Q, and where (ii) we concur with the substantive assertion represented by "Q." Should we be willing in all these cases, at least, to say that X has indeed come to know (and not merely to believe) that Q?

This question raises a point of general importance regarding the attribution of knowledge: Some writers on the subject have recognized a weak and a strong sense of *know that.*[2] The answer to our question

---

[1] The letter Q occurs here, and in discussions to follow, sometimes framed by quotation marks, sometimes not. The letter *without* quotation marks stands in place of a sentence, fully displayed at the location of the occurrence in question. The letter *with* quotation marks, on the other hand, stands in place of a name of the sentence in question—typically, in place of the sentence-name which consists of the sentence itself framed by quotes.

[2] For example, Jaakko Hintikka, *Knowledge and Belief* (Ithaca, N.Y.: Cornell University Press, 1962), pp. 18–19.

will depend on which sense we have in mind. In the weak sense, *knowing that* depends solely on having true belief: in the strong sense, it requires something further—for example, the ability to back up the belief in a relevant manner, to bring evidence in its support, or to show that one is in a position to know what it affirms. If we take the weak sense of *know that*, we shall then answer our question in the affirmative. If X has learned that Q and has therefore come to believe that Q, and if, further, we are willing to concur with the claim made by "Q" (i.e., to affirm it as true), we must acknowledge that X has come to believe truly, hence to know (in the weak sense) that Q.

If we take the strong sense of *know that*, however, we must answer our question in the negative. For a person may believe correctly or truly that Q, and yet lack the ability to provide adequate backing for his belief or to show that he is in a position to know that Q. Though he has learned that Q and has come to believe truly that Q, he will then not *really* know, or know in the strong sense, that Q. He has, for example, learned in school that $E = mc^2$, but cannot, unless he can supply suitable supporting reasons, be said to know (in the strong sense) that $E = mc^2$.

We may summarize our discussion to this point as follows: If X has learned that Q, he has come to believe that Q. If we deny "Q," we will directly rule out that X has also come to know that Q, no matter how well X is able to support "Q." On the other hand, if we grant that "Q" is true, it is not directly ruled out that we shall say X has come to know that Q. We shall, indeed, say this immediately if we employ the weak sense of *know*, but only upon the satisfaction of further conditions if we employ the strong sense of *know*.

Often, perhaps typically, however, we do not make a direct test to determine whether these further conditions have indeed been satisfied; we operate rather on general presumptions that seem to us plausible. The presumption that the relevant conditions have been satisfied varies, for example, with the difficulty, technicality, or complexity of the subject. Thus, it seemed quite natural to us earlier to say that a student who has learned that Boston is the capital of Massachusetts has indeed come to know this. Nor does this seem to be simply a result of using the weak sense of *know*. The question "He has learned it, but does he really know it?" springs less easily to our lips in this case than in the case of "$E = mc^2$." For what sort of complex technical backing could possibly be needed here? Granted that the strong sense of *know* is operative, we are more likely to presume, on general grounds, that a student who has learned a "simple" fact can support it appropriately than we are likely to make the same presumption for a relatively "complex" or technical affirmation.

Another source of variation seems to be the method by which the belief has been acquired. To have merely been made aware or informed by somebody that Q leaves open the practical possibility that one does not really know (in the strong sense) that Q, even where "Q" is true.

To have found out for oneself that Q, lends greater credence to the presumption that one really has come to know that Q, for it suggests, though it does not strictly imply, that one has been in a good position to realize that Q, either relatively directly or on the basis of clues or reasons pointing to "Q."

This suggests why the discovery use of *learning that* seems to imply *knowing that* in the strong sense. Consider again our reporters, who learned (found out) after extensive investigation that the negotiations had been in progress for three weeks before the publicly announced agreement. The question "Granted they found out, but did they really know?" does not strike us as immediately relevant or natural. Those educators who stress so-called discovery and problem-solving methods in schooling may, in fact, be operating upon the general presumption that such methods lead to strong knowing as an outcome. And emphasis on *teaching*, with its distinctive connotations of rational explanation and critical dialogue, may have the same point: to develop a sort of learning in which the student will be capable of backing his beliefs by appropriate and sufficient means. To have learned that Q as a consequence of genuine teaching, given that "Q" is true, does seem to lend some weight to the presumption that one has come to know.

The notion of "teaching," unlike "learning," has, typically, *intentional* as well as *success* uses.[3] That is to say, teaching normally involves trying, whereas learning does not. To say of a child that he is learning to walk, that he is learning several new words every day, that he is learning how to conduct himself socially, that he is learning to express himself well in speech, does not in itself normally convey that he is *trying* to accomplish these things. It does not even convey that he is engaged or occupied in them, in the sense of thinking of what is going on, focusing his attention, and acting with care. Learning, it might thus be said, is not an *activity* but rather more nearly a *process*. We may surely distinguish the different stages of a process, and we may separate those situations in which the process has run its course to completion from those in which it has not. But such analyses do not presuppose either deliberateness or intention, although the latter *may*, in particular circumstances, be involved. We *can* try to learn this or that, but we often learn without trying at all; there is, moreover, no general presumption that any given case of learning is intentional.

Teaching appears quite different, by comparison. To say of someone that he is teaching conveys normally that he is engaged in an activity, rather than caught up in a process. It is to imply contextually that what he is doing is directed toward a goal and involves intention and care. He is, in short, trying, and what he is trying to bring about represents *success* in the activity, rather than simply the end-state of a process. We can, to be sure, speak of so-called "unintentional teaching," in which a

---

[3] On this point, see Israel Scheffler, *The Language of Education* (Springfield, Ill.: Charles C Thomas, 1960), pp. 42, 60–61.

person actually brings about a certain sort of learning, although without trying or even awareness on his part. But such reference will require that the word *teaching* be suitably qualified (e.g., by the word *unintentional*), or that supplementary explanation of the case be offered. Without such further information, a bare ascription of *teaching* contextually implies intention, whereas a success use of the verb (e.g., "Jones has taught his son how to swim") signifies intention brought to successful fruition.

What does teaching have as its goal? What does a person engaged in teaching intend or try to bring about? Obviously, an appropriate bit of learning. In the particular case of *teaching that* with which we have so far been concerned, a person X teaching Y that Q, is trying to bring about Y's learning that Q. As we have seen, this involves Y's coming to accept "Q" or to believe that Q. If X has been successful in teaching Y that Q, Y has indeed learned that Q, has come to believe that Q.

The converse, of course, does not hold: One may learn that Q without having been taught it by anyone. Furthermore, we must not suppose that teaching can be *reduced to* trying to achieve someone's coming to believe something. One may try to propagate a belief in numerous ways other than teaching—for example, through deception, insinuation, advertising, hypnosis, propaganda, indoctrination, threats, bribery, and force. Nor must we be quick to identify teaching with schooling generally, for formal agencies of schooling have employed and often do employ methods other than teaching—for example, indoctrination, suggestion, threats, and force. Thus, if we think of *learning that* as referring to the acquisition of belief just in the context of schooling, we still cannot take teaching as simply directed toward learning as its goal, although teaching does have learning as its goal.

What distinguishes teaching, as we remarked earlier, is its special connection with rational explanation and critical dialogue: with the enterprise of giving honest reasons and welcoming radical questions. The person engaged in teaching does not merely want to bring about belief, but to bring it about through the exercise of free rational judgment by the student. This is what distinguishes teaching from propaganda or debating, for example. In teaching, the teacher is revealing his reasons for the beliefs he wants to transmit and is thus, in effect, submitting his own judgment to the critical scrutiny and evaluation of the student; he is fully engaged in the dialogue by which he hopes to teach, and is thus risking his own beliefs, in lesser or greater degree, as he teaches.

Teaching, it might be said, involves trying to bring about learning under severe restrictions of *manner*—that is to say, within the limitations imposed by the framework of rational discussion. Since teaching that Q presupposes that the teacher takes "Q" to be true (or at least within the legitimate range of truth approximation allowable for purposes of pedagogical simplification and facilitation) and since the activity of teaching appeals to the free rational judgment of the student, we might say that the teacher is trying to bring about knowledge, in the strong sense earlier discussed. For the presumption is that a person who is encouraged to form his beliefs through free rational methods is likely to be in a position to provide proper backing for them. The teacher does not strive merely to get the student to learn that Q, but also to get him to learn it in such a way as to know it—i.e., to be able to support it properly.

We must, however, admit that there will generally be differences of opinion as to the success or failure of the whole teaching operation. Cross-cultural cases provide the clearest illustrations. Consider the teacher of a distant age who strove to teach that evil spirits cause disease. He was (we have said) *trying* to get his students really to know this. Now we may admit that he was successful in getting them to believe that evil spirits cause disease and even in supporting this belief in a way that may have been reasonable in their cultural environment. We cannot, however, admit his *success* in getting his students to *know* that evil spirits cause disease, for *we* hold this doctrine to be false.

Is there not a difficulty here from the point of view of appraisal of teaching? We want to distinguish successful from unsuccessful teaching in this ancient era, but our present analysis forces us to judge all of it (at least with respect to such false doctrines as we have been considering) to have been uniformly unsuccessful. To meet this problem, we may propose a secondary or "subjective" notion of success to supplement the primary or "objective" notion we have been using. According to this secondary or subjective notion of success, we assume that the truth of the doctrine taught is to be judged from the teacher's point of view; we also judge the question of proper backing in a way that makes allowances for the prevalent standards and available data in the culture in question. Then we judge success in the normal manner. We can now make the wanted cross-cultural distinctions between successful and unsuccessful teaching even where, from an objective point of view and judged from our standpoint, it has been unsuccessful.

Any teaching is geared to what the teacher takes to be true and his aim is not merely that his student learn what he takes to be true but that he be able to support it by criteria of proper backing taken to be authoritative. Insofar as the teacher is *teaching*, he is, in any event, risking his own particular truth judgments, for he is exposing them to the general critique of these criteria and to the free critical judgment of the student's mind.

One point of general importance should be especially noted. *Knowing* that attributions reflect the truth judgments and critical standards of the speaker; they commit him substantively to the beliefs he is assigning to others, and they hinge on the particular criteria of backing for beliefs, which he adopts. Thus, unlike attributions of *belief, learning that*, and *teaching that*, they reveal his own epistemological orientation to the items of belief in question; in this sense, they do more than merely describe the person to whom knowledge is being attributed.

We have, in sum, connected the educational ideas of learning and teaching with the cognitive ideas of knowledge and belief, as follows: Learning that Q involves coming to believe that Q. Under certain further conditions (truth of "Q" and, for the strong sense of *knowing*, proper backing of "Q"), it also involves coming to know that Q. Teaching that Q involves trying to bring about learning that (and belief that) Q, under characteristic restrictions of manner, and, furthermore, knowing that Q, as judged by the teacher from his own standpoint.

Now, there are certain classes of counterexamples that might be offered in opposition to these generalizations. A student might say, in reporting what he had learned on a certain day, "I learned that the gods dwelt in Olympus," or, if a student of philosophy, "I learned that the world of sense is an illusion." These reports might indeed be true, without the student's actually coming to *believe* that the gods dwelt on Olympus or that the world of sense is an illusion. Such reports are, however, plausibly interpreted as elliptical. What is really intended is, "I learned that it was believed (by the Greeks) that the gods dwelt on Olympus," or, "I learned that it was said (by such and such a philosopher) that the world of sense is an illusion."

Another sort of counterexample is provided by the case of X, who is teaching Y that metals expand when heated but who does not really care whether Y believes this or not. He is not trying to get Y to believe or to qualify (from his point of view) as knowing that metals expand when heated. He is only preparing Y to do what is necessary to pass the end-term examination. He may not even care about that; he may only be trying to get through the day. First, as to the latter case, it is quite possible for a *teacher* not to be engaged in *teaching* at a given time. To be called a teacher is, typically, to be described as having a certain institutional role in the process of schooling, rather than as engaging in teaching activity; we must avoid the assumption that whatever a teacher does on the job is properly describable as teaching. Secondly (as to the former case we might well differentiate teaching Y that metals expand when treated from teaching Y how to handle examination questions relating to this subject in order to facilitate passing. It is, in fact, possible to do one of these without doing the other; from the time of the Sophists (at least), it has been recognized that teaching might be geared not toward knowledge of propositions taken as true but rather toward the acquisition of skills in handling the outward manifestations of such knowledge. There are analogous cases, moreover, where the latter aim is quite respectable—for example, where teaching is geared toward the development of skills in handling and applying theories rather than toward acceptance of these theories as true.[4]

---

[4] The criticisms of Marcus Brown, "Knowing and learning." *Harvard Educational Review*, XXXI (Winter 1961), 10–11, and note 19, thus seem to me to be taken care of.

RANGES OF COGNITIVE AND EDUCATIONAL TERMS

Our discussion of the previous section dealt with certain general connections between the educational terms *learning* and *teaching* and the cognitive terms *knowing* and *believing*. Our discussion was restricted, however, to comparable uses of these terms—i.e., *learning that, teaching that, knowing that,* and *believing that.* We must now turn to the question of their several ranges of use, which differ in important ways. We shall then have a clearer idea of the landscape within which our previous considerations may be located. Further, we shall find reason to avoid identifying the range of *education* with the range of *knowledge.* Following our exploration of the larger territory, we shall turn to detailed analyses of the region where educational and cognitive ranges overlap.

We may begin by suggesting that *know* is a term of wider range than *believe.* We can speak not only of *knowing that* but also of *knowing how to;* we can speak only of *believing that.* We may say not only "X knows that Napoleon was defeated at Waterloo" but also "X believes that Napoleon was defeated at Waterloo." However, though we may say "X knows how to ride a bicycle," we *cannot* say "X believes how to ride a bicycle." This fact may be conveniently formulated by labeling the *that* use *propositional* and the *how to* use *procedural,* and saying that whereas there is a propositional use of both *know* and *believe,* there is a procedural use only of *know.*

It must immediately be acknowledged, to be sure, that we have the construction *believing in* but not *knowing in.* X may be said to believe in God, in God's benevolence, in the future of the U.N., in democracy, or in John Jones. However, it seems possible to suggest plausible interpretations of *believing in* as propositional, in context: To believe in God is, in many typical contexts, for example, to believe that there is a God; to believe in God's benevolence is to believe that God is benevolent; to believe in the future of the U.N. is to believe that the U.N. has a future; to believe in democracy is to believe that democracy is good or that it has a future; to believe in Jones is to believe that Jones will satisfy the trust placed in him or the hopes for his good performance or achievement. There is, it would appear, no single formula of reduction for *believing in* statements; yet, with the help of contextual clues, it does seem plausible to suppose that reduction can be carried through along the lines just suggested, singly or in combination.

Assuming such reduction, belief will be construable as solely propositional, while knowing will clearly be not only propositional but also procedural. Nor is an extra procedural use the only prima facie indication of a wider range for *know* as contrasted with *believe.* We can speak, first of all, of knowing why there are tides but not of believing why there are tides, of knowing who committed the murder, or how or when it was committed, but not of believing who did it nor of believing how or when it was done. We can, to take a second set of examples, speak of knowing chess, music, or Scrabble but not of believing chess, music, or Scrabble. The first set of cases involves implicit reference to *questions* of one or another sort ("Why are there tides?" "Who committed the murder?" etc.); we will tag these as *question* uses. The second set we will label as *subject* uses, since they refer to the "subjects" chess, music, etc.

It is true that for some subjects we can also apply *belief* notions. For example, we can speak not only of knowing the theory of evolution but of believing the theory of evolution. Nonetheless, we cannot apply *belief* notions analogously throughout the whole category of knowable subjects—e.g., to chess or music.

Moreover, even in cases of subjects where *belief* does apply, it is propositional where the corresponding knowing is *not*; it is, furthermore, not implied by (nor included in) the corresponding *knowing*, as is the case with propositional uses. That is to say, *knowing that* metals expand when heated implies *believing that* metals expand when heated, but knowing the theory of evolution does not imply believing the theory of evolution. To say that someone believes the theory of evolution is to say he accepts it or takes it as true. To say he knows it is, normally, to say not *more* than this but something *different*: it is to say rather that he is acquainted with this theory or that he can recognize, handle, and perhaps state it. To *believe* a theory is, in short, to believe *that* it is correct or true; to *know* a theory is *not* to know *that* it is correct or true. The relevant sense of *know* is different from that of the *propositional* use we have discussed.

Now it may, in fact, be suggested that subject and question uses of *know* are reducible to procedural ones: To *know a theory* is to *know how to* formulate and possibly work with it; to *know why* there are tides is to *know how to* answer correctly the question why there are tides. Alternatively one might propose to reduce question uses, at least, to propositional ones, taking "X knows who the murderer is" as "There is a true answer to the question 'Who is the murderer?' and X knows that this answer is true." These suggestions may be thought plausible or they may not, but we need not decide whether they are adequate, at least for our present purposes. It is sufficient if we recognize that belief may be interpreted as, in any event, propositional. On the other hand, knowing is not always propositional; it is not always, nor always reducible to, *knowing that*. Even if the above mentioned reductions were to be carried out, we should still be left with a procedural as well as a propositional use of *know*. Nor could it be plausibly proposed to reduce the procedural use itself to the propositional: To what *knowing that* expression would "knowing how to type" correspond?

The range of *knowing* may thus be said to be larger than that of *believing*. If we now turn to the terms *learning* and *teaching*, we find that they are applicable in all the cases so far discussed; they are not limited to simply propositional users. The student may learn or be taught that Napoleon was defeated at Waterloo. He may learn or be taught how to ride a bicycle or how to type. He may learn or be taught why there are tides. He may learn or be taught chess or the theory of evolution. Since, however, the notion of belief is not applicable in any but the first and the last of these cases (i.e., believing that Napoleon was defeated at Waterloo, believing the theory of evolution), it cannot be generally tied to learning and teaching as it was in the specifically propositional cases earlier discussed. Taking learning first, we cannot say, for example, that if X has learned how to type, he has come to believe how to type, as we *can* say that if he has learned that Napoleon was defeated at Waterloo, he has come to believe it. We cannot say that if X has learned why there are tides, he has come to believe why there are tides. Nor can we say he has come to believe chess if he has learned chess. Rather, we need to say that if he has learned how to type, he has come to know how to type; if he has learned why there are tides, he has come to know why there are tides; if he has learned chess, he has come to know chess. Moreover, even though it *is* possible to speak of believing the theory of evolution, as it is not possible to speak of believing chess, it is false to say that if X has learned the theory, he has come to believe it; we should rather say he has come to know the theory—which, as we have seen, is a different thing from coming to accept the theory as true.

Analogously, we cannot introduce belief into our general account of teaching as we did earlier. For example, we cannot say that, in teaching Y how to type, the teacher is trying to bring about Y's believing how to type. Rather, we need to say he is trying to get Y to know how to type. Similarly, he wants the student to know the theory of evolution, or chess, or why there are tides.

The main result to be noted is that, while the range of *knowing* is larger than that of *belief, learning* and *teaching* are at least as large in range as *knowing*. Education outstrips belief in its range, we might say, concerned as it also is with the development of skills, procedural techniques, subject familiarity—in short, with everything that might be characterized in terms of knowing. Nonetheless, we must not suppose that the range of education coincides with that of knowing. In fact, it goes beyond it; the concepts of learning and teaching are applicable in cases where *knowing* is not.

This point may be introduced by the consideration that *learning to* and *teaching to* have no counterparts such as *believing to* or *knowing to*. The child, for example, may *learn to* be punctual or be *taught to* be punctual, but he cannot then be said to *believe* or *know to* be punctual. His learning here is best thought of not in terms of knowledge but rather in terms of active propensities, tendencies, or habits of conduct. He has not necessarily nor simply come to believe something new, nor has he simply or necessarily achieved a new procedural facility or a new subject familiarity. He has, rather, acquired a new trait or pattern of action. His conduct now, though not before, is characterizable as generally displaying punctuality.

The *learning to* and *teaching to* expressions are, furthermore, not limited to the case of active propensities; they extend also to other cases, which are difficult to classify but which might perhaps be here labeled *attainments:* The child might, for instance, learn to *appreciate* music or to *understand* the relation between multiplication and addition, but he could not be said to *believe* or to *know to* appreciate or understand. So in respect of attainments as well as propensities our educational terms outstrip *knowing* in range.

But perhaps to understand something is reducible to knowing it, so learning to understand X is learning to know X. While, however, there may indeed be contexts in which knowing X conveys the connotation of understanding X, it does not seem plausible to make the proposed *general* reduction. A person may say without contradiction, "I know the doctrines of the existentialists, but I don't understand them." Or we may say of a child, "He knows Newton's laws (or Shakespeare's plays) but doesn't yet understand them." The limits of such knowing are perhaps elastic, involving at times familiarity, recognition, acquaintance, and ability to formulate, paraphrase, and use but not in every case including understanding. What constitutes understanding if it is not simply familiarity or skill of a certain sort is a separate question. Some have suggested that understanding involves something analogous to perception: seeing the point. Or it might be construed to include having explained or paraphrased the doctrine in question in special terms, initially intelligible to the person. Or, again, it might be thought to require a certain degree of experience or maturity (as in understanding Shakespeare's plays). However, we interpret it, it seems *not* to reduce to the subject use of *know.*

It might now be suggested that, although there are no *believing to* or *knowing to* locutions, a certain kind of *believing that* or *knowing that* accompanies *learning to.* The idea, in effect, may be to reduce the latter to *learning that:* The child who has learned *to* be punctual has come to believe or know *that he ought to* be punctual; the child who has learned to appreciate music has come to believe or know that he ought to appreciate music; having learned to understand multiplication, he has come to know that he ought to understand multiplication.

This suggestion does not, however, seem to be tenable. Certainly, the converses fail even though in some contexts we interpret, for example, the child's knowing that he ought to be punctual as implying that he is punctual. But even the inferences from *learning to* statements to the proposed *believing that* or *knowing that* statements break down. A boy may learn to bite his nails or to smoke without coming to believe or to know that he ought to bite his nails or to smoke. A person may come to appreciate a painting or to understand the concepts of atomic theory without holding that he ought to; indeed, the question may be raised whether it can meaningfully be said that one ought to appreciate or understand, as distinct from trying to appreciate or understand. Nor, in coming to appreciate a painting, does a person always come to believe that it is a *good* painting; and surely the converse here fails also. (Appreciation may, to be sure, involve liking, but liking is itself not reducible to a belief in the goodness of the object.)

Finally, it might be suggested that *learning to* is really *procedural*, a matter of acquiring more or less complex skills or techniques, describable in terms of *knowing how*. There are some examples in which this suggestion seems to find a plausible interpretation: To say that someone has learned to swim or to drive a car is indeed to say that he has come to know how to swim or to drive—he has acquired swimming or driving skills. These are, however, cases in which the *learning to* expression could well be supplanted by *learning how to*: To have learned to swim or to drive is to have learned how to swim or to drive. Not every case of *learning to* can, however, be thus rewritten in terms of *learning how to*, nor can it be interpreted as a matter of acquiring some relevant bit of know-how. To learn to be a good neighbor or citizen is not the same as learning how to be a good neighbor or citizen. To learn to pay one's debts is not the same as learning how to pay one's debts; it is not, for example, simply the sort of thing that is involved in learning the proper use of a checkbook.[5] Learning various techniques for ensuring one's punctuality is not yet learning to be punctual. To acquire a skill is one thing, to acquire a habit or propensity quite another.

The case seems even stronger with respect to what we have called *attainments*. For, whereas active propensities often have strictly associated techniques (e.g., a person who enjoys swimming and swims regularly knows how to swim), attainments do not have strictly associated techniques. A person who appreciates music is not properly said to know how to appreciate music; one who understands quantum theory is not well described as knowing how to understand quantum theory. (It would certainly seem strange if someone said that he knew very well *how* to appreciate music but didn't choose to, or that he knew *how* to understand quantum theory but hadn't in fact understood it lately.) Certainly there are techniques *embedded* in attainments: One who understands quantum theory knows how to read, and one who appreciates music knows how to listen. But these bits of know-how are not strictly associated; they are not equivalent to knowing how to *understand*, and knowing how to *appreciate*, respectively. Understanding and appreciation cannot, it would seem, readily be said to be exercises of technique or know-how, as swimming might be said to be an exercise of swimming know-how. For there seems to be no such thing as an *understanding know-how* or an *appreciating know-how*. Much less can learning to understand or to appreciate be suggested to reduce to mere acquisition of such know-how.

Skills, or procedures and elements of know-how, carry with them a cluster of associated notions that do not all apply *either* in the case of propensities *or* in the case of attainments. First of all, a skill or element of know-how, once acquired, may or may not be exercised, given the

[5] See Scheffler, *The Language of Education*, p. 98.

relevant opportunities; a person may be said to have a skill or the relevant know-how even though he never (or very rarely) exercises it after having acquired it, although he has ample opportunity to do so. There are many people who have learned and who know how to swim but who do not any longer swim at all, or only very rarely, though they have the chance. We may conjecture that their technique is rusty, but we do not feel compelled to deny that they *can* swim. By contrast, a person who has the habit or trait of punctuality is a person who *is* generally punctual on relevant occasions. If a person who had been punctual began to show up late for all, or nearly all, of his appointments and continued thus consistently for an appreciable length of time, we should wish to say he had lost the habit of punctuality. A person could not claim still to be punctual on the grounds that he had once been, though for a long time he had never, or hardly ever, arrived anywhere on time. In short, it is quite possible to say that X knows how to swim but never does; it would, however, strike us as self-contradictory to say that X has the habit of punctuality but never shows up on time. For attainments, the very notion of repeated performance is suspect: We may speak of one who knows how to swim as swimming every Tuesday, of a punctual student as showing up on time to class twenty times in a row. But what would it mean to say of a person who understands the quantum theory that he had understood it every Tuesday last month, or of a person who appreciates modern art that he had appreciated it twenty times in a row?

Secondly, in the case of skill or know-how a person may clearly decide not to exercise it. There is nothing puzzling in saying that a man knows how to play tennis but chooses not to. An analogous description is indeed possible also for habits, for a man may deliberately control his own propensities on particular occasions; a smoker may decide not to smoke now, for example. There seems, however, to be no such analogue for attainments: A person with an understanding of quantum theory cannot choose not to understand it; one who appreciates poetry cannot decide not to appreciate poetry on Mondays. Even for habits, moreover, the analogy is limited; where control goes far enough, it turns into elimination of the habit in question.

Thirdly, the notion of practice seems clearly relevant to skills and know-how; they are, indeed, typically built up through repeated trials or performances. Analogously, we may speak of habits, too, as being formed through repeated trials; through smoking again and again one may, for example, develop a genuine smoking habit. A parallel description seems, however, out of the question in the case of attainments. One cannot develop an understanding of the quantum theory by understanding it over and over again, nor can one strengthen or deepen one's understanding by repeated performances of understanding; the very notion of repeated performances is here suspect, as argued above. It makes sense to tell a student to practice playing a certain piece of music; it makes no sense to tell him to practice appreciating what he plays.

Finally, the notions of proficiency or mastery seem peculiarly applicable to skills. One may attain proficiency in driving or become a master in chess, but one cannot well be described as proficient in punctuality or honesty nor as having become a master of the habit of taking a walk before breakfast. Neither can one be said to be proficient in understanding a theory nor to have mastered the appreciation of Bach. A person may have more or less understanding of a topic, he may appreciate a poem less or more, but he cannot be called a good understander or appreciator as he might be called a good driver, typist, or chess-player. Similarly, a person's habit of smoking or of fingernail-biting may be weak or strong, deeply or less deeply ingrained, easy or difficult to break, but he cannot well be described as a good smoker or fingernail-biter.

The upshot is that neither propensities nor attainments can well be assimilated to the category of skills or know-how, nor can *learning to* and *teaching to* be construed as really procedural. It follows that the range of educational concepts is not only larger than that of belief, as we saw earlier; it is also larger than that of knowing. Education outstrips cognitive notions altogether in its range, embracing, as we have seen, also the formation of propensities and traits, and the development of understanding and appreciation.

ILLUSTRATIVE DEFINITION OF PROPOSITIONAL KNOWLEDGE

Having seen the wide range of educational notions, we now turn to a consideration of that part of the range which overlaps the range of *knowing*. The case of knowing that has figured most prominently in classical discussions in epistemology is the propositional case, and to this we address ourselves first. We shall find it convenient to introduce here a sample definition of *knowing that* as an anchor for our future discussions of the propositional case. This definition sets three conditions for *knowing that*, and we shall refer to these as the *belief* condition, the *evidence* condition, and the *truth* condition.[6]

$$X \text{ knows that } Q$$

if and only if

    (i) X believes that Q,

    (ii) X has adequate evidence that Q,

and   (iii) Q.

This definition takes all three stated conditions as jointly defining *knowing that* and thus corresponds to the "strong sense" of *know* discussed early in the first section of the present chapter. The "weak sense" is easily gotten by simply omitting condition (ii).

---

[6] Variants of this definition may be found in Roderick M. Chisholm. *Perceiving: A Philosophical Study* (Ithaca, N.Y.: Cornell University Press, 1957), p. 16, and in D. J. O'Connor, *An Introduction to the Philosophy of Education* (New York: Philosophical Library, 1957), p. 73.

Toward Dialogue

In summarizing his discussion of "knowing that" kind of knowledge, Scheffler offers a formula-set of conditions for knowing:
X knows that Q, if and only if:
(1) X believes that Q
(2) X has adequate evidence that Q
(3) Q
To give a concrete illustration, X knows that bats are blind if and only if:
(1) he believes that bats are blind
(2) he has adequate evidence that bats are blind
(3) bats are, in fact, blind
It would appear from this analysis that the first two conditions relate to the knower's psychological state and to what he has done—gathered evidence—to place him in that state. However, condition number three is an ontological condition. According to Scheffler, something must actually be the case in order for anybody to know it. Later in the same book, speaking of condition number three, he says, ". . . knowing requires not only the proper state of X's mind but the proper state of the world." Or again, ". . . knowing that does not, in general, have purely psychological reference, for it also makes independent reference to an appropriate state of the world."

But how does anyone know what is actually the case? Presumably, there was an original investigator who arrived at the discovery Q. But when he turned away from his inquiry and said, "I know that Q," are not the same three conditions applicable to him? And if so, what authority is there for saying that Q is the case?

Scheffler's argument is flawed either by an infinite regress or by a massive assumption that the world's Q's are somehow obtainable. Science makes no such promises. In fact, the bulk of scientific assertions contained in the world's books are wrong. Scientific knowledge, by its very character, is corrigible.

So, nobody knows for certain that Q.

THOMAS F. GREEN

A Topology of the Teaching Concept

THE TEACHING CONTINUUM

A concept is a rule. When someone learns a concept, without exception, what he has learned is a rule, a rule of language, or more generally, a rule of behavior. But some of the rules we observe in action and speaking are enormously complicated. Some are "open textured" in the sense that they do not specify with accuracy and precision what is permitted under the rule and what is not. These are the kinds of rules which are vague. They circumscribe the limits of vague concepts.

We can imagine what a vague concept is like by picturing a modern painting in which the different colors are blurred, one blending into another in degrees more imperceptible and gradual even than those which we discover in the spectrum. Such a painting, when viewed at a distance, clearly possesses a certain order among its several parts. There is a pattern of light and colors which constitutes the structure of the figures in the painting, but which when seen in close proximity, conceals the order of the painting.

How could we draw a clear and precise representation of what is found in such a painting? Here is a certain place where the colors change from red to orange and thence to yellow. Yet we cannot, with any certitude, point to a place and say at that point the color ceases to be red and becomes orange, or ceases to be orange and becomes yellow. Any attempt to specify precisely where the colors change, any attempt to eliminate the delicate blending of one color into another, would misrepresent the order or pattern of the painting. There are many points at which such a line can be drawn. They would all be equally right and all equally wrong.

A vague concept is like such a picture. It is a rule which is enormously complicated, and a part of its complication arises for no other reason than that it is not precise. It allows differences of opinion and differences of judgment at precisely those blurring points where people try to specify where one color begins and another leaves off. Nonetheless, the difficulty of making such differences precise does not mean that there is no order, or that we cannot find it. It means simply that we must not insist on too much precision in the order that we find.

We can, in fact, give a description of such a picture without sacrificing anything in the way of a faithful representation. For if we discover that there are two patches of paint which can be cut out and substituted

From *Studies in Philosophy and Education*, 3 (Winter, 1964–65), pp. 284–319.

one for another without in any way changing the picture, then we would be justified in saying that these two patches are related in a certain sense, namely, in the sense that they are exactly similar. And if we discovered that the color in the space intervening between them could be reproduced by imperceptibly and gradually blending the pigment in each of these patches with some second color in ever increasing proportions, then we would be justified in saying that we understand, in a different sense, *how* these two patches of color are related. We would have specified the rule which will suffice to relate the two patches of color. In this fashion we could develop a topology of such a canvas, showing by what rule each point on the canvas is related to every other point by the gradual blending of the pigments. Thus we could reveal the structure of the painting without converting it into a line drawing.

The concept of teaching is like such a blurred picture. It is a vague concept. Its boundaries are not clear. However accurately we may describe the activity of teaching there will, and always must, remain certain troublesome border-line cases. In admitting this, the point is not that we have failed to penetrate the darkness and to discover that juncture at which an activity ceases to be teaching and becomes something else. The point is rather that beneath the darkness there is simply no such precise discrimination to be found. There is therefore an initial presumption against the credibility of any analysis which yields precise criteria, which, without a trace of uncertainty assigns to every case a clear identity.

We can, nonetheless, describe the structure of the teaching concept, or if you wish, map its terrain, by standing at a distance and by asking not about teaching itself, but about such patches or parts of teaching as training, indoctrinating, conditioning, showing and instructing. We need not insist that the blur between these patches be removed. We need only show how they are related and how the gradual transition from one to the other may be reproduced. When we have done that, we will have drawn a map of the teaching concept; we will have described a rule or complex set of rules which formulate the structure of the concept.

At the outset, one must recognize then, that the concept of teaching is molecular. That is, as an activity, teaching can best be understood not as a single activity, but as a whole family of activities within which some members appear to be of more central significance than others. For example, there is an intimate relation between teaching and training which can be observed in many ways. There are, for example, contexts in which the word "teaching" may be substituted for "training" without any change of meaning. One reason for this is that teaching is often conceived to involve the formation of habit, and training is a method of shaping habit. Thus, when engaged in training, we may often say with equal propriety that we are engaged in teaching. The two concepts are closely related.

Nonetheless teaching and training are not identical. Training is only a part of teaching. There are contexts in which it would be a rank distortion to substitute the one concept for the other. For example, it is more common, and perhaps more accurate, to speak of training an animal than to speak of teaching him. I do not mean there is no such thing as teaching a dog. I mean only that it is more accurate in this context to speak of training. We can, indeed, teach a dog to fetch, to heel, to point, and to pursue. There is in fact a common saying that you cannot teach an old dog new tricks. The use of the word "teaching" in each of these cases has its explanation. It has to do with the fact that the actions of a trained dog are expressive of intelligence; they involve obedience to orders. Indeed, a well trained dog is one which has passed "obedience trials."

But the intelligence displayed in such cases is limited, and it is this which renders the education of an animal more akin to training than to teaching. What should we think of a trainer of dogs attempting to explain his orders to an animal, giving reasons for them, presenting evidence of a kind that would tend to justify them? The picture is absurd. Dogs do not ask "Why?" They do not ask for reasons for a certain rule or order. They do not require explanation or justification. It is this limitation of intelligence which we express by speaking of training rather than teaching in such circumstances. Moreover, those rare occasions in which animals most clearly display intelligence are precisely those in which they appear to ask "Why?" They are the occasions when they do precisely what they have been trained *not* to do, or when they do *not* do what they have been trained to do. The horse, trained to pull the carriage, saves his master's life in the darkness of the night by stopping at the edge of the washed out bridge and refusing to go on. The dog trained not to go into the street, is killed because he rushed into the path of a truck to push a child to safety. On such occasions, it is as though the animal had obeyed an order which was not given. It is as though he had given himself a reason for acting contrary to his training.

I am not concerned whether this, or something like it, is a correct explanation of such remarkable happenings. I am concerned only to observe that training resembles teaching insofar as it is aimed at actions which display intelligence. In this respect, training has a position of central importance in that congerie of activities we include in teaching. Ordinarily, however, the kind of intelligence aimed at in training is limited. What it excludes is the process of asking questions, weighing evidence and, in short, demanding and receiving a justification of rules, principles, or claims of fact. In proportion as training is aimed at a greater and greater display of intelligence, it more and more clearly resembles teaching, and one of the clues as to how closely training approaches teaching is the degree to which it involves explanations, reasons, argument, and weighing evidence. It is because training sometimes approaches this point, that we can in many cases substitute the word "teaching" for the word "training" without any change in meaning.

This point is strengthened when we consider what happens in proportion as training is aimed less and less at the display of intelligence.

In that case, the concept fades off imperceptibly into what we would commonly call conditioning. It is natural to speak of teaching a dog to fetch, to heel, to walk in time to music. It is more of a distortion to speak of teaching a dog to salivate at the sound of a bell. It is in precisely this latter context that we speak of conditioning. Conditioning does not aim at an intelligent performance of some act.[1] Insofar as training does not aim at the display of intelligence, it resembles conditioning more and teaching less. Thus, we can see that training is an activity which is conceptually of more central importance to the concept of teaching than is conditioning. We teach a dog to fetch; we condition him to salivate. And the difference is a difference in the degree of intelligence displayed.

Instruction also must be numbered among the family of activities related to teaching. Instructing, in fact, is so closely bound to teaching that the phrase "giving instruction" seems only another way of saying "teaching." There seems to be no case of an activity we could describe as "giving instruction" which we could not equally and more simply describe as teaching. Nonetheless, teaching and giving instruction are not the same thing. For there are almost endless instances of teaching which do not involve instruction. For example, it is acceptable, and even correct, to speak of *teaching* a dog to heel, to sit, or to fetch. It is, however, less acceptable, more imprecise, and perhaps even incorrect to speak of *instructing* a dog in sitting and fetching.

But why, in such contexts, is it more awkward to speak of instructing than to speak of teaching? We need not go far to discover the answer. When we train a dog, we give an order and then push and pull and give reward or punishment. We give the order to sit and then push on the hindquarters precisely because we cannot explain the order. We cannot elaborate its meaning. It is precisely this limitation of intelligence or communication which disposes us to speak of training a dog rather than instructing him. What we seek to express by the phrase "giving instruction" is precisely what we seek to omit by the word "training." Instruction seems, at heart, to involve a kind of conversation, the object of which is to give reasons, weigh evidence, justify, explain, conclude and so forth. It is true that whenever we are involved in giving instruction, it follows that we are engaged in teaching; but it is not true that whenever we are engaged in teaching, we are giving instruction.

This important difference between training and instructing may be viewed in another way. To the extent that instructing necessarily involves a kind of conversation, a giving of reasons, evidence, objections and so on, it is an activity of teaching allied more closely to the acquisition of knowledge and belief than to the promotion of habits and modes of behavior. Training, on the contrary, has to do more with forming modes of habit and behavior and less with acquiring knowledge and belief. Instructing, in short, is more closely related to the quest for understanding.

---

[1] There may be circumstances, however, in which it would be intelligent, i.e., wise, to "teach" with the aim of producing a conditioned response.

We can train people to do certain things without making any effort to bring them to an understanding of what they do. It is, however, logically impossible to instruct someone without at the same time attempting to bring him to some understanding. What this means, stated in its simplest and most ancient terms, is that instructing always involves matters of truth and falsity whereas training does not. This is another reason for observing that instructing has more to do with matters of belief and knowledge, and training more with acquiring habits or modes of behaving. It is not therefore a bit of archaic nonsense that teaching is essentially the pursuit of truth. It is, on the contrary, an enormously important insight. The pursuit of truth is central to the activity of teaching because giving instruction is central to it. That, indeed, is the purpose of the kind of conversation indigenous to the concept of giving instruction. If giving instruction involves giving reasons, evidence, argument, justification, then instruction is essentially related to the search for truth.

The point is not, therefore, that instructing necessarily requires communication. The point is rather that it requires a certain *kind* of communication, and that kind is the kind which includes giving reasons, evidence, argument, etc., in order to approach the truth. The importance of this fact can be seen if we consider what happens when the conversation of instruction is centered less and less upon this kind of communication. It takes no great powers of insight to see that in proportion as the conversation of instruction is less and less characterized by argument, reasons, objections, explanations, and so forth, in proportion as it is less and less directed toward an apprehension of truth, it more and more closely resembles what we call indoctrination. Indoctrination is frequently viewed as a method of instruction. Indeed, we sometimes use the word "instruction" to include what we quite openly confess is, in fact, indoctrination. Nonetheless, indoctrination is a substantially different thing from instruction, and what is central to this difference is precisely that it involves a different kind of conversation and therefore is differently related to matters of truth.

We can summarize the essential characteristics of these differences by saying that indoctrination is to conditioning as beliefs are to habits. That is to say, we may indoctrinate people to *believe* certain things, but we condition them always to *do* certain things. We do not indoctrinate persons to certain modes of behavior any more than we condition them to certain kinds of beliefs. But the important thing is to observe that *insofar as* conditioning does not aim at an expression of intelligent doing, neither does indoctrination aim at an expression of intelligent believing. Conditioning is an activity which can be used to establish certain modes of behavior quite apart from their desirability. It aims simply to establish them. If a response to certain stimuli is trained or conditioned, or has become a fixed habit, it will be displayed in the fact that the same stimuli will produce the same response even when the person admits it would be better if he responded otherwise. This is an unintelligent way of behaving. In an analogous way, indoctrination is aimed at an unintelligent way of holding beliefs. Indoctrination aims simply at establishing certain beliefs so that they will be held quite apart from their truth, their explanation, or their foundation in evidence. As a practical matter, indoctrinating involves certain conversation, but it does not involve the kind of conversation central to the activity of giving instruction. Thus, as the teaching conversation becomes less related to the pursuit of truth, it becomes less an activity of instruction and more a matter of indoctrination. We may represent these remarks schematically as shown in the figure below.

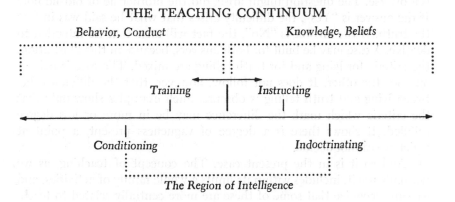

THE TEACHING CONTINUUM

The Region of Intelligence

The diagram is not meant to suggest that the distinction between conditioning, training, instructing and indoctrinating are perfectly clear and precise. On the contrary, each of these concepts, like the teaching concept itself, is vague. Each blends imperceptibly into its neighbor. It is as with the well-known case of baldness. We cannot say with precision and accuracy at precisely what point a man becomes bald. There is nonetheless a distinction, clear enough in its extremities, between a bald head and a hairy head. One might say that the difference is a matter of degree. But if the difference between conditioning and training or between instructing and indoctrinating is simply a difference of degree, then one must ask, "What is it that differs in degree?" The fact is that instructing and indoctrinating are different in kind, but the respects in which they differ may be exemplified in different degrees. Thus, we may be uncertain in many concrete cases whether the conversation of a teaching sequence more nearly resembles instructing or indoctrinating. But it does not follow from this that the difference between them is obscure, that we are uncertain about it or that they differ only in degree. It follows only that in such specific instances the criteria that mark the difference though perfectly clear in themselves, are neither clearly exemplified nor clearly absent.

A parallel example may suffice to make this clearer. To lie is to tell a falsehood with the intent to deceive. But now consider the following circumstances. Two brothers go to bed on the eve of one's birthday. He whose birthday is coming wishes to know what in the way of gifts the next day may hold in store for him; and so he questions, prods, cajoles, and teases his brother to tell him. But he receives only the unsatisfactory but truthful answer from his brother that he does not know. And so the teasing continues and sleep is made impossible. The only recourse for the weary one is to invent a lie. It must, however, be a lie that is believable. It must satisfy and yet must be most assuredly a lie. And so he says what is most improbable, "You will get a bicycle." But now suppose they discover on the morning after that indeed the principal gift is a bicycle. The question might arise, did the brother lie or did he not? If the answer is "Yes", the difficulty arises that what he said was in fact the truth. If the answer is "No", the fact will arise that he intended to deceive. A case may be built for both answers, because in this illustration, the criteria for lying and for truth telling are mixed. The case is neither one nor the other. It does not follow, however, that the difference between lying and truth telling is obscure. Such examples show only that the criteria which mark the difference may be in more or less degree fulfilled. It shows there is a degree of vagueness present, a point at which we cannot decide.

And so it is in the present case. The concept of teaching, as we normally use it, includes within its limits a whole family of activities, and we can recognize that some of these are more centrally related to teaching than others. We have no difficulty, for example, in agreeing that instructing and certain kinds of training are activities which belong to teaching. We may have more difficulty, and some persons more than others, in deciding whether conditioning and indoctrinating legitimately belong to teaching. There is, in short, a region on this continuum at which we may legitimately disagree, because there will be many contexts in which the criteria which tend to distinguish teaching and conditioning or teaching and indoctrination will not be clearly exemplified. Thus, there is an area of uncertainty on this continuum, an area of vagueness neither to be overcome nor ignored, but respected and preserved.

Nonetheless, were we to extend this continuum, we would discover another region of agreement. For we would surely stretch a point too far were we to extend the line on the left and include such activities as intimidation and physical threat, or on the right and include such things as exhorting, propagandizing and just plain lying. The continuum would look like [the figure on page 239].

We would have to strain and struggle to include within the teaching family such things as extortion, lying and deceit. The point is not that such things *cannot* be included among the assemblage of teaching activities. The point is rather that to do so would require an extension and distortion of the concept of teaching. It is clear in any case that such activities are less central to the concept of teaching than condi-

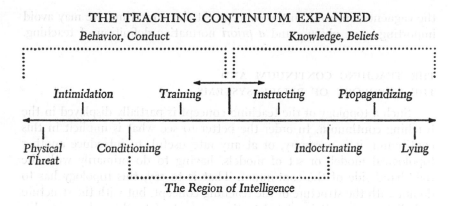

tioning and indoctrination, and that these are, in turn, less central than training and instruction. Thus as we extend the extremities of this continuum we depart from a region of relative uncertainty and enter a segment within which we can agree with relative ease. Lying, propagandizing, slander and threat of physical violence are not teaching activities, although they may be ways of influencing persons' beliefs or shaping their behavior. We know in fact, that these activities are excluded from the concept of teaching with as much certainty as we know that training and instructing are included. This shows approximately where the region of vagueness occurs in the concept of teaching. It occurs in respect to matters of behavior, somewhere between the activities of training and conditioning, and in respect to matters of knowledge and belief, it occurs somewhere between instructing and indoctrinating. The most central properties of the concept of teaching are revealed, in short, within the limits of what we have called the region of intelligence. Or, to put the matter in another way, we can say that teaching has to do primarily with the relation between thought and action.

It is a matter of no consequence that there have been societies which have extended the concept of teaching beyond this limit of vagueness and have thus included even the most remote extremities of this continuum. That propaganda, lies, threats, and intimidation have been used as methods of education is not doubted. But the conclusion warranted by this fact is not that teaching includes such activities, but that education may. Propaganda, lies, and threats are more or less effective means of influencing and shaping beliefs and patterns of behavior. It follows that teaching is not the only method of education. It does not follow that the use of propaganda, lies and threats are methods of teaching.

The concept of teaching is thus a molecular concept. It includes a congerie of activities. In order to more clearly understand the concept it may suffice to simply describe in schematic form what are the logical properties most central to this family of activities and to display in what respects other less central activities do or do not bear the marks of teaching. In this way we may gain in clarity without doing violence to the vagueness inherent in the concept. At the same time, we may avoid importing some obscure and *a priori* normative definition of teaching.

THE TEACHING CONTINUUM AND
THE TOPOLOGY OF BELIEF SYSTEMS

Such a topology of the teaching concept is partially displayed in the teaching continuum. In order the better to see what is implicit in this continuum, it is necessary, or at any rate useful, to introduce another topological model, or set of models, having to do primarily with the right-hand side of the continuum. That is to say, this topology has to do not with the structure of the teaching concept, but with the structure of belief systems. It is related to the concept of teaching, however, because teaching has less to do with *what* we believe and more to do with *how* we believe; and this contrast is best displayed in the structure of belief systems.[2]

This contrast between what beliefs we hold and how we hold them is not, however, altogether obvious. For it may seem, initially at least, that a person must either believe a thing or not, and that there can be no question as to *how* he believes it. A belief, after all, is either true or doubtful, precise or muddled, clear or confused. But these differences all have to do with the belief itself and not with the *way* it is believed. One might suppose there cannot be different ways of believing a thing as there are different ways of planting corn or skinning a cat. When a person believes something, he believes it to be true, and in addition to arriving at some decision on its truth, he does not need to decide also *how* to go about believing it.

There are, nonetheless, certain adjectives which appear in belief statements but which do not qualify the truth or falsity, clarity or precision of the belief. They have to do instead with the *way* we believe something. They delineate, as it were, a "style" of belief. We can, for example, believe something strongly or not, with passion or not, for good reasons or not. Two persons may hold the same belief with a different measure of strength, with more or less adequate reasons, or on more or less adequate evidence. They may, on the contrary, believe different things with equal strength, reasons, or evidence.

These adjectives of belief style fall roughly into two categories. In the first, there are those which have to do with the way beliefs are held in relation to each other. In the second class are those words which describe the way beliefs are held in relation to evidence or reasons. To understand these differences, we have to recognize that people seldom if ever hold to

[2] The following account of belief systems is suggested by but not derivable from nor identifiable with the views of Milton Rokeach. In many ways this account goes beyond what Rokeach has done, and goes beyond it in a way he would find unacceptable. See his *The Open and Closed Mind* (New York: Basic Books Incorporated, 1960).

a belief in isolation, in total independence of other beliefs. Each of us, in fact, possesses a whole system of beliefs, and we can understand that in this system there may occur different arrangements. Thus two persons may hold to similar beliefs and yet they may hold them in quite different arrangements. Thus the order of one's beliefs is a property of belief systems conceptually distinct from their content, and this can be described as a contrast between the beliefs we hold and how we hold them.

For example, in the order of anyone's beliefs there are quite often identifiable relations of a logical sort. That is to say, there are always certain beliefs which people may tend to reject because they understand them to be logically incompatible with others they accept. The point is not that such beliefs *are* logically inconsistent, but only that they are thought so. Similarly, we can identify some beliefs which a person may tend to accept because he finds them implied by others he accepts or consistent with others he accepts. Given any three beliefs in a system we shall say that if C is held to as implied by B, then B is primitive in respect to C. But if B in turn is held to as implied by A, then B, which is primitive in respect to C, is derivative in respect to A. When a belief has the status of a primitive belief and is not itself held to be derivative from any other belief, then we may say it is a primary primitive belief.

In short, the concept of primitive and derivative beliefs is a quasi-logical concept. That is to say, it has nothing to do with the actual objective logical relation between beliefs. But it does have to do with the logical order they receive in a belief system. A primitive belief is one which is not itself questioned. In this respect it resembles a postulate. It is itself appealed to in determining the acceptability of other beliefs. A belief which is seen to be implied by a primitive belief will *tend* to be more acceptable. One which is seen to contradict a primitive belief will *tend* to be rejected. A primitive belief then has the status of an arbiter, so to speak, in determining which beliefs can be received and which must be rejected. But the important point is that this adjudicative function is performed on the basis of a logical claim: It is the claim that what is implied by a truth must be true, what is contradicted by a truth must be false.[3]

But this relationship between primary and derivative beliefs is not

[3] See Leon Festinger, A *Theory of Cognitive Dissonance* (Evanston, Illinois: Row, Peterson and Company, 1957). His thesis roughly is that when one receives a message which is dissonant with an established belief held by a person, then one or more of three different things may happen, either the message will be rejected and some reasons developed to justify its rejection, or it will be modified so as to become "consonant" with the belief system and therefore suitable for internalization, or finally, the belief system itself may be modified so as to become "consonant" with the message. Festinger is not always clear concerning the meaning of the terms "consonant" and "dissonant," but they are reminiscent of the logical notions of "consistent" and "inconsistent," and are actually given "a more formal conceptual definition" in terms of negation and the phrase "follows from." Although his discussion lacks precision at the level of definition, there is no doubt that he is pointing to the fact that belief systems do have a logical structure of the kind I have tried to

a fixed or stable one, nor is it the objective order which logicians may establish between propositions. It has to do with the logical order which beliefs receive in a system. It has long been observed that men have the untidy disposition to hold in logical relation beliefs which are in fact wholly independent. The objective order of beliefs discoverable through logic, is based upon their content and structure. It has to do with *what* is believed. But the order we are concerned to describe has to do with the order beliefs may be given. It can be described only as having to do with *how* they are believed.

The second point to observe is really a facet of what has been said already. It is simply that belief systems are in many respects not logical systems at all. When, for example, the theory of evolution is found in some person to conflict with some logically primitive belief concerning the authority of scripture, it is true that one or the other belief will *tend* to be rejected or modified; but we must ask *which* it shall be, the belief in evolution or the belief in the authority of scripture. And this question has to do less with the logical structure of a belief system than with its psychological or spacial order. It is not uncommon for students in the course of study to discover that they must alter certain of their beliefs and cancel out others altogether. The facts of social life and the order of institutions may conflict with one's idealized conceptions of the world. Some cherished myths of our national heroes may become shattered in the pursuit of the truth about our history. If one is to live in the company of others, some cherished standards of judging them may have to be abandoned along with some treasured estimates of one's self. It is often with respect to some beliefs an easy thing to change and with respect to others wholly beyond the realm of possibility. A belief which one person may be quite prepared to doubt, another may be incapable of questioning.

Thus some beliefs are more important than others, and the measure of their importance, in this sense, is not whether they are logically primitive but whether they are psychologically central. Thus, we can visualize a belief system as having a spacial dimension, as having the structure of a set of concentric circles. Within the core circle will be those beliefs held with greatest psychological strength, those which we are most prone to accept without question, and, therefore, least able to debate openly and least able to change. As we move from circle to circle toward the perimeter there will be distributed those beliefs which we hold with progressively less strength and are more prepared to examine, discuss, and alter.

Psychologically central beliefs do not cluster together because they are logically primitive. It is quite conceivable, in fact, that beliefs could be logically derivative and yet psychologically central. Beliefs which are quite independent in the logical dimension of a belief system may nonetheless be related by the fact that they are "core" beliefs. Whether a belief is central or peripheral has, therefore, little to do with its content;

it has to do not so much with what a person believes, as with how he believes it. Thus, the same belief may be psychologically central to one person and peripheral to another. The spacial location of a belief is determined not by its logical properties, but by the manner of its psychological possession.

A belief system is not a logical system. It is not at all uncommon that men hold strongly to certain beliefs which if ever set side by side would clearly conflict. But until they be set side by side, and their inconsistency revealed, there need be no problem in believing both. Indeed, two beliefs equally central psychologically, may be logically incompatible. Thus one may hold certain central convictions concerning matters of economics—that competition among men is the only basis for social progress, that individual initiative is the supreme requirement for merit, that a man is entitled to keep what he can secure, that if a person does not "succeed," he has no one to blame but himself. Similarly, one may hold to a set of beliefs in matters of public morality— that only by cooperation among men can society be improved, that one must be charitable in assisting those who are less fortunate, that a good member of society is one who does not "take advantage" of his neighbors.

Such conflicting sets of beliefs may all be held as psychologically central. This is possible because we tend to order our beliefs in little clusters encrusted about, as it were, by a protective shield which prevents any cross-fertilization among them or any confrontation between them. Thus we may praise the value of competition as an article of economic faith and the necessity for cooperation as a fundamental demand of social ethics. In this way we can hold psychologically central, certain beliefs which are at many points logically incompatible. This is perfectly possible provided we never permit our cluster of economic beliefs to influence our ethical convictions or permit our ethical beliefs to influence our economic thought. We can do this effectively by protecting certain clusters of beliefs by a hard coating as the germ of a seed is protected from the corrosive influences of the winter. This impregnable shield appears disguised as a belief itself. "Ethics has nothing to do with business" or "Religion ought to stay out of politics." A student, for example, may possess a religious faith which militates against the demands of inquiry. He may nonetheless be a successful student provided he never permits his religious faith to influence his life as a student, and conversely never permits his life as a student to influence his understanding of his religion. Such a segregation of concerns can be accomplished by adopting certain beliefs. "Matters of faith are beyond the reach of reason to appraise." Or, again, it is not uncommon to find those who devote their lives to scientific study and yet hold to a religion which is fundamentally a matter of magic. "Science is one thing and religion is quite another."

We may therefore identify a third dimension of belief systems. First, there is a logical relation between beliefs. They are primary or derivative. Secondly, there is a relation between them which has to do with their special location or psychological strength. But there is a third dimension in every belief system by which certain clusters of beliefs are held more or less in isolation from other clusters and protected from any relationship with other sets of beliefs. Each of these dimensions has to do not with the content of our beliefs, but with the *way* we hold them. None of these dimensions need be stable. Indeed, the belief systems of different persons can be described in relation to the ease with which different clusters of beliefs can be related, the number and nature of the logically primitive and psychologically central beliefs, the ease with which they may move from center to periphera and back, and the correspondence or lack of it between the objective logical order of beliefs and the order in which they are actually held.

There is a second way of marking this distinction between beliefs we hold and how we hold them. It has to do not with the relation between beliefs, but with their relation to evidence or reasons. When beliefs are held without regard to evidence or contrary to evidence, or apart from good reasons or the canons for testing reasons and evidence, then we may say they are held non-evidentially. It follows that beliefs held non-evidentially cannot be modified by introducing evidence or reasons or by rational criticism. When beliefs, however, are held "on the basis of" evidence or reasons, can be rationally criticised, and therefore can be modified in the light of further evidence or better reasons, then we shall say they are held evidentially.

This contrast between holding beliefs evidentially and non-evidentially corresponds closely to a fundamental point on the teaching continuum. It has to do with a conventional contrast between teaching and indoctrinating. This difference has nothing to do with the contents of beliefs. It is perfectly possible that two persons may hold to the same belief and yet one may do so evidentially and the other non-evidentially. It is possible, in other words, to indoctrinate people into the truth. The only problem is that they will not *know* that it is the truth. They will only know that it is a *correct* belief. That is to say, they will hold to certain true beliefs, but will be unable to give any adequate reasons for them, any clear account of them, or offer any sound evidence in their support beyond the logically irrelevant observation that they are commonly held beliefs. And yet we cannot be said to *know* that a belief is true, if we cannot give any reasons for it, any explanation of it or any evidence in support of it. In short, even though the beliefs one holds are true, one cannot be said to know they are true, if they are believed in this non-evidential fashion. They can only be known to be *correct* beliefs, and that is one of the features of beliefs held as a consequence of indoctrination.

But this contrast between teaching and indoctrination cuts more deeply. Consider the following context.[4] At some conferences there is

[4] The following illustration was suggested by a student of mine, Mr. William Lauderdale.

a period set aside to lay out the work of the conference, to set the limits to be observed and the methods to be followed. It involves the presentation of decisions already arrived at and now presented as "the ground rules," so to speak, within which the work of the conference shall proceed. A sales conference, for example, may be concerned with the study and discussion of a single method of selling, excluding all others from consideration.

Such a period is sometimes called an orientation period. But it may also appropriately, more accurately, but less wisely, be called a period of indoctrination because of the place and function served by debate. In such a period, persons may raise questions; there may be a discussion and a certain amount of disagreement expressed with decisions arrived at. This process overtly resembles the process of debate carried on for the purpose of informing and arriving at decisions. But in this context questions are raised, information given and discussion permitted only for purposes of persuasion, never for purposes of *arriving* at conclusions.

Both teaching and indoctrination may involve debate, questions, discussions and argument. Both appear to involve instruction, and, in that respect, there is a striking resemblance between them. But there also is a great difference. In indoctrinating, the conversation of instruction is employed only in order that fairly specific and predetermined beliefs may be set. Conflicting evidence and troublesome objections must be withheld because there is no purpose of inquiry. The conversation of instruction is adopted without its intent, without the "due regard for truth" so essential to instruction. Not every point on the teaching continuum is, therefore, equally a point where truth is significant. Indoctrination begins precisely where a concern for truth ends. In short, the intent of indoctrination is to lead people to hold beliefs as though they were arrived at by inquiry, and yet to hold them independently of any subsequent inquiry and therefore secure against the threat of change by later introduction of conflicting reasons or conflicting evidence. The intent, in other words, is to produce persons who hold their beliefs non-evidentially.

That this is the intent of indoctrination is proved by the fact that the process of indoctrinating, unlike the process of teaching, is *logically* dispensable to success. Consider, for example, the following illustration.[5] Suppose we identify two persons, Adams and Barnes, neither of whom knows the identity of the discoverer of the American continent. Let us suppose that with Adams we present certain evidence, give explanations, enter into arguments, examine the statements of authorities, and finally Adams concludes that there are reasonably good grounds for the claim that the discoverer of the American continent was Columbus.

Let us use a different method in the case of Barnes. He is told to respond with the name "Columbus" whenever asked for the identity of the discoverer of the American continent. He is then asked the question

[5] Another student of mine, Mr. Gerald Reagan, suggested this illustration, although to make a slightly different point.

at intervals, rewarded for the correct answer and punished in some way for a wrong answer. In this manner, he may learn to respond correctly and without hesitation.

But could we say that Barnes had been taught that Columbus discovered America? Certainly not. One reason is that at no point in such a process need it be asserted that Columbus *did* discover America. We could say that Barnes had been trained to make a certain response, a response which, by the way, need not manifest intelligence; but we could not say he had been taught that Columbus discovered America. Indeed, he could have learned to make this response without having learned that Columbus discovered America. For this reason, we could not say that Adams and Barnes had learned the same thing, even though by certain observable measures they will appear to give the same response. What Barnes knows is how to respond. What Adams knows is that Columbus discovered America. What one knows is a skill; what the other knows is a truth—or at least a reasonably well-founded belief. But what is most important is that Adams has arrived at this knowledge or belief by a process which we call teaching; and he could not arrive at this truth or come to hold this belief as he does hold it, except by that process or by a process resembling it in certain important logical respects.

The creation of an evidential style of belief is inextricably and logically tied to the process of instruction, or to another process which closely resembles instruction. A non-evidential style of belief, however, is conceptually independent of the process by which beliefs are acquired. A belief is held non-evidentially when it is held quite apart from any reasons, evidence or canons for testing reasons and evidence; and, therefore, the process by which the belief comes to be held is logically a matter of no consequence. But when a belief is held evidentially, it is held always in relation to its grounds in reasons or evidence; and thus the process by which the belief comes to be held is logically decisive.

This is an extraordinarily important and far-reaching mark of difference between instructing and indoctrinating. It follows that insofar as teaching has to do with the acquisition of knowledge and beliefs held evidentially, it is an activity which necessarily involves instruction.

This does not imply that the way of knowing and believing aimed at in instructing can be achieved only by instruction. It does imply, however, that it can be achieved only by a process which resembles instruction in certain important respects. Study, for example, is an activity which aims at accomplishing the results of instruction; yet it does not require the presence of an instructor. Study, in short, is a method of learning and not a method of teaching. Although study is an activity more intimately related to learning than to teaching, it is nonetheless an activity which in its anatomy starkly resembles instruction. Study, as distinguished from other methods of learning—practice, drill, memorization—always involves asking questions, weighing evidence, giving and testing reasons, and so forth. The conversation of study, in short, is the same as the conversation of instruction. What is aimed at in teaching, insofar as it involves instruction, can also be accomplished by study. This fact we acknowledge when we speak of the need for independent study rather than the need for independent learning. In this way we acknowledge that study is another way of accomplishing precisely what is aimed at in teaching.

Suppose, however—to return to our example—that after extensive periods of instruction, Adams refused to acknowledge that Columbus was the discoverer of the American continent. Would it follow that we had failed in teaching? Not necessarily.[6] We would need to know *for what reasons* he refuses to assent to such a commonly held opinion. It may be, in fact, that the reasons for his judgment are better than can be offered for the more widely received opinion. He might say something like this: "There seems to be good evidence for the view that Columbus was not the first European to set foot on the American continent. Indeed, it seems a well established fact that many years before Columbus' voyage, there were visitors to this continent of some Scandinavian descent. But the visits of these people seem not to have had the far-reaching historical consequences of Columbus' discovery. If you consider the historical consequences of great importance, then one might say Columbus discovered America; but if you mean by that that this was the *first* discovery of America, then you would be mistaken."

This kind of reply would not signal the failure of instruction. It would be evidence of singular success. Instruction is an activity which has to do not with what people believe but with how they believe it. It has to do not so much with arriving at "the right answer" as with arriving at an answer on the right kind of grounds. It is no objection to point out the many areas of knowledge in which it is important to lead students to the right answer. For all that is usually pointed out is that there are many areas of knowledge in which the grounds of decision are decisive, and in which therefore there *is* a correct answer which it is important to know. Even in mathematics, however, where a "right answer" is often discoverable, a concern simply to lead students to that answer, or to equip them to find it, is a fundamentally defective kind of instruction. Even in such a formal science where certitude is common, we are concerned that students be brought to an evidential style of knowing. To focus simply upon securing a right solution without understanding the nature of mathematical operations is the mathematical equivalent of indoctrination. Indeed, when indoctrination is seen to involve a certain style of knowing or believing, we can discover the possibility of indoctrination in nearly every area of human knowledge and not simply in those having to do with what we would more commonly call "matters

---

[6] Note, however, that a failure to get the "right answer" in the case of Barnes would constitute a failure to succeed in teaching. Indoctrination aims at inculcating the "right answer," but not necessarily for "the right reasons" or even for good reasons.

of doctrine." In other words, when, in teaching, we are concerned simply to lead another person to a correct answer, but are not correspondingly concerned that they arrive at that answer on the basis of good reasons, then we are indoctrinating; we are engaged in creating a non-evidential style of belief.

There is one further curious fact to observe about the concept of indoctrination and its relation to a non-evidential way of holding beliefs. It has to do with the difficulty in identifying concrete cases of indoctrination as opposed to teaching. We have already suggested that there is an area of vagueness between instructing and indoctrinating. The difference between them is clear, but the criteria that mark the difference may, in specific instances, be mixed. For example, a person who has received his beliefs by indoctrination will be able to give reasons for them, offer evidence, and in other ways display every mark of holding his beliefs in an evidential way. But this is an illusion, albeit an illusion to which each of us, in some measure, submits. A person who is indoctrinated can sometimes give reasons and evidence for his beliefs, because as a practical matter, reasons and evidence were necessary in the process of establishing his beliefs. The difference, however, is betrayed in his *use* of reasons and evidence. He will use argument, criticism, evidence, and so forth, not as an instrument of inquiry, but as an instrument establishing what he already believes. He will display a marked incapacity to seriously consider conflicting evidence or entertain contrary reasons. That is to say, such a person will hold his beliefs as matters of ideology. It is indeed the characteristic of an ideology that it requires reason and argument, not for inquiry, but for defense. It requires reason as a weapon. This is not required for the defense of a belief held evidentially.

The point is that the differences between instruction and indoctrination, clear enough conceptually, are extraordinarily difficult to detect in specific cases. It requires, in ourselves, the capacity to discriminate between beliefs which are held evidentially and those which are not. To do this, we must not only have the capacity to detect sophistry in ourselves, but the courage to reject it when discovered, and the psychic freedom to follow where the pursuit of truth may lead. The detection of non-evidential beliefs in ourselves, therefore, requires not simply the logical skill to examine and appraise the adequacy of reasons, but the psychic freedom to give up or alter those beliefs which are non-evidential. In short, the distinction between instruction and indoctrination, easy enough to grasp intellectually, is immensely difficult to detect in practice, because it involves nothing less than the most radical examination of our belief systems in their psychological dimensions. To possess such a capacity is a mark of rare courage and honesty.

This psychic difficulty corresponds to a certain interesting logical difficulty. It is a curious but quite understandable fact that it is both grammatically and logically impossible for a person to say of himself truthfully and in the present tense, that he holds his beliefs as a consequence of indoctrination. It is something which cannot be said. Suppose I walk into a room where I find someone lying down in an attitude of blissful sleep. I ask, "Are you asleep?" Without hesitation, with clarity and firmness of voice, he answers, "I am." His answer is strong evidence that in fact he is not asleep. Similarly, if a person says with sincerity and conviction "My beliefs *are* indoctrinated," (there is no satisfactory way of putting it) it must follow that his beliefs are no longer held as a consequence of indoctrination only, and he is already on his way toward an evidential style of belief. Indoctrination is successful only if people *think* they hold their beliefs evidentially and in fact do not, only when they use reason as a weapon under the illusion that they are seriously inquiring. Indoctrination then is the intentional propagation of an illusion. All of us live with this illusion to some extent. Insofar as teaching is directed at matters of knowledge and belief, it involves instruction and may be described as the effort to free us from this illusion to whatever extent that is possible. Teaching might be described then as the unending effort to reconstitute the psychic structure of our ways of believing. But in order to begin, instruction presupposes that there is already a certain kind of structure of beliefs. The death of innocence is needed before teaching can begin. At this point teaching and indoctrination both become intimately related to the formation of attitudes.

To say this, however, is merely to repeat an observation at least as old as Socrates' attempt at the moral reform of Athens, namely that the beginning of inquiry is the confession of ignorance and the ensuing willingness to follow where the truth may lead. This is an attitude, a disposition, which like most other attitudes can be described as the manifestation of a certain kind of belief system, a certain way of holding beliefs. He cannot be taught who is convinced there is no truth to be appropriated or none he does not possess already. But it takes no great fund of experience to observe how rare is the capacity to admit one's ignorance, to seriously entertain new ideas, alternative ways of doing things, and to change one's point of viewing the world. Every mind is fettered to some extent, ridden with presuppositions and stereotypes which stand in the way of mental freedom. Every man knows some point at which he cannot earnestly confess his ignorance. It would come as a personal affront; it would endanger the self.

These are the points which teaching cannot touch. For teaching, insofar as it involves matters of knowledge and belief, begins with posing questions to be answered, or answers to be questioned. It begins by placing such matters in the open where they cannot be avoided. But there are those who cannot allow certain questions to be raised, who cannot permit certain doubts because they touch upon themselves too directly, threaten them too deeply. In proportion as such questions are greater and greater in number, in proportion as one's psychologically central beliefs are multiplied and segregated, teaching has less and less scope for success. Teaching is ineffectual in those whose minds are enchained by prejudice or who cannot face the questions which must be raised. Teaching aims to remove these fetters; it seeks by instruction to reconstitute the order of our beliefs so that even our psychologically central beliefs are evidentially held. But in this it presupposes already some measure of psychic freedom. For instruction to proceed, it must, in effect, find some foothold from which to push back the darkness and let in the light.

It is in this sense that the practice of teaching presupposes certain attitudes the cultivation of which is at the same time the consequence of teaching. The attitudes it presupposes, constitute that posture toward the self and toward the world which permits new questions to present themselves and new answers to be entertained. When a teacher can, in effect, find no foothold from which to proceed, he must try directly to change attitudes in order to begin teaching. The formation of attitudes is, in this sense, a precondition for teaching. It is also a consequence, however, insofar as teaching is concerned with the *way* we hold our beliefs. To the extent that it has this consequence, we may say that teaching is that activity which preeminently aims at enhancing the human capacity for action. It is concerned with the nurture of that state of being which we might describe as the posture of the pilgrim, the capacity, within limits, to tolerate an increasing measure of aliena-tion, to be free to wander in the world.[7]

One of the clearest illustrations of the failure to teach, in this sense, is found in the Church. For in the Church, as in the political arena of our society, there are those who think the aim of teaching is to get people to hold certain specific beliefs even though the evidence does not always support them, though they are not believable to the person taught and cannot be defended on the basis of good reasons. The result of so-called Christian education is sometimes, from the perspective of the uni-

---

[7] The topology of teaching helps us to discriminate between those considerations which enter as a part of the teaching activity and those which enter only as pre-suppositions of the teaching act. For example, there are some views of teaching which focus upon the personal relation of teacher and student, emphasize the need for mutual trust and acceptance, and thus, stress in the teaching relation those matters having to do primarily with mental health and self-understanding. Such views tend to picture the teaching activity as primarily therapeutic. Such views have nothing to do with the teaching activity. Though they have much to do with satisfying the conditions without which teaching cannot succeed or even begin. In short, they deal with the presuppositions of teaching and not with its substance.

This does not mean that such views are irrelevant to what teachers are con-cerned to do. For there are many actual settings in which teachers, for psychological and institutional reasons, are called upon to forsake the task of teaching and attend to those matters which must be satisfied in order that teaching may begin. It ought always to be kept in mind that the "office" of teacher often requires more than a talent for teaching. It requires also that one be now a counselor, now a clinician, now a friendly guide, and another time a public relations officer. To say that these activities have to do with the presuppositions of teaching does not mean they must temporarily precede the activity of teaching. It means simply that though they are always involved in the "office" of teacher, they are not logically central to the activity of teaching.

versity, disastrous. Sometimes it destroys the possibility of teaching because it results in a non-evidential style of belief. There is learning in such education, but the kind of learning which results in holding beliefs so that henceforth further learning is made more difficult and further teaching rendered all but impossible.

No one who has long been a university teacher will fail to detect how often those students most at home in the Church, most articulate in matters doctrinal, are those whose minds are most bound and restricted and who are least able to learn or seriously inquire. They are often the ones least capable of doubt and most lacking in the courage to follow where the truth may lead them. They are, in short, often lacking in the moral courage which their lives as students require. Their education in the Church often has had the consequence of multiplying their "core" beliefs by an endless list of prohibitions, and segregating their beliefs into such well protected and isolated clusters that neither facts nor reasons may penetrate. It is a strong indictment of the Church that in its education it often produces such a nonevidential style of belief.

It is a serious charge, however, not only because of its social consequences, but because it contradicts what it is the Church's task to affirm. Such education is a subtle form of unbelief within the Church itself. It is a denial of the view that men are justified by faith, in favor of the view that they are justified by their opinions. Education in and by the Church has often, as a consequence, had damaging results.

It is not, however, the presence of the faith which creates a nonevidential style of belief; it is its absence. Those whose minds have been enchained by their education, are men of little faith. To say that men shall abide in faith does not mean they shall abide in their opinions, not even in their opinions about God. To think otherwise would be to suppose that God loves men because of their beliefs. There may be those who entertain such a faith, but it is surely not the kerygma that it has been the historic concern of the Church to affirm. The man of faith should be the most fearless in the search for truth because he knows that in the end it is not decisive. Being freed even from that most worldly of all concerns, namely the concern for his own salvation, he may be fearless even in his search for the truth about God.

One must add, however, that the Christian Church is not the only party in the modern world guilty of fostering a non-evidential style of belief. Our schools, including universities, have often been barbaric in the same way. Some years ago, in his studies on dogmatism, Rokeach and others tested many college freshmen in the east and middle west.[8] They were concerned to study the belief systems of these students, not only *what* they believed but *how* they believed it. The results were astonishing. The test included a series of statements accompanied by a series of reasons. The students were to indicate the statements and

---

[8] Milton Rokeach and Albert Eglash, "A Scale for the Measurement of Intellectual Convictions," *Journal of Social Psychology*, XLIV (August, 1956), 135–141.

reasons with which they agreed. Remarkable numbers agreed with such statements as the following: "We ought to combat communism because communism means longer working hours and less pay," or "Hitler was wrong because otherwise he wouldn't have lost."

These are responses of persons who have been led to hold the "right beliefs" but never have been taught good reasons for them. There has been learning which has resulted in the observable and verbal responses of the right kind, but for entirely erroneous reasons or for none at all except that such beliefs are "correct."

THE TOPOLOGY OF ENABLING BELIEFS

This emphasis on an evidential system of belief is susceptible to misunderstanding in a dangerous way. It could be understood to imply that one should not have *any* passionate convictions. A belief held evidentially is amenable to examination, and therefore open to change in the light of better reasons and more substantial evidence. Thus the possession of firm convictions seems to conflict with the cultivation of evidential beliefs. He who has passionate convictions is to that extent and at those points no longer open-minded, and he who is at *every* point open-minded must be without any passionate convictions. He is that completely flexible man, whose placid and weak mentality marks him off as dangerous, because he thinks nothing is really very important.

An evidential belief style does not commit us to such a mentality. The problem is rather to seek closure of mind at precisely those points and on those matters which will permit us to be open to the evidence on all other matters of belief. The only beliefs, in short, which must be rejected are those which prevent us from being open to reasons and evidence on all subsequent matters. As Chesterton has put it in another context: "There is a thought that stops thought. That is the only thought that ought to be stopped."[9] He might have added that there are beliefs without which no beliefs can be warranted and these are the only beliefs which at all cost must be affirmed.

Such beliefs, in fact, ought to enlist our most passionate loyalty; for they are the ones which enable us to hold all other beliefs in an evidential way. For example, a thorough skepticism in regard to reason, a kind of complete anti-intellectualism, if held to as a deep conviction, would successfully prevent the examination of any subsequent beliefs. It could lead only to a non-evidential way of believing. On the other hand, a "due regard for truth,"—the belief that truth is powerful, attainable and to be treasured whenever identified—such a belief is indispensable if *any* belief is to be held evidentially. Such a conviction does not commit us to the naive faith that all men have a due regard for truth or are equally moved to dispassionately weigh and consider the evidence on important

[9] *Orthodoxy*, 58.

questions. Nor does it commit us to the truth of any specific belief. It commits us only to a certain *way* of holding beliefs, and that way is an evidential way. Indeed, a "due regard for truth," understood in this way and passionately held to, is indispensable if we are to hold to *any* beliefs in an evidential way. A deep conviction concerning the value of truth is in this sense rationally defensible because without it there can be no rational defense of any belief whatsoever.

It is not, therefore, the aim of teaching to eliminate all passionate convictions. The aim, on the contrary, is to seek every possible assurance that our passionate convictions, our enabling beliefs, are also rationally or evidentially held. Such enabling beliefs may be open for examination, capable of refinement and elaboration, but under no conditions can they be exchanged for others. Their abandonment cannot be warranted on the basis of evidence or reasons, because they are precisely those beliefs without which we could not seriously entertain the evidence.

These comments also are susceptible to a dangerous misappropriation. At the point of enabling beliefs, there is only the most tenuous line between the fanatic and men of less singular devotion. For at this point, the difference between what is believed and how we believe it is obscured. How a person believes something can be reduced, at this point, to an account of what he believes. The actions of the inquisitor, after all, may be defended on grounds of the most passionate regard for truth, a regard for truth so strong, in fact, that it becomes necessary to stamp out every trace of error that the truth may receive the recognition it deserves. The difficulty with the fanatic at every point, however, is that he confuses a due regard for truth with passionate concern to propagate certain *specific truths*.

But it may be answered, "Is not a due regard for truth also a specific set of beliefs?" It is indeed. It is the belief that truth is attainable, powerful, and to be treasured. But the belief that truth is attainable does not entail the belief that we have attained it. Such a regard for truth does not permit us the illusion that we have appropriated more than a fragmentary vision of the truth. It does not permit us with ease to identify the truth. Rather, it places upon us the difficult and tortuous task of weighing with great care whatever beliefs we may regard as true, holding them always as open to challenge, and to change in the light of further evidence and fresh reasons. In short, although a due regard for truth involves a passionate and unswerving loyalty to certain specific beliefs, although it involves a kind of fanaticism, it is an unyielding commitment to just those beliefs which will not permit the fanatic to develop.

It is at this point again that the Christian faith provides an interesting illustration. The Christian faith is often thought to be contained in certain doctrinal assertions. As such, it is commonly conceived to have more to do with *what* men believe than with *how* they believe. There is in this view a considerable burden of truth. But faith is not simply a matter of credal recitation; it is also a matter of fidelity. The fact is that *what* is believed in faith is precisely what is sufficient in order that all subsequent beliefs may be surveyed, examined, and held in an evidential way. What is believed, in short, has to do not so much with the beliefs we hold, as with the way we hold our beliefs. It has to do, in short, with the conditions without which we could not have a "due regard for truth," i.e., the conditions which permit us to develop an evidential "style of belief."

For example, one of the greatest barriers to a free and fearless search for truth is the tendency of men to identify their ideas with themselves, so that one cannot attack ideas without attacking their author. The result is that in debate beliefs are held non-evidentially, and reason is used in the fashion required by ideology, not as an instrument of inquiry, but as a weapon for defense of self. A "due regard for truth" then becomes extraordinarily difficult, and men find it virtually impossible to value the emergence of truth more highly than they value their own victory in debate. When we find such an attitude expressed in the practice of teaching, we recognize the authoritarian personality, the person who is less concerned that his words *be* truthful and more that they be *regarded* as the truth. Perhaps one ought to expect no more; for our beliefs are indispensable to ourselves; an attack upon them is an attack upon us.

This is, theologically speaking, the expression of man's unceasing effort to achieve salvation by works, to value his own ideas more highly than the truth, not because his thoughts carry a greater burden of truth, but simply because they are his. The man of faith is like any other man. He does not escape his condition, but along with others he may at least understand it, and understanding it place his hope elsewhere than in the fruits of his labor. For to walk in faith is to walk in the confidence that in death there is life, that beyond the death of self, there is hope for the freedom to think without any limitations except those imposed by the demands of thought itself. The quest for knowledge then holds no fears. Though it may displace one's ideas, it cannot endanger one's person. On the contrary, it can hold only inexhaustible surprises.

It is precisely the possibility of this kind of psychic freedom which lies at the heart of teaching. It is a due regard for truth which serves to distinguish the conversation of instruction from that of indoctrination. In indoctrination we are concerned primarily with *what* people believe and as a consequence are we concerned with *how* they believe it. In teaching, however, we are concerned primarily with *how* persons believe a thing and, therefore, can afford less concern with *what* they believe. If we adhere to the practice of teaching, we shall not be permitted a great anxiety over those who do not believe as we do, *provided* they can be led to a psychologically central regard for truth. For given that enabling belief, held with passionate conviction, it will follow that their beliefs, and our own as well, may be open to subsequent alteration in the face of reasons, evidence, and further reflection upon our experience. Apart from such beliefs, however, the hope that men's opinions may be changed by teaching is a hope in vain. Their beliefs will either be unalterable or else so easily changed as to fluctuate with every changing wind of doctrine or fashion of opinion. Without a due regard for truth, we must resort to indoctrination, force, or outright lies. With it, we may instruct. We may then say to men, in effect, "Come let us reason together." A due regard for truth is an indispensable condition for that civilizing community in which not men but ideas are perpetually on trial.

Indoctrination, nonetheless, has a perfectly good and important role to play in education. There is nothing in these remarks which would suggest otherwise. Like the development of attitudes, indoctrination may be useful as the prelude to teaching. Just as we need not cut off the hand of every child or thrust one of every fifty into the street in order that they may understand the dangers of knives and highways, and learn to obey the rules established to protect their lives, so we need not offer reasons for every belief we think important for children and adults to hold. On the other hand, we have no warrant to inculcate beliefs for which there is no good reason, or for which we can offer no good reason; and we must be prepared to offer reasons or evidence when they are requested. Though indoctrination may, in many contexts, be both good and necessary, it can never be justified for its own sake. It can only be justified as the nearest approximation to teaching available at the moment. Indoctrination, in short, may be sanctioned only in order that beliefs adopted may later be redeemed by reasons, only that they may be vindicated by teaching.

TEACHING, LEARNING, AND EDUCATION

To say that indoctrination plays a legitimate role in education, but is, nonetheless, peripheral to the concept of teaching, is already to strike at an immensely important and powerful distinction. It is already to begin to describe the logical relations that exist between teaching and learning on the one hand, and teaching and education on the other.

Learning is commonly defined as any change of behavior. This definition or one like it, has certain advantages for the science of psychology. It makes it possible to deal with learning as an observable phenomenon, which is important if the study of learning is to remain a scientific inquiry. Such a definition, nonetheless, is wholly inadequate to capture what we normally mean by "learning." Ordinarily, we would regard a change of behavior at best as only *evidence* of learning, and we would not regard it as either necessary or sufficient evidence. A change of behavior in many contexts is not evidence that one has *learned* something new, but only that he has decided *to do* something new. A bank cashier who begins to embezzle, has not necessarily learned anything not learned by the cashier who does not embezzle. And this is so, because it is not obvious that learning to embezzle is distinguished in any way from simply learning to keep books. In this case, as in unnumbered others like it, a change of behavior is not sufficient evidence that anything new has been learned. But for exactly the same reasons it cannot be necessary evidence either. A person may learn to do something and yet never in his life decide to do it, or in any other way display his knowledge or capacities. Unless such a supposition can be shown to be absurd or meaningless, it cannot be held that a change of behavior is a necessary part of what we *mean* by learning.

The important point to observe, however, is that regardless of our definition of learning, it must remain true that *every* point on the teaching continuum is *equally* a point of learning. Or, more precisely, every point on the teaching continuum, as much as any other, represents a method of bringing about learning. It is not therefore anything implicit in the concept of learning itself which distributes the teaching activities in certain logical relations along the teaching continuum. They are distributed by the logic of the concept 'teaching' and not by the logic of the concept 'learning.' People can and will learn by propaganda, indoctrination, and lies. They can be brought to adopt certain patterns of behavior by conditioning, by intimidation, by deceit, by threats of physical violence. Indeed, these different methods appear on the teaching continuum *because* they are all ways of bringing about learning, and because it is true *in some sense*, that teaching aims at bringing about learning. It is not true, however, that every method of bringing about learning is equally a method of teaching. Some are more central to the concept of teaching than are others.

It is because of this logical fact that the teaching concept can yield a continuum of the kind I have described. It is an immensely important fact, however, that the concept of learning cannot yield such a continuum, and that it cannot for the following reasons. The concept of teaching includes within its limits a whole assemblage of human activities. Teaching stands related to instruction, training, indoctrination, and conditioning as genus to species. But it is not the relation between genus and species which is represented on the teaching continuum. Every point within the limits of teaching is a species of a certain genus, and *in this respect*, no point is different from any other. The continuum, however, is directional; it is directional in a way that membership in a certain genus would not warrant. What is represented by the direction of the continuum is a logical relation between the *members* of the genus, indicating the extent to which they do or do not instantiate the properties of central importance in the logic of the concept. The concept of teaching is peculiar in the respect that not only does it stand related to certain activities as genus to species, but there is also *between* its species a discernible order.

If we consider learning to be a human activity, then it will also stand related to such things as drill, memorization, practice, and study, as genus to species. But among the species of learning there is *no* corresponding logical order of the kind that exists among activities of teaching. That is to say, the activities of learning fall under the concept as members of a class. It makes no sense to ask whether insight is more central logically to the concept of learning than, say, drill or practice or any other learning activity. But it *does* make sense to ask whether instruction is more central to the concept of teaching than, say, indoctrination. In short, teaching is a vague concept, but learning is not.

We might discover that some activities on the teaching continuum are more efficient or effective than others in bringing about learning, or that some methods of teaching are more appropriate to certain types of materials to be learned. But these distinctions cannot be discovered in the concept of learning itself. They must be discovered by empirical study. And such studies might show that the most effective methods of bringing about learning do not fall within the province of teaching at all. If that were to happen, it would follow that teachers ought *not* to adopt the most effective or efficient means of bringing about learning. In short, teaching and learning are conceptually independent *in the sense that* we cannot discover in the concept of learning, any principles sufficient to distinguish those kinds of learning aimed at in teaching from those which are not.

Now this may sound like an utterly fantastic and unwarranted claim, but it is not. Suppose it is true that by their consequences, we can identify many different kinds of learning. We can discriminate between learning habits and learning to obey certain principles, between acquiring belief sets and conditioned responses, or between learning by insight and by rote memorization. It is quite conceivable that different kinds of learning can be related to different points on the teaching continuum, and therefore, can be ordered in a certain relation to each other and some identified as more appropriate to teaching than others. For example, there may be a certain kind of learning which would result in a non-evidential belief set, and which might therefore be related to the methods of propaganda or indoctrination. Similarly, learning certain habits or skills might be related, more or less, to training or conditioning.[10] If this is so, then different kinds of learning can be placed in an order similar to the order of the teaching continuum. But the point is that this order is imposed upon the phenomena by the logic of the concept 'teaching.' There is no such order discoverable among species of learning. We can, in short, discriminate between kinds of learning and identify which are appropriately aimed at in teaching only if we *bring to* the concept of learning some principles or presuppositions which are derived from the concept of teaching. This is, in fact, what we usually do when we "select" from studies of learning those insights and truths which we think will be of practical use in classroom instruction. The fact remains

---

[10] I do not suppose there is in fact such a correspondence between kinds of learning and methods of enhancing learning. On the other hand, I see no logical reason why there should not be.

that no species of learning is more centrally related to the concept of learning than is any other, and therefore when we discover how to bring about learning, it does not follow necessarily that we have discovered how to do anything we are concerned to do in teaching.

But what is the significance of this fact? The most immediate and far-reaching conclusion is a somewhat negative one. It is not clear within what limits or on what grounds we are warranted in deriving a theory of teaching from a theory of learning. To what extent, in other words, can our knowledge of learning be made to yield, in a logically defensible way, some principles which can be normative for the conduct of teaching? Indeed, one may ask whether there is any logically well-founded principle which will suffice to mediate the inference from the management of learning to the practice of teaching.

The problem arises because the concept of learning is of greater dimensions than the concept of teaching described in our topology. But the concept represented in that topology is the one we normally employ when we think about teaching in the setting of the school. How do we know then, that when we study certain phenomena of learning we are concerned with phenomena which fall within the more narrow limits of teaching? The fact is that apart from assumptions or presuppositions concerning the activity of teaching we do not know when our studies are relevant to the activity of teaching and when they are not. The methods of instruction and the techniques of deceit are both ways of inducing learning. On what possible grounds then, are we more concerned to master one than the other? Can it be that at this point we manifest a presupposition that one is in some sense more relevant to the practice of teaching than the other? On what grounds can we justify such a presupposition? Apart from some theory of teaching, assumptions of this kind have no warrant; and yet without such assumptions, we have no grounds for an inference from the principles of learning to the principles of teaching. In order to profit from our studies of learning, the logically prior problem is not to develop a general theory of learning, but to develop a theory of teaching. The topology of teaching described in these pages is a step in that direction.

There are, however, at least two other ways of meeting the logical problem posed by the conceptual relation between teaching and learning. The most attractive alternative is simply to extend the teaching concept so that it has a scope of equal dimensions with the concept of learning. Teaching understood in such an inclusive sense may be defined as any activity the primary purpose of which is to induce learning. Thus, the concept of teaching can be made to include within its limits all the endless activities which appear on the extended continuum, including the use of deceit, propaganda and outright lies. Such a move would suffice to guarantee that every discovery about the conduct of the learning process would have immediate and valid implications for the conduct of teaching. But the logical problem would not be solved. It would simply be made to appear at a different point. We would then have two concepts of teaching, a very inclusive sense and another more narrow sense. The problem then remains. Apart from some unexamined assumptions or presuppositions, we have no way of knowing when our knowledge of teaching in the wider sense is relevant to the conduct of teaching in the more restricted sense. We are left without any logical principle which will mediate the inference required.[11]

The second method of resolving this logical difficulty has to do less with the relation between teaching and learning and more with the relation between teaching and education. It may be argued that the construction of the teaching continuum is merely the consequence of certain social values which we share. It is because of our liberal-democratic tradition or because of our rational-humanistic inheritance that we do not regard the use of lies, propaganda and deceit as proper instruments of teaching. Apart from certain assumed values, it may be argued, any means of inducing learning, however barbarous they may seem to us, are perfectly bona fide methods of teaching. Thus, what we have been concerned with is not the difference between activities of teaching on the one hand, and other methods of bringing about learning on the other hand. Instead, it may be argued, that we have been concerned only to discriminate between good or socially sanctioned methods of teaching and bad or socially proscribed methods. In short, it might be held that the construction of the teaching continuum is possible only because of certain values which are presupposed in it, and that all we require in the way of presuppositions about teaching is adequately provided by our commitment to these values.

This view, however, is fundamentally mistaken. The teaching continuum is in fact neutral as regards the different options of value from

---

[11] There is a third way of meeting this problem. It could be argued that the kinds of learning aimed at in teaching are only a special case of the wider phenomena of learning. Thus whatever one discovers about the process of inducing learning must *a fortiori* be true also of the activity of inducing learning by teaching. But what is the meaning of the phrase "special case of"? Does it point to a relation of class membership, class inclusion or to some other deductive relation?

Consider the following concepts and the relations of the members of the classes generated by each.

(a) 'activities aimed at inducing learning'
(b) 'activities aimed at inducing learning by teaching'

The class (b) is said to be a special case of (a) in the sense that $b < a$. Thus whatever is true of every member of the class (a) is true of every member of (b). But the class generated by (b) has a greater intension than the class whose members fall under (a). Thus the members of the class generated by (b) have certain properties *not* shared by other sub-sets falling under (a), and the problem is that in the present case, our concern is with exactly those features of the intension of the class (b) by virtue of which it is a sub-set of (a) and *not* those by virtue of which it is a "special case of" (a). Thus, it may be admitted that (b) is a "special case of" (a) in the sense that $b < a$. But this observation, though true, is not the kind of observation which will meet the difficulty posed by the relation between teaching and learning. What we need to study about the activity of teaching has to do with those respects which are not relevant to its being "a special case of" activities aimed at inducing learning.

which men may choose. The relation between instruction and indoctrination, for example, has nothing to do with any presupposed values. The relation between them has been described on grounds of logic only. Between the activities of instructing and indoctrinating, there are certain striking resemblances. But there are also substantial differences. They are activities with different purposes. They aim at the development of different kinds of belief systems. They are differently related to a concern for truth. The process of each is differently related to the purpose of each. These relationships have nothing to do with the acceptance or rejection of any social values whatever. The logical relations will be the same whether we approve of indoctrination as a method of education or not. These distinctions will hold whether in our moral sentiments we are inclined to aristocracy, democracy or fascism. In this sense, the constructing of the teaching continuum does not rest upon any prior assumptions concerning what is valuable and what is not. All the difficult questions of values concerning the goals of education remain undecided and untouched by the topology of teaching. In this sense, such a topology is genuinely formal and neutral.

Moreover, the view that instruction is more centrally related to teaching than indoctrination has nothing to do with the relative value of one over the other, or with our preference of one. It has to do simply with the fact that in so far as the conduct of indoctrination possesses certain properties, it resembles instruction, and as it lacks these properties it resembles propaganda. And as this change occurs and indoctrination tends to assume the characteristics of propaganda, it becomes increasingly difficult to substitute the concept of "teaching" for the concept of "indoctrination" without a change in meaning. The topology of teaching therefore is not based upon any value presuppositions, but only on a series of logical distinctions.

From the topology of teaching it does follow, however, that education may be accomplished by other methods than teaching. In short, the idea of education, like the idea of learning, is of considerably larger dimensions than the idea of teaching. Education includes all of the enormously diverse means by which we learn, and these range all the way from the intricate processes of socialization to the rather formal methods of teaching mathematics and grammar. Propagandizing, lying, and intimidating are all methods we may use to educate. Education is therefore like an instrument. It can be used for any purpose men may adopt. It may be used to barbarize or to civilize. It may be used to liberate the heroic capacities of men and make them free or it may be used to make them cowards and slaves. Education is the kind of activity which may be adopted for many purposes. That is why the problem of value is important for educators. We must seek some grounds for determining what shall be our purposes. But though it is true that education can be used to accomplish many different purposes, it is not true that teaching is a method of education adequate to every purpose. One of the most difficult of all questions in educational theory is the question to what extent and within what limits shall we employ or be permitted to employ teaching as the method of education. In the construction of the teaching continuum, no resolution to these perpetual questions of value is presupposed. Education is an adequate instrument for barbarization, but teaching is not. Teaching is that human activity which is preeminently suited to enhance the human capacity for action. It is that activity of men which being engaged in, contains the conditions for the nurture of free human beings.

Toward Dialogue

Sometimes footnotes are as revealing as the text. Take a look at footnote 7 on page 250. It refers to a paragraph in which Green is widening the concept of teaching to a generic dimension, as "that activity which preeminently aims at enhancing the human capacity for action." In the footnote, however, he brushes aside many teaching behaviors whose main contribution is to this very enhancement. He says of them that they "have nothing to do with the teaching activity . . . they deal with the presuppositions of teaching and not with its substance."

This will come as a surprise to those for whom teaching is precisely what Green dismisses. For example, many people choose teaching because it offers an opportunity to have a direct effect on other people. One of these effects, in Green's own words, is the cultivation of "that posture toward the self and toward the world which permits new questions to present themselves and new answers to be entertained."

How is it possible for anybody, even a hard-boiled philosophical analyst, to dismiss this aspect of teaching as merely the establishment of "the conditions without which teaching cannot succeed or even begin?" It must mean that what goes on in a psychiatrist's office is not teaching and learning. But if not, then what is it?

B. PAUL KOMISAR AND JAMES E. McCLELLAN

The Logic of Slogans

It is simple enough to notice that educational literature contains a surprisingly large number of such expressions as "Education for Life Adjustment," "Return to the Fundamentals," "The Ideal of Disciplined Intelligence," and "Pursuit of Excellence." These expressions *apparently* do not give any specific information, and we disparage them with the title of "slogans." When we find slogans in educational language we frequently become indignant. Moreover, our umbrage is magnified if the convicted slogan-user, be he administrator or philosopher of education, is not properly shameful when his error is pointed out to him.

Why is this so? Why should we hold pedagogical slogans in such disdain? Is it because of our failure to understand how slogans actually function in educational discourse? Do we not tend to judge pedagogical slogans according to models taken from other linguistic domains and applied uncritically to the language of education? If we would escape being the victims of both the sloganizers and the anti-sloganizers, we should ask ourselves these questions: What role do slogans play in educational language? How can we judge whether a particular slogan is playing its appropriate role? If so, is it acquitting itself well in this role?

THE CEREMONIAL AND NON-CEREMONIAL USES OF SLOGANS

It requires no exceptional perspicacity to recognize that slogans are chosen to appeal to the feelings of the listener or reader. Sometimes slogans are used to do *only* this. Let us call this the ceremonial use of slogans, from the context in which this use is most typically encountered[1] —a dedication, a convocation, an inauguration, or the like. On such a propitious occasion, a slogan may be a very useful device for emotive purposes, arousing interest, inciting enthusiasm, engendering loyalty, or achieving a unity of feeling and spirit. "Educational Leadership for a Free World" is a recent and notable example of a slogan used in this way.[2]

When used ceremonially, slogans do not usually refer or point to

[1] It's very doubtful that these ceremonial occasions are the most *usual* instances of a ceremonial use of slogans. But the ceremonial occasion provides the "point" of the slogan when used on other kinds of occasions.

[2] The expression was the "theme" of the Inauguration Year at Teachers College, Columbia University, 1955–56.

From *Language and Concepts in Education*, eds. B. O. Smith and Robert H. Ennis, (Chicago: Rand McNally & Company, 1961), pp. 195–214.

anything in particular. But this lack of concrete reference, while it infuriates many, probably confuses very few people. From the point of view of the sloganizer, the only criterion to apply to the ceremonial use of slogans is an empirical one: Does the slogan arouse the intended feelings? As the level of sophistication of the average educationist rises, slogan-makers will probably find it increasingly difficult to satisfy this criterion.

We call attention to this use of slogans only to avoid it. The study of how the ceremonial use of slogans may be handled more effectively (or avoided more skillfully) is not a matter for logical inquiry; it is a matter of skill in public relations or personal sanity. All slogans are chosen to appeal to feelings to some extent, but not all have this as their sole or primary function. Slogans sometimes occur in textbooks, lectures, seminars, and in meetings of educational policy-makers. Here slogans are used to give information and direction to educational activity, to create and establish rather definite language customs for the profession. These we call non-ceremonial uses of slogans, and our analysis is intended to apply to them.

Rarely, it would appear, does one have genuine difficulty in distinguishing between the ceremonial and non-ceremonial uses of a slogan. If a person asks for the meaning of *Lux et veritas*, we should ordinarily respond by translating the Latin into English. But suppose he then says, "Oh, I know how to translate the words. But I want to know what the motto means; that is to say, in what way an educational institution is different because it adopts this slogan as its motto rather than, say, *In lumine tuo videbimus lumen*."

Now this represents a case of mistaking a ceremonial use of slogans (putting them on the covers of college catalogues) for a non-ceremonial use of slogans (to convey, in a distinctive sort of way, information and directions). But usually we know when slogans are being used purely ceremonially, and we know that one does not ask from slogans so used, "What does it mean?" or "What should I do?"

THE LOGIC OF SLOGANS

Slogans Considered as Summarizing Assertions

The educationally important uses of slogans are not the purely ceremonial ones. The important uses are those for which it does make sense to ask of a slogan, "What does it mean?" To understand these uses we propose the general rule: *When trying to find out what a slogan means, see what other assertions it summarizes.*[3] Some insight can be gained into the functioning of slogans by comparing them with gen-

[3] The word "slogan" is applied even more widely than we will here consider it. The expression "Boost Soap Sales," bandied about by the salesmen of a soap company, would commonly be called a slogan. The expression is relatively specific; it does not resemble a generalization. In the remainder of this chapter we will concentrate on *general* slogans since an elucidation of the features of general slogans is important for understanding educational language.

eralizations, the assertion-form which they most closely resemble. Up to this point we have mostly used expressions as examples of slogans. If we are to compare them with generalizations, we must extend the word "slogan" to include utterances which have the grammatical form of assertions. Please note that we are using "assertion" in its most general sense, to include optative and prescriptive as well as descriptive utterances.

Slogans and Generalizations: Similarity

The first point is one of *resemblance* between generalizations ("all teachers are college graduates") and slogans ("we learn what we live"). Both are typically used to summarize other assertions not explicitly stated in the general assertion itself. How is this done? Imagine a hypothetical foreign lecturer who tells his audience that the disciplinary methods of teachers, standards of pupil achievement, and courses of study found in his country differ from those he has observed here. He might stop there or go on (later in the lecture, perhaps) to state that public education in this country differs from public education in his homeland. In this case the general statement "public education differs in the two countries" is simply a restatement in *general* form of the many *particular* differences discussed in the lecture. The general statement summatively asserts the particular assertions; these *are* its meaning. Slogans in educational language often function in this way. On specific occasions when they are so used, they literally *mean* some list of other assertions.

The matter we want to call attention to is the relation between assertions of great generality on the one hand and particular assertions to which they are related on the other. The former act as (or are used as) summaries of the latter. For our purpose a particular assertion can be viewed as one in which a unique reference is made, and some simple, non-ambiguous assertion is then made about this reference; for example, "Miss Jones, teacher of Grade 5B in Smith School, should stress phonetics."

It is not uncommon for a generalization or slogan to summarize other generalizations or slogans. But these sub-slogans or generalizations may be reducible to more specific assertions. For example, we may be told that the task of a liberal education is to liberate the student to freedom through discipline (a very general slogan). Asking what this means, we may be told that, in part, this includes "Emphasizing the Rational Faculties of Students" (sub-slogan). More specifically (or prosaically), we might find that a proposal is being made to give instruction in logic and semantics. The last, when given a unique reference, would constitute a particular assertion subsumed under the slogans stated.

Slogans and Generalizations: Differences

When slogans are used as summaries, they differ from generalizations in several respects. When we speak of a generalization we ordinarily mean a general statement that is itself a descriptive assertion and summarizes more particular descriptive assertions. Of course, we can speak of prescriptive generalizations, but we must add the qualification "prescriptive" explicitly, else the descriptive will be understood. But in either case there is agreement in logical form between the generalization and its particulars: if the generalization is descriptive, all of its particulars will be descriptive; if prescriptive, all prescriptive.

Educational slogans, however, *always* contain a prescriptive element. There is a very good reason for this. Since education is a practical enterprise, aimed at the achievement of certain results through action, the language of education will inevitably be studded with assertions that are prescriptive. These particular assertions will be proposals and recommendations for action. The slogan itself may even be in the imperative form (e.g., "Make Learning Meaningful for Students"). But even if the slogan itself is in the indicative form, many of the assertions summarized by the slogan will not be. For example, the slogan "Good Teaching is Meaningful Teaching" may be summarizing, among others, such *proposals* to teachers as "discuss the practical application of the ideas presented," "give students reasons for the rules they are expected to obey," and "use visual devices."

Slogans, then, that seem to be nothing but *descriptions* of practice to the extent that they are summarizing at all, end up summarizing assertions that do not merely describe educational practice but recommend, advise, exhort, hint, or suggest that certain educational practices should be followed and others avoided.

Let us look at the logic of this a bit more closely. When our foreign lecturer mentioned above says "education differs in the two countries," we realize in the context of his speech that he is summarizing what has gone before. Since his statement is not being used as a slogan and since it is in the indicative mood, we know that *all* the particular statements summarized by it will be indicative statements also (e.g., education differs in the two countries with respect to the average length of the school year). But contrast the slogan "Good Teaching is Meaningful Teaching." Although this assertion also has the form of an indicative statement, at the level of particulars it will be found to summarize not only descriptive statements but also, and more importantly, proposals for action. In fact, the descriptive statements and definitions it summarizes receive their relevance from their relation to the proposals. For example, in the context in which the slogan is used, perhaps an article in an educational journal, we might find the descriptive statement, "Miss Jones of Smith School reports a 50% greater enjoyment in the study of history by students who were shown films regularly in their history course." The point of this descriptive statement is to be found in its support of the proposal to the reader, "Use more visual devices in *your* teaching."

Slogans, then, may have one or more of these features usually not found in generalizations. (1) A slogan invariably summarizes, among other things, proposals for action. (2) There may be a disparity between the form or mood of the slogan and the assertions summarized by the slogan. (3) Slogans usually summarize assertions of differing logical types (descriptions, definitions, prescriptions), while a generalization does not.

Slogans and Generalizations: A Theoretical Explanation

Both slogans and generalizations may summarize particular assertions, but slogans summarize with much broader latitude than do generalizations. In explaining the differences, we wish to make two points: (1) Generalizations imply their particulars in a way that slogans do not; (2) Slogans are systematically ambiguous, in a demonstrable sense, until the systematic ambiguity is eliminated through a process of arbitrary delimitation of meaning.

(1) What we would call a generalization in common-sense or in scientific discourse can be said to *imply* a definite (or defined) set of particulars. Now this is no startling revelation, nor is it a statement likely to be contested on any philosophical grounds. Philosophers of different persuasions may wish to explain or interpret the concept of implication in different ways, but none would wish to deny that it holds between a generalization and its own defined set of particulars. In a perfectly straightforward, if not completely precise, fashion we may say that "all roses are red" means that if any object is a rose (thus defining a set of particular statements—"Object O_1 is a rose," "Object O_2 is a rose," and so on), then that object is red. The inverse square law of gravitation defines a set of particular statements—those describing the masses and distances of all objects in the same physical universe—and implies the existence of a certain accelerative tendency between any two such objects. The latter example should make clear, if the first did not, that a set of particular statements need not be finite in length nor even knowable in principle.

Now this last feature of generalizations makes it possible to speak of the meaning of a generalization as something over and above any limited set of particulars that are offered as evidence or explanation of the generalization. Thus we may say that the meaning of "all roses are red" is not exhausted by any finite list of statements like "the rose in John's garden is red," "the rose in Mary's hand is red," and so on. From this it is a short step to the Whiteheadian idea that the complete explication of (i.e., making explicit what is necessarily implied in) any true generalization must reveal the necessary structure of the universe.

This may seem far removed from the logic of educational slogans; and so it is. But its relevance is not far to seek. When pedagogical slogans are translated into complete sentences, they typically take the form of statements of the purposes, aims, goals, ends, ideals, or ultimate values of education, and these statements closely resemble generalizations. Hence arises the quite common notion that the proper way to decide upon practices in a concrete situation is to formulate generalizations of aims or purposes of education and to draw the implications of these statements for the particular situation. If slogan-like statements of purposes or ends were logically identical with generalizations, and, further, if it were possible to formulate true statements of purposes or ends, then this commonly accepted procedure would have much to recommend it.

Sad to say, however, neither of these conditions can be met. We can assert at this point what remains to be demonstrated just below: slogans and generalizations differ in *how* they summarize their particulars; slogans do not *imply* their particulars in the way generalizations do. Slogans merely become connected or attached to a more or less clearly specified group of proposals, together with definitions and empirical evidence used as argument in favor of the proposals made. (Therein lies the genius or horror of slogans, however you would have it.) Assuming the satisfactory demonstration of that point, it follows that seeking to find the particulars summarized by a slogan is logically a quite different kind of procedure from that of finding the particular implications of a generalization. Between the generalized slogan and its application to a particular case stands a somewhat arbitrary act of interpretation.

(2) Initially, slogans are systematically ambiguous. Consider, for example, "More Democracy in the Classroom," a sometimes popular pedagogical slogan. There is no limit to the variety of conceivable practices this slogan could be summarizing. Does it propose ability grouping within the classroom or not? Is a student government being recommended or a discussion of problems of democracy? The list could be extended indefinitely. Some proposals that might be made under this slogan will probably be inconsistent or, at least, incompatible with other possible proposals ("leadership by the teacher" or "more pupil planning"; "same instruction for all" or "vary instruction with ability"). This is what we mean when we speak of the *systematic* ambiguity of a slogan. A slogan that remains in this state is empty; it does not summarize. This is the sense in which we speak of a slogan as meaningless. Not that it has no reference, but that it is embarrassingly rich in this commodity. So to say that a slogan is meaningless is to say that no attempt is made (or that there is no other way) to restrict this great diversity of *possible* particulars.

Now let us pull together these two comments on slogans: that they do not imply particulars, and that they are systematically ambiguous. The two are obviously related, but we must note a qualification before stating this obvious relation.

Insofar as a slogan has the grammatical form of a statement, we may say that the slogan implies what the statement of its implies. For example, "Good Teaching is Meaningful Teaching" implies "for any X, if X is not meaningful teaching, then X is not good teaching." This is a valid implication from the statement. Or again, "All Teachers Ought to Transmit the Culture" implies "if Miss Jones is a teacher, then Miss

Jones ought to transmit the culture." But notice we did not say that slogans do not imply *something*; we said that they did not imply their *particulars*. The implications drawn from the slogans just above are quite clearly not the particulars, that is, not the proposals to teach one set of materials rather than another, by one method rather than another, etc., that we have in mind when we talk about what the slogan *summarizes*.

Now it is clear that the implications drawn from a generalization (descriptive or normative) exclude otherwise possible states of affairs. Thus it can*not* be the case that at the same time (1) all crows are black and (2) object F is a non-black crow. Therefore, the *acceptance* of a generalization is logically tied to the *denial* of certain possibilities. But, since slogans do not imply their particulars, to accept a slogan does not logically require one to deny any proposals for teaching. Thus when one accepts "More Democracy in the Classroom" he has logically denied "Less Democracy in the Classroom," but he still has a bewildering plethora of possible particulars not excluded by his acceptance of the slogan. For non-ceremonial (informative, directive) purposes, a slogan left in this state is useless.

Slogans and Their Interpretations

But slogans need not remain in such a useless state. Slogans may come to summarize some definite set of particulars. That is, in our term, it can come to acquire an *interpretation*.[4] For we can reduce the initial systematic ambiguity of a slogan by *deliberately* restricting or delimiting its application to some limited set of proposals within the larger amorphous class. So from all the possible particulars a slogan could conceivably be used to summarize, the slogan is made to apply to some sub-set of them. Notice, however, that, when performed, this is not only a *deliberate* act but largely an *arbitrary* one as well.[5] Some person or group

---

[4] It might seem more natural to speak of the "meaning" of a slogan rather than employing the unwieldy term "interpretation." We do in fact quite often ask "What do you mean?" when we want someone to interpret their slogan, i.e., give us the proposals they are summarizing with it. But the question "What does this slogan mean?" can be asked for different purposes. It could be a request for its historical or sociological significance ("What has the slogan 'Child-Centered School' meant to the Progressive Education movement?"). Or it might be taken as a request for a personal reaction ("What does it mean to you?"). To avoid these and other possible confusions, we use the word "interpretation" to refer to the proposals or program a slogan is used to summarize, and "interpreting a slogan" refers to the act of elucidating (indicating, specifying) the proposals. This retains one sense of the question "What does the slogan mean?" while avoiding contamination with the other senses.

[5] There is a sense of "arbitrary" in which it means "without justification." This is not the sense of the term we adopt. Actually, there may be good reasons for any particular restriction of meaning, not the least of which is the act of delimitation itself. For this act reduces the slogan to manageable form.

We call the giving of an interpretation an arbitrary act for two reasons: (a) Language permits the interpretation but does not demand it as it does with generalizations. (b) It is always possible to give an entirely new interpretation to an old slogan even when the slogan enjoys a standard interpretation.

actually *makes* this slogan mean this or that kind of educational program. They *give* the slogan this interpretation. In a sense, they are legislating or establishing a rule for the interpretation of their slogan (or of *the* slogan when *they* use it).

This is the essential difference between generalizations and slogans. Those who make "Democracy in the Classroom" *mean* "more teacher-pupil planning" cannot claim to be drawing an implication. They are arbitrarily legislating one into existence (for they might have ignored this point and made it *mean* something else, such as "teaching the Constitution"). Suppose generalizations got their meaning through the same kind of arbitrary act. Imagine, for example, a basketball coach who refers to a roomful of boy and says, "All those boys are on the second team." We can legitimately infer that for *each* boy it is true to say that "he is on the second team." This is what it means to draw the implications from a generalization. But suppose the coach really did not want to include boys over six feet tall in his statement, though he neglected to tell us. This would be an arbitrary reservation (restriction), and we could not be expected to be aware of it. We could properly claim that he is misusing language or that on this occasion he is not using the assertion as a generalization at all. The fact that we can blame the coach for his use of language marks an important difference between slogans and generalizations. The arbitrary element is always present in slogans; it is not present (or should not be present) in generalizations.

This feature of slogans has the consequence that we cannot discover a slogan's interpretation by examining only the slogan itself. If some group asserts the slogan, "Teach the Structure of the Subject," they must explicitly inform us (or in some way let it be known) what educational program they have in mind. They must inform us what pedagogical practices are being prescribed and what proscribed with this slogan. There are two qualifications to this requirement. (1) It is not necessary for each and every detailed proposal to be made explicit. Vagueness, in the sense of incompleteness and lack of precision, may remain after systematic ambiguity is removed or reduced. (2) Logically, an arbitrary

---

To explain our use of "arbitrary" we must return to the difference between ambiguity and vagueness. The systematic ambiguity of a slogan is to be found in the range of linguistic expressions which it summarizes. The vagueness of a generalization is in the range of concrete objects to which it applies. In the latter case, for example, a court may have to exercise an arbitrary judgment in deciding whether "breaking and entering a building" applies to an act of forcing a latch on a chicken coop. But there is nothing arbitrary linguistically: If it is breaking and entering, then it is a felony. But whether the recommendation "Use more visual aids" is or is not included in the slogan, "Good Teaching is Meaningful Teaching," must be decided in a manner not determined by the rules of common sense language but by the preference of the user of the slogan. *In that sense,* it is arbitrary.

No one, of course, is required to provide an interpretation *de novo* each time he uses a slogan. Indeed, to the extent that a person wishes to take advantage of well known programs, he is not even permitted to. The logic is seen more clearly in simpler cases when it is possible to identify one man with one interpretation. See section on *Slogan Systems*, pp. 273–280.

act of delimitation has to occur, but there are different ways of conduct-ing it; that is, there are different procedures for reducing systematic ambiguity.

(1) As noted above, the difficulty we encounter when dealing in slo-gans is discovering the educational proposals some slogan is being made to summarize. From a larger array (or disarray) of possibilities a selec-tion must be made. But this does not require that a complete detailed list of precise proposals be given. It is usually acceptable if some indica-tion is given of the *kind* of educational program that is being proffered. Though this will probably be done by giving actual sample proposals embraced by the program, the proposals may lack precision, and the entire program may never be completely specified. Thus, under the same slogan, "Produce Students Who Think," one person may indicate an educational program wherein "the basic disciplines are rigorously taught." Another may author a program in which "significant social problems are exhaustively studied." Now, the programs have not been stated with any exactness; yet the systematic ambiguity has been considerably reduced. We now have a fairly good idea of the kind of thing that is meant by the slogan in each case. So the systematic ambiguity may be reduced, though a kind of vagueness remains.

(2) There are diverse modes of communication a spokesman may adopt to interpret his slogan. Of course, the usual procedure is to list some of the intended proposals. Or the sloganizer may indicate his in-terpretation by referring us to previous writings of his own or his col-leagues. Or he may attach himself publicly to some well-known public-school program. But some writers on educational matters eschew such procedures. A Broudy or a Ulich will indicate his meaning by a wealth of allusion. The very language they choose to present their views may suggest (by form and cadence especially) the kind of education they are proposing. This latter mode of presentation serves the additional purpose of attracting favorable attention to the interpretation being offered. Yet even in these cases the act of delimiting the usage of a slogan is precisely the legislative, as opposed to the implicative, procedure that has been pointed out above as the necessary condition for eliminating the sys-tematic ambiguity of slogans.

Slogans and Standard Interpretations

A mark of exceptional success in interpreting slogans is, without doubt, the occasion when others accede to or adopt it. Thus, custom comes to bless some slogans with a standard interpretation (though it is doubtful if this common awareness will ever extend down to the level of specific proposals). For example, educationists in general are aware of (if not always in agreement with) the proposals commonly sum-marized by the slogan "Education for Life Adjustment." This slogan has come to be a summary of the program expressed by the Ten Impera-tive Needs of Youth. (Note: The needs themselves are sub-slogans that probably receive various interpretations in practice.) The man who utters this slogan on some occasion, *to mean this program*, need not present an explicit interpretation of the slogan. He can assume, under normal circumstances, that his audience is familiar with the proposals being offered to school people.

Much of the accepted activity of educational debate and discussion is to establish and disestablish standard interpretations of certain slogans. Educators spend a good deal of time attempting to capture slogans for one set of proposals rather than for another. They try to get such adjectives as "vital," "democratic," and "creative" attached to one program rather than another. Perhaps the natural history of such a dispute might run somewhat as follows. A foreign country's scientific achievements lead many to want more highly trained scientific personnel than our schools currently produce. A rash of slogans appear as promissory notes for programs that will yield more such people than are currently available. Interpretation provides a few postulates; research (some of it of high quality, most not) is carried on in the interest of determining whether a given set of particulars in the program will produce people who have the skills required by employers. Then a contradiction appears: some of these new particulars are seen to be just those rejected in some rather well accepted slogan. So a reinterpretation of the older slogan (e.g., "Education for Democratic Citizenship") is called for, and usually provided. What occurs simultaneously is that certain administrators take the promissory slogans and provide their own interpretations for them in practice. At one time all these may be going on at once, and the uninitiated may find the controversy very disconcerting. This is one situation in which argument over words is not trivial. He who can successfully claim squatter's rights on, say, "developing the leadership potential of American youth" has gained a real advantage over the man who has to call his program "I.Q.-segregated training program for future military executives."

Of course, other educational strategy and tactics may be viewed as attempts to alter or even dissolve standard interpretations. Criticism is aimed at showing that some proposals should be added or deleted or revised. Continued debate on these matters may lead to the formation of different camps, each campaigning for a slightly different version of a slogan which once enjoyed a standard interpretation. "Traditional Education" and "Teaching the Fundamentals" seem to have suffered this fate, and it is probably no longer appropriate to speak of these slogans as possessing a common interpretation.[6] At least three claimants for the appealing "Basic Education" are currently disputing the title.

---

[6] The process of reinterpreting (or interpreting out of existence) certain summarizing assertions in education can be seen clearly in the contemporary public discussion of education. See C. Winfield Scott and Clyde M. Hill, eds., *Public Education Under Criticism* (New York: Prentice-Hall, Inc., 1954), esp. Chaps. II, III, and IV.

Résumé

The distinction we have drawn between interpreted and uninterpreted slogans tends to be irrelevant to an examination of the ceremonial use of slogans. For that use, however, we are not at all interested in the meaning of the slogan but solely in its emotive impact on the hearers. This laissez faire attitude is inappropriate, however, when slogans are used non-ceremonially. On these occasions a failure to maintain this distinction can result in abuses. Rugg's use of "future-centered education" is an example of such an abuse. The context (a textbook) calls for a slogan with some more or less definite interpretation. This is made obvious when educators are charged with *failing* to have supplied a "future-centered education." Rugg does not interpret his slogan, but without an interpretation there is no criterion of success; and without a criterion of success it makes no sense to speak of failure. A similar case is the administrator who gets support for his policy at *only* the slogan level. He may take this as sufficient warrant to engage in all kinds of *particular* activities never explicitly connected with the slogan. This, too, is an abuse of slogans. It comes from a failure to realize that when a slogan is used non-ceremonially, an interpretation is required.

Note that we do not require that a slogan be *completely* interpreted. There is a sense in which we do not know exactly what a slogan means until we know all the particulars (with specific time and space restrictions) summarized by it. But there is a difference between knowing what the slogan means and knowing *exactly* (in that sense) what it means. Let us therefore modify the rule announced above to read: *When trying to find the meaning of a slogan, seek its interpretation.* Corollary: *Never use a slogan in such a way that you encourage asking for its meaning without being prepared to offer an interpretation.* Corollary: *Do not change interpretations without giving clear, and preferably prior, notice.*

Perhaps someone might object that ours is an unwarranted application of the term "slogan." The objector might claim that this label is reserved for assertions that are uninterpreted and *only* used to arouse feelings. In the next section we apply the term to a body of educational writing that is renowned for its seriousness and austerity of purpose. It is essential, therefore, that we answer this objection.

Now, it is true that there may be a few people who persist in employing the term "slogan" to defame statements found in educational discourse. These people will no doubt be incensed at our failure to condemn sloganizing in general. But there are many general assertions encountered in educational writing and discussion that are neither descriptive nor prescriptive generalizations. The logic of slogans fits them. In educational psychology and methods textbooks they are often called principles or even general methods. Now when we apply the label and logic of slogans to them, we are not making an unwarranted extension of usage. We merely clarify an established practice. There are, for example, political expressions such as "Fifty-Four Forty or Fight," "Speak Softly but Carry a Big Stick," "Manifest Destiny" which are called slogans. Though these expressions quite obviously have a hortatory function, they do more than merely exhort. They summarize, but do not *imply*, a rather clearly specified program. This program includes *proposals* for what to do in the field of foreign relations as well as other assertions in the indicative form. Now these are the logical features of interpreted slogans as we have discussed them. These political slogans are the counterparts of similar assertions found in the educational literature ("Education is not Preparation for Life; It is Life"). Since they share the logical characteristics of slogans, why call them by any other name?

SLOGAN SYSTEMS
Analyzing Slogan Systems

Up to this point we have devoted exclusive attention to the isolated educational slogan and its interpretation. This approach seemed necessary in order to explain the distinctive logical characteristics of interpreted slogans. But in educational discourse, it is not the individual slogan that is of most significance; it is the slogan which, in context with other slogans, serves to unify a range of different proposals for education.

The activity commonly called "philosophy of education" (or its product, called sometimes by the same name and sometimes "theory of education") is in large part a matter of constructing and interpreting slogans. Customarily, one grand slogan—in which the fundamental "purpose" or "definition" of education is stated—is used to summarize many sub-slogans covering the accepted areas of educational activity. For example, consider Professor Ulich's statement, "Education, rightly conceived, is the process by which a growing person, according to his individual capacity, is prepared to understand himself, his relation to the universe, and to act upon this understanding."[7] This assertion, itself clearly a slogan in the sense of this essay, does not answer directly any educational questions. It does not propose that certain materials be taught to certain kinds of students under certain administrative conditions. Nor is there a standard interpretation for "rightly conceived education." But in Professor Ulich's own works and in those of his followers we see that this slogan summarizes more particular slogans which are interpreted by Ulich in such a way that systematic ambiguity is reduced to a minimum, and more importantly, those various sub-slogans have an interconnectedness that permits us to call the whole a slogan system.

In this sense a philosophy of education is literally a *system* of slogans. It is, indeed, the apex of educational sloganizing. In a well-constructed philosophy of education we find not only interpretations given for sub-slogans, we find also more general slogans which encompass

---

[7] Robert Ulich, *Crisis and Hope in American Education* (Boston: Beacon Press, 1951), p. xi.

the sub-slogans and give to the whole scheme an inner consistency and an outward charm.

The manifold advantages of a slogan system as compared with other forms of educational discourse can be seen clearly if we glance at two quite similar slogans, "The Objective of Self-Realization," as found in the 1938 statement of the Educational Policies Commission, and "The Principle of Self-Realization," as found in Broudy's *Building a Philosophy of Education*.[8] In the E.P.C. statement we have a congeries of slogans; in Professor Broudy's work, a system. In the former the interpretations of the slogan are crude, abrupt, disconnected. According to what we have already said, the E.P.C. has a perfect right to use this slogan to summarize such sub-slogans as "The Educated Person Knows How to Write the Mother Tongue" and "The Educated Person Knows How to Read the Mother Tongue." But the transition is neither smooth nor appealing.

In Professor Broudy's work, however, an entire language system has been skillfully developed just in order, or so it would appear, that the general slogan merges easily downward to the particulars he proposes and upward to still more general ethical and epistemological assertions. This slogan system enables him to relate the proposed changes in educational practice to the basic moral commitments and spiritual aspirations of his society. What appear at first blush to be mere metaphysical impedimenta actually function as quite useful baggage. A fully developed slogan system must necessarily cover a lot of ground; the metaphysical slogans, those of greatest generality, make it possible to take this journey in comfort.

But these advantages of a slogan system may be bought at too high a price. If we confuse the slogans with generalizations, if we try to argue the metaphysical assertions of a slogan system as if they had a meaning over and above their summarizing function, the price may be exorbitant. The most promising solution would seem to be the issuing of a general caveat to the users of slogan systems. If slogans are unavoidable in educational discourse, then we would do well to attend to the slogan systems; for in these we find slogans in their most useful form. But we must not permit the generalization form, in which we express well-developed slogans, to conceal from us their true nature. The slogans in a slogan system mean what the system's author interprets them to mean; or rather, the particulars summarized by the slogan system are those the system's author has decided it shall summarize. Any given statement within a slogan system may have a non-slogan meaning over and above its slogan function, but that meaning is ordinarily carefully distinguished (it must, in any event, be distinguished) from its meaning as a statement in a slogan system. This last injunction is nothing but common sense. If we have before us a statement such as "the school should promote self-

---

8 Educational Policies Commission, *Policies for Education in American Democracy* (Washington: The Commission, 1946), pp. 193–213. Harry Broudy, *Building a Philosophy of Education* (New York: Prentice-Hall, Inc., 1954), Chap. 3.

realization," and we are asked what it means, we know, if we are at all wise, to ask where it comes from, what is its context, before trying to explain its meaning. The meaning of a statement within a slogan system is determined by the interpretation of that system.

At this point an objection might be raised against the analysis of philosophies of education as slogan systems. Imagine Mr. B. raising the point in this way:

> Mr. B: "You say, then, that educational theories or philosophies of education are helpfully analyzed by the logic of slogans. The very general assertions encountered in these theories do not resemble generalizations, but slogans. And the specific assertions made in the same contexts are not descriptions *implied* by generalizations but proposals *arbitrarily attached* to slogans."
>
> "Yes, that is essentially correct."
>
> Mr. B: "But you know as well as I that we often charge people with misinterpreting or misapplying the theories of someone else. What could this charge mean but that improper implications have been drawn from general statements given in the theory? But on your account this is impossible. Since you do not admit the existence of an implicative track, how can you account for these implicative derailments? On your view, how can anyone ever misinterpret the intent or meaning of another's theory?"

This is a serious objection. We do in fact frequently speak of someone violating or misinterpreting in practice a theory invoked to justify the practice. Any analysis that is unable to account for misinterpretation is automatically suspect.

But Mr. B is mistaken in his contention that misinterpretation is an implicative fallacy. This notion that from a number of general statements in an educational theory, we deduce some specific statements is just another philosophical myth. Rather, misinterpretation is sometimes just what the name suggests—a "missed" interpretation. The practitioner might completely overlook the relevant specific proposals actually given somewhere in the context of the theory. But this is not so much misinterpretation as simply an error.

The occasion for misinterpretation arises when proposals are offered that go beyond those found in the theory itself. The interpretor develops additional practical proposals not given by the original author of the theory. In this sense the practitioner is extending the interpretation of the author's slogans. Since there is no strict rule dictating these extensions, how can we say that they are rightly or wrongly made? Though it is not uncommon to find the charge of misinterpretation leveled, there always is some difficulty in substantiating it. We *do* have trouble in deciding whether extensions of some theory are justified. The matter is not as simple as the "implicative model" would have us believe. We are rather generous in our appraisal of different interpretive extensions of the same root theory when these interpretations do not differ radically. Is it proper to interpret Dewey, a leading educational philosopher, as a supporter of the "planned curriculum"? Did he *really* have a strong social dimension in his theory? These are difficult questions, and we are quite willing to entertain differences of opinion over answers to them.

But if pressed to give a positive or negative appraisal of someone's interpretation of Dewey, how might we answer? Ultimately, the only test we have is whether the author of the theory himself would have welcomed this additional interpretation of his slogan. But, of course, when we charge someone with misinterpretation, we do not resort to this ultimate test. In deciding whether a person has properly interpreted some slogan in a slogan system, we take into account two aspects of the system. First, if the original theorist gave any interpretation to this slogan at all, we judge whether the later interpreter is giving the same *kind* of interpretation. Secondly, we judge the interpretation of one slogan against the backdrop of the other slogans (the "metaphysical baggage") in the system. Every teacher of philosophy of education has learned to fear the day when a student takes an isolated assertion from Dewey and offers the practical implications of it. Yet if Dewey's famous general assertions were generalizations rather than slogans, this procedure would be quite acceptable.

In principle, the process of judging whether a theorist has been misinterpreted is relatively simple. If Mr. X gives an interpretation of Dewey's slogan system, we ask whether Mr. X's interpretation is the sort of proposal Dewey would have included, given Dewey's slogans and the kind of interpretation Dewey himself gave them. *In practice*, of course, it is excruciatingly difficult to make such a judgment. But if it were simply a matter of checking a new proposal by whether or not it can be deduced from the theory, this difficulty would not make sense.

Mr. B, in raising this objection, has actually pointed to a major difficulty in the "generalization-deduction" model of educational philosophy. As it turns out, when we use the model of a slogan system, we can account for both the existence of misinterpretation and also the difficulty we encounter in judging whether a charge of misinterpretation is justified.

Appraising Slogan Systems

(1) Any student recently emerged from instruction in philosophy can recite the standard tests of a good "theory." Among other things, to be acceptable, a theory must be consistent, comprehensive, and parsimonious. That is, the constituent elements in the theory must be internally consistent, all the relevant "facts" must be accounted for by the theory, and this must be accomplished with the fewest possible number of basic terms.

These tests, of course, apply also to slogan systems; they do so, however, quite differently from the way they might be applied to a scientific theory. In dealing with slogan systems, these tests become simply convenient names for an indefinite number of challenges a slogan system might be exposed to. So when we say that a slogan system has passed these tests, we are not calling direct attention to any *particular* feature present in the slogan system. Instead we are attending to a whole assortment of features and indirectly reporting that the theory has either forestalled certain questions or has been able to answer them satisfactorily by adroit manipulation within the system.[9]

Thus, for example, under the label of comprehensiveness a slogan system might be challenged because it failed to make proposals concerning the emotional development of children or because it contained no provisions to help students prepare for careers in science. Such demands, however, vary with time and social context, and a mark of deficiency at one time may be a positive boon at another. These factors account for the difficulties one encounters in trying to specify, exactly, how much "ground" an educational theory has to cover to be comprehensive. These positive features are not easily identifiable, but we do know specifically that a theory is not comprehensive if we detect a certain particular and currently relevant deficiency.

Similarly with the tests of parsimony and consistency. Suppose a theory contained proposals aimed at refining the emotional responses of young children, constituting an interpretation of the slogan "Teach the Whole Child." We might question whether these proposals might not be better summarized under another slogan already included in the same system. In the name of parsimony, then, we would request that the theorist expunge all reference to "the whole child" in his slogan system.

A special difficulty arises when applying the test of consistency. The questions we ask of a slogan system under this label are not concerned, by and large, with issues of formal contradiction as the name might suggest. This may be part of the story, of course, but we mainly ask whether certain proposed practices are compatible with others on sheer empirical grounds even though no formal contradiction is involved. We might take account of this by construing the test as one of compatibility. For example, there is no formal contradiction between these two proposals: (1) Schools should focus attention on the great literary heritage of our civilization; and (2) Schools should provide essentially the same education for all youth. But for quite obvious reasons, the person who tried to act on both these proposals would find them incompatible.

Finally, it is important to note that none of these tests (i.e., the challenges they summarize) can be applied to slogans *per se*. This follows from the very nature of a slogan. Except in a very trivial sense, one slogan cannot contradict another, although their interpretations may conflict. It

---

[9] These concepts (consistency, comprehensiveness, and parsimony) are *defeasible* in much the same way as certain legal concepts ("voluntary") and ordinary concepts ("responsibility"). See H. L. A. Hart, "On the Ascription of Rights and Responsibilities," in *Logic and Language*, A. G. N. Flew, ed., First Series (Oxford: Basil Blackwell, 1952), pp. 145–66.

is amazing that such a number of critics overlook this very obvious point. It is not at all uncommon to find people who criticize slogans without paying the slightest attention to the interpretation or interpretations given to them in educational discourse. The critic feels perfectly free to give his own interpretation (which is legitimate) and then to criticize it as if his constituted the standard interpretation. A further analysis in these terms of certain writings on public education by people only superficially acquainted with educational discourse would be instructive.

(2) Some charges that might be leveled against a slogan system cannot be satisfactorily categorized by the three standard tests discussed above. For example, granting that some educational theory has a slogan covering the emotional development of children, we can ask whether this slogan has been sufficiently interpreted. But once again this positive sounding criterion, "a philosophy of education must be interpreted," does not demand a certain predetermined level of interpretation. We only require that present demands for specification be met. So this criterion, also, is simply a convenient general label for an assortment of specific questions that might be put to a sloganizer, specifically, in this case, questions concerning the systematic ambiguity of his slogans (e.g., "What do you mean by 'logical order of knowledge'?" or "What do you mean by 'adjustment to the universe'?"). We may say that a slogan system must be capable of interpretation, not already interpreted, to any level of specificity desired. The amount of interpretation required depends on how much is asked for. As long as the questioner will detail the actual conditions under which the theory is supposed to operate, the author or supporter of the slogan system must be prepared to offer practical proposals. But, as indicated below, he is unwise if he interprets in too detailed fashion within his general statement.

Finally we may test a slogan system against the criterion of attractiveness.[10] The theory must have the power to charm. For if it fails to attract

[10] In connection with this discussion, see Joseph Justman's plea for a new slogan system in *School and Society*, May 12, 1956. Jerome Bruner's *The Process of Education* (Cambridge: Harvard University Press, 1960) seems the most promising slogan system to appear in many years. Indeed this book represents an almost classic case of the natural history of a slogan system as discussed earlier, especially in passages like the following (p. 9): "We may take as perhaps the most general objective of education that it cultivate excellence [a most persuasive slogan-word currently]. . . . It here refers . . . to helping each student achieve his optimum intellectual development. [This is hoary but still effective.] Good teaching that emphasizes the structure of a subject is probably more valuable for the less able student than for the gifted one. . . ." Here not only are currently conflicting slogans reconciled, but the key word in the synthesis, "structure," has such a solid sound that one is not put off when regard is shown for the currently unfashionable less able student. If Mr. Bruner and his associates can provide the necessary interpretations of the slogan system when called on, they may perform a most valuable function, perhaps providing at least a linguistic basis for overcoming the "tragic" fragmentation between academics and educationists. *Cf.* Gordon B. Turner: "A Report on the Conference of the National Commission on Teacher Education and Professional Standards," *Newsletter* of the American Council of Learned Societies, Oct. 1960. This group also had a slogan, "New Frontiers in Teacher Education and Professional Standards," but they lacked a common slogan system.

serious defenders and critics, if it does not enlist disciples and opponents, it has failed as a slogan system. It may still serve some ends; it may be an interesting intellectual exercise or contribute proposals to other slogan systems. But as a slogan system its days are numbered outside of academic circles. Here, more obviously than anywhere else, it is apparent that a successful slogan system does not possess some one feature not found in other, less fortunate, theories. This single criterion is a label for a concatenation of features and the way they are organized. We might be asking about any one of these features by questioning its attractiveness.

Let us give attention to one component of charm. Confronted with a slogan system, we can always ask if it has the potential for growth and development. As indicated above, some theories may be over-interpreted to the level of stultifying detail. There is a strong presumption that over-interpretation reduces a slogan system's attractiveness. Such a system may not enlist creative minds to its camp, since it leaves so little working room for imagination. A little too much interpretation may be a dangerous thing.

At the practical level the situation is reversed. For whether or not teachers and administrators are actually influenced by the theory is apt to depend upon the presence of specific proposals. The slogan system must tell the practitioner what, where, when, and how to do something. In this requirement we have one goad to system building in education. The educational theorist finds himself facing a task that only the most imaginative and disciplined mind could complete successfully. The sloganizer must produce a system that is, at one and the same time, *vague* enough to attract theorists and sufficiently *specific* to direct the practitioner. No mean assignment!

The only appropriate response is a slogan system. The logic of slogans admits the richness, flexibility, and subtlety in using language that are essential to doing the jobs that an educational theory must do. The history of Western educational thought is a rich storehouse for those who wish to understand the logic of slogans.

As a criterion against which to appraise slogan systems, attractiveness may well be a general test embracing all the others that have been mentioned. For slogan systems do not die from explicit rejection, but through lack of attention. With theories, as with lovers, it is the little attentions that count. When the general slogans in the system fail to capture imagination, no longer command loyalty, and creative disciples fade away, the system dies. But the less general sub-slogans survive, become modified and temporarily involved with other systems. Some of the proposals attached to these sub-slogans become accepted tools in the teacher's repertoire regardless of theoretical commitments. After a time we even cease to speak of these as parts of slogan systems; they become simply good advice to teachers. Prospective teachers may be advised to organize their subject matter into units of study that have some degree of wholeness in themselves and also some point of initial interest and appeal to students, without the prospective teachers ever being aware of the existence of the systems of Kilpatrick or Morrison. Research is done at this level, testing the consequences when this advice is followed. But the stimulus to significant, imaginative research comes from the slogan system in which the proposal is temporarily housed, although the positive results of this research outlives, usually, the slogan system that inspired it. This is the level at which we can speak of progress in pedagogical knowledge. This advice accumulates and one can always criticize a slogan system for failure to include it or otherwise take account of it.

Toward Dialogue

Each age has its slogans. Here are some for the current epoch:
"Tell it like it is."
"Make love, not war."
"Educate for creativity."
"Black power for black identity."
If one were to apply the Komisar-McClellan test, it is apparent that some of these would not score too well on the scale of meaning. Indeed, all of them have a large "ceremonial" element. If they are summarizing assertions, we shall have to wait upon the fleshing out of the "particulars" to which they allegedly refer. Or perhaps, as Komisar and McClellan point out, these slogans are so rich in particulars that they cannot possibly restrict and focus the reader's mind on those particular particulars referred to.

One may wish to ask, though, whether the educational world is becoming more or less addicted to sloganeering. Is our new preoccupation with urban educational problems, the disadvantaged child, the ghetto ethic, merely ushering in a new batch of slogans? Or are American educators getting more sophisticated about the use of their "slogan system" language?

Further Readings

Archambault, Reginald, ed. *Philosophical Analysis and Education.* New York: The Humanities Press, 1965.

Komisar, B. Paul, and Jerrold B. Coombs. "The concept of equality in education," *Studies in Philosophy and Education,* 3 (Fall, 1964), pp. 223–244.

Macmillan, C. J. B., and James E. McClellan. "Can and should means-ends reasoning be used in teaching?" *Studies in Philosophy and Education,* 5 (Fall, 1967), pp. 375–406.

Mosier, Richard D. "From inquiry logic to symbolic logic," *Educational Theory,* 18 (Winter, 1968), pp. 32–38.

Peters, Richard S. "Must an educator have an aim?" in *Philosophy of Education,* ed. William K. Frankena. New York: The Macmillan Company, 1965.

Reid, Louis A. *Philosophy and Education.* New York: Random House, 1965.

Soltis, Jonas F. *An Introduction to the Analysis of Educational Concepts.* Reading, Massachusetts: Addison-Wesley Publishing Company, 1968.

5

Existential
Philosophy
in
Educational
Thought

Existential Philosophy

The history of philosophy could be described as a fairly steady progression from metaphysics to epistemology to axiology. Plato and Aristotle, who invented and established philosophy as a discipline, were preoccupied with ontological and metaphysical notions. They had theories of knowing and conceptions of "the Good," but in the end everything depended on their metaphysical designs, that is, on certain assumptions concerning the structure of ultimate reality. The influence of this ontological orientation lasted for a millennium and a half, coming to a kind of final, total summation in the massive work of St. Thomas Aquinas in the 13th century.

After that, from the 15th century to our own day, men began roaming the earth, poking at nature, and stirring themselves from the slumber of a very long night of sweet dreams about a world they finally realized they would never know. They put away metaphysics not exactly as "a childish thing" but as a project that did not seem to be providing useful returns for mankind on the move. From Copernicus and Galileo through Descartes, Hume, and Kant to Russell, Whitehead, and Dewey there has been a gradual but inevitable turning away from grand designs to the problems of knowing and understanding. It is too early to say, but perhaps science is the "final, total summation" of this epoch just as Aquinas' theology was the culmination of the metaphysical epoch. For science seems always to have the last word when we want to know something, and it could well be, from the philosophical historian's point of view, the climax and culmination of the epistemological "period."

Whether or not this turns out to be the case, we now seem to be moving into a third epoch. We want to know the world, but we also want to know ourselves. And when we turn to ourselves, we are not entirely satisfied with what science can tell us. There is in human existence a "fifth dimension," beyond space and time, which we are curious about but which does not yield to the conventional, canonical logic of science: the zone of human feeling, of wanting, desiring, purposing, and valuing. We are puzzled by the phenomenon of a sentient organism, man, with vast powers of knowing and comprehending at his disposal, yet still incapable of moving toward a more humane and, let's say it again, good life. We have knowledge, but the good seems as far away as ever.

There is no assurance, of course, that turning to problems of value will yield spectacular solutions. But we turn to them nevertheless because they seem to be the next order of philosophical business. We want to know not what being is, as the metaphysicians talked of it, but what human being is. Existential philosophy may be thought of as the initial probe in this direction.

In the selections to follow, an essay of my own provides a brief prologue to this discussion. Fernando Molina, working from Kierkegaard, explores the "category of the individual" from which much Existential thinking begins. Robert Olson expands this theme by considering "the anguish of freedom" and Existentialism's manner of dealing with it. Finally, Huston Smith investigates one side of a question we have raised earlier (see page 204 ff.) concerning the meaning of cognitive as against valuational statements. In short, what meaning, if any, does Existential language carry?

VAN CLEVE MORRIS

Existentialism as a Philosophy

Existentialism is a theory of individual meaning. It asks each man to ponder the reason for his existing.

As philosophies go, Existentialism may be said to be something of a "special case." Voiced a century ago by a tormented man, then ignored

From *Existentialism in Education* by Van Cleve Morris (New York: Harper and Row, 1966), pp. 1–5. Copyright © 1966, Harper and Row.

by an age of reason, suddenly springing to life out of the rubble of tragedy and crisis, Existentialism would seem to be a philosophy fit only for men and worlds gone mad. As a view of life, its career so far offers only the most questionable of credentials.

Søren Kierkegaard, the Danish theologian of the early 1800s generally regarded as the first major Existential thinker, was a man beset by public scorn and personal heartbreak. As a philosopher, he was an iconoclast in the classic tradition, trying, among other things, to erase the pretty diagrams which the Hegelians had chalked on the European conscience. In a stream of monologues and diary entries, published under thinly veiled and not very cryptic pseudonyms, he ridiculed the Grand Designs of the "system builders," preferring instead to record the struggle of a single individual questioning the meaning of his own existence.

The nineteenth century paid little attention to Kierkegaard. At least in the West, men were preoccupied with proving out the big systems by seeking truth in the outside world. Nobody was interested in the prattlings of a man searching for truth within himself. And it did seem, at the time, that the search for objective, scientific truth was indeed the right pursuit. For science *did* produce knowledge; it did, indeed, rationalize experience.

By the twentieth century, however, the Grand Designs began to collapse; like cardboard boxes in the rain, they quietly folded into grotesque shapes of irrelevance. Science, having promised so much, had not delivered. As a logic for explaining the world, it seemed helpless before the juggernaut of modern events. How, one might ask, can science and system rationalize an age in which men schedule two world wars in every lifetime and casually discuss, as just another problem in social affairs, the prospect of total human annihilation?

In this unlikely environment, Existential thought has finally found a place to speak. Becoming articulate especially in war-rent, post-Occupation France and in spent and beaten Germany, Existentialism has spoken the troubled thoughts of the bewildered, "cornered" European people. In drama and fiction, as well as technical philosophy, such writers as Martin Heidegger, Karl Jaspers, Gabriel Marcel, Albert Camus, and Jean-Paul Sartre have addressed the West's attention once again to Kierkegaard's question.

It is said that Existentialism is a philosophy of crisis, a theory of life and man particularly suited to our anxious time. But this can be understood two ways. If it means that Existentialism is the spiritual medicine which can quiet man's nerves and steady him for living in an age of peril, then it is certainly false. Existentialism is no analgesic. If Existentialism is a philosophy of crisis, let this be understood to mean that it is a *feature of* the crisis rather than a *shield against* it.

This is not, it must be said, a very promising note to sound. It explains, I suppose, why Existentialism's reception beyond the Continent has been so unenthusiastic. Imported into the United States over the past couple of decades, Existentialism has had to buck not only the happy insouciance of a fun-geared, thing-ridden society but also the more sophisticated notion that the experimental sciences and the positive logics have taken us philosophically as far as we can go, and that further discussion of the meaning of man in the world is useless and silly.

Existentialism therefore enjoys only the most precarious of reputations today. Many people, even intellectuals who presumably should know better, have the vague feeling that it is a new and somewhat illicit poetry concocted in a nihilist atmosphere on the Parisian Left Bank by intense characters who wear little beards. Some of our national magazines have depicted it as a movement of the Big No, the strident dogma of the beatniks, who have merely made a convention of negation and who parade their negativisms, in dirty sweat shirts and stringy hair, before the tourists in the coffeehouses of Greenwich Village and North Beach. Some people feel even more strongly about it, registering agreement with the Italian philosopher Guido de Ruggiero, who calls Existentialism "metaphysical pornography."

Yes, the credentials are dubious, the reactions unflattering.

It is difficult to counter this impression. But, strangely enough, the Existentialists feel no urgency to do so. Existentialism is not a missionary movement. It does not promise anything. Rather, it tells us what is at stake in the task of being human. Its one claim to our attention is its shattering candor, betokened in its starting ground rule: There is a real possibility that we live in a meaningless world. Are we, it asks, equal to the task of living in such a world?

Most people, Americans in particular, find this difficult to listen to. It gives them a spiritual headache, a dizziness of the metaphysic. They are disenchanted by a philosophy which seems so bleak, which declines to offer reassurance that man has a reason for being and that the universe is somehow "on our side."

This reaction can possibly be traced to places deep within the American psyche. It must be remembered that the American people, not discounting what individuals and minority groups may encounter, have never really known the meaning of tragedy. Spared the crunching boot and the 2:00 a.m. doorknock, lacking experience with violence and holocaust, twentieth-century style, never having known the feeling of the constant fear of death, the American people cannot be expected to share the mood and temper of those in other parts of the world for whom mere survival has become a deliberate daily project. This is, I suggest, the real significance of the word "tragedy"—not simply defeat and grief, but the pain of having to struggle to establish and certify one's own significance in the world. In this sense, the American people have not yet developed, in Unamuno's phrase, the tragic sense of life.

Americans approach Existentialism the way they approach an automobile accident or a train wreck—slowing down their own vehicle, stepping out, edging forward, repelled at the sight they see, yet attracted and pressing toward the vortex of suffering, peering over shoulders lest they miss something even more bizarre and gruesome, finally retreating like spectators from a stadium. And they will most certainly devour—to the very last paragraph—next morning's newspaper accounts of the smashup. At arm's length almost anything is mentally digestible!

So with this philosophy. A kind of intellectual train wreck, it has attracted a gallery of track-side curiosity seekers. If you, the reader, are in the gallery, may I greet you. At least you are not home reading the newspaper. And don't be in a hurry to leave. For here, at the scene of the crash, is where we can best carry on our dialogue. It is only when men are in the presence of extremity that they can best talk about the meaning of life. This is what Existentialism proposes to do: examine the meaning of human life.

As such, it is the kind of philosophy which addresses each one of us—you, the reader, and me, the author—in the most personal of ways. It asks us to ask ourselves what significance we can attach to our own presence in the world. This is a sobering assignment, and quite probably an unpleasant one, too. Yet, for all its unpleasantness, it is a task we seem unable to turn from. We are chained to this puzzle, the meaning of our own existing. And the surprise is that, as study continues and awareness grows, the unpleasantness slowly turns to a new and somehow deeper sense of what it means to be a man. If Existentialism must begin in agony, it is capable of issuing in exhilarating sensations of human power. It is these affirmative thrusts of the philosophy which have been too much overlooked and which shall therefore be accentuated in this discussion.

Because Existentialism asks the kinds of questions it does, its rhetoric differs from that of other philosophies:

Existentialism is more interested in particulars than in universals. It is more interested in trying to fathom the import of a single human life than in coming to some grand category which allegedly explains the "All" and the "One."

It discusses the subjective. And since the subjective is, in a manner of speaking, undiscussable, there is need to invoke the services of metaphor, allegory, and symbol.

It discusses the individual. Our response to it, yours and mine, is likely to be personal. Hence the conversational tone of this book.

One may reasonably ask just what the prospects are for a theory of education to come out of this unorthodox set of ideas. There *are* difficulties—admittedly. We are, for one thing, working from a very small library, a bookshelf maybe not even two feet long. Few Existentialist writers have taken up questions in what we have come to call the social sciences. Even fewer have ventured into a discussion of education. For another thing, and perhaps more decisive, in the field of philosophy we continue to work these days in the rigorous and unyielding climate of Anglo-American Positivism, a movement dedicated to the analysis of logic and language. Existentialism does not flourish in such a climate; the air is too heavy with p's and q's. Under analysis, Existentialist prose gets lost in a thicket of equations. But what is more disturbing is the Positivist contention that no prescriptions—for education or anything else—can logically be drawn from any philosophical position, including Existentialism. From an "is" there issues no "ought." What this dictum has to mean is that, logically speaking, philosophy is useless as a guide to conduct. Since this principle presumably applies to the philosophy of Positivism also, it would appear to be self-canceling. At any rate, I have chosen to ignore it.

Toward Dialogue

It may be true, as I suggest in this essay, that the American experience has not been sufficiently tragic to make Existential thinking viably understandable by the American mind. However, I may have spoken rather too soon.

The United States is rapidly building up a national inventory of tragic events. At the top of the list, of course, are senseless individual actions such as the assassinations of John Kennedy, Martin Luther King, Jr. and Robert Kennedy, all of which plunged the nation into paroxysmal convulsions of public mourning. Then there are the urban riots of the 1960's—the seemingly senseless burning, looting, and wanton pillage by city dwellers of their own neighborhoods. While all this has been going on, college and university students across the land have fomented in themselves such hatred for "the system" that their bodily take-overs of the nation's campuses call to mind newsreels of a few years ago showing Latin-American mobs turning over streetcars, a form of protest then totally mystifying to the American conscience.

Finally, the tragedy for which American history provides neither precedent nor clue: the slaughter and sack of Vietnam. This massive and brutal blunder in Asia has wounded the American spirit. We have achieved the ultimate tragedy: we have violated ourselves!

Are we then eligible? Have we caught up with the others in acquiring "the tragic sense of life?" Have we finally passed the test for insanity? Or will it take more to get "into the club?"

FERNANDO MOLINA

Kierkegaard: The Category of the Individual

---

*The individual is the category through which
. . . this age, all history, the human race as a
whole, must pass.*

SÖREN KIERKEGAARD, The Point of View

More than one hundred years ago, the Danish philosopher and theologian Sören Kierkegaard asserted, somewhat cryptically, that *truth is subjectivity*. Whatever debate has since arisen as to what Kierkegaard intended by this statement, the extent to which its presumed meaning has been influential in determining the form of contemporary existentialism is above argument. Furthermore, I suggest that the statement, if viewed against the intellectual background of the time in which it was set down, is clear and unambiguous in its meaning.

The intellectual background in question is the all-encompassing philosophical system of the German philosopher G. W. F. Hegel, which, as Walter Lowrie has indicated in his classic study, *Kierkegaard*, dominated the thinking of the intellectual youth of Copenhagen at that time, a group of which Kierkegaard was a member.[1] For the moment then, we shall concern ourselves with the notions of truth and subjectivity as they were developed by Hegel, viewing them as a point of departure for understanding Kierkegaard's statement that truth is subjectivity. Of truth Hegel says:

> In common life truth means the agreement of an object with our conception of it. We thus presuppose an object to which our conception must conform. In the philosophical sense of the word, on the other hand, truth may be described, in general abstract terms, as the agreement of a thought-content with itself. This meaning is quite different from the one given above. At the same time the deeper and philosophical meaning of truth can be partially traced even in the ordinary usage of language. Thus we speak of a true friend; by which we mean a friend whose manner of conduct accords with the notion of friendship. In the same way we speak of a true work of art. Untrue in this sense means the same as bad, or self-discordant. In this sense a bad state is an untrue state; and evil and untruth may be said to consist in the contradiction subsisting between the function or notion and the existence of the object.[2]

[1] Walter Lowrie, *Kierkegaard* (London: Oxford University Press, 1938), p. 78.
[2] G. W. F. Hegel, *The Logic of Hegel*, trans. Wallace (London: Oxford University Press, 1950), pp. 51–52.

In this passage from Hegel's *Logic*, the point to be noted as relevant to an understanding of Kierkegaard is the somewhat peculiar meaning which Hegel gives to the concept of truth. The definition of truth proposed by Hegel differs from that generally accepted by such modern philosophers as Bertrand Russell, for whom truth was once a correspondence between belief and fact.[3] On the basis of the passage cited above, it appears that truth for Hegel is an *ontological* notion; that is, truth is "in the ordinary usage of language" something ascribed to a *thing*, rather than to a belief or a sentence or a proposition. For Hegel, a thing is true if its character is in accordance with its notion, its essence or function. A *true* soldier is a man who is a soldier in the fullest sense possible; that is, he exhibits in his professional life all the virtues of a military man; his conduct *is in accordance with* the essence of soldiering. Moreover, and by way of making the transition from the adjective "true" to the noun "truth," we can speak of the *truth* of an individual as *the state of being in accord with* the essence of individuality, with what an individual *ought to be*.

In view of this analysis of Hegel's notion of truth, we can now partially clarify Kierkegaard's statement that truth is subjectivity by stating it in a less truncated form: the truth of the existing individual is in accordance with the notion of subjectivity.[4]

To this notion of subjectivity we now turn our attention, first examining Hegel's views on a related problem, the nature of the self:

> By the term "I" I mean myself, a single and altogether determinate person. And yet I really utter nothing peculiar to myself, for every one else is an "I" or "Ego," and when I call myself "I," though I indubitably mean the single person myself, I express a thorough universal. "I," therefore, is mere being-for-self, in which everything peculiar or marked is renounced and buried out of sight; it is as it were the ultimate and unanalyzable point of consciousness. We may say [that] "I" and thought are the same, or, more definitely [that] "I" is thought as a thinker.[5]

The significance of this passage to the present discussion can best be seen by raising the question of what, for Hegel, is the truth of the self; what character ought the self to have if it is to be in accord with its notion? The answer is not difficult to obtain; this passage leaves little doubt that the "I," the self, is *thought*. The "I" is conceived by Hegel to be a thinker. The existing person is identified with the thought.

The comparison of Hegel's conception of the self with Kierkegaard's approach to the problem of subjectivity is stated clearly and forcefully by Kierkegaard himself:

> The systematic Idea [of Hegel's] is the identity of subject and object, the unity of thought and being. Existence, on the other hand,

---

[3] Bertrand Russell, *The Problems of Philosophy* (New York: Oxford University Press, 1959), p. 123.

[4] The interpretation of this point opposes that of Walter Kaufmann. Cf. Kaufmann's *From Shakespeare to Existentialism* (New York: Doubleday & Company, Inc., 1960), p. 193 ff.

[5] Hegel, *Logic*, p. 48.

is their separation. It does not by any means follow that existence is thoughtless; but it has brought about, and brings about, a separation between subject and object, thought and being.[6]

What purpose is served by this insistence on the separation of subject and object in (human) existence? Kierkegaard, in his answer to this question, rightly points out that for Hegel the thought in question is not *someone's thought*, but pure thought, thought in itself. Yet the self *is* the thought; and this self is, as seen in the last passage cited from Hegel, itself a universal thinker *in general, not* a particular thinker. It is then easy to see why Kierkegaard is troubled by the fact that for Hegel "the existing subjectivity tends more and more to evaporate."[7] Whatever else may be at stake, Kierkegaard's main point here is certainly an insistence on the primacy of the subject, a subject who may or may not think but who certainly exists:

> The existing subject . . . is engaged in existing, which is indeed the case with every human being.[8]

In pointing up the contrast between Hegel and Kierkegaard on the truth of the individual, it is important not to overstate the case against Hegel in order to delineate Kierkegaard's conception of subjectivity. Rather, to see what, besides thought, the individual may possess according to Hegel, is to enable oneself to see the significant difference between him and Kierkegaard. My point is not that Hegel does not admit into the concept of the individual *subjective elements* such as volition and freedom, but that Hegel denies the *subjectivity* of the individual, if only by omission.

The relation that holds, according to Hegel, between the "I" and the subjective elements of the individual is illustrated in this short passage:

> What I have in my consciousness, is for me. "I" is the vacuum or receptacle for anything and everything: for which everything is and which stores up everything in itself. Every man is a whole world of conceptions, that lie buried in the night of the "Ego." . . . it [the "Ego"] is not a mere universality and nothing more, but the universality which includes in it everything.[9]

In the earlier examination of Hegel's views on the self, the self as thought is a universal, the same for different individuals. In the passage just cited, the relation between the self, a universal, and the particulars that constitute it is described by Hegel by means of the repeated use of metaphors of *containment*: the "I" is a *vacuum* or *receptacle*, it *stores* up things in itself, and these things are *buried*, and *included in* it. I submit that these metaphors of containment are not merely accidentally chosen by Hegel, but are related bits of evidence that Hegel is viewing

---

[6] Sören Kierkegaard, *Concluding Unscientific Postscript*, trans. Swenson (Princeton, N.J.: Princeton University Press, 1944), p. 112. This reference hereafter cited as *CUP*.

[7] *CUP*, p. 112.

[8] *CUP*, p. 112.

[9] Hegel, *Logic*, p. 48.

the individual by means of objective categories; that is, by means of general ideas borrowed from the world of *things* and *events* instead of the world of persons. But only persons may be subjects, may have subjectivity; it is to an awareness of one's own subjectivity that Kierkegaard would have us direct our attention.

There is also an element missing in Hegel's viewpoint. Is the self, for example *your* self, essentially a thinking being? Is a self primarily a *container* of various thoughts and feelings? If these questions can be answered negatively, Hegel's analysis of the self has somehow "left something out." My own use of metaphor here has to be clarified, for, in a sense, no-thing has been "left out" of the analysis. The Hegelian analysis cannot be completed by pointing to some other factor, there for inspection, needing only to be included in the formula of the self.

On the contrary, what has been "left out," subjectivity, could not possibly have been included, given Hegel's mode of approach to the problem at hand. A strange question may clarify what is meant by Hegel's "mode of approach." How could we characterize a situation in which a blind person were to serve as judge in a photography contest? The answer to this question must explain the obvious absurdity involved in trying to conceive of a blind person as judge of photographs; the answer must demonstrate in a logically forceful manner why the situation in question is absurd. Certainly the answer would be that the categories with respect to which a photograph is judged are visual categories; for example, contrasts of shades, balance of parts, unity of impression. Indeed, the pictures themselves are visual objects. We would say, then, that the categories with respect to which a blind person can make a judgment are simply not adequate to the task of judging visual objects; the blind person's *mode of approach* is such that he can never encounter the object which, in such a contest, he would be called upon to judge.

Thus Hegel approaches the analysis of the self with categories such as those with which he would analyze an object or event. But can the self be so approached? Is it a universal that somehow encloses or contains within itself a set of particulars? Or would it be less misleading to speak of the self as *living in* its particulars? Or, perhaps even better, as *unfolding itself* by means of its particulars?

A problem that these questions are intended to illustrate centers around the virtual impossibility of avoiding the use of metaphor in any attempt to discuss the self. In philosophy, especially in those areas of contemporary philosophy in which the meaningfulness of an assertion is held to be dependent upon its empirical confirmability, the use of metaphor is actively discouraged in favor of the literal employment of language. Language literally employed, however, is singularly ill-suited to deal with human subjectivity; it tends to *objectify* that portion of the world about which discourse is taking place. And, when we are seeking to describe a world of *subjects* rather than objects and events, objectification is tantamount to mutilation or destruction.

In brief, to the question, "What is subjectivity," there is no literal answer. Any hints, descriptions, explanations, or definitions can, at best, serve (1) to clarify what subjectivity is not, (2) to illustrate figuratively what some of its aspects are, and (3) to orient the questioner towards what might enable him to become aware of his own subjectivity. Clarification of what the subject is not we shall postpone until the discussion of Sartre, for whom the self is nothing; Sartre's paradoxical use of the word "nothing" will then also be examined. Our attention has been engaged in this chapter . . . on the figurative illustration of some of the aspects of subjectivity. The third objective, to bring about an awareness of subjectivity on the part of the individuals in his audience, is one to which Kierkegaard devoted much of his intellectual energy. Since, as noted above, it is virtually impossible to speak *literally* about human existence, Kierkegaard, to make his readers aware of existence, usually employed indirect communication; that is, he used such forms as journal, pseudo-diary, fiction, and religious polemic and commentary. Whereas in direct communication the importance lies in the objective truth which is communicated without regard for the manner of its reception, in indirect communication the emphasis is placed on the manner in which the thought is appropriated—received into the reader's subjectivity. For further illustration of the technique of indirect communication, the reader is referred to the works of Kierkegaard themselves, since the task of bringing about an awareness of existence is not a proper part of this study, which is a survey of certain aspects of existentialism rather than itself an existential essay.

According to Kierkegaard, not only is subjectivity the essence of man, but freedom and the responsibility that goes with it are the essence of subjectivity. This primacy of freedom in Kierkegaard's thinking is no doubt responsible for some of his exaggerations regarding it, exaggerations whose echoes are still found in Sartre. But the significance which this concept has for Kierkegaard can be put in an interesting perspective by again looking at Hegel. For Hegel, freedom is an attribute reserved ultimately only for God. Although Hegel writes that individuals achieve freedom by virtue of their participation in the state, a closer look at the *precise* meaning that this concept of human freedom has for Hegel reveals the meaningless of the concept. This meaninglessness of freedom, when freedom is attributed to individuals living in a state, stems from the fact that the freedom in question is defined by Hegel as the submission of the will of man to the will of God, for Hegel believed that the will of God takes the form of law in a state or nation.[10] God's will, manifested as the laws or *spirit* of a nation, is particularized, is *ingredient* in persons, but Hegel unambiguously states that it entirely dominates these persons from within. The individuals composing a nation take this spirit—which appears to them in the guise of a personal aim—as their true being.

[10] Hegel, *Selections*, ed. J. Loewenberg (New York: Charles Scribner's Sons, 1929), p. 387.

Thus, without any selective reflection, the person performs its duty as his *own* and as something which *is*; and in this necessity *he* has himself and his actual freedom.[11]

Thus in Hegel's conception of the ethical, one is free precisely when one is really not free. It is to thinking of this type that Kierkegaard's conception of the individual and of the ethical is a reply.

First, in speaking of the individual, Hegel had disclaimed knowledge whose aim was to detect the peculiarities and passions of men, which would ". . . lay bare what are called the recesses of the human heart." He continues:

> Information of this kind is, for one thing, meaningless, unless on the assumption that we know the *universal*—man as man, and, that always must be, as mind.[12]

We have already seen that Kierkegaard rejects this definition of man as essentially mind; he especially rejects Hegel's emphasis on what is universal in man, thereby giving preference to the existing individual:

> . . . for my task was as a humble servant . . . to provoke, if possible, to invite, to stir up the many to press through this defile of "the individual," through which, however, no one can pass except by becoming the individual. . . .[13]

Second, regarding the ethical, Kierkegaard bluntly states his opposition to the Hegelian misallocation of responsibility: the ethical makes everyone ". . . responsible for the use to which he puts his life. . . ."[14] Unlike the Hegelian, whose thought addresses itself to man in general, Kierkegaard chooses to remind us that we exist as particular men; and in contrast to Hegel's belief that individuals perform their duty because of the controlling immanence of God's will, Kierkegaard maintains that the individual's ethical reality is exclusively his own, realizable only by him.

For Kierkegaard, ethics is a task in which the individual neither receives help from the "world-historical" nor concerns himself with it, the term "world-historical" being Hegel's means of referring to those individuals whom God employs in shaping the course of history because of their sense for the "ripeness of the times." Kierkegaard's ethical individual is an individual concerned inwardly with his spirit, not with the course of universal history.[15] He sees in ethics the highest task encountered by a human being, the task of becoming subjective, of achieving the truth of man.[16]

---

[11] Hegel, *Philosophy of Mind*, trans. Wallace (Oxford: The Clarendon Press, 1894), pp. 119–120.

[12] Hegel, *Philosophy of Mind*, p. 3.

[13] Sören Kierkegaard, *The Point of View, etc.*, trans. Lowrie (London: Oxford University Press, 1939), pp. 130–131.

[14] *CUP*, p. 307, footnote.

[15] *CUP*, p. 128.

[16] *CUP*, p. 119.

Of central importance to the task of becoming subjective is the realization of decisiveness.[17] Although there is no decisiveness without subjectivity, neither can there be subjectivity without decisiveness. Hegel, on the other hand, by defining man as essentially rational rather than subjective, effectively eliminated human freedom from his world view. He was therefore unable to give proper weight to the factor of decisiveness in the makeup of the person.

The decisiveness that is rooted in subjectivity is not a *mere* decisiveness for Kierkegaard, however; there is a matter of *interest*, of passionate involvement respecting one's death, one's eternal happiness after death, and one's very existence.[18] The contemplative individual, the *purely* objective individual, neither feels the need for decision nor sees decision anywhere.[19] But for the subjective individual, an Abraham, for example, even the fact of a revelation involves that individual in a process of unending reflection regarding the source, the meaning, and the validity of the revelation. The point is that a revelation in itself settles nothing, and reflection, if unlimited by decisiveness, goes on endlessly and fruitlessly.[20] Sartre has cogently restated this belief for our own century by declaring that, from the point of view of existentialism, not even the existence of God would make a difference to a responsibly decisive individual.[21]

... man himself interprets the sign as he chooses.[22]

But decisiveness, even when passionate, still does not fully constitute the subject, for there remains the possibility that the subject's decisiveness might be exercised sporadically. One needs personal continuity, and such continuity, for Kierkegaard, is not a mere fact but an *achievement* on the part of subjectivity. This achievement requires that the individual not only arrive at a decision regarding a project, but also that he renew that decision to pursue the project.

This need for renewal of one's decisions obviously presents problems which we all recognize independently of any acquaintance with existentialism. But for Kierkegaard the role of this need attains heroic proportions because of the very fact *that* the need has to be met in order for the subject to attain personal continuity. Differently stated, there is no personal continuity *already there* to guarantee or even to aid the renewal of a decision. Thus a renewal can only be approached in dread. The recurrent emphasis in existentialism on the mood of dread or anxiety stems from just this absence of personal continuity, for the subject who seeks to constitute his personal continuity by renewal of a decision does so as

---

[17] *CUP*, p. 33.
[18] *CUP*, p. 51, p. 148; see especially p. 279.
[19] *CUP*, pp. 34–35.
[20] *CUP*, p. 35, footnote.
[21] Jean-Paul Sartre, "Existentialism Is a Humanism," *Existentialism from Dostoevsky to Sartre*, ed. Kaufmann (New York: Meridian Books, The World Publishing Company, 1951), p. 311.
[22] Sartre, "Existentialism Is a Humanism," p. 295.

a free individual, but free *in two different respects*. On the one hand, he is free in that he is *self-determined;* the choice and the would-be renewal of it are acts for which he alone is responsible. But, on the other hand, he is also free in that he is *indeterminate;* prior to his successful renewal of decision, there is no continuity, no fixity of self, to see him *with certainty* through the act of renewal of choice and pursuit of the original project. An individual who sees that his freedom—his choices—in the future is not now guaranteed enters a state of anxiety.[23] The concept of anxiety, which has achieved such prominence in many commentaries and discussions of existentialism, is undeniably important to the structure of existentialistic thinking, but too emphatic a discussion of anxiety tends to detract from what, I would suggest, is by far the more fundamental point. This basic realization, appearing in Kierkegaard and reaching its culmination in Sartre, permits freedom to be at once the *essential* characteristic of man yet not a *defining* or *delimiting* characteristic. Freedom is determinate as a *source* of spontaneity, yet it is indeterminate with respect to the *direction* that the exercise of spontaneity will take. Finally, and most important, freedom is not something we *have;* it is something we *are*.

Kierkegaard's commitment to so extreme a conception of human freedom, although developed explicitly in his *The Concept of Dread,* appears implicitly throughout the massive *Concluding Unscientific Postscript* in the many references to the *becoming* of the subject in time:

> The principle that the existing subjective thinker is constantly occupied in striving, does not mean that he has . . . a good toward which he strives, and that he would be finished when he had reached this goal. No, he strives infinitely, *is constantly in process of becoming.*[24]

Existence is a striving in time, a *venture*. Our task is not only to become subjective and to achieve the personal continuity of our subjectivity; it is also, for Kierkegaard, to *become* a Christian, a task made difficult by the paradoxical nature of the Christian truth, the appearance of an *eternal* God in the *historical* person of the Christ.

Too many discussions of this aspect of Kierkegaard's thinking, it seems to me, have been vitiated not by overemphasis placed on the task of becoming a Christian, but rather by underemphasis of Kierkegaard's insight here—an insight which obtains, to put it frankly, whether or not one is a Christian, and even whether or not one is religious at all. In Kierkegaard's position regarding the Christian paradox, especially as it relates to the significance of *the instant* (to be contrasted with *the moment* in the discussion that follows), there is a real contribution to philosophical thinking about the nature of time and time-consciousness, a contribution as valuable as those advanced by Kant and Bergson.

[23] Sören Kierkegaard, *The Concept of Dread,* trans. Lowrie (Princeton, N.J.: Princeton University Press, 1957), pp. 38–40, 55, 99–100.
[24] *CUP,* p. 84. Italics mine.

Stated first only in its specifically Christian guise, Kierkegaard's thesis is that the truth of Christianity which the existing subject must appropriate and then renew is, logically, an absurdity; for how can God, an *eternal* being, make an appearance in *time* in the person of the Christ?[25] How much of the substance of Christianity rests on the fact of there being meaningful relatedness between God in heaven, the eternal, and the Christ and men on earth, the temporal? But how can this relatedness possibly be conceived? For Kierkegaard it cannot, and in that fact rests the absurdity of Christianity:

> In my God-relationship I have to learn precisely to give up my finite understanding. . . .[26]

Kierkegaard's interest in the absurdity of Christianity lies strongly in the consideration that, if Christianity is absurd, then the truth of Christianity remains objectively uncertain. This uncertainty regarding the objective truth of Christianity makes faith (as contrasted with knowledge) possible, for without the element of risk in believing what is uncertain, there can be no faith.[27]

This statement of Kierkegaard's irrationalism indicates the questionable nature of a faith, the very meaning of which is absurd to human reason. I suggest, however, that the genuinely philosophical issue with which Kierkegaard is dealing here, an issue that continues to merit study, is his concern with the absurdity of Christianity *not* in its relation to the possibility of faith, but rather in its relation to the problem of time-awareness. This problem concerns the human awareness of a particular moment as having a significance that transcends the moment in question. This point can be developed by illustrating the difference between a *moment* and what Kierkegaard calls an *instant*.[28] In philosophy we often make the distinction between physical time, on the one hand, and psychological time, on the other. Physical time refers to the flow of events in nature considered without regard to the presence or experience of an observer; this is the time measured by clocks of whatever kind. Psychological time, on the contrary, is the time of the flux of one's experience. It is the time which passes quickly when we are happily engaged in an agreeable task, and slowly when our circumstances are not of so pleasant a nature. We can say of both of these types of time, physical and psychological, that they are composed of moments, units of time each capable of being viewed in and by itself.

Disregarding physical time, we can say that units of psychological time are not always capable of being exhaustively described if they are treated merely as self-contained units; some of them have the *significance*

---

[25] *CUP*, p. 188.
[26] *CUP*, p. 159.
[27] *CUP*, p. 182.
[28] What follows includes of necessity a great deal of interpretation of some often unclear points made by Kierkegaard in *The Concept of Dread*, pp. 73–83.

which qualifies them as *instants* in the generalized Kierkegaardian sense suggested here.[29] The moment of insight into a law of the universe by a Newton or an Einstein illustrates the difference between a moment and an instant.[30] Many moments may pass in the reflective life of a thinker, some slowly, some quickly. Then at one point in his reflection the person reflecting may *see* that a certain principle regarding the nature of the universe is true, or at least highly possible, on the basis of his reflections. This insight has taken place at one moment, but that moment, in virtue of the insight, is transformed, is different in a striking way from the moments that preceded it. For in that moment a truth about the universe, timeless in itself, has made its appearance, not just in the experience but in the understanding of an individual existing essentially, as Kierkegaard would say, *in time*. That moment of insight constitutes itself as an *instant* in virtue of its being not just "an atom of time," but also "an atom of eternity":

> Such a moment has a peculiar character. It is brief and temporal indeed, like every moment; it is transient as all moments are; it is past, like every moment in the next moment. And yet it is decisive, and filled with the eternal. Such a moment ought to have a distinctive name; let us call it the *Fullness of Time*.[31]

For Kierkegaard the instant is the moment of apprehending the truth of Christianity. But if, as has already been noted, the truth of Christianity is an absurdity, how then can the individual *truly* become a Christian, Kierkegaard's notion of the instant notwithstanding? The answer to this question brings together two of Kierkegaard's main theses in a somewhat unusual fashion. For, if *the truth of man is subjectivity*, inwardness, then the individual seeking to become a Christian has to maximize his inwardness. But what better means, for Kierkegaard, can there be for maximizing one's inwardness than by being passionately concerned with truth of Christianity, *if only because the absurdity, and therefore the uncertainty, of Christianity call for passionate concern in the absence of an objectively attainable truth?*

> Without [an intellectual] risk [regarding the objective truth of one's beliefs] there is no faith. Faith is precisely the contradiction between the infinite passion of the individual's inwardness and the objective uncertainty.[32]

Thus Kierkegaard's approach to the paradox that is Christianity itself culminates in a paradox; for if the individual is in the right God-relation-

---

[29] Only the extreme case is being illustrated here; it may be that in human consciousness all or nearly all moments are instants.

[30] Cf. José Ortega y Gasset, *What Is Philosophy?* (New York: W. W. Norton & Company, Inc., 1961), p. 21 ff.

[31] Sören Kierkegaard, "Philosophical Fragments," *A Kierkegaard Anthology*, ed. Bretall (New York: The Modern Library, Random House, 1946), p. 161.

[32] *CUP*, p. 182.

ship, in the proper state of intensified inwardness, he is *in truth* even if the object to which he is so related (the Incarnation) be itself false.[33]

This awkward conclusion on Kierkegaard's part (which has been the occasion for much well-deserved criticism of him) reflects a tension in Kierkegaard's thinking. He sometimes keeps the two main aspects of his thought apart; but at other times, as in his conclusion just noted above, they are merged with not always happy results. These two aspects, unless one's attention is carefully focused upon them, are easy to confuse with each other, and Kierkegaard's failure to keep them separated, or at least *explicitly interrelated,* is understandable. The two aspects in question are, first, the concern with awakening his audience to the true meaning of existence, subjectivity, and second, the concern with identifying the process of becoming a Christian with a certain mode of existence rather than with the purely formal acceptance of a certain set of "beliefs." Insofar as the task of achieving the true meaning of existence involves an emphasis on responsibility, decisiveness, passionate involvement, and risk, it is not unreasonable to grant that only an individual whose existence fully exhibits these characteristics could be said to be capable of truly becoming a Christian. But if the truth of Christianity is an absurdity and thereby unjustifiable, it is not reasonable to assert the reverse of this last point; namely, that only by becoming, or seeking to become, a true Christian can one achieve the richest possible existence. That the absurdity of Christianity makes the process of becoming a Christian a risky venture is true, to be sure; but so also are other tasks whose demands upon us are not without rational meaning or evidence.

My point here is that Kierkegaard's personal commitment to a form of Christianity for which no justification can be asked, although perhaps the dominant aspect of his thinking, reveals an unfortunately antirationalistic fact about Kierkegaard, the person. It is not, however, his essential contribution to existentialism, if by existentialism we mean responsible philosophizing regarding the truth of human existence. Kierkegaard contributes significantly to the development of existentialism when he addresses himself to his age, an age which has forgotten what inwardness signifies and what it means to exist.[34] Nowhere is this forgetfulness of existence more easy to see than in the behavior of a crowd, which, as Kierkegaard is quick to see and underscore, is really the behavior of *each individual* in the crowd:

> For "Crowd" is an abstraction and has no hands; but each individual has ordinarily two hands, and so when an individual lays his two hands on Caius Marius [an ancient Roman whose life was once spared when no one of his captors could steel himself to carry out the group's death decree; cf. Plutarch's *Lives*] they are the two hands of the individual, certainly not those of his neighbor, and still less those of the . . . crowd which has no hands.[35]

33 *CUP,* p. 178.
34 *CUP,* p. 216.
35 *The Point of View,* p. 115.

To be *part of a crowd* is to be in untruth; for Kierkegaard, truth, as we have already seen, lies only in the individual's existence and his reflection on it. That his own concern with the task of awakening the awareness of existence in his audience by means of indirect communication is developed within the domain of Christianity is interesting and important; it is not essential.

What is essential is the energy—and historically speaking, the success—of Kierkegaard's development of his thesis that *the individual stands alone.*[36] For Kierkegaard there is no *settled* human nature. There is no truth or revelation which is not an occasion for reflection regarding its validity or source. There is not even a personal continuity which man can simply take for granted. But there is insight into the uniqueness of human subjectivity, the spiritual development of which is not an object of presumption but of self-activity.[37] There is also insight into the fact that such activity on the part of the self is not essentially rational, but involves coordinately reason, imagination, and feeling[38]—and not just as three separate factors:

> The task is not to exalt the one at the expense of the other, but to give them an equal status, to unify them in simultaneity; the medium in which they are unified is existence.[39]

Toward Dialogue

Kierkegaard used to respond, when asked if he were a Christian, "No, I'm trying to become one," by which he meant that it was the wrong question to ask. The individual is not anything about which one can inquire what it is: it is not an is-ing thing. The individual is a phenomenon of becoming: not a "thing" at all, but an event, a "happening," a working toward meaning.

This is why, as Molina points out, Hegel always talked in absurdities about the self. He approached the self the way a blind man approaches a photograph; he discussed it as if it were a thing which could be examined objectively like a microbe under glass. Instead, the self is a phenomenon which has to be approached with altogether different kinds of awareness.

What blinded Hegel is the same thing that blinds modern science when it tries to understand human beings, a tendency to objectify the targets of its inquiry. But subjects can never be objects, or at least we will

---

36 *CUP*, p. 287.
37 *CUP*, p. 309.
38 *CUP*, p. 310.
39 *CUP*, p. 311.

never come to know them that way for, as Molina puts it, "when we are seeking to describe a world of subjects . . . objectification is tantamount to mutilation and destruction."

One is led to wonder, then, what sort of thinking is appropriate. If we are searching for understanding of the individual, what problems can we raise and what questions can we ask which in the answering will not destroy what we're trying to understand?

And what about the mode of our discourse? Molina reminds us that Kierkegaard always communicated indirectly through journals, diaries, and polemical commentaries. And we know that our latter-day Existentialists, Camus and Sartre in particular, often employ the novel and the drama for their message. But what can the ordinary person use as a medium of expression? How can all of us—you and I—better understand "the individual" in ourselves and how can we share this understanding with others?

ROBERT G. OLSON

The Human Condition

ANGUISH OF FREEDOM

The expression "anguish of freedom" may seem puzzling. Is not freedom something wholly desirable? The bafflement will be largely dispelled by fixing firmly in mind that the type of freedom before which the existentialist stands in anguish is not the ability to achieve chosen goals. If one has decided to be a doctor and is free to do so in the sense that there are no obstacles in his way (he has the money, a good medical school has accepted him, there are no other commitments which take priority, etc.), it would be silly to speak of anguish. But even with this qualification the expression may still seem puzzling. Why should anyone be anguished simply because he has the ability to choose? The wider the range of choice, the more possible lines of conduct from which the individual may select, the greater will be his sense of power and mastery. The answer to this last question is that "anguish of freedom" is a somewhat misleading expression. What is called the anguish of freedom would more accurately be called "anguish before the necessity of choosing." The anguish of freedom is really anguish over the fact that one *must* choose. And this is something that everybody can understand. Im-

From Robert G. Olson: *An Introduction to Existentialism* (New York: Dover Publications, 1962), pp. 51–57 and 86–99.

portant decisions affecting the entire course of one's life are rarely made without some form of mental distress; and it is a commonplace of contemporary social criticism that modern-day men try very hard to escape this form of distress by having others (the state, public opinion, or the corporation) make decisions for them.

This does not mean, however, that the anguish of freedom is to be identified with the mental distress which a responsible person experiences when he is obliged to make a crucial decision. The anguish of freedom arises only with the realization that one must always decide for oneself and that efforts to shift the burden of responsibility upon others are necessarily self-defeating. Not to choose is also to choose, for even if we deliver our power of decision to others, we are still responsible for having done so. It is always the individual who decides that others will choose for him. At times he may dull the awareness of his original and inalienable responsibility, but he can never wholly suppress that awareness. It will always be there even on the surface of consciousness as a vague sense of guilt or uneasy feeling of personal inadequacy.

The relationship between the anguish of freedom and the other two forms of anguish are subtle and complex. As already seen, the anguish before the here and now leads inevitably to the anguish of freedom. Since the individual is tied to a limited portion of space and time and since he is actively engaged in the historical process as a unique and irreducible factor, he must be free. For the existentialists freedom of choice means autonomy of choice, and autonomy of choice means undetermined choice. But what does it mean to say that man's choices are undetermined if not that he is a unique and irreducible part of the historical or social scene? If man makes history, it is because man himself is not made by history.

The relationship between these two forms of anguish also works in reverse. If man is free to choose, then he cannot merge with the whole of being. "Every choice is a choice of finitude," as Sartre says, since every choice involves elimination. The voracious appetite for being displayed by Spinoza and Hegel cannot coexist with respect for human freedom. If one chooses to be a doctor, then one chooses the world of a doctor. Everything about one's life—the source of one's income, one's daily work, daily surroundings, relationships with others, even the odors one breathes—has a particular character and will separate one from the world of those who have made a different choice. The doctor cannot see things *sub specie aeternitatis* without ceasing to be a doctor. His attention will have to be focused on individual human beings and their specific ailments.

The relationship between the anguish of being and the anguish of freedom is also reciprocal. In rough and general terms it can be put this way: To the extent that man is free, it is by his choices or decisions that the natural and social world becomes meaningful. A shivering lump of human flesh in the agonies of death means one thing for the doctor who has chosen to take a professional interest in it, but something very different for the man who has decided to call that lump of flesh his wife. It follows from this that in so far as a man is conscious of his freedom, his natural and social environment will take on the character of a brute fact, something contingent, absurd, alien; for consciousness of freedom is also consciousness of the fact that meaning comes to being through us. In Sartrean terms the consciousness or anguish of freedom is the means by which "the world" dissolves and "being-in-itself" is revealed. Conversely, the consciousness or anguish of being is the means by which we take cognizance of our freedom; for it is only when the world dissolves and being-in-itself stands revealed to us that we understand the utter emptiness of our own being as persons in so far as we are not engaged in a process of choice, i.e., in so far as we fail to construct for ourselves a habitable world.

Of all the existentialists Sartre has most stressed the anguish of freedom. The manner in which he has developed the set of ideas connected with this form of anguish has, therefore, a special interest. Sartre's major antagonists are the Thomistic-minded Christians and the Marxists. For them, as for determinists of every variety, man is so made by God or Nature, as the case may be, that he automatically pursues certain goals. He has a given nature which determines him to realize certain ends. The motives of his acts are, so to speak, "ready-made and prehuman." According to Sartre, however, man freely chooses his own goals and in terms of his choice of goals confers upon the ready-made and prehuman whatever meaning it may possibly have. The determinist asks Sartre: If my action "cannot be understood either in terms of the state of the world or in terms of my past taken as something irremediable, how can it possibly not be gratuitous?"[9] Sartre counters by asking: If the world and my past are not understood in terms of my personally chosen projects, how can the world and my past possibly not be gratuitous? The determinist, in other words, says that man's life would be vain and meaningless if it did not have a place in an objective and meaningful scheme of things. Sartre says the universe would be vain and meaningless if man did not endow it with meaning by an unceasing act of choice.

It follows from Sartre's fundamental contention that "no state of fact, whatever it may be (political or economic structure of society, psychical 'state,' etc.), is by itself capable of motivating any act whatsoever."[10] He invites us to consider the case of the individual who revolts against certain bitter material conditions in his life. According to the common-sense point of view, in this respect similar to that of the determinist, these objective conditions constitute in themselves a sufficient cause for the action of the individual. But common opinion, if pressed, will recognize that the objective situation stimulates action only to the extent that the individual is aware of a better state of affairs in terms of which the actual circumstances of his life are seen to be unsatisfactory.

9 Sartre, Being and Nothingness, p. 453.
10 Ibid., p. 435.

In order to reconcile the recognition of this fact with the belief that external circumstances are sufficient to cause action, the determinist and the common man tend to explain the awareness of a better situation to be realized in the future as itself a strict causal consequence of the objective situation. Sartre, however, finds it necessary to "invert the common opinion and recognize that it is not the severity of a situation or the sufferings it imposes which give rise to the conception of another state of affairs . . . ; on the contrary, it is from the day we conceive a different state of affairs that a new light falls upon our misery and our sufferings and that we *decide* they are no longer tolerable."[11] In so far as man is a part of nature or "sunk in the historical situation, it will not even occur to him to conceive the defects or the insufficiencies of the given political or economic organization. . . . He grasps it in its fullness of being and cannot even imagine that it could be different."[12] The worker subjected to extreme hardship "will have to go beyond the objective situation and his suffering, to put a distance between himself and it and to effect a double nihilation: on the one hand he will have to pose an ideal state of affairs as a pure nothingness with respect to the present; on the other hand he will have to pose the present situation as a nothingness with respect to that ideal state of affairs."[13]

Resuming this argument briefly, human action is always to be interpreted as a reaction against an existing state of affairs and an effort to establish an ideal state of affairs. It implies both the recognition of a given situation as undesirable and the conception of an ideal situation as desirable. These two factors appear simultaneously, complementing one another; but neither of them can be determined by the objective situation in itself, since "no state of fact can determine consciousness to grasp it as a negative quantity or as a lack."[14]

In order to advance further into Sartre's thinking it will be necessary to introduce a bit of his technical terminology and to clarify his conception of man. Opposed to the being of fact or being-in-itself stands the being of consciousness, which Sartre also calls "being-for-itself." The choice of the term being-in-itself for objective fact is easily understood, since this region of being is merely a network of undifferentiated things and objects which point to no ideal value, which refer dumbly and meaninglessly to themselves alone. The choice of the term being-for-itself is also easily understood, since for the existentialists consciousness is fundamentally characterized by purpose or intention. As the names of these two regions of being indicate, they are radically opposed to one another. The in-itself has the properties of Platonic Being: its timelessness, self-sufficiency, and immutability. It is being par excellence. The for-itself, on the other hand, is a temporal being with all the properties of Platonic Becoming. Its existence is derivative and unstable. In the full sense of

---

[11] *Ibid.*, pp. 434–35.
[12] *Ibid.*, p. 434.
[13] *Ibid.*, p. 435.
[14] *Ibid.*, pp. 435–36.

the term it *is* not. It merely exists. Etymologically, the term "existence" means to stand out of, and to mark their close adherence to the etymological meaning of the term existentialists frequently hyphenate the word, writing "ex-istence" instead of "existence."

Despite the radical duality of the in-itself and the for-itself, man or the "human reality," to use Sartre's favorite expression, is itself made up of this duality. Whereas the in-itself is defined as a being "which is what it is," man or the human reality is defined as a being "which is what it is not and is not what it is." Man is, as the determinists say, an empirical being born at such and such a time and living under such and such conditions. In this sense, he is what he is. But in another sense man is not this empirical being living in a given situation, assuming a place in a chain of empirical facts going back to his birth or further. He is also a complex of desires or pattern of values which does not empirically exist, which empirically is not, since its factual being, if it ever has one, must await realization in the future. In this sense, man is not what he is.

It is important to realize that although the Sartrean definition of human reality is most definitely paradoxical, the paradox is largely verbal. It can best be understood as a forceful rhetorical device for illustrating the irreducibility of the distinction between the being of fact and the being of ideals or values and for emphasizing that it is man's fate to be simultaneously both types of being. It is especially important to bear this in mind in interpreting a second, but strictly convertible, Sartrean definition of man. Man, says Sartre, is a "nihilating nothingness." If again we follow the common-sense approach and take as the primary definition of being the being of fact, that is, the being which points to no ideal goal and which is simply what it is without reference to any system of values, then conscious human existence is pure nothingness; for consciousness is nothing more than a complex of desires tending toward the realization of an ideal state in the future. This ideal state of affairs being nonexistent, the desire or motive behind it is likewise nonexistent, the desire and its ideal value being but two aspects of a single phenomenon. "The motive can only be understood by its end, that is to say, by a nonexistent; the motive of action, therefore, is in itself a negative quantity."[15] But this nothingness of desire and of value, of motive and end of human behavior, can only exist for the individual in so far as he nihilates the being which he is, i.e., the objective situation and the conditions which constitute his being of fact, by posing a better ideal world in terms of which the objective situation and his empirical being are viewed as nothingness. In other words, to exist, man must perpetually transcend himself.

If this theory is correct, it necessarily follows that we must abandon all hope of attaining a secure and harmonious integration with the surrounding objective world. In desiring, valuing, and existing we necessarily

[15] *Ibid.*, p. 437.

reject the world in which we live. All projects which are turned toward acceptance of the world as constituted imply a diminution of our being and a loss of self-respect in so far as they tend to reduce the tension which constitutes the necessary condition of free human action. Freedom is a "lack of being with respect to a given being."[16] In technical language Sartre expresses this fact by saying that the human reality is a "detotalized totality" of in-itself and for-itself. Man is both in-itself and for-itself, but the two dimensions of his being are radically different. There is a deep rent in his being, and it will never be closed.

If Sartre's theory is correct, it also follows that "man is the foundation without foundation" of his values. "Nothing," says Sartre, "absolutely nothing, justifies me in adopting this or that value, this or that scale of values. As the being through whom values exist, I am incapable of justification."[17] The price of human existence is alienation—from God, from nature, and from society. Man is "condemned to freedom."

* * *

THE EXISTENTIALIST ALTERNATIVE

The existentialists answer the question "What can man know?" by saying that man can know the human condition. To the question "How can man know?" their answer is: by intuitive insight resulting from affective experiences such as anguish. To the question "What is the value of knowledge?" they answer that a proper understanding of the human condition is essential to the experience of existentialist values, the only values genuinely available to mankind.

The answer to the first of these questions is overly simplified and could be misleading. The rationalists say that man can know nothing but the eternal and the universal. The empiricists say that man can know nothing but matters of empirical fact and man-made a priori truths. The existentialists do not, however, say that man can know *nothing but* the human condition. Their position is rather that nothing but the human condition is ultimately worth knowing. They often deny that an alleged object of knowledge exists, and they often deny that the object could be known if it did exist. But the essence of their position is much more likely to be that even if the object existed and even if it could be known, the knowledge of this object would be without human significance. Existentialism is first and foremost an axiology, or theory of value.

Sartre, for instance, does not believe in the existence of God, and if he did he would certainly agree with Christian existentialists, who say that man cannot have an adequate knowledge of the divine nature. Yet, as he has repeatedly declared, emphasis should be placed upon the fact that even if God did exist and even if man could know God, nothing would be changed. Since man is free, he must choose his own values and

[16] *Ibid.*, p. 485.
[17] *Ibid.*, p. 38.

take upon himself the responsibility for his choice. He cannot shift this responsibility to God. The rationalist who says that knowledge of eternal objects is valuable because the good life in the world of becoming should be modeled upon the eternal objects has simply forgotten that finitude means freedom and that freedom means man must choose for himself.

Similarly, few existentialists have shown much interest in determining whether abstract ideas have any ontological status, and none of them has hailed the empiricist attempt to reduce Platonic Ideas or Aristotelian essences to linguistic conventions. Most often they simply ignore the problem, apparently allowing that abstract ideas do have some sort of being. Heidegger goes so far by way of concession to the rationalists as to house abstract ideas in a special region of being. The principal existentialist argument is that whether abstract ideas exist or not they are uninteresting and unimportant to the existing individual who has to make concrete decisions.

Again, the existentialists agree with the anti-scientism of the empiricists; even more than the empiricists they are prone to insist that the totality of being has no ground and that there is no pattern or system of order lying beyond what we directly observe which explains the visible sequence of events. But even on this point there are exceptions. Kierkegaard, for instance, declared that nature does exist as a unitary system, adding simply that the system exists for God alone, not for man who is tied to the here and now. And of the majority, who wholeheartedly reject monism and scientism, few show any great interest in tracing the implications of this stand so far as it concerns the status and knowability of laws of nature. Are laws of nature merely observed regularities among different kinds of things in the world? Or are they, Kantian-fashion, forms imposed upon a nameless and shapeless matter? Sartre and Heidegger lean strongly toward a Kantian interpretation, but it would be hazardous to say much more on the subject. All existentialists agree, however, that knowledge of the laws of nature has no human value. Television and automobiles have not made man happy, and the chief accomplishment of medical science has been to prolong senility. Countries such as Switzerland, Sweden, and the United States with their high level of material prosperity and long average life span are also countries with an extremely high incidence of suicide, mental illness, alcoholism, and dope addiction.

The existentialist arguments against the behavioral sciences have a similar focus. The value of psychoanalysis has yet to be proved; no satisfactory study has yet been made showing that the rate of recovery for persons treated on the couch is higher than the rate of recovery among persons with similar ailments who have received no treatment at all. Experimental psychologists have successfully predicted the behavior of rats and of certain types of human behavior closely resembling that of rats. Sociologists have successfully predicted which segments of the population are most likely to buy striped toothpaste or powdered coffee. But neither the experimental psychologists nor the sociologists have much else to show for their efforts. And so on down the line of the behavioral sciences.

To be sure, the existentialists explain the failure of the behavioral sciences by asserting the necessary unpredictability of human behavior in so far as it depends upon choices of vital concern to the individual. If a sociologist can successfully predict the proper time and place to market striped toothpaste, this is only because the choice of a dentifrice is a matter of little importance and most persons are quite willing to allow that choice to be made for them. None the less, even here axiological considerations predominate over ontological considerations. The existentialist does not say simply that since man is free human behavior cannot be predicted. The existentialist also says that since man is free he ought to take consciousness of the fact and act in a manner appropriate to a free man. Specifically, this means that although freedom is inalienable, it is still possible for the individual to *choose* that his behavior be dictated by others, thus permitting himself to become a manipulable and predictable object for the social engineer. This kind of behavior is what the existentialists call "flight from freedom," an attempt to make life easy which succeeds only in depriving life of existential intensity. And it is their opposition to the flight from freedom, far more than their commitment to the ontological doctrine that freedom is ultimately inalienable, which lies at the source of their attitudes toward the behavioral sciences.

In sum, the proper object of human concern for the existentialists is not God, abstract ideas, laws of nature, or empirical knowledge of human beings. What man should strive to know is the human condition. And by an understanding of the human condition the existentialists do not mean knowledge of human history, of man's natural and social environment, or of the so-called laws of human behavior. An understanding of the human condition is rather a knowledge of certain general traits of human existence which remain the same in all ages: of man's contingency, particularity, and freedom; of man's fundamental aspirations; and of the basic ways in which the individual can relate to the world and to other human beings.

With regard to the means by which man can know what is worth knowing, the existentialists are closer to the rationalists than to the empiricists. It is characteristic of them to assert that the fundamental features of the human condition are "ontological necessities" which can and must be known a priori. Their language itself often smacks of old fashioned rationalism. In this connection, therefore, two problems arise. How does the method of the existentialists differ from that of the rationalists? And how can the existentialists defend their claim to know a priori certain necessary features of human existence?

Between the existentialists and the rationalists there are two important differences. First, for almost all rationalists intuitive insight is exclusively the function of the intellect; the passions, it was said, obscure the intellect. The existentialist, on the other hand, either denies that any sharp distinction exists between intellect and passion or else regards the latter as a condition for the successful operation of the former. The human condition is revealed to us in anguish. Second, almost all traditional philosophers regarded the acquisition of knowledge as an act of grasping or apprehending some external object. What is known lies outside the knowing subject, and in the act of knowing the individual comes into possession of the known for the first time. The existentialists, on the contrary, maintain that the insights delivered in the experience of anguish are merely a rendering explicit of a state of affairs in which the individual is himself deeply involved and that in some sense the individual already knows what anguish reveals to him.

The historical origins of the existentialist position are not easy to trace. Ironically, however, Plato himself with his doctrine of knowledge by reminiscence must be held partially responsible. A less distant source is St. Augustine, who held not only that God, the true object of human knowledge, is to be discovered in the inmost recesses of the human soul, but also that man can know the truth only if God first grants him the privilege of believing without understanding. Still nearer in time is Pascal, who said "the heart has its reasons which the mind does not know."

Whatever the sources, the logical connection between the view that knowing is an act of making explicit what we already know and the view that passion is a condition of knowing becomes clear when one remembers that for the existentialist what is known is the human condition and that the index of involvement in the human condition is passion or intensity. When the tendency to incorporate into one's very concept of a thing the necessary conditions of its existence is taken into account, one can also readily understand why some existentialists should prefer to say that passion is a mode of knowing rather than merely a condition of knowing. Wealth, for instance, is perhaps most properly regarded as a necessary condition of happiness, happiness itself being a subjective state of enjoyment or contentment. Many persons, however, do not bother to keep the concept of happiness as a subjective state rigidly separate from the concept of wealth. For them, wealth is not simply a condition of happiness; it is a part of happiness.

The sense in which we already know what is explicitly revealed in the experience of anguish is by no means clear. Through Freud the notion of the unconscious has become exceedingly popular in the twentieth century. When, therefore, the existentialists say that anguish merely makes explicit what we have in some sense known prior to the experience, the contemporary reader finds nothing exceptionally puzzling in this and almost irresistibly understands that what was already known was known by a kind of Freudian unconscious. This interpretation could lead to serious misunderstandings. For one thing, Freud's unconscious consists among other things of biological needs or innate drives, in which the existentialists do not believe. In the existentialist view what makes man go is not a set of innate drives or biological needs but free and fully conscious choices. Man is not driven by animal exigencies; he makes himself by his own choices. For another thing, several existentialists have denied the existence of the unconscious as an ontological entity. Sartre even argues that the concept of the unconscious is self-contradictory.

Is it then possible, without invoking the notion of the unconscious, to make sense out of the contention that we know what is revealed through the experience of anguish prior to that experience even though we have no explicit awareness of it? It would seem that we can in either of two ways.

One way in which we may know something without being explicitly aware of it is illustrated by the act of remembering. It frequently happens that one knows another person's name without being able to think of it. A second way is illustrated in certain problem-solving situations. It frequently happens that a person has present to mind all the ideas needed to resolve a problem on which he is working, that the solution is somehow there in his mind the way the conclusion of an argument is in the premises, but that he is unable to articulate the solution. In this case, as in the first, we often say that we know something even though there is no explicit awareness of it.

No doubt, these two kinds of situations have helped to give rise to the concept of the unconscious. Since one of the criteria of knowing is having explicitly present to mind and being able to articulate what is known, we tend to say that we do not know the name or the answer to the problem. But since there are other criteria of knowing which permit us to say that we do know the name or do know the answer to the problem, we introduce the idea of an unconscious. On one level of consciousness we know; on another level we do not.

There is no need, however, to invoke the idea of the unconscious to explain these situations. There is no more reason to believe that the solution to a problem is literally in the mind so long as we are unable to articulate it than there is to believe that the conclusion of an argument is literally in the premises. And the same remark applies to the name we have forgotten. The mind is not a box, and to say that something is "in" the mind could be a purely metaphorical mode of speech.

Since, therefore, many existentialists do not believe in the unconscious as an ontological reality, it would probably be best to interpret their doctrine that anguish merely makes explicit or fully conscious what we already know in the light of the above remarks. Their probable intent is to suggest that in the experience of anguish either facts which we have always known in the noncontroversial sense of "to know" take on a new significance and we draw from them their full logical conclusions, or else facts which we had known before are recalled. An example of drawing the logical implications of what we already know would be the anguish before the here and now. We all know that we are tied to a limited region of space and time; but how many of us have drawn from this simple item of knowledge the logical implications which the existentialists claim to have drawn from it? An example of recall might be the anguish of freedom. All of the existentialists insist that man can and frequently does conceal from himself fundamental facts about his being. We "flee" from freedom by refusing to focus attention upon it, by deliberately diverting the mind to other things. The anguish of freedom could therefore be produced by a simple act of recall.

How does the existentialist support his claim to have an a priori intuition of necesary features of human existence? According to the empiricist we can know nothing about mankind except by induction from particular instances of human behavior in determinate natural and social conditions. If in the past men have always behaved in a certain way in a certain type of situation, then one can infer with a high degree of probability that they will continue to behave that way in similar situations in the future. But no empiricist would admit that a universal pattern of behavior is an "ontological necessity" or that any pattern of human behavior can be known a priori.

It would be possible to present the existentialist argument by taking any one of the features of the human condition revealed in the three basic types of anguish as a basis of discussion. The issues will emerge most clearly, however, by considering the fact of freedom. The existentialist cannot and does not pretend to prove that man is free by logical argument or by empirical observation. Freedom, he insists, is a directly and immediately intuited fact of human existence, and the person who does not intuit it cannot be made to accept it by a process of reasoning. The existentialist, therefore, limits himself to showing that the empiricist contention according to which man is not free is itself incapable of rational demonstration, that if it can be known that man is not free this will have to be known by an intuitive insight of exactly the same character as the one by which the existentialist claims to establish human freedom.

Belief in determinism is closely associated in empiricist thinking with belief in the validity of the principle of induction. If, says the empiricist, two kinds of events have been uniformly conjoined in the past, then we have good reason to believe that they will continue to be conjoined in the future. If human beings have behaved in certain ways in the past, then they will continue to behave in the same way under similar conditions in the future. They are not free to do otherwise. What, then, asks the existentialist, is the status of these statements? What reason has the empiricist for believing them to be true? If he cannot present an argument for these statements he is in ńo position to criticize the existentialist for maintaining their contraries.

Since the time of Hume, of course, empiricists have recognized that the principle of induction and along with it the belief in determinism cannot be established by rational argument unless one invokes God to guarantee that the course of nature will remain uniform. And since they are unwilling to do this, they have usually admitted that there is no argument by which their position can be confirmed.

Hume's view was that man believes in the principle of induction and in determinism because he cannot help doing so, because it is psychologically impossible for him to do otherwise. To this the existentialist retorts by saying that if it were psychologically impossible for man not to believe in determinism then he would not be subject to the anguish of freedom, which in fact he is. Hume conceded that in the quiet of his study a man could imagine the course of nature not remaining uniform, but added that his doubts on this subject would be merely hypothetical and could not be maintained over any period of time. To this the existentialists reply that the anguish of freedom is a concrete fact of life from which no man ever really escapes.

The logical positivists and pragmatists have typically taken a different position. They claim, not that men are psychologically compelled to believe in determinism, but rather that men ought to act as if determinism were a fact. When they say that the course of nature will remain uniform or that men will behave in the future as they have behaved in the past, they are not asserting the truth of a factual proposition. They are rather exhorting us to persist in the search for undiscovered uniformities and to utilize the results of past scientific inquiry for the purpose of predicting and controlling future behavior. The grounds for so exhorting us are purely pragmatic: it is only by acting in this way that we may hope to contribute to human progress. Here, too, however, the existentialist has a retort. How can the logical positivist or the pragmatist support his contention that by acting as if the course of nature would remain constant we advance the cause of human progress, without presupposing that the course of nature will remain uniform? If the course of nature does not remain uniform, then the results of past scientific inquiry will be utterly useless for the purpose of prediction and control and future discoveries will be equally useless.

Still a third position has been taken by members of the analytic movement. Many of them argue that the statement "These two types of events have always been conjoined in the past" is logically substitutable for the statement "We have good reason to believe that these two types of events will probably be conjoined in the future," in much the same way that "10" and "X" are substitutable. Rules governing linguistic usage decree that the person who asserts the former must also assert the latter, and vice versa. In effect, this is to make the principle of induction an a priori truth. "If two types of events have always been conjoined in the past, then we have good reason to believe that these two types of events will probably be conjoined in the future" becomes a statement of the same kind as "All bachelors are unmarried men." Most existentialists have never heard of this argument and would probably consider it beneath their dignity to answer it if they had. But, no doubt, if they did answer it they would point out that linguistic rules require a justification, and the only possible justification for making the principle of induction an a priori truth in the sense in which empiricists have analyzed a priori truths is that one first accept it as a statement of fact and that one believe in its truth in so far as it is taken as a simple statement of fact.

The upshot of all this is that the existentialist refuses to accept criticism from the empiricist, since he believes that ultimately the empiricist uses the very same method of intuitive insight he uses himself. And once the indispensability of intuitive insight in order to found a philosophical position is admitted, there is no reason to accept as correct only those insights required to found an empiricist theory of knowledge.

As remarked above, the case of the indispensability of intuitive insight could also be made out with respect to traits such as the contingency of being and the particularity of human existence. On the face of it, it seems absurd to claim that man's being limited to the here and now is a fact known by induction. On the contrary, this appears to be a fact which each of us knows immediately and directly; it is a condition of our making any empirical observations at all, not a fact established by empirical observation. At the same time, it would not be difficult for the existentialist to argue that the empiricist proof for the contingency of being based on their theory of knowledge is circular. If the empiricist did not know by intuitive insight that the whole of things is contingent, he would never have been led to adopt a theory of knowledge according to which only particulars and the relationships between particulars can be known. Since, however, empiricists and existentialists agree about the contingency of being and about human particularity, there is no compelling reason to go into these matters.

There is, however, one further point which does require consideration. If the empiricists' fundamental "intuitions" are correct, then any trait of human existence which could be established by induction can only be established by induction. Heidegger, for instance, claims that death is an ontological necessity, but since there is no reason to say that mortality as a fact of human existence could only be established by intuitive insight, the empiricist will have to deny Heidegger's claim. The empiricist does not, of course, believe that someday man will become immortal; there are very good inductive grounds for asserting the contrary. Nor does he object strongly, if at all, to listing mortality among the defining properties of man. The issue is how and with what degree of certainty we can know that the objective property of mortality characterizing the beings presently denoted by the word "man" will continue to characterize these or similar beings in the future. Heidegger claims to know this with absolute certainty by intuitive insight. The empiricist asserts that we know it by induction from particular instances and that our knowledge of this fact, as of all matters of fact, is probable. The degree of probability is so high that for all practical purposes no harm is done by claiming complete certainty. Still we cannot exclude a priori the possibility of man's becoming immortal unless we choose to define man as mortal. And if we define man as mortal, we are no longer asserting that man is mortal; we are simply resolving not to use the word "man" to denote immortal things. According to the empiricist, Heidegger has surreptitiously defined man as mortal and has illegitimately attributed to an objective state of affairs the subjective impossibility of imagining a being without the property of mortality whom he would be prepared to call man. A confusion of this kind would not be difficult to make, especially by philosophers who have little sympathy with Anglo-American philosophy and who have often not kept up with its latest developments.

Moreover, whether one accepts or rejects the empiricistic theory of knowledge, one must distinguish between the contention that certain issues must and consequently should be decided by intuitive insight and the contention that one may and should use intuitive insight to establish facts which could be established by other methods. Unfortunately, it is very common for a person who believes himself to have proved the indispensability of intuition in deciding certain issues, to feel himself justified without further reason to use intuition in order to decide any and all issues.

After this unavoidably long review of the major answers to the three questions raised at the beginning of this chapter, it is now possible to ask "Are the existentialists irrationalists or are they not?" Like the word "happiness" and its synonyms, the word "rationalist" and its synonyms have both a general and several more specific meanings. In the widest and most general sense of the term, a rationalist is one who believes that there exists some method by which those things which it is humanly desirable to know may be known. Now, if the existentialist ontology, epistemology, and axiology are acceptable, the existentialists have almost as much right to call themselves rationalists as either the philosophical rationalists or the empiricists. To the extent that they do not do so, it is largely because they wish to avoid misunderstandings due to the crowd of associations which have accrued to the term "rationalist" in the course of Western history.

The qualification "almost as much right" is owed to the fact that most of the existentialists, especially Kierkegaard and the religious existentialists, do not fully believe that a method exists for knowing what it is humanly desirable to know. The anguish of the religious existentialists stems in good part from their belief that God cannot be known. But even this qualification may be unwarranted; for if the universal existentialist conviction that life is fundamentally tragic is accepted, it would make as much sense to qualify the definition of rationalism as to qualify the existentialists' claim to the term. Why not define a rationalist as one who believes that it is possible for man to know whatever it is desirable for a being irrevocably condemned to incompleteness and tragedy to know?

The pragmatists have actually done something similar. To take a specific example, Dewey believed that rationality consists in the ability to adjust oneself to the circumstances of one's life, where by "adjustment" is meant either "accommodation," i.e., a kind of Stoic renunciation of impossible desires, or "adaptation," i.e., a transformation of the physical and social environment permitting the realization of desire. Where possible we transform the environment; where this is not possible, we accommodate ourselves to it. But according to Dewey, perfect adjustment is an impossible ideal both for the individual and for the race. The rational being does not attempt to create a paradise on earth, nor does he deceive himself into believing that he can be happy even on the rack. The rational man is one who attempts by a gradual and piecemeal process to eliminate the hardships of life which it is within his power to eliminate and to accommodate to those hardships which he cannot eliminate—but bearing always in mind that total adjustment is impossible.

Some persons, of course, would argue that the essence of rationality is a willingness to accept the elementary principles of logic and would refuse existentialists the title of rationalists on the grounds that they disdain these principles. In fact, however, the existentialists do not disdain the principles of logic. The existentialists do have a penchant for paradox, but almost all of their paradoxes are purely verbal. When Jaspers says that he who loves everybody loves nobody or when Sartre says that man is not the being which he is, neither of them is betraying the logical principle of contradiction. They are merely expressing themselves in a rhetorically arresting manner.

The closest one comes to genuine logical paradoxes in the whole of existentialist literature is in the elaboration of the Christian existentialist doctrine of faith. For the empiricists faith means a willingness to act on the basis of probable knowledge. If one has good but not conclusive evidence that a friend is trustworthy, one nevertheless reposes faith in him. This kind of faith is in no sense irrational. For the traditional Christians faith meant belief in a proposition for which there is no evidence one way or the other, but which might so far as logic is concerned be true. St. Augustine and St. Thomas speak of Christian mysteries, but they emphatically deny that any article of faith contradicts reason. Faith is nonrational, but not irrational. Faith surpasses reason, but it does not cancel it out. The Christian existentialists, however, strenuously insist that Christian dogma, notably the dogma of creation, of the Man-God, and of the Trinity, do contradict reason. It is logically impossible that God be a creator, that he be both wholly divine and wholly human, that he be simultaneously one and three persons. Thus faith becomes belief in the logically impossible—or so it would seem.

In fact, Kierkegaard did occasionally define faith in this manner. But so long as he did, he insisted that he was not a Christian—that he was arguing for honesty, not Christianity. Nobody believes in the logically impossible. The logically impossible cannot be conceived, much less believed in. That was Kierkegaard's despair. He was a man who wanted to be a Christian, who wanted to believe in the absurd, but who could not succeed. He was merely the "poet of Christianity." The source of his despair, it should be observed, was nothing other than his extreme respect for the principles of logic. The irrationality is all on the side of the traditional Christian who either ignored the essentials of Christian doctrine or refused to recognize the evident logical contradictions in those essentials.

Since, however, faith defined as belief in the logically impossible is a human impossibility, Kierkegaard more frequently used a different definition of faith. Faith became simply the desire to believe, intense care or concern for one's fate. "Faith," he says, "is precisely the contradiction between the infinite passion of the individual's inwardness and the objective uncertainty." At the same time Kierkegaard redefined religious truth. Religious truth, he declared, was not objective belief, but subjective passion. The savage who worshipped an idol with passion was in the truth, whereas the civilized man who worshipped the "true God" without passion was false. Nothing would be more illogical, however, than to take the Christian existentialists' redefinitions of faith and religious truth as evidence of illogicality. These existentialist redefinitions are a tribute to logic of the very highest order. They may also be a *reductio ad absurdum* of Christianity, but in this case Christianity, not logic, is the loser.

Toward Dialogue

One of the peculiarities of Existentialist rhetoric is its personal quality. It enunciates ideas, propositions, and theories which have their locus not in the outside world but in ourselves. Hence, to accept or even understand what Existentialists are talking about, one has to identify personally with what they allege to be the qualities of human living. One has to be able to say, "Yes, I've felt that way myself sometimes!" And if one is unable to do this, while reading an Existentialist tract, then there is very little possibility of dialogue.

Perhaps we should first consider the following ideas which Olson develops in order to see how each of us, as individuals, responds to them. In short, have you ever "felt that way"?

"The anguish of freedom is really anguish over the fact that one must choose. And this is something that everybody can understand."

". . . even if we deliver our power of decision to others, we are still responsible for having done so. It is always the individual who decides that others will choose for him."

As Sartre says, "I am incapable of justification." I am absurd. My presence in the world has no meaning. I *create* meanings.

". . . even if God did exist and even if man could know God, nothing would be changed." I would still have to choose how to live my life and take responsibility for living it that way.

Do you identify with these notions, or do they sound like a foreign language to you?

HUSTON SMITH

An Analytic Approach to Existential Meaning

Philosophers have been even more occupied with the problem of meaning than have psychologists or anthropologists. A recent review of the subject points out that "the notorious obscurity of the word 'meaning' [has] in the past two generations provoked almost every active philosophical thinker to seek some resolution of the concept into clearer and sharper outlines."[1] But the kind of meaning that has inspired this concerted attack differs significantly from the kind we have been speaking of. The philosophers whom the author of the above quotation has in mind (as evidenced by the ones he discusses in this book) are English-speaking, analytic philosophers, and the meaning that occupies this dominant Anglo-American school wears a noticeably different guise from that which interests anthropologists and therapy-oriented psychologists.

How shall we describe this difference? It seems to come down to something like this: Whereas anthropologists and psychologists have been occupied with man's concern for the meaning of *life*—whether life as a whole or specific situations within it—analytic philosophers have been concerned with the meaning of *words*. How completely the latter half of this statement holds is evidenced by the treatise cited in the preceding paragraph. Titled *The Diversity of Meaning*, the book was written deliberately to show "that any single theory of meanings. . . . is bound to do less than justice to the complexity of problems about meaning [because] there are . . . importantly different ways of talking about meanings and correspondingly . . . several important kinds of query about meanings."[2] But the diversity the author emphasizes turns out to be within a single camp. He is at pains to alert us to the varieties of *linguistic* meaning; nowhere does he deem it pertinent to remark—if indeed he allows—that there are kinds of meaning other than linguistic.

It has remained for Continental or existentialist-phenomenological philosophers to make this latter point. Thus, with respect to the problem of meaning, the Western philosophical world falls into halves. On the one hand are the Continental philosophers who are interested in the way meanings can inhere in life-situations; the kinship of such meanings to

[1] L. Jonathan Cohen, *The Diversity of Meaning* (New York: Herder and Herder, 1963), p. 24.
[2] *Ibid.*, pp. 105–106.

the kinds that interest anthropologists and psychologists is evidenced by the fact that "philosophical anthropology" and "existentialist psychology" are both Continent-originated designations. On the other hand, there are the analytic philosophers who consider meaning almost exclusively as a function of language.* Something of the feel of the difference between the two schools may come through if we juxtapose a characteristic sentence from each camp. In *The Myth of Sisyphus* the Continental philosopher-novelist Albert Camus writes: "Judging whether life is or is not worth living amounts to answering the fundamental question of philosophy. . . . I therefore conclude that the meaning of life is the most urgent of questions."[3] A comparatively representative sentence from the most prestigious journal of analytic philosophy reads as follows: "When philosophers attempt to say what a meaning is, they generally do so in the course of trying to make explicit what it is we say about a *word* when we specify its meaning; i.e., in the course of trying to analyze meaning-*statements*."[4]

Thus, with respect to the problem of meaning, the academic world presents us with a curious schism. Where we might most hope to find one world, in the world of the mind, we find in fact two. On one side are anthropologists, therapy-oriented psychologists, theologians, and existentialist philosophers who are on (or polarized by) the Continent and interested in philosophical anthropology. On the other side are linguists and most English-speaking or analytic philosophers. With due allowance for the vagueness of the phrases, the former may be said to be concerned with life-meanings, the latter with language-meanings.† No iron curtain divides the two camps, but a near-vacuum does. It would be too much to describe them as locked in a cold war, but essentially accurate to describe each as giving the other the cold shoulder.

* If one counts Soviet philosophy as Western, Western philosophy divides into thirds instead of halves. Until recently Soviet philosophy has not been much concerned with either life meanings or linguistic meanings. Officially committed to dialectical materialism as *the* scientific (and hence true) philosophy, it has dismissed all other philosophies and their special preoccupations as rationalizations of bourgeois mentality. Consequently, the recent publication of *The Philosophy of Man* by the Polish philosopher Adam Schaff (London: Lawrence and Wishart, 1963) assumes importance, not only generally as marking a thaw in Marxist philosophical orthodoxy, but specifically for our problem of meaning by arguing that Marxists must pay more attention than they have to issues the existentialists have been raising with regard to the meaning of man's individual and personal life. The book is a symptom of a small but growing movement which might be called Marxist existentialism. Its favorite Marx is the Marx of the *Economic-Philosophic Manuscripts*, who was concerned with the problem of alienation, and its representatives tend to be more interested in the quality of individual life than in tactics of ideological class struggle.

  ³ (New York: Vintage Books, 1955), pp. v, 4.
  ⁴ W. P. Alston, "The Quest for Meanings," *Mind*, 72, No. 205 (1963), 80.
  † This distinction corresponds closely to the one noted by Michael Polanyi in his *Personal Knowledge* (Chicago: University of Chicago Press, 1958), p. 58:
    "The distinction between two kinds of awareness allows us readily to acknowledge . . . two kinds of meaning. . . . We may describe the kind of meaning which a context possesses in itself as *existential*, to distinguish it especially from *denotative* or, more generally, *representative* meaning."

The factors that account for this split in interest among philosophers provide materials for an interesting chapter in the history of ideas, if not the sociology of knowledge. The chapter would pursue such questions as whether analytic philosophers may, consciously or unconsciously, have turned from life-meanings not only to emphasize philosophy's distinctness from theology to which she had been subservient for a millennium, but also because—what is less the case on the Continent—they have been largely ignored by men of affairs and left with students (relatively unversed in life) and one another to talk to. This could produce a vicious circle: shunned by those most involved with life, these philosophers might lapse into saying less and less about life, accepting the dominant feeling that life is not their concern and hence coming to deserve and justify this shunning. Simultaneously, English-speaking philosophers may have been attracted to linguistic meanings by the positivistic notion that philosophy's true function is to provide a language and logic for science, as well as the Englishman's native enjoyment of language in its own right.

But it is not history that concerns us here; it is the present and the impending future. Is it healthy for philosophy to remain divided between the entirely analytic and the entirely existential, or does the disjunction represent an updated version of Kant's "the empty and the blind"? Is it possible that America's contribution to philosophy in the balance of this century may be to capitalize on the virtues of both schools and move them into creative synthesis? Today not only philosophy, but humanistic education as a whole, stands in need of revitalization. The humanities must be opened to society-at-large as the Church was opened four centuries ago. Even on the Continent, where philosophers are (as we noted) in closer touch with men of affairs than are their counterparts in English-speaking countries, humanists are speaking only to men of letters, men still rooted in the genteel tradition. In the face of this under-relevance of the humanities as currently practiced, American philosophy may possess a unique asset in being less specialized than either British or Continental philosophy, for biology teaches that the least specialized species is the one most capable of radical advance. This suggests that American philosophy may be specially equipped for a new departure—a breakthrough into incisive relevance—if it should catch a vision of what might provoke it.

Meaning might be a good topic on which to test whether a creative union of talents now separated by the English Channel holds promise of such a breakthrough into heightened relevance. An obvious way for American philosophy to proceed with the test would be for it to accept Continental philosophy's contention that life-situations constitute legitimate referents for meaning and then bring its British-derived analytic techniques to bear in analyzing these situations and the meanings to which they give rise.

In addition to the possibility of breaking important new ground, such a move would bring to American philosophy, which today is predominantly analytic, two more specific benefits. First, it would provide proof—needed at this juncture—that analytic philosophy is essentially a method, not a doctrine (the doctrine that meanings inhere only in language), nor a preserve (the preserve of language analysis), nor an epistemology (which has only partially outgrown its positivistic past).

The second benefit can be indicated through some words from Abraham Kaplan's chapter on "Analytic Philosophy" in his *New World of Philosophy*. The chapter begins with compliment:

> There is no doubt that the broad philosophical movement which I am loosely designating as "analytic philosophy" is far and away the most influential one in the English-speaking world. In almost every American university, certainly in the British ones, philosophy has virtually come to mean just this kind of enterprise. For the younger generation of students of philosophy, at any rate, the ideas of this movement are thought to be by far the most exciting and promising.[5]

The chapter ends, however, with a criticism which for its pertinence merits quoting in full.

> If I had to express in one word the defect of character that I find in analytic philosophy, it would be *remoteness*—it simply is too withdrawn from so much that I feel to be so important. It is a bracing, antiseptic air, but too rarefied to make my home in. When Aristotle formulated his conception of God, the question confronted him of what God could conceivably be engaged in doing. The only activity that Aristotle found worthy of deity was what he and other philosophers were engaged in—namely, thinking; and the only subject worthy for God to think about was, naturally, thought itself. So Aristotle's God was endlessly engaged in thinking about thinking. With very little paraphrase—only replacing "thought" by "language"—this might be said of analytic philosophy as well. It is a noble enterprise, and indeed, there is something divine about it. But most of us, I believe, want a philosophy which is more—human.[6]

What more effective way for analytic philosophy to overcome its remoteness and become more humanistic than by turning part of its attention to analyzing meanings that arise directly from life-situations?

* * *

An airline hostess dreams that while waiting to board her plane a passenger kicks a hole in her suitcase; she asks her psychiatrist what the dream means. A couple driving home from seeing *The Seventh Seal* find themselves absorbed in discussing what the producer wanted to get across, what the film means. Anthropologists discover that primitive peoples in widely scattered areas bury their dead in a crouching position and wonder what this fact, too consistent to be dismissed as chance, means; since the posture is that of the infant in the womb, does burial

[5] (New York: Vintage Books, 1963), p. 53.
[6] *Ibid.*, p. 90.

in this position express hope for regeneration? A survivor writes of his months in a Nazi concentration camp: "The question . . . was, 'Has all this suffering, this dying around us a meaning?' If not, then ultimately there is no sense in surviving." In *The Adventures of the Black Girl in Her Search for God*, George Bernard Shaw writes that if a person moves through life "without ever asking 'What the devil does it all mean?', he (or she) is one of those people for whom Calvin accounted by placing them in his category of the predestinately damned."

Whether the meaning such persons seek to wrest from the life-situations in question has anything substantive in common with the meaning analytic philosophers find resident in words and propositions is not at issue. Suppose for the sake of argument that they have no more in common than the dual meanings of a pun; the present inquiry would remain unaffected. For we are not trying to compose a theory of meaning which will show analytic and existential meanings to be species of a common genus. Instead we are asking (at this point in the discussion) if there is any reason why analytic *methods* cannot be brought to bear on existential meanings—defined as meanings that arise directly from concrete life-situations—however close or removed these be from the verbal meanings on which these methods are usually employed. It would seem as if, sooner or later, analytic philosophy must be driven to the task by its own principles. For if, faithful to the later Wittgenstein, analytic philosophy is committed to trying to understand "the job words do," "the roles they perform,"[7] it seems only a matter of time before it must ask what job "meaning" does when men speak—as they repeatedly do—about the meaning of life and episodes within it.

The methodological principles of analytic philosophy are precise statement, rigorous argument, careful scrutiny of detailed examples, and suspicion of premature generalizations and oversimplifications. To suppose that these principles can receive even the beginnings of adequate exemplification here would be ludicrous; the difficulties inherent in the attempt to analyze existential meanings are enough to mock a lifework, to say nothing of an occasion piece. In tackling the problem one feels as if he were sitting down, not to a fabric to study its weave, but to a heap of knotted threads which would take hundreds of hands years to untangle even if the threads were not so brittle as to break at the gentlest touch. The most that can be expected from the present discussion is the drawing of several initial distinctions. But the limitations of the discussion can double for success. Insofar as its statements are imprecise, its arguments erroneous, its examples misleading, or its generalizations excessive, to just this extent will the discussion give evidence of analytic work that needs to be done in this area. Meanwhile, if anything constructive is achieved, it will support the contention that existential meanings are not in principle inaccessible to analysis.

[7] Cf. Ludwig Wittgenstein, *Philosophical Investigations* (New York: The Macmillan Co., 1953), p. 20. "For a *large* class . . . in which we employ the word 'meaning' it can be defined thus: the meaning of a word is its use in the language."

MEANINGS *WITHIN* LIFE AND THE MEANING *OF* LIFE: ATOMIC *VERSUS* GLOBAL MEANING

Analysis usually begins by identifying the major parts or features of its object. An obvious distinction with which to begin the analysis of existential meaning is the distinction between meanings that derive from specific situations within life as opposed to the meaning of life as a whole.

Suppose a young man who had planned to become a doctor were drafted for a role in a community theater production for no reason more far-reaching than that he seemed to be the type for the part. Suppose further that the response from the audience and the press was spectacular; that he turned out to have a talent not only far greater than that of the other actors, some of whom were contemplating the theater as a career, but also a talent that drew him into the enterprise to the point where he felt more alive than in anything else he had heretofore undertaken. It is easy to imagine that the man in question might assess the meaning of this experience to be that he should seriously rethink his vocational intent.

In doing so he may find himself reflecting on the meaning of life as a whole. Is its purpose to make money, achieve status, enjoy oneself, derive satisfactions deeper than enjoyment, contribute to the happiness of others? The relation of partial or atomic meanings (his brush with the theater) to global meaning (the meaning of his life) invites reflection. Is it possible to assess the meaning of any experience within life without to some extent appraising life's meaning as a whole? A recent book in the history of science argues that our scientific concepts have theories built into them to such an extent that to abandon a major scientific theory without providing an alternative would be to let our concepts crumble.[8] Does the same hold for existential meanings? Do our assessments of the meaning of specific life-situations have assessments of life as a whole built into them to such an extent that to alter one involves altering the other? Are meanings within life related to the meaning of life in ways analogous to the relation between semantic and syntactic meaning in language? We shall not pursue these questions. The point here is not to show how atomic and global meanings are related; it is to show that they are distinguishable and need at times to be considered separately.

INTRINSIC *VERSUS* EXTRINSIC MEANING

Epileptic seizures are preceded by a distinctive brain wave pattern. Electroencephalographic monitors have been built that trigger a buzzer when they register the pattern, thus warning the epileptic wearing the

---

[8] N. R. Hanson, *Patterns of Discovery* (Cambridge: Cambridge University Press, 1958).

monitor that a seizure is in the offing. The buzz *means* that a seizure is approaching.

Such meaning is extrinsic, for it derives from the fact that it points to something beyond itself. There are, by contrast, other meanings that are relatively self-contained, that refer primarily to themselves. An evening at the theater can be a significant, in the sense of meaningful, experience in itself; similarly, a day, a task, a friendship. The distinction is reflected in our language where "X means that Y" is idiomatic for extrinsic and "X is meaningful" for intrinsic meaning. The former bespeaks a transitive relation; the latter is intransitive, a suppressed reflexive wherein the subject is taken as its own object. As the suffix "-ful" in "meaningful" suggests, intrinsic meanings are self-complete. They indwell, each part referring only to what is present as another part. None refers to anything lacking, for nothing else is needed to make sense of the experience or episode in question. An experience is meaningful insofar as its meaning is fully filled (fulfilled) in the experience itself.

Although we are primarily engaged at this point in distinguishing different kinds of meanings, we interrupt for a passing observation about how they are related. Whereas atomic meanings can be either intrinsic or extrinsic—the presence of a boy on a basketball court could mean either that he hoped to make the team or only that he enjoyed shooting baskets —global meanings seem invariably to be intrinsic. Again, our language bears out the point. If someone were to say, "The fact that John got up in time to shoot baskets for half an hour before going to school [an atomic fact] must mean that he has decided to try out for the team," the sentence would sound completely natural. The "means that" phrase would *not* sound as natural if made to follow a global subject. To say, "Miller's life is (was) meaning*ful*," implies straightforwardly that Miller leads (led) a life of fulfillment. To say, "Miller's life *means that . . . ,*" would seem like a curious way to begin. If the point to be made were that Miller's life provides evidence for a conclusion distinct from that life itself—that the good die young, for instance, or that the evil flourish like the green bay tree—we would think it clearer to say, "His life *shows* that . . ."

Obviously, intrinsic meanings will have afterglows and other repercussions that spill across arbitrarily stipulated cutoff points. But this does not compromise the fact that their meaning is basically self-contained. The epileptic's buzz derives its significance from its relation to an occurrence temporally removed from it. Not so those experiences whose meaning is intrinsic.

ARTICULATE *VERSUS* INARTICULATE MEANING

There are meanings that can be stated in words, and others that cannot be.

As an indication of the former, we cite an autobiographical passage from Havelock Ellis' *The Dance of Life:*

It so chanced that at this time I read the "Life in Nature" of James Hinton. . . . Evidently . . . my mind had reached a stage of saturated solution which needed but the shock of the right contact to recrystallise in forms that were a revelation to me. Here evidently the right contact was applied. Hinton in his book showed himself a scientific biologist who carried the mechanistic explanation of life even further than was then usual. But he was a man of highly passionate type of intellect, and what might otherwise be formal and abstract was for him soaked in emotion. Thus, while he saw the world as an orderly mechanism, he was not content . . . to stop there and see in it nothing else. As he viewed it, the mechanism was not the mechanism of a factory, it was vital, with all the glow and warmth and beauty of life; it was, therefore, something which not only the intellect might accept, but the heart might cling to. The bearing of this conception on my state of mind is obvious. It acted with the swiftness of an electric contact; the dull aching tension was removed; the two opposing psychic tendencies were fused in delicious harmony, and my whole attitude toward the universe was changed. It was no longer an attitude of hostility and dread, but of confidence and love. My self was one with the Not-Self, my will one with one with the universal will. I seemed to walk in light; my feet scarcely touched the ground; I had entered a new world.

The effect of that swift revolution was permanent. At first there was a moment or two of wavering, and then the primary exaltation subsided into an attitude of calm serenity towards all those questions that had once seemed so torturing.[9]

This passage is not itself an instance of articulate meaning, but it points to such an instance. To Mr. Ellis' satisfaction, at least, the author of *The Life of Nature* had succeeded not only in catching a vision of life-in-its-world as luminously meaningful. He had succeeded in forging this vision into words.

What about meanings that cannot be verbalized? The basic fact to note is that they exist. Therapists (trying to help patients understand atomic meanings) and theologians and traditional philosophers (trying to understand global meanings) labor at articulating meanings directly; poets and myth-makers give voice to meanings indirectly. But direct and indirect articulations do not exhaust meaning's domain. There are meanings we sense but cannot say. When on the death of President Kennedy, his successor said, "We have a sense of loss too deep for words," he was not speaking in hyperbole.

Meanings fall away from words by degrees. At first remove are tacit meanings.[10] These are meanings we can sense, sometimes very vividly, without being able to put them adequately (if at all) into words. "There have been days at my home in the desert," wrote John van Druten.

days of an intense stillness, when the whole place seemed as though it were imprisoned in a crystal globe, bright with sunshine, murmur-

9 (Boston: Houghton Mifflin Co., 1923), pp. 215–217.
10 On tacit knowledge in general, see Michael Polanyi, "Tacit Knowing: Its Bearing on Some Problems of Philosophy," *Review of Modern Physics*, 34, No. 4 (October 1962), 601–616. Also his *Personal Knowledge*, Chicago: University of Chicago Press, 1958), passim.

ous with life: as though there were an invisible Presence standing on the threshold of one's consciousness, or of the garden—one was never quite sure which—so that one wanted to say, in a breath no louder than a whisper: "Oh, come in."[11]

Who could have said what this Presence was? There are meanings that move between lovers who understand each other without speech; meanings that settle over broken nations and vanquished leaders and all who have failed; meanings that come with age, too laden with experience to be intelligible to those who have not lived great regions of life. If we could give adequate voice to such meanings we would be poets, but if we were poets there would be deeper meanings we could not describe. For when depths are encountered, speech falters or grows dumb.

Farthest removed from articulation are meanings that exist without our being aware of them at all. The fact that there are things we know without knowing that we know them is an important recent discovery. Here are three examples. A number of nonsense syllables were shown briefly to a subject with certain of the syllables followed by an electric shock. Presently the subject anticipated shock on the sight of "shock syllables," but on being questioned he wrongly identified these syllables —clear instance of a knowing that influenced his behavior but of which he was unaware. A second example is from the work of Smith and Hendrickson.[12] They exposed the picture of a smiling face so briefly that it could not be identified, and found that unsmiling faces exposed (long enough to be identified) immediately afterwards were seen as smiling slightly. The third example is from the work of Hefferline, Keenan, and Harford. They seated subjects in reclining chairs and attached recording electrodes to various parts of their bodies, including their left thumbs, telling them that the study concerned the effects on body tension of static superimposed upon music. While the subjects relaxed and listened to tape-recorded music, the experimenters spotted for each subject a thumb position which occurred less than 20 per cent of the time. Thereafter, static was superimposed on the music except when the thumb was in that position. After an hour of such conditioning, subjects showed a marked tendency to hold their thumbs in these unnatural positions, thereby eliminating the static. But when interviewed, "all . . . still believed that they had been passive victims with respect to the onset and duration of noise, and all seemed astounded to learn that they themselves had been in control.[13]

Following Lazarus and McCleary, who coined the term "subcept" (as contrasted with "concept") to refer to things we know without

11 "One Element," *Vedanta and the West*, XIII, No. 4 (July–August, 1950), 104.
12 Smith and Hendrickson, *Acta Psychologia*, II (1955), 346. This and the preceding example are cited in Michael Polanyi, "Tacit Knowing," *op. cit.*
13 R. F. Hefferline and others, "Escape and Avoidance Conditioning in Human Subject without Their Observation of the Response," *Science*, 130 (1959), 1338–1339.

knowing that we know them[14] we shall refer to meanings that affect our lives but of which we are oblivious as "subceptual meanings."

These three levels at which meanings function—articulate, tacit, and subceptual—stand proof that meaning is layered, its strata lying at various removes from speech. But though the layers are distinct, no meaning need remain fixed at a given level. "Where id was, there shall ego be. It is reclamation work, like the draining of the Zuyder Zee."[15] We quote Freud not for his conviction that the more our psychic life becomes conscious, the better, but for his recognition that meanings can shift registers. Whether they are improved by being raised first to awareness and then to articulation we leave an open question. Sometimes they are, but not necessarily.

INDIVIDUAL *VERSUS* GENERIC MEANING

Viktor Frankl reports that when he was taken to the concentration camp at Auschwitz a manuscript ready to be published was confiscated from his pocket. In retrospect he is convinced that his wish to write this manuscript anew was a decisive factor in enabling him to survive the ordeals which proved too much for most of his fellow-prisoners, many of whom were physically more robust than he.

This illustrates Nietzsche's contention that "he who has a *why* to live can bear almost any *how*"; likewise Dostoevski's conviction that "the secret of man's being is not only to live but to have something to live *for*." But the *whys* for which men live differ. For Frankl it was to rewrite a manuscript; for a mother it might be to care for her child; for a Marxist it could be to hasten a revolution. Nor have we reached the limits of legitimate relativity when we admit this; we must add that meaning need not be founded on *any* sense of task. The world of the Zen Buddhist—the *sunyat*—is replete with significance, but this significance does not derive from any contribution the Zennist might make to it, for the *sunyat* is self-sufficient. W. T. Stace quotes a correspondent who felt likewise:

> I think I said to you that once my life was meaningless and that now it had meaning. That was misleading if it suggested that human life has a purpose and that I now know what that purpose is. . . . On the contrary I do not believe that it has any purpose at all. As Blake put it "all life is holy" and that is enough; even the desire for more seems to me mere spiritual greed. It is enough that things are; a man who is not content with what is simply does not know what is.[16]

Given a sufficiently important *why* to live for, man can indeed bear almost any *how*, but it does not follow that no man without a *why* (in

[14] R. S. Lazarus and R. A. McCleary, *Journal of Personality*, 18 (1949), 171; and *Psychological Review*, 58 (1951), 113.

[15] Sigmund Freud, *New Introductory Lectures on Psychoanalysis* (New York: W. W. Norton, 1933), p. 112.

[16] *Mysticism and Philosophy* (Philadelphia: J. B. Lippincott Co., 1960), p. 75.

the sense of a purpose extrinsic to immediate experience) can bear his *hows* equally well. People are different and the sources of their meanings differ correspondingly. What "rings a bell" for one may not for another, and the sum of one life's experiences are certain to add up in ways different from those of every other life.

Literary artists and biographers tend to be interested in meanings which vary from person to person and from group to group; their aims are achieved when they succeed in revealing the unique way experience shapes up inside a specific person or relationship. With comparable interests historians portray the meaning of a past epoch or historical personage. But interest in meaning does not end with such variegated depictions. In addition to the question of what life meant to Benvenuto Cellini or men living in Tang China, there is the question of the meaning of *life*—period—and of features it invariably embodies: time, history, freedom, sex, death, and the-world-as-life's-matrix. Originating as they do in experiences that men share, such meanings are generic as distinct from individual meanings that vary from person to person.

Toward Dialogue

Smith has argued strenuously that "existential meanings are not incapable of analysis" but what seem to remain, after the analysis is complete, are meanings—"life-meanings" he calls them—which are still essentially alien to the plain talk which the analytic philosophers have been urging on us for so long.

Take Smith's own language: "Meanings fall away from words by degrees." What does that mean? It is a metaphor. Through the illustrations which follow on page 323, we get a dim glimpse of what it signifies. But as language it is highly impressionistic, and unlikely to satisfy the criterion of verifiability which we met on pages 185–187.

Or, take a favorite phrase of the Existentialists—"existence precedes essence." It means that man is the being who defines himself. He has no a priori essence, no definition or "whatness" already waiting for him when he comes into the world; on the contrary, man exists first, then realizes that he must choose his essence, his whatness, by the way he lives his life. Now, what could analysis do with such a remark as this? It is one of those "global," "intrinsic," "inarticulate" meanings of which Smith speaks. Indeed, it is another grand metaphor.

But perhaps life is all metaphor.

Further Readings

Buber, M. *I—Thou*. New York: Scribner's, 1958.

Camus, Albert. *The Stranger*, tr. Stuart Gilbert. New York: A. A. Knopf, 1946.

Harper, R. *Existentialism: A theory of man*. Cambridge: Harvard University Press, 1948.

Kauffman, Walter, ed. *Existentialism from Dostoevsky to Sartre*. Cleveland: The World Publishing Company, 1956.

Sartre, Jean Paul. *Being and Nothingness*. New York: Philosophical Library, 1956.

Existential Philosophy in Education

As we mentioned in the Preface, the relationship between philosophy and education is always close. What philosophers set down as a program or attitude toward life naturally suggests itself to educators as a possible recommendation to the young: if science is the persuasion of the age, then let education be scientific; if culture is the medium by which man tries to civilize himself, then let education be "culture therapy;" if analysis of language is the only avenue to clarity of thought and effective human functioning, then let education be analytic.

When it comes to Existentialism, however, the passage from philosophical theory to educational principle is not so easy; there is no ready equivalent of the "if-then" statements offered above. All we have from the Existentialists is a stance, a posture, a way of "bearing oneself" toward the art of educating.

This, admittedly, is not much to go on, but perhaps it's just as well. Existentialists would not want to find themselves—in this book or in any other—the sponsors of a "philosophy of education" in the customary, school-of-thought, "ism" sense. To be so characterized would itself be proof that their message, whatever it is, had been misunderstood.

We owe it to them, therefore, to back off from drawing inferences from their thinking for educational policy-making or school practice. Instead, we are called upon to concentrate on the "bearing toward" educational work which is perhaps implicit, but never explicit, in their rhetoric. What would this "bearing" be?

For one thing, there is a personal motif which runs through Existentialists' language. Their words always seem to be addressed to one person at a time—to you the reader or to me, the editor. As noted elsewhere (page 286), if you cannot identify with an Existentialist idea from your own experience, it is possible that you don't understand it. When Existentialists speak or write, they seem to approach human beings as individuals rather than as members of a class. This tends to be unsettling; we are not used to being so addressed by philosophers. It requires a certain psychic adjustment. We have to listen not in the hope of acquiring some new cognitive truth, as with other philosophies, but in the hope of sharing some insight, some feeling, some moment's wonder about being human.

Is there a "bearing toward education" suggested by all this? Here again, one must somehow sense it without full understanding. We could say, for instance, that Existentialist ideas make it easier to comprehend the notion that teaching and learning is above all else a personal encounter, a dialogue not of cognition between minds but of feeling between subjectivities.

There is also in Existential thinking a summons to the normative. Where other philosophies have suggested ways of understanding and comprehending the world about us—nature, society, or language—this philosophy wishes to awaken us to the human career itself and how we as individuals interpret that career in our own lives. We are asked to worry less about whether the square of the hypotenuse is equal to the sum of the squares of the two opposite sides and more about what qualities of goodness we personally can bring into existence by the way we live. If man is the creator of value, if he is the author of the definition of Man, then the hypotenuse may bear certain relationships to its neighbors and we can be glad to know what they are; but when all such splendid truths are known, we realize that they are essentially trivial.

Teaching and learning is a process of growing, for both teacher and student. Growing, essentially, is growing beyond science, beyond culture, beyond language analysis to assume personal responsibility for the values we choose to live by. It is difficult; but since teachers and students are at the center of the growing process, this highest form of growth should never be absent from their relationship.

The following selections provide indirect access to the possible impact of Existential thinking on educational life. William Barrett explains Existentialism as derived "from concrete and everyday human experience." Martin Buber finds a theme in the "creative, originative" powers of the individual child. An essay of my own makes a comparison with Experimentalism in education and suggests that Existentialism may have something significant to add.

WILLIAM BARRETT

What Is Existentialism?

What is Existentialism?

This question had a lively and journalistic, though somewhat superficial, ring at the end of World War II when we first heard news of this philosophic movement from France. Nowadays Americans are asking this question with a great deal more earnestness and seriousness. As Americans, of course, with our inherited prejudice for plain speech, we tend to be suspicious of any big "ism"; and the label "Existentialism" seemed to suggest something eccentric or exotic or both. Many of us,

---

From *The Saturday Evening Post*, November 21, 1959, pp. 45 ff.

after all, had had our first news of this philosophy from some rather bizarre and Bohemian settings in Paris after the war. But these accidents of misunderstanding have now largely faded into the past; and in recent years Americans have begun to give serious attentions to this new—and yet very old—philosophy.

There are many reasons for this change in attitude. For one thing, we have just learned here that in Europe for more than the past twenty years a well-developed movement in existential psychoanalysis has been going on; and, further, that this movement, far from being the creation of Bohemian intellectuals, is headed by practicing psychiatrists, directors of hospitals, sanatoria and mental clinics. When healers of the mind have to go to a new philosophy for help in understanding human psychology, we, too, begin to feel that we may have more to learn from this philosophy than we might have supposed.

Another reason for this new and more serious interest is the continuing and mounting influence of modern art and literature. As we reflect more and more upon the strange and powerful art of the first fifty years of this century—upon the disturbing world of a Kafka or Joyce or the early Faulkner, or upon the baffling image, or lack of image, of man in modern painting and sculpture; as we search for ourselves and our time in all this art, we begin to find our life today riddled with more questions than we had suspected. And we also see that Existentialism is the one philosophy of this period that has raised the themes that have obsessed modern art to the level of explicit intellectual questioning.

The immense vogue of such popular works of social analysis as Riesman's The Lonely Crowd and W. H. Whyte's The Organization Man has led people to reflect uneasily about what is taking place in modern society. These books have one central theme: that modern mass society, while it raises the material level of all, tends to swallow up the individual in its intricate machinery. Modern society becomes a kind of bureaucratically organized flight from the Self; a flight into which everybody can easily drift. These criticisms, however, do not originate with our own social analysts; more than a century ago Kierkegaard inveighed against the depersonalizing forces of modern society far more powerfully than do Riesman and Whyte. The same line of critcism has been developed with great subtlety by Ortega y Gasset, Jaspers, Marcel and Buber. Present-day sociologists have provided some admirable documentation of the way in which these depersonalizing forces work, but they have hardly attacked the philosophical root of the matter. For this we have to go to the Existentialists themselves.

Finally, a simpler and more direct reason for this keener interest in Existentialism is the increasing number of translations of the existentialist writings. As we get more English versions of the books of Martin Buber, Gabriel Marcel, Martin Heidegger, Karl Jaspers, José Ortega y Gasset, the name of Jean-Paul Sartre no longer pre-empts the field; and we see that Existentialism is a basic movement among European thinkers, one that is neither peripheral nor faddist but central to our time. It becomes apparent that the body of the existentialist writings constitutes a commentary upon the human situation as rich and profound as any produced in our century, and that it would be folly for Americans to ignore it.

What, then, is Existentialism?

The question is relatively easy to answer; for the irony here is that, despite its portentous label, this philosophy derives from concrete and everyday human experience rather than from any abstract or specialized areas of knowledge. Existentialism is a philosophy that confronts the human situation *in its totality* to ask what the basic conditions of human existence are and how man can establish his own meaning out of these conditions. Its method is to begin with this human existence as a fact without any ready-made preconceptions about the *essence* of man. There is no prefabricated human nature that freezes human possibilities into a preordained mold; on the contrary, man exists first and makes himself what he is out of the conditions into which he is thrown. "Existence precedes essence," as the formula puts it.

Here philosophy itself—no longer a mere game for technicians or an obsolete discipline superseded by science—becomes a fundamental dimension of human existence. For man is the one animal who not only can, but must ask himself what his life means. We are all philosophers in this sense whenever we reach a point in life where total reflection upon ourselves is called for. Most of the time we try to avoid such occasions for total reflection by temporary expedients: we plug leaks in the ship without bothering to ask where it is heading. But if the problem is fundamental, expedients do not serve and we are faced with such questions as: What am I ultimately interested in? What is the point of it all? What meaning does my life have?

With these questions we become actively engaged with the problems of philosophy. The existential philosopher spends a lifetime asking these questions that assail the ordinary man only in unusual or extreme moments. One of the achievements of existential philosophers is that they have restored to the philosophical profession the true meaning of the latter word: a full-time vocation to which a man feels summoned or called. If the old saying that "Philosophy bakes no bread" has its point, it is also true that in the end we do not bake bread or in fact do anything else without a philosophy.

So much by way of a schematic answer to the question what Existentialism is. But Existentialism itself is opposed to schematic and abstract answers about human facts, which are always concrete, individual, situated in a definite place and time. Man is a historical being—that is his uniqueness among all other animals—and he can never be understood apart from his history. This is true of existential philosophy itself as a historical human fact. To understand it concretely we have to see where its roots lie in the history of modern thought and what urgencies of the modern spirit drive it onward.

The existential philosophers themselves have taught us to reread in a new and more profound way the whole history of modern thought. By showing us philosophy as an essentially human enterprise they have enabled us to see the whole history of philosophy for the momentous human drama it really is. Most of us tend to think of the history of philosophy as a succession of contradicting opinions held by rival philosophers or rival schools decade after decade or century after century. The dramatic parts of human history seem to be wars and battles, or great political decisions that change the external patterns of our lives. But for the Existentialist the history of philosophy is one of the most dramatic and fateful chapters in human history; the great philosophers, far from being mere airy speculators, are in fact the real prophets. Their thinking illuminates the problems that mankind as a whole, in its external and social history, will have to live out for generations.

Our modern epoch in philosophy—and with it our whole modern world—begins with the great French philosopher René Descartes (1596–1650). Descartes, who was also a mathematician and a physicist, wanted his philosophy to establish a basis for the then "new science" of mathematical physics. For this, the first step needed was to establish the solid objectivity of the world of physical things, and particularly those aspects of things that are quantitative and measurable and so can be expressed in mathematical laws. Hence Descartes declared that matter was essentially extension: that is, the real properties of any physical object are the quantitative ones. What about the qualities of things? They are declared to be merely subjective effects in the human mind. Here the world of the new science is no longer the ordinary human world in which we live. This qualitative world of our everyday life, with all the color, warmth and vibrancy of its texture, is thrust out of the real world and relegated to the human mind as a kind of shadowy specter. Such is the famous Cartesian dualism: the world of matter (objects) is split off from the human mind (subject). More significantly, it splits the human and the scientific worlds.

Today, we are still experiencing the consequences of this dualism. Descartes is a founder and a prophet of the historical era in which mathematical physics comes more and more to dominate the whole of human life. Today, when we tremble before the possibilities of atomic bombs and missiles, when the mathematical physicists and technicians are more important instruments of power than any military general, we need hardly be told that this Cartesian era of mathematical physics approaches its violent climax. But also, with all the human turmoil of our period, with its political unrest and individual rootlessness, we are aware of the skeleton that lurks in the Cartesian closet: our power to deal with the world of matter has multiplied out of all proportion to our wisdom in coping with the problems of our human and spiritual world.

Descartes could bear the consequences of his philosophy because in the rest of his person he was still a Catholic of the Middle Ages. Descartes the thinker was one thing; Descartes the man something else; although in Descartes' philosophy there was no place for the two to meet, in his life—for very practical human purposes—he had established a concordat between them by remaining a faithful son of the church. When he discovered analytic geometry, he promptly made a pilgrimage of gratitude to the shrine of the Virgin of Loretto. So too in his philosophy: however much the prophet of the new science, he still retained the medieval conviction that human reason has its own luminous and direct access to the transcendent reality of God. So long as Descartes could prove to his own satisfaction that God exists, this omnipotent and benevolent God could heal the breach between man's physical and spiritual being.

But this comforting assurance of the Middle Ages receded more and more as "the new science" of Descartes and Newton made astounding progress through the next century. The trouble—and it is a trouble at the heart of our whole modern epoch—comes to the surface again with Immanuel Kant (1724–1804). Writing at the end of the great century of Rationalism in 1781 in his *Critique of Pure Reason*, Kant showed that the transcendent ideals of our traditionally Christian civilization—God, the human soul and its possible immortality, the freedom of man as a spiritual person—could not be known by human reason. Like everything human, reason has its history; and here, in the course of its evolution, it had at last become strictly scientific reason. Insofar as reason sought to be scientific and exact it had to exclude all references to the ultimate things that man had lived by in his ethical and spiritual life.

Had Kant been merely what is now called a "scientific philosopher," like the modern positivists, he would at this point simply have thrown out God and the human soul as "meaningless" and gone off in search of new values. Since he retained the vestiges of a pious Protestant upbringing, however, he chose to live by the values of traditional Christianity. Hence he went on to write a *Critique of Practical Reason* in which he argued that, though science could never deal with these ultimate things, man in the seriousness of his ethical striving is called upon to live as if he had an immortal soul, and as if there were a God who providentially guided the destinies of the world. Kant held that in our inner conscience we touch a reality more absolute than anything in science.

The human, or existential, import of Kant's whole philosophy comes then to this: what Kant, the man, lived by as an ethical and spiritual person, Kant, the scientific thinker, could not even bring into thought. The split between the scientific and the human world with which Descartes launched our modern epoch has here become more sharply drawn. Kant, like Descartes before him, had that naïveté which sometimes accompanies great genius, and hardly anticipated the explosive effects of his philosophy. When his first *Critique* dropped like a bombshell on intellectual Germany, Kant himself was most astonished that his contemporaries were shocked.

The idealist philosophers after Kant felt that he had dug a chasm between two parts of the human personality, and by one means or another they sought to restore the spiritual wholeness or integrity of man. One of the greatest of these was G. W. F. Hegel (1770–1831). Hegel's means of restoring the wholeness of man was an imperialism of reason so audacious that it eventually brought Existentialism into being as a necessary corrective. If there are ethical and spiritual realities that concern us ultimately as human beings, Hegel argued, then these must be accessible to reason. Reason takes in all areas of human experience; nothing can be denied to it. In making reason all-inclusive, however, Hegel also made it omnivorous: wishing to give it wings to soar, he also gave it the devouring beak of a vulture. Everything vital and individual is swallowed up in the maw of the Hegelian system. In Hegel's thought, religion—even a religion like Christianity in which the central faith revolves around the unique and unreasonable moment in history when God became man in order to save the human race—becomes merely a crude approximation, by parable and myth, of the absolute truth that reason can spin out of its own ideas.

Enter now Existentialism. The moment was perfectly timed in this great human drama of western thought—for the situation was ripe for revolt. The revolt came in the persons of Sören Kierkegaard (1813–55) and Friedrich Nietzsche (1844–1900), who are now accepted as the founding fathers of existential philosophy. Neither was an academic philosopher, though Nietzsche had earlier been a professor of classical philology; and perhaps just because they were outsiders to academic philosophy, they had sharper eyes for the real human root of the trouble. Sometimes an outsider coming into a family can see more clearly the source of its dissensions than can those blinded by their intramural quarrels.

Kierkegaard put an end to the totalitarian claims for reason made by philosophers like Hegel. If religion could be reduced to reason, said Kierkegaard, there would be no need for religion—least of all a religion like Christianity whose central belief in the God-man is altogether paradoxical to reason. As a believing Christian, Kierkegaard insisted on the necessity of faith as a vital act beyond reason. But beyond this message as a Christian apologist, Kierkegaard brought to the attention of philosophers—and more recently to psychologists—the fact that human existence can never be totally enclosed in any system. To exist as an individual is to strive, change, develop, stand open to the future, be incomplete —while a system by its very nature is closed, complete, static, dead. The philosopher or scientist who thinks he can freeze our human existence into a system does so by substituting a pallid and abstract concept for the living and concrete reality. Life is lived forward and understood backward, says Kierkegaard. If we were ever to understand it completely, we would have to be already dead, without a future and with no untried and novel possibilities before us.

In one sense Kierkegaard returns us to the situation of Kant before

Hegel: he gives a more urgent and powerful expression to the Kantian view that each of us, as individuals, touches reality inwardly in our moments of serious moral decision rather than in the detached speculations of reason. In another sense, however, Kierkegaard destroys the makeshift supports of Kantian ethics by calling attention to the fact that the values Kant espouses—and espouses in spite of scientific reason—live or die with the Christian faith. These values are not rooted in the eternal nature of the human conscience, but historically and existentially derive from the Christian religion; and the central crisis of the modern period is that this religion now stands on trial. Kant's values cannot be kept alive by mere rational reflection on the so-called "postulates of practical reason"; in the end they can be kept alive only by the energy of faith.

Nietzsche starts from this same historical insight, but attacks Kant from just the opposite direction. If, says Nietzsche, the development of human reason along the line of science has brought us to the point in human history where scientific reason rules out those transcendent ideals—God, the immortal soul, our essential freedom as moral agents— that Christians have lived by for centuries, then why persist in Kant's blind old prejudice for these concepts? Why not throw them on the dust heap of history? Besides, is not Christianity already dead or at least dying in our time when, though some people may give it lip service, it no longer rules the total life of man as it did in the earlier ages of faith?

Had Nietzsche stopped here, he would have been merely one among many nineteenth-century atheists; more brilliant and incisive in his language than the others, but hardly a founder of existential philosophy. Nietzsche was, however, a man of great imagination and perhaps even greater religious yearning. He could see that the abolishing of the transcendent world in which the human spirit had hitherto sought its home would not solve all problems, as some of the rationalists of his century thought, but would only bring into desperate relief the pathos of our human situation. For when God is at last dead for man, when the last gleam of light is extinguished and only the impenetrable darkness of a universe that exists for no purpose surrounds us, then at last man knows he is alone in a world where he has to create his own values. The disappearance of religion would be the greatest challenge in human history —perhaps the ultimate challenge—for man would then be fully and dreadfully responsible to himself and for himself. Moreover, the natural sciences that helped bring about this situation could not help here, for they can never explain to man what he really is. Man steps beyond the world of natural objects in the very act of asking what this world means, what he himself means, and in seeking to create this meaning for himself. The natural sciences are tools that man can use in the service of his own values, but these sciences will never create a guiding ideal for human life.

This slow, unfolding development of modern philosophy is like a great symphony which Descartes opens with the leading theme, andante;

other philosophers enrich with variations and counter-themes, allegro; and Kierkegaard and Nietzsche bring to a furious and boiling presto. It might be tempting to hope that the existential philosophers of the twentieth century have at last brought us the grand finale; but unlike a symphony, the process of human thought admits no finale so long as man continues to be man, a being perpetually open to the future. The existentialists of this century are the heirs of Kierkegaard and Nietzsche, and their task has been, first, to save the great revolt of these two giants from being buried under the apathy of academic philosophers; and secondly and more importantly, to enrich and carry on the line of thought initiated in that revolt.

The very richness and diversity of existential thought in this century makes it difficult to fashion any easy summary of its conclusions. How sum up the philosophies of such men as Karl Jaspers and Martin Heidegger of Germany, Gabriel Marcel and Jean-Paul Sartre of France, Unamuno and Ortega y Gasset of Spain? Or the thought of such existential theologians as Nikolai Berdyaev and Paul Tillich? These men have different problems, attack the problems by different methods, and on a number of points are in disagreement. Hence some critics have declared that Existentialism is not a unified movement at all, with the implication that it may not even be a definite philosophy. On the contrary, a movement is alive and vital only when it is able to generate differences among its followers; when everybody agrees, we may be sure that it has declined into the stereotyped rigidity of death. Moreover, despite the differences among Existentialists, there is a common core to their thinking. Let us try now to see what some of the main points of this common core are.

If the modern era began with the way of thinking launched by Descartes, then we must, to save ourselves, recast our fundamental way of thinking. The world Descartes portrays—of material objects stripped of all qualities, extended in mathematical space of three dimensions, and with only quantitative and measurable properties—is not the world in which we live as human beings, but a high-level abstraction from the world that surrounds and involves us, exalts or enchants or terrifies us. We live in the human world, not in the world of science. And it is from the context of this human world that all the abstractions of science ultimately derive their meaning.

So, too, those fateful abstractions, the body and the mind. Man is not basically a body to which a mind is annexed in some incomprehensible way. Man is first and foremost a concrete involvement or enmeshment with the world, and within this concreteness of his being we distinguish the opposed poles of body and mind. We do not first exist inside our bodies and then proceed to infer a world existing beyond ourselves; on the contrary, in the very act of existing we are beyond ourselves and within the world. The verb "ex-ist" means, etymologically, to stand outside or beyond oneself. It is this self-transcendence that makes man what he is and distinguishes him from all the other animals whose existence does not reach backward and forward in time and history, and which remain rooted in space to their own natural habitat.

Because he is this perpetually self-transcending animal, man cannot be understood in his totality by the natural sciences—physics, chemistry, biology, or purely behaviorist psychology—as materialists have held. Man has expressed the truth of his existence in art and religion as well as in science; we would get less than the truth about human life if we left out any of these expressions of truth. One great achievement of existential philosophy has been a new interpretation of the idea of truth in order to point out that there are different kinds of truth, where a rigid scientific rationalism had postulated but one kind: objective scientific truth.

Kierkegaard introduced this difference by his analysis of religious truth. The truth with which religion is ultimately concerned, said Kierkegaard, has nothing to do with questions of rational proof. We do not exclaim, "There is a genuinely religious person!" when we happen to encounter a man who is an expert in all the subtle dialectic of theology. If we have ever encountered a genuinely spiritual person, we know that the heart of the matter lies elsewhere: in the being of the total person, not in the cerebrations of reason. Religious truth is realized actively and inwardly in the life of the individual man; it is not something embodied in a system of concepts, like science. Hence the fact that seemed so catastrophic to Kant—that the existence of God could not be proved rationally—is perfectly acceptable. For God is never real in our lives when He is considered a mere object of scientific proof or disproof.

Similarly, Heidegger has elucidated the unique kind of truth found in art. Truth is that peculiar relation of man to the object in which he lets the object be seen for what it is. Science is truth in this sense, but so too is art, though its way of letting the thing be seen is distinctly different from that of science. What kind of truth would we have about the long life of man upon this planet without those great works of art that have appeared in the tortuous course of human history? Here Existentialism, a new philosophy, goes back to a tradition before Plato, who on purely intellectualist grounds condemned all art as illusion. The older tradition among the Greeks was that their great poets were seers who voiced the hidden wisdom of the race. The Greek people of that earlier age were wiser than Plato.

A contemporary poet, our own Robert Frost, seems to speak from this ancient wisdom. Though he can hardly be called an Existentialist, Frost, in a recent address on television, epitomized this central point of Existential philosophy with the simplicity and directness of insight that only a great poet can manage:

"This present of ours I hope will be found all right for what it was. That is, that it will have made its point in history.

We're going to discriminate once and for all . . . what can be made a science of and can't be made a science of. And we're going to settle that. There's a whole half of our lives that can't be made a science of, can't ever be made a science of. And we're going to know more about that before we get through this period. That's what it will be remembered for."

If the poet is right in his prophecy for our age, if we really do discriminate what can and cannot be made a science of in human life, then this would be an achievement more significant for the future of mankind than the creation of jet planes, missiles or atomic bombs.

Because it denies the restrictions of scientific rationalism, Existentialism sometimes has been labeled a form of Irrationalism. This accusation is both glib and ungrounded. We do not cast all doubt upon an instrument by pointing out its functional limitations. A crowbar is not a key, and even if we wanted to pick the lock, we should do better with a hairpin. In making this observation we can hardly be called guilty of anticrowbarism.

Scientific reason is abstract and universal; life as we live it is individual and concrete. There are bridges between the two, but the former can never claim to supersede the latter without doing violence to it. You may use the crowbar to batter down the door, but then you will have to stand the expense of having the door repaired. We smile at the absurdity of the remark by the French mathematician Laplace after he had witnessed, without being moved, a performance of Racine's *Phèdre:* "What does it prove?" The mind of this great mathematician was geared to only one kind of truth. In considering Laplace's question absurd we are only using plain human judgment, not espousing a philosophic system of Irrationalism. When scientific rationalists raise the facile cry of "irrationalism," they are exposing their own mental blind spots. The danger to our civilization is that as this rigid rationalism attempts to embrace all areas of life we will not only profit from its vision but also be the victim of its blindness.

Reason, after all, is *human* reason and we should expect it, like everything human, to have its limitations. There is no positive without a correlated negative. Being always involves non-Being. As reason becomes more abstract, it seems to soar beyond the human conditions from which it took its initial leap; but it has perpetually to return to the solid earth of our human condition for refueling. What we need is neither a blind exaltation nor an empty rejection of reason, but a new concept of what Ortega y Gasset calls "vital reason"—a reason rooted in the fundamental conditions of human existence. The man who exists and the man who thinks is in the end (as in the beginning) one and the same; and if as thinker he chooses to forget that he is a man, he will end, as Kierkegaard pointed out in rebutting Hegel, by becoming humanly absurd.

One final and central point common to the Existentialists is their emphasis upon time and history as fundamental dimensions of human existence. Among all the animals man stands in a unique relation to time because he stands open to a future in which the present conditions of life can be transformed. Standing open to this future, he orders his present and connects it with his past. Hence our lives become meaningful to the degree that we bind together tomorrow, today and yesterday in an active whole. Time is thus the fundamental condition of our human existence; without time there would be no human meaning. But time, real time, is never the abstract "once upon a time" of the fairy story; it is always time here and now, urgent and pressing upon us. We are temporal beings not because we reckon with abstract mathematical time sequences, but because we experience time in the historical pressure of our generation with its challenging and fateful tasks.

Here, clearly, Existentialism emerges as a philosophy that summons us to responsible social action. This is a far cry from the earlier impression among Americans that this philosophy merely expressed a mood of despair or nihilism or Bohemian eccentricity. To be sure, this summons to social action is subordinated by the Existentialists to the more basic human task of becoming an authentic individual in our own right: we cannot meaningfully go outward into the world unless we have also gone inward and downward into the Self. Nevertheless, the authentic Self (all Existentialists agree) is never found in some Platonic realm beyond time and history, but only within the world. All significant thinking points toward the future; the historical challenge that the existential philosophers call upon us to face during the second half of this twentieth century is nothing less than this: Are we, at long last, to decide whether this coming epoch shall be the Age of Man or the Age of Mathematical Physics?

Toward Dialogue

Some day, Barrett intimates, our age will be noted in history as the time when a major decision was reached; we are determining, in the words of Robert Frost, "what can be made a science of and can't be made a science of." We are living through one of the not infrequent periods in history when man's tools of inquiry are not adequate to his curiosities. His puzzlements outrun his powers.

If education is, in some measure, the preparation for managing life's problems, and if man is now identifying problems that do not yield to the scientific method, what stance is the modern educator to take? Is he simply going to run the unyielding problems out of the curriculum? Or is he going to tell the learner frankly that a new situation is upon us in which all the learning and scholarship so far accumulated are unavailing?

The latter option, more difficult but more honest, cannot be postponed too long. The first order of business would be a catalogue of those spheres of human inquiry which "can't be made a science of," and therefore need a wholly new kind of approach.

MARTIN BUBER

Education Between Man and Man

EDUCATION

"The development of the creative powers in the child" is the subject of this conference. As I come before you to introduce it I must not conceal from you for a single moment the fact that of the nine words in which it is expressed only the last three raise no question for me.

The child, not just the individual child, individual children, but the child, is certainly a reality. That in this hour, while we make a beginning with the "development of creative powers," across the whole extent of this planet new human beings are born who are characterized already and yet have still to be characterized—this is a myriad realities, but also one reality. In every hour the human race begins. We forget this too easily in face of the massive fact of past life, of so-called world-history, of the fact that each child is born with a given disposition of "world-historical" origin, that is, inherited from the riches of the whole human race, and that he is born into a given situation of "world-historical" origin, that is, produced from the riches of the world's events. This fact must not obscure the other no less important fact that in spite of everything, in this as in every hour, what has not been invades the structure of what is, with ten thousand countenances, of which not one has been seen before, with ten thousand souls still undeveloped but ready to develop—a creative event if ever there was one, newness rising up, primal potential might. This potentiality, streaming unconquered, however much of it is squandered, is the reality *child*: this phenomenon of uniqueness, which is more than just begetting and birth, this grace of beginning again and ever again.

What greater care could we cherish or discuss than that this grace may not henceforth be squandered as before, that the might of newness may be preserved for renewal? Future history is not inscribed already by the pen of a causal law on a roll which merely awaits unrolling; its characters are stamped by the unforeseeable decisions of future generations. The part to be played in this by everyone alive to-day, by every adolescent and child, is immeasurable, and immeasurable is our part if we are educators. The deeds of the generations now approaching can illumine the grey face of the human world or plunge it in darkness. So, then, with education; if it at last rises up and exists indeed, it will be able to strengthen the light-spreading force in the hearts of the doers—how much it can do this cannot be guessed, but only learned in action.

From *Between Man and Man* by Martin Buber, tr. R. G. Smith (London: Routledge and Kegan Paul, Ltd., 1947), pp. 83–108.

The child is a reality; education must become a reality. But what does the "development of the creative powers" mean? Is *that* the reality of education? Must education become that in order to become a reality? Obviously those who arranged this session and gave it its theme think this is so. They obviously think that education has failed in its task till now because it has aimed at something different from this development of what is in the child, or has considered and promoted other powers in the child than the creative. And probably they are amazed that I question this objective, since I myself talk of the treasure of eternal possibility and of the task of unearthing it. So I must make clear that this treasure cannot be properly designated by the notion of "creative powers," nor its unearthing by the notion of "development."

Creation originally means only the divine summons to the life hidden in non-being. When Johann Georg Hamann and his contemporaries carried over this term metaphorically to the human capacity to give form, they marked a supreme peak of mankind, the genius for forming, as that in which man's imaging of God is authenticated in action. The metaphor has since been broadened; there was a time (not long ago) when "creative" meant almost the same as "of literary ability"; in face of this lowest condition of the word it is a real promotion for it to be understood, as it is here, quite generally as something dwelling to some extent in all men, in all children of men, and needing only the right cultivation. Art is then only the province in which a faculty of production, which is common to all, reaches completion. Everyone is elementally endowed with the basic powers of the arts, with that of drawing, for instance, or of music; these powers have to be developed, and the education of the whole person is to be built up on them as on the natural activity of the self.

We must not miss the importance of the reference which is the starting-point of this conception. It concerns a significant but hitherto not properly heeded phenomenon, which is certainly not given its right name here. I mean the existence of an autonomous instinct, which cannot be derived from others, whose appropriate name seems to me to be the "originator instinct." Man, the child of man, wants to make things. He does not merely find pleasure in seeing a form arise from material that presented itself as formless. What the child desires is its own share in this becoming of things: it wants to be the subject of this event of production. Nor is the instinct I am speaking of to be confused with the so-called instinct to busyness or activity which for that matter does not seem to me to exist at all (the child wants to set up or destroy, handle or hit, and so on, but never "busy himself"). What is important is that by one's own intensively experienced action something arises that was not there before. A good expression of this instinct is the way children of intellectual passion produce speech, in reality not as something they have taken over but with the headlong powers of utter newness: sound after sound tumbles out of them, rushing from the vibrating throat past the trembling lips into the world's air, and the whole of the little vital body vibrates and trembles, too, shaken by a bursting shower of selfhood. Or watch a boy fashioning some crude unrecognizable instrument for himself. Is he not astonished, terrified, at his own movement like the mighty inventors of prehistoric times? But it is also to be observed how even in the child's apparently "blind" lust for destruction his instinct of origination enters in and becomes dominant. Sometimes he begins to tear something up, for example, a sheet of paper, but soon he takes an interest in the form of the pieces, and it is not long before he tries— still by tearing—to produce definite forms.

It is important to recognize that the instinct of origination is autonomous and not derivatory. Modern psychologists are inclined to derive the multiform human soul from a single primal element—the "libido," the "will to power," and the like. But this is really only the generalization of certain degenerate states in which a single instinct not merely dominates but also spreads parasitically through the others. They begin with the cases (in our time of inner loss of community and oppression the innumerable cases) where such a hypertrophy breeds the appearance of exclusiveness, they abstract rules from them, and apply them with the whole theoretical and practical questionableness of such applications. In opposition to these doctrines and methods, which impoverish the soul, we must continually point out that human inwardness is in origin a polyphony in which no voice can be "reduced" to another, and in which the unity cannot be grasped analytically, but only heard in the present harmony. One of the leading voices is the instinct of origination.

This instinct is therefore bound to be significant for the work of education as well. Here is an instinct which, no matter to what power it is raised, never becomes greed, because it is not directed to "having" but only to doing; which alone among the instincts can grow only to passion, not to lust; which alone among the instincts cannot lead its subject away to invade the realm of other lives. Here is pure gesture which does not snatch the world to itself, but expresses itself to the world. Should not the person's growth into form, so often dreamed of and lost, at last succeed from this starting-point? For here this precious quality may be unfolded and worked out unimpeded. Nor does the new experiment lack demonstration. The finest demonstration I know, that I have just got to know, is this Children's Choir led by the marvellous Bakule of Prague, with which our Conference opened. How under his leadership crippled creatures, seemingly condemned to lifelong idleness, have been released to a life of freely moving persons, rejoicing in their achievement, formable and forming, who know how to shape sights and sounds in multiform patterns and also how to sing out their risen souls wildly and gloriously; more, how a community of achievement, proclaimed in glance and response, has been welded together out of dull immured solitary creatures: all this seems to prove irrefutably not merely what fruitfulness but also what power, streaming through the whole constitution of man, the life of origination has.

But this very example, seen more deeply, shows us that the decisive influence is to be ascribed not to the release of an instinct, but to the forces which meet the released instinct, namely, the educative forces. It depends on them, on their purity and fervour, their power of love and their discretion, into what connexions the freed element enters and what becomes of it.

There are two forms, indispensable for the building of true human life, to which the originative instinct, left to itself, does not lead and cannot lead: to sharing in an undertaking and to entering into mutuality.

An individual achievement and an undertaking are two very different matters. To make a thing is mortal man's pride; but to be conditioned in a common job, with the unconscious humility of being a part, of participation and partaking, is the true food of earthly immortality. As soon as a man enters effectively into an undertaking, where he discovers and practises a community of work with other men, he ceases to follow the originative instinct alone.

Action leading to an individual achievement is a "one-sided" event. There is a force within the person, which goes out, impresses itself on the material, and the achievement arises objectively: the movement is over, it has run in one direction from the heart's dream into the world, and its course is finished. No matter how directly, as being approached and claimed, as perceiving and receiving, the artist experiences his dealings with the idea which he faces and which awaits embodiment, so long as he is engaged in his work spirit goes out from him and does not enter him, he replies to the world but he does not meet it any more. Nor can he foster mutuality with his work: even in the legend Pygmalion is an ironical figure.

Yes; as an originator man is solitary. He stands wholly without bonds in the echoing hall of his deeds. Nor can it help him to leave his solitariness that his achievement is received enthusiastically by the many. He does not know if it is accepted, if his sacrifice is accepted by the anonymous receiver. Only if someone grasps his hand not as a "creator" but as a fellow-creature lost in the world, to be his comrade or friend or lover beyond the arts, does he have an awareness and a share of mutuality. An education based only on the training of the instinct of origination would prepare a new human solitariness which would be the most painful of all.

The child, in putting things together, learns much that he can learn in no other way. In making some thing he gets to know its possibility, its origin and structure and connexions, in a way he cannot learn by observation. But there is something else that is not learned in this way, and that is the viaticum of life. The being of the world as an object is learned from within, but not its being as a subject, its saying of I and *Thou*. What teaches us the saying of *Thou* is not the originative instinct but the instinct for communion.

This instinct is something greater than the believers in the "libido" realize: it is the longing for the world to become present to us as a person, which goes out to us as we to it, which chooses and recognizes us as we to it, which is confirmed in us as we in it. The child lying with half-closed eyes, waiting with tense soul for its mother to speak to it—the mystery of its will is not directed towards enjoying (or dominating) a person, or towards doing something of its own accord; but towards experiencing communion in face of the lonely night, which spreads beyond the window and threatens to invade.

But the release of powers should not be any more than a *presupposition* of education. In the end it is not the originative instinct alone which is meant by the "creative powers" that are to be "developed." These powers stand for human spontaneity. Real education is made possible—but is it also established?—by the realization that youthful spontaneity must not be suppressed but must be allowed to give what it can.

Let us take an example from the narrower sphere of the originative instinct—from the drawing-class. The teacher of the "compulsory" school of thought began with rules and current patterns. Now you knew what beauty was, and you had to copy it; and it was copied either in apathy or in despair. The teacher of the "free" school places on the table a twig of broom, say, in an earthenware jug, and makes the pupils draw it. Or he places it on the table, tells the pupils to look at it, removes it, and then makes them draw it. If the pupils are quite unsophisticated soon not a single drawing will look like another. Now the delicate, almost imperceptible and yet important influence begins—that of criticism and instruction. The children encounter a scale of values that, however unacademic it may be, is quite constant, a knowledge of good and evil that, however individualistic it may be, is quite unambiguous. The more unacademic this scale of values, and the more individualistic this knowledge, the more deeply do the children experience the encounter. In the former instance the preliminary declaration of what alone was right made for resignation or rebellion; but in the latter, where the pupil gains the realization only after he has ventured far out on the way to his achievement, his heart is drawn to reverence for the form, and educated.

This almost imperceptible, most delicate approach, the raising of a finger, perhaps, or a questioning glance, is the other half of what happens in education.

Modern educational theory, which is characterized by tendencies to freedom, misunderstands the meaning of this other half, just as the old theory, which was characterized by the habit of authority, misunderstood the meaning of the first half. The symbol of the funnel is in course of being exchanged for that of the pump. I am reminded of the two camps in the doctrine of evolution, current in the seventeenth and eighteenth centuries, the animalculists, who believed that the whole germ was present in the spermatozoon, and the ovists who believed it was wholly present in the ovum. The theory of the development of powers in the child recalls, in its most extreme expressions, Swammerdam's "unfolding" of the "preformed" organism. But the growth of the spirit is no more an unfolding than that of the body. The dispositions which would be discovered in the soul of a new-born child—if the soul could in fact be analysed—are nothing but capacities to receive and imagine the world. The world engenders the person in the individual. The world, that is the whole environment, nature and society, "educates" the human being: it draws out his powers, and makes him grasp and penetrate its objections. What we term education, conscious and willed, means *a selection by man of the effective world*: it means to give decisive effective power to a selection of the world which is concentrated and manifested in the educator. The relation in education is lifted out of the purposelessly streaming education by all things, and is marked off as purpose. In this way, through the educator, the world for the first time becomes the true subject of its effect.

There was a time, there were times, where there neither was nor needed to be any specific calling of educator or teacher. There was a master, a philosopher or a coppersmith, whose journeymen and apprentices lived with him and learned, by being allowed to share in it, what he had to teach them of his handwork or brainwork. But they also learned, without either their or his being concerned with it, they learned, without noticing that they did, the mystery of personal life: they received the spirit. Such a thing must still happen to some extent, where spirit and person exist, but it is expelled to the sphere of spirituality, of personality, and has become exceptional, it happens only "on the heights." Education as a purpose is bound to be summoned. We can as little return to the state of affairs that existed before there were schools as to that which existed before, say, technical science. But we can and must enter into the completeness of its growth to reality, into the perfect humanization of its reality. Our way is composed of losses that secretly become gains. Education has lost the paradise of pure instinctiveness and now consciously serves at the plough for the bread of life. It has been transformed; only in this transformation has it become visible.

Yet the master remains the model for the teacher. For if the educator of our day has to act consciously he must nevertheless do it "as though he did not." That raising of the finger, that questioning glance, are his genuine doing. Through him the selection of the effective world reaches the pupil. He fails the recipient when he presents this selection to him with a gesture of interference. It must be concentrated in him; and doing out of concentration has the appearance of rest. Interference divides the soul in his care into an obedient part and a rebellious part. But a hidden influence proceeding from his integrity has an integrating force.

The world, I said, has its influence as nature and as society on the child. He is educated by the elements, by air and light and the life of plants and animals, and he is educated by relationships. The true educator represents both; but he must be to the child as one of the elements.

The release of powers can be only a presupposition of education, nothing more. Put more generally, it is the nature of freedom to provide the place, but not the foundation as well, on which true life is raised. That is true both of inner, "moral" freedom and of outer freedom (which consists in not being hindered or limited). As the higher freedom, the soul's freedom of decision, signifies perhaps our highest moments but not a fraction of our substance, so the lower freedom, the freedom of development, signifies our capacity for growth but by no means our growth itself. This latter freedom is charged with importance as the actuality from which the work of education begins, but as its fundamental task it becomes absurd.

There is a tendency to understand this freedom, which may be termed evolutionary freedom, as at the opposite pole from compulsion, from being under a compulsion. But at the opposite pole from compulsion there stands not freedom but communion. Compulsion is a negative reality; communion is the positive reality; freedom is a possibility, possibility regained. At the opposite pole of being compelled by destiny or nature or men there does not stand being free of destiny or nature or men but to commune and to covenant with them. To do this, it is true that one must first have become independent; but this independence is a foot-bridge, not a dwelling-place. Freedom is the vibrating needle, the fruitful zero. Compulsion in education means disunion, it means humiliation and rebelliousness. Communion in education is just communion, it means being opened up and drawn in. Freedom in education is the possibility of communion; it cannot be dispensed with and it cannot be made use of in itself; without it nothing succeeds, but neither does anything succeed by means of it: it is the run before the jump, the tuning of the violin, the confirmation of that primal and mighty potentiality which it cannot even begin to actualize.

Freedom—I love its flashing face: it flashes forth from the darkness and dies away, but it has made the heart invulnerable. I am devoted to it, I am always ready to join in the fight for it, for the appearance of the flash, which lasts no longer than the eye is able to endure it, for the vibrating of the needle that was held down too long and was stiff. I give my left hand to the rebel and my right to the heretic: forward! But I do not trust them. They know how to die, but that is not enough. I love freedom, but I do not believe in it. How could one believe in it after looking in its face? It is the flash of a significance comprising all meanings, of a possibility comprising all potentiality. For it we fight, again and again, from of old, victorious and in vain.

It is easy to understand that in a time when the deterioration of all traditional bonds has made their legitimacy questionable, the tendency to freedom is exalted, the springboard is treated as the goal and a functional good as substantial good. Moreover, it is idle sentimentality to lament at great length that freedom is made the subject of experiments. Perhaps it is fitting for this time which has no compass that people should throw out their lives like a plummet to discover our bearings and the course we should set. But truly *their* lives! Such an experiment, when it is carried out, is a neck-breaking venture which cannot be disputed. But when it is talked about and talked around, in intellectual discussions and confessions and in the mutual pros and cons of their life's "problems," it is an abomination of disintegration. Those who stake themselves, as individuals or as a community, may leap and crash out into the swaying void where senses and sense fail, or through it and beyond into some kind of existence. But they must not make freedom into a theorem or a programme. To become free of a bond is destiny; one carries that like a cross, not like a cockade. Let us realize the true meaning of being free of a bond: it means that a quite personal responsibility takes the place of one shared with many generations. Life lived in freedom is personal responsibility or it is a pathetic farce.

I have pointed out the power which alone can give a content to empty freedom and a direction to swaying and spinning freedom. I believe in it, I trust those devoted to it.

This fragile life between birth and death can nevertheless be a fulfilment—if it is a dialogue. In our life and experience we are addressed; by thought and speech and action, by producing and by influencing we are able to answer. For the most part we do not listen to the address, or we break into it with chatter. But if the word comes to us and the answer proceeds from us then human life exists, though brokenly, in the world. The kindling of the response in that "spark" of the soul, the blazing up of the response, which occurs time and again, to the unexpectedly approaching speech, we term responsibility. We practise responsibility for that realm of life allotted and entrusted to us for which we are able to respond, that is, for which we have a relation of deeds which may count —in all our inadequacy—as a proper response. The extent to which a man, in the strength of the reality of the spark, can keep a traditional bond, a law, a direction, is the extent to which he is permitted to lean his responsibility on something (more than this is not vouchsafed to us, responsibility is not taken off our shoulders). As we "become free" this leaning on something is more and more denied to us, and our responsibility must become personal and solitary.

From this point of view education and its transformation in the hour of the crumbling of bonds are to be understood.

It is usual to contrast the principle of the "new" education as "Eros" with that of the "old" education as the "will to power."

In fact the one is as little a principle of education as the other. A principle of education, in a sense still to be clarified, can only be a basic relation which is fulfilled in education. But Eros and the will to power are alike passions of the soul for whose real elaboration a place is prepared elsewhere. Education can supply for them only an incidental realm and moreover one which sets a limit to their elaboration; nor can this limit be infringed without the realm itself being destroyed. The one can as little as the other constitute the educational attitude.

The "old" educator, in so far as he was an educator, was not "the man with a will to power," but he was the bearer of assured values which were strong in tradition. If the educator represents the world to the pupil, the "old" educator represented particularly the historical world, the past. He was the ambassador of history to this intruder, the "child"; he carried to him, as the Pope in the legend did to the prince of the Huns, the magic of the spiritual forces of history; he instilled values into the child or he drew the child into the values. The man who reduces this encounter between the cosmos of history and its eternally new chaos, between Zeus and Dionysos, to the formula of the "antagonism between fathers and sons," has never beheld it in his spirit. Zeus the Father does not stand for a generation but for a world, for the olympic, the formed world; the world of history faces a particular generation, which is the world of nature renewed again and again, always without history.

This situation of the old type of education is, however, easily used, or misused, by the individual's will to power, for this will is inflated by the authority of history. The will to power becomes convulsive and passes into fury, when the authority begins to decay, that is, when the magical validity of tradition disappears. Then the moment comes near when the teacher no longer faces the pupil as an ambassador but only as an individual, as a static atom to the whirling atom. Then no matter how much he imagines he is acting from the fulness of the objective spirit, in the reality of his life he is thrown back on himself, cast on his own resources, and hence filled with longing. Eros appears. And Eros finds employment in the new situation of education as the will to power did in the old situation. But Eros is not a bearer or the ground or the principle any more than the will to power was. He only claims to be that, in order not to be recognized as longing, as the stranger given refuge. And many believe it.

Nietzsche did not succeed in glorifying the will to power as much as Plato glorified Eros. But in our concern for the creature in this great time of concern, for both alike we have not to consider the myths of the philosophers but the actuality of present life. In entire opposition to any glorification we have to see that Eros—that is, not "love," but Eros the male and magnificent—whatever else may belong to him, necessarily includes this one thing, that he desires to enjoy men; and education, the peculiar essence bearing this name which is composed of no others, excludes precisely this desire. However mightily an educator is possessed and inspired by Eros, if he obeys him in the course of his educating then he stifles the growth of his blessings. It must be one or the other: either he takes on himself the tragedy of the person, and offers an unblemished daily sacrifice, or the fire enters his work and consumes it.

Eros is choice, choice made from an inclination. This is precisely what education is not. The man who is loving in Eros chooses the beloved, the modern educator finds his pupil there before him. From this unerotic situation the *greatness* of the modern educator is to be seen—and most clearly when he is a teacher. He enters the school-room for the first time, he sees them crouching at the desks, indiscriminately flung together, the misshapen and the well-proportioned, animal faces, empty faces, and noble faces in indiscriminate confusion, like the presence of the created universe; the glance of the educator accepts and receives them all. He is assuredly no descendant of the Greek gods, who kidnapped those they loved. But he seems to me to be a representative of the true God. For if God "forms the light and creates darkness," man is able to love both—to love light in itself, and darkness towards the light.

If this educator should ever believe that for the sake of education he has to practise selection and arrangement, then he will be guided by another criterion than that of inclination, however legitimate this may be in its own sphere; he will be guided by the recognition of values which is in his glance as an educator. But even then his selection remains suspended, under constant correction by the special humility of the educator for whom the life and particular being of all his pupils is the decisive factor to which his "hierarchic" recognition is subordinated. For in the manifold variety of the children the variety of creation is placed before him.

In education, then, there is a lofty asceticism: an asceticism which rejoices in the world, for the sake of the responsibility for a realm of life which is entrusted to us for our influence but not our interference—either by the will to power or by Eros. The spirit's service of life can be truly carried out only in the system of a reliable counterpoint—regulated by the laws of the different forms of relation—of giving and withholding oneself, intimacy and distance, which of course must not be controlled by reflection but must arise from the living tact of the natural and spiritual man. Every form of relation in which the spirit's service of life is realized has its special objectivity, its structure of proportions and limits which in no way resists the fervour of personal comprehension and penetration, though it does resist any confusion with the person's own spheres. If this structure and its resistance are not respected then a dilettantism will prevail which claims to be aristocratic, though in reality it is unsteady and feverish: to provide it with the most sacred names and attitudes will not help it past its inevitable consequence of disintegration. Consider, for example, the relation of doctor and patient. It is essential that this should be a real human relation experienced with the spirit by the one who is addressed; but as soon as the helper is touched by the desire—in however subtle a form—to dominate or to enjoy his patient, or to treat the latter's wish to be dominated or enjoyed by him other than as a wrong condition needing to be cured, the danger of a falsification arises, beside which all quackery appears peripheral.

The objectively ascetic character of the sphere of education must not, however, be misunderstood as being so separated from the instinct to power and from Eros that no bridge can be flung from them to it. I have already pointed out how very significant Eros can be to the educator without corroding his work. What matters here is the threshold and the transformation which takes place on it. It is not the church alone which has a testing threshold on which a man is transformed or becomes a lie. But in order to be able to carry out this ever renewed transition from sphere to sphere he must have carried it out once in a decisive fashion and taken up in himself the essence of education. How does this happen? There is an elemental experience which shatters at least the assurance of the erotic as well as the cratetic man, but sometimes does more, forcing its way at white-heat into the heart of the instinct and remoulding it. A reversal of the single instinct takes place, which does not eliminate it but reverses its system of direction. Such a reversal can be effected by the elemental experience with which the real process of education begins and on which it is based. I call it experiencing the other side.

A man belabours another, who remains quite still. Then let us assume that the striker suddenly receives in his soul the blow which he strikes: the same blow; that he receives it as the other who remains still. For the space of a moment he experiences the situation from the other side. Reality imposes itself on him. What will he do? Either he will overwhelm the voice of the soul, or his impulse will be reversed.

A man caresses a woman, who lets herself be caressed. Then let us assume that he feels the contact from two sides—with the palm of his hand still, and also with the woman's skin. The twofold nature of the gesture, as one that takes place between two persons, thrills through the depth of enjoyment in his heart and stirs it. If he does not deafen his heart he will have—not to renounce the enjoyment but—to love.

I do not in the least mean that the man who has had such an experience would from then on have this two-sided sensation in every such meeting—that would perhaps destroy his instinct. But the one extreme experience makes the other person present to him for all time. A transfusion has taken place after which a mere elaboration of subjectivity is never again possible or tolerable to him.

Only an inclusive power is able to take the lead; only an inclusive Eros is love. Inclusiveness is the complete realization of the submissive person, the desired person, the "partner," not by the fancy but by the actuality of the being.

It would be wrong to identify what is meant here with the familiar but not very significant term "empathy." Empathy means, if anything, to glide with one's own feeling into the dynamic structure of an object, a pillar or a crystal or the branch of a tree, or even of an animal or a man, and as it were to trace it from within, understanding the formation and motoriality of the object with the perceptions of one's own muscles; it means to "transpose" oneself over there and in there. Thus it means the exclusion of one's own concreteness, the extinguishing of the actual situation of life, the absorption in pure æstheticism of the reality in which one participates. Inclusion is the opposite of this. It is the extension of one's own concreteness, the fulfilment of the actual situation of life, the complete presence of the reality in which one participates. Its elements are, first, a relation, of no matter what kind, between two persons, second, an event experienced by them in common, in which at least one of them actively participates, and, third, the fact that this one person, without forfeiting anything of the felt reality of his activity, at the same time lives through the common event from the standpoint of the other.

A relation between persons that is characterized in more or less degree by the element of inclusion may be termed a dialogical relation.

A dialogical relation will show itself also in genuine conversation, but it is not composed of this. Not only is the shared silence of two such persons a dialogue, but also their dialogical life continues, even when they are separated in space, as the continual potential presence of the one to the other, as an unexpressed intercourse. On the other hand, all conversation derives its genuineness only from the consciousness of the element of inclusion—even if this appears only abstractly as an "acknowledgement" of the actual being of the partner in the conversation; but this acknowledgement can be real and effective only when it springs from an experience of inclusion, of the other side.

The reversal of the will to power and of Eros means that relations characterized by these are made dialogical. For that very reason it means that the instinct enters into communion with the fellow-man and into responsibility for him as an allotted and entrusted realm of life.

The element of inclusion, with whose recognition this clarification begins, is the same as that which constitutes the relation in education.

The relation in education is one of pure dialogue.

I have referred to the child, lying with half-closed eyes waiting for his mother to speak to him. But many children do not need to wait, for they know that they are unceasingly addressed in a dialogue which never breaks off. In face of the lonely night which threatens to invade, they lie preserved and guarded, invulnerable, clad in the silver mail of trust.

Trust, trust in the world, because this human being exists—that is the most inward achievement of the relation in education. Because this human being exists, meaninglessness, however hard pressed you are by it, cannot be the real truth. Because this human being exists, in the darkness the light lies hidden, in fear salvation, and in the callousness of one's fellow-men the great Love.

Because this human being exists: therefore he must be really there, really facing the child, not merely there in spirit. He may not let himself be represented by a phantom: the death of the phantom would be a catastrophe for the child's pristine soul. He need possess none of the perfections which the child may dream he possesses; but he must be really there. In order to be and to remain truly present to the child he must have gathered the child's presence into his own store as one of the bearers of his communion with the world, one of the focuses of his responsibilities for the world. Of course he cannot be continually concerned with the child, either in thought or in deed, nor ought he to be. But if he has really gathered the child into his life then that subterranean dialogic, that steady potential presence of the one to the other is established and endures. Then there is reality *between* them, there is mutuality.

But this mutuality—that is what constitutes the peculiar nature of the relation in education—cannot be one of inclusion, although the true relation of the educator to the pupil is based on inclusion. No other relation draws its inner life like this one from the element of inclusion, but no other is in that regard like this, completely directed to one-sidedness, so that if it loses one-sidedness it loses essence.

We may distinguish three chief forms of the dialogical relation.

The first rests on an abstract but mutual experience of inclusion.

The clearest example of this is a disputation between two men, thoroughly different in nature and outlook and calling, where in an instant—as by the action of a messenger as anonymous as he is invisible—it happens that each is aware of the other's full legitimacy, wearing the insignia of necessity and of meaning. What an illumination! The truth, the strength of conviction, the "standpoint," or rather the circle of movement, of each of them, is in no way reduced by this. There is no "relativizing," but we may say that, in the sign of the limit, the essence of mortal recognition, fraught with primal destiny, is manifested to us. To recognize means for us creatures the fulfilment by each of us, in truth and responsibility, of his own relation to the Present Being, through our receiving all that is manifested of it and incorporating it into our own being, with all our force, faithfully, and open to the world and the spirit. In this way living truth arises and endures. We have become aware that it is with the other as with ourselves, and that what rules over us both is not a truth of recognition but the truth-of-existence and the existence-of-truth of the Present Being. In this way we have become able *to acknowledge.*

I have called this form abstract, not as though its basic experience lacked immediacy, but because it is related to man only as a spiritual person and is bound to leave out the full reality of his being and life. The other two forms proceed from the inclusion of this full reality.

Of these the first, the relation of education, is based on a concrete but one-sided experience of inclusion.

If education means to let a selection of the world affect a person through the medium of another person, then the one through whom this takes place, rather, who makes it take place through himself, is caught in a strange paradox. What is otherwise found only as grace, inlaid in the folds of life—the influencing of the lives of others with one's own life—becomes here a function and a law. But since the educator has to such an extent replaced the master, the danger has arisen that the new phenomenon, the will to educate, may degenerate into arbitrariness, and that the educator may carry out his selection and his influence from himself and his idea of the pupil, not from the pupil's own reality. One only needs to read, say, the accounts of Pestalozzi's teaching method to see how easily, even with the noblest teachers, arbitrary self-will is mixed up with will. This is almost always due to an interruption or a temporary flagging of the act of inclusion, which is not merely regulative for the realm of education, as for other realms, but is actually constitutive; so that the realm of education acquires its true and proper force from the constant return of this act and the constantly renewed connexion with it. The man whose calling it is to influence the being of persons that can be determined, must experience this action of his (however much it may have assumed the form of non-action) ever anew from the other side. Without the action of his spirit being in any way weakened he must at the same time be over there, on the surface of that other spirit which is being acted upon—and not of some conceptual, contrived spirit, but all the time the wholly concrete spirit of this individual and unique being who is living and confronting him, and who stands with him in the common situation of "educating" and "being educated" (which is indeed one situation, only the other is at the other end of it). It is not enough for him to imagine the child's individuality, nor to experience him directly as a spiritual person and then to acknowledge him. Only when he catches himself "from over there," and feels how it affects one, how it affects this other human being, does he recognize the real limit, baptize his self-will in Reality and make it true will, and renew his paradoxical legitimacy. He is of all men the one for whom inclusion may and should change from an alarming and edifying event into an atmosphere.

But however intense the mutuality of giving and taking with which he is bound to his pupil, inclusion cannot be mutual in this case. He experiences the pupil's being educated, but the pupil cannot experience the educating of the educator. The educator stands at both ends of the common situation, the pupil only at one end. In the moment when the pupil is able to throw himself across and experience from over there, the educative relation would be burst asunder, or change into friendship.

We call friendship the third form of the dialogical relation, which is based on a concrete and mutual experience of inclusion. It is the true inclusion of one another by human souls.

The educator who practises the experience of the other side and stands firm in it, experiences two things together, first that he is limited by otherness, and second that he receives grace by being bound to the other. He feels from "over there" the acceptance and the rejection of what is approaching (that is, approaching from himself, the educator)— of course often only in a fugitive mood or an uncertain feeling; but this discloses the real need and absence of need in the soul. In the same way the foods a child likes and dislikes is a fact which does not, indeed, procure for the experienced person but certainly helps him to gain an insight into what substances the child's body needs. In learning from time to time what this human being needs and does not need at the moment, the educator is led to an ever deeper recognition of what the human being needs in order to grow. But he is also led to the recognition of what he, the "educator," is able and what he is unable to give of what is needed—and what he can give now, and what not yet. So the responsibility for this realm of life allotted and entrusted to him, the constant responsibility for this living soul, points him to that which seems impossible and yet is somehow granted to us—to self-education. But self-education, here as everywhere, cannot take place through one's being concerned with oneself but only through one's being concerned, knowing what it means, with the world. The forces of the world which the child needs for the building up of his substance must be chosen by the educator from the world and drawn into himself.

The education of men by men means the selection of the effective world by a person and in him. The educator gathers in the constructive forces of the world. He distinguishes, rejects, and confirms in himself, in his self which is filled with the world. The constructive forces are eternally the same: they are the world bound up in community, turned to God. The educator educates himself to be their vehicle.

Then is this the "principle" of education, its normal and fixed maxim?

No; it is only the *principium* of its reality, the beginning of its reality —wherever it begins.

There is not and never has been a norm and fixed maxim of education. What is called so was always only the norm of a culture, of a society, a church, an epoch, to which education too, like all stirring and action of the spirit, was submissive, and which education translated into its language. In a formed age there is in truth no autonomy of education, but only in an age which is losing form. Only in it, in the disintegration of traditional bonds, in the spinning whirl of freedom, does personal responsibility arise which in the end can no longer lean with its burden of decision on any church or society or culture, but is lonely in face of Present Being.

In an age which is losing form the highly-praised "personalities," who know how to serve its fictitious forms and in their name to dominate the age, count in the truth of what is happening no more than those who lament the genuine forms of the past and are diligent to restore them. The ones who count are those persons who—though they may be of little renown—respond to and are responsible for the continuation of the living spirit, each in the active stillness of his sphere of work.

The question which is always being brought forward—"To where, to what, must we educate?"—misunderstands the situation. Only times which know a figure of general validity—the Christian, the gentleman, the citizen—know an answer to that question, not necessarily in words, but by pointing with the finger to the figure which rises clear in the air, out-topping all. The forming of this figure in all individuals, out of all materials, is the formation of a "culture." But when all figures are shattered, when no figure is able any more to dominate and shape the present human material, what is there left to form?

Nothing but the image of God.

That is the indefinable, only factual, direction of the responsible modern educator. This cannot be a theoretical answer to the question "To what?", but only, if at all, an answer carried out in deeds; an answer carried out by non-doing.

The educator is set now in the midst of the need which he experiences in inclusion, but only a bit deeper in it. He is set in the midst of the service, only a bit higher up, which he invokes without words; he is set in the *imitatio Dei absconditi sed non ignoti*.

When all "directions" fail there arises in the darkness over the abyss the one true direction of man, towards the creative Spirit, towards the Spirit of God brooding on the face of the waters, towards Him of whom we know not whence He comes and whither He goes.

That is man's true autonomy which no longer betrays, but responds.

Man, the creature who forms and transforms the creation, cannot create. But he, each man, can expose himself and others to the creative Spirit. And he can call upon the Creator to save and perfect His image.

THE EDUCATION OF CHARACTER

Education worthy of the name is essentially education of character. For the genuine educator does not merely consider individual functions of his pupil, as one intending to teach him only to know or be capable of certain definite things; but his concern is always the person as a whole, both in the actuality in which he lives before you now and in his possibilities, what he can become. But in this way, as a whole in reality and potentiality, a man can be conceived either as personality, that is, as a unique spiritual-physical form with all the forces dormant in it, or as character, that is, as the link between what this individual is and the sequence of his actions and attitudes. Between these two modes of conceiving the pupil in his wholeness there is a fundamental difference. Personality is something which in its growth remains essentially outside the influence of the educator; but to assist in the moulding of character is his greatest task. Personality is a completion, only character is a task. One may cultivate and enhance personality, but in education one can and one must aim at character.

However—as I would like to point out straightaway—it is advisable not to over-estimate what the educator can even at best do to develop character. In this more than in any other branch of the science of teaching it is important to realize, at the very beginning of the discussion, the fundamental limits to conscious influence, even before asking what character is and how it is to be brought about.

If I have to teach algebra I can expect to succeed in giving my pupils an idea of quadratic equations with two unknown quantities. Even the slowest-witted child will understand it so well that he will amuse himself by solving equations at night when he cannot fall asleep. And even one with the most sluggish memory will not forget, in his old age, how to play with x and y. But if I am concerned with the education of character, everything becomes problematic. I try to explain to my pupils that envy is despicable, and at once I feel the secret resistance of those who are poorer than their comrades. I try to explain that it is wicked to bully the weak, and at once I see a suppressed smile on the lips of the strong. I try to explain that lying destroys life, and something frightful happens: the worst habitual liar of the class produces a brilliant essay on the destructive power of lying. I have made the fatal mistake of *giving instruction* in ethics, and what I said is accepted as current coin of knowledge; nothing of it is transformed into character-building substance.

But the difficulty lies still deeper. In all teaching of a subject I can announce my intention of teaching as openly as I please, and this does not interfere with the results. After all, pupils do want, for the most part, to learn something, even if not overmuch, so that a tacit agreement becomes possible. But as soon as my pupils notice that I want to educate their characters I am resisted precisely by those who show most signs of genuine independent character: they will not let themselves be educated, or rather, they do not like the idea that somebody wants to educate them. And those, too, who are seriously laboring over the question of good and evil, rebel when one dictates to them, as though it were some long established truth, what is good and what is bad; and they rebel just because they have experienced over and over again how hard it is to find the right way. Does it follow that one should keep silent about one's intention of educating character, and act by ruse and subterfuge? No; I have just said that the difficulty lies deeper. It is not enough to see that education of character is not introduced into a lesson in class; neither may one conceal it in cleverly arranged intervals. Education cannot tolerate such politic action. Even if the pupil does not notice the hidden motive it will have its negative effect on the actions of the teacher himself by depriving him of the directness which is his strength. Only in his whole being, in all his spontaneity can the educator truly affect the whole being of his pupil. For educating characters you do not need a moral genius, but you do need a man who is wholly alive and able to communicate himself directly to his fellow beings. His aliveness streams out to them and affects them most strongly and purely when he has no thought of affecting them.

The Greek word character means *impression*. The special link between man's being and his appearance, the special connexion between the unity of what he is and the sequence of his actions and attitudes is impressed on his still plastic substance. Who does the impressing? Everything does: nature and the social context, the house and the street, language and custom, the world of history and the world of daily news in the form of rumour, of broadcast and newspaper, music and technical science, play and dream—everything together. Many of these factors exert their influence by stimulating agreement, imitation, desire, effort; others by arousing questions, doubts, dislike, resistance. Character is formed by the interpenetration of all those multifarious, opposing influences. And yet, among this infinity of form-giving forces the educator is only one element among innumerable others, but distinct from them all by his *will* to take part in the stamping of character and by his *consciousness* that he represents in the eyes of the growing person a certain *selection* of what is, the selection of what is "right," of what *should* be. It is in this will and this consciousness that his vocation as an educator finds its fundamental expression. From this the genuine educator gains two things: first, humility, the feeling of being only one element amidst the fullness of life, only one single existence in the midst of all the tremendous inrush of reality on the pupil; but secondly, self-awareness, the feeling of being therein the only existence that *wants* to affect the whole person, and thus the feeling of responsibility for the selection of reality which he represents to the pupil. And a third thing emerges from all this, the recognition that in this realm of the education of character, of wholeness, there is only *one* access to the pupil: his *confidence*. For the adolescent who is frightened and disappointed by an unreliable world, confidence means the liberating insight that there is human truth, the truth of human existence. When the pupil's confidence has been won, his resistence against being educated gives way to a singular happening: he accepts the educator as a person. He feels he may trust this man, that this man is not making a business out of him, but is taking part in his life, accepting him before desiring to influence him. And so he learns to *ask*.

The teacher who is for the first time approached by a boy with somewhat defiant bearing, but with trembling hands, visibly opened-up and fired by a daring hope, who asks him what is the right thing in a certain situation—for instance, whether in learning that a friend has betrayed a secret entrusted to him one should call him to account or be content with entrusting no more secrets to him—the teacher to whom this happens realizes that this is the moment to make the first conscious step towards education of character; he has to answer, to answer under a responsibility, to give an answer which will probably lead beyond the alternatives of the question by showing a third possibility which is the right one. To dictate what is good and evil in general is not his business. His business is to answer a concrete question, to answer what is right and wrong in a given situation. This, as I have said, can only happen in an atmosphere of confidence. Confidence, of course, is not won by the strenuous endeavour to win it, but by direct and ingenuous participation in the life of the people one is dealing with—in this case the life of one's pupils—and by assuming the responsibility which arises from such participation. It is not the educational intention but it is the meeting which is educationally fruitful. A soul suffering from the contradictions of the world of human society, and of its own physical existence, approaches me with a question. By trying to answer it to the best of my knowledge and conscience I help it to become a character that actively overcomes the contradictions.

If this is the teacher's standpoint towards his pupil, taking part in his life and conscious of responsibility, then everything that passes between them can, without any deliberate or politic intention, open a way to the education of character: lessons and games, a conversation about quarrels in the class, or about the problems of a world-war. Only, the teacher must not forget the limits of education; even when he enjoys confidence he cannot always expect agreement. Confidence implies a break-through from reserve, the bursting of the bonds which imprison an unquiet heart. But it does not imply unconditional agreement. The teacher must never forget that conflicts too, if only they are decided in a healthy atmosphere, have an educational value. A conflict with a pupil is the supreme test for the educator. He must use his own insight wholeheartedly; he must not blunt the piercing impact of his knowledge, but he must at the same time have in readiness the healing ointment for the heart pierced by it. Not for a moment may he conduct a dialectical manœuvre of the real battle for truth. But if he is the victor he has to help the vanquished to endure defeat; and if he cannot conquer the self-willed soul that faces him (for victories over souls are not so easily won), then he has to find the word of love which alone can help to overcome so difficult a situation.

Toward Dialogue

Reading Buber is like roaming through a woods on a dark, misty night. We are not actually lost, nor is the experience particularly scary, but murkiness obscures landmarks we cannot quite identify. We have the uneasy feeling that somewhere in the mist lies important truth. An occasional lightning flash illuminates the landscape, and we see, for an instant, what Buber is thinking. But then the picture fades and we have to trudge on. With each subsequent walk through his prose, the lightning strikes new images, and if memory were accurate and cumulative, we might gradually acquire a working picture of the territory. But it is difficult, and we long for daylight.

For example, early in the foregoing essay, Buber develops the idea that there is some incompatibility between the development of creativity on the one hand and the nurturing of mutuality and communion on the other. As he says, "An education based only on the training of the instinct of origination would prepare a new human solitariness which *would be the most painful of all." As it stands, there is a certain luminosity to this assertion, but since it runs counter to some of our so-called common sense in education, it is not easy to fit into our other ideas. What does he mean by this? Is "the saying of Thou" in human mutuality made more difficult in group enterprises?*

Or, consider this: ". . . the true meaning of being free of a bond: it means that a quite personal responsibility takes the place of one shared with many generations. Life lived in freedom is personal responsibility or it is a pathetic farce." His meaning here is more accessible. But it raises questions. If we want our young to grow in freedom and if we dread their lives becoming a farce, we are left with the obligation of lifting them out of shared values with other generations into the loneliness of their own. What then becomes of the I and Thou in the educational encounter? Is it possible for one human being to teach another "personal responsibility," or is that something we must awaken to by ourselves?

VAN CLEVE MORRIS

Existentialism and Education

American education continues in search of a guiding principle by which to order its affairs. Hardly a week passes but another statement of educational aims and purposes is run from the nation's presses.

Most of this debate swirls around the protagonistic head of Experimentalism which in a short half century has initiated truly remarkable changes in educational theory and practice. Platonic Idealists, Aristotelian Neo-Thomists, and even Rousseauian Naturalists almost daily in the public prints hurl themselves against the house of Experimentalism, hoping, if not to storm and rout, at least to infilter and infect it with the germs of what to them is a more reasonable and truthful view of things. There are few signs that the struggle is likely to abate.

In fact, if portents are accurate, we are about to witness a new and vigorous assault, originating in this case not from one of the older, more conventional traditions but rather from a fresh and genuinely modern theory of man—Existentialism. The intellectual, to say nothing of the lay, world knows so precious little about this philosophical infant (or better, adolescent) that the full fury of the assault may be some years off. But the issue shall be joined sooner or later.

From *Educational Theory*, 4, (October, 1954), pp. 247–258.

This paper is an effort (1) to state the substance of the Existentialist point of view, (2) to note points of contrast and comparison with Experimentalism, and (3) to suggest from our study of Existentialism some implications for education. Unfortunately, for this final section we have little to go on; Existentialist writers have not as yet systematically turned their attention to the education of man. At this point therefore we shall be on our own.

WHAT IS EXISTENTIALISM?

The casual reader has no doubt run across references to Existentialism with increasing frequency in recent years. It is said, as it is probably said of every new philosophy, that Existentialism is a philosophy of crisis, a theory of life and man particularly fitted for our anxious times. It is not clear what actually is meant by this; for if this means that Existentialism is the spiritual medicine which can quiet man's nerves and can steady and strengthen him for living in an era of peril, then it is certainly false. For, as we shall see, Existentialism is hardly a comforting analgesic. On the contrary, it leaves man more exposed than he has ever been to the pains and agonies of existence. It leaves him alone, completely alone, bereft of any shield whether it be of the grace of a supernatural God or the comforting company of men. Indeed, if Existentialism is a philosophy of crisis, then it certainly must be considered as a part *of* the crisis rather than a foil *against* it.[1]

The reader will also recall vague references to Existentialism which have suggested its apparent disinterest in morals. One hears that Existentialists are vulgar and obscene and that Existentialism means quite literally 'each one his own judge of right and wrong.' The implication is that there is no such thing as right and wrong, and therefore no need for personal responsibility for moral choices. This feeling has been the unfortunate result of the total misinterpretation of the writings of the French Existentialists, most notably Jean-Paul Sartre. Sartre is an accomplished novelist and playwright, as well as philosopher, and his nonphilosophic works might be accused of vulgarity. And it is true that he considers each individual his own judge not only of right and wrong but of the criteria by which one judges right and wrong. But it is erroneous to construe this to mean that right and wrong do not exist and an outright inversion of actual fact to intimate that Sartre believes personal

---

[1] In a sense Existentialism may become man's bulwark. Absolutistic doctrines, promising safety and security, have revealed a nasty habit of disintegrating just when men needed them most. When these card houses collapse men find themselves with nothing left on which to build. Existentialism refuses to erect these marvelous but fragile edifices and therefore avoids deluding men into what can only be false security. Existentialists therefore consider their point of view an improvement if only because it is more trustworthy, because it is so radically realistic in describing the world men live in. A life without pretense, even if difficult and hazardous, is to be preferred to a life full of confident hopes for security and salvation which turn out to be mere illusions.

responsibility for ethical choices has become unnecessary. On the contrary, as we shall see, the radical necessity for individual responsibility in making moral decisions is practically the central principle in the Existentialist network of ideas.

Incidentally, the name of Sartre has gained such popularity in recent years on both sides of the Atlantic that people have begun to think of Sartre and Existentialism almost as synonymous. As a matter of actual fact, Sartre is only a late comer on the Existential stage, and is surprisingly enough, only partially representative of genuine Existentialism today.

Although the philosophical problem of existence has been touched on in classical and medieval writings, it never came to the fore as a central philosophical theme until Sören Kierkegaard (1813-1855) began its development about a century ago. This turbulent and complex Danish figure remained obscure for more than half a century, until early in the nineteen hundreds when his works began to appear in German translation. English translations did not begin to arrive until 1935. Most of the systematic elaboration of existential philosophies has therefore taken place quite recently and the major Existentialist figures are still living.

Of these men, Karl Jaspers (1883–   ) and Martin Heidegger (1889–   ) have been responsible for the German development and Gabriel Marcel (1889–   ) and the aforementioned Sartre (1905–   ) the French development of what has come to be known as the philosophy of Existence, or Existentialism. Generally speaking, Jaspers and Marcel, both Catholics, represent the Christian 'wing' and Heidegger and Sartre the secular and (in the case of Sartre) atheistic 'wing' of the movement.

As the philosophic sightseer circles 'round this complex chamber of wonders (or horrors), he is assailed by doubt as to which of the few small doors he should most profitably enter first. For, in a sense, Existentialism is not merely a set of new answers to old metaphysical questions but instead a bold attempt to provide new kinds of answers by considering the questions in an entirely new setting.

> Classical philosophy comes to an end in Hegel, because it has become folly to construct intellectual totalitarian systems in which everything is taken up, harmonized, rationalized, and justified. Such palaces are still marvelous, but nobody can live in them. The savour and reality of human existence, its perils and triumphs, its bitterness and sweetness, are outside in the street.[2]

To begin with, classical philosophy and in fact all philosophy from Plato to Hegel has traditionally centered its attention on the question of essence; philosophers have repeatedly felt that the main business of philosophy is to answer the question "What is reality?" Study of this central question is customarily carried on through study of other com-

[2] H. J. Blackham, *Six Existentialist Thinkers*, London, Routledge and Kegan Paul, Ltd., 1952, p. 44.

panion questions of essence: What is man?, What is God?, What is the Universe?, What is Knowledge, Truth, Beauty, Good, Evil?

Existentialism turns its attention elsewhere, relegating questions of essence to subordinate status. The Existentialists claim that the question "What is man?" must wait upon an answer to the problem of explaining what it means to say that man *is*. How can we search for essence before we have even explained the *existence* of the thing we seek the essence of?

Older philosophies have merely assumed existence or have engaged in flashy ratiocinations like the Cartesian 'Cogito ergo sum' to "prove" it. The Existentialist says this will not do, that a thorough study of existence must precede any intelligent attack on the problem of essence. This then becomes the primary *new kind* of question that Existentialism raises, i.e., What does it mean to say 'I am'?

Among some of the Existentialists, the argument goes even further, to the point of stating that existence should take priority over essence in philosophic study because in fact it precedes essence in terms of cosmic development. Sartre is most apt to use this thesis and he puts it in this wise: When an artisan makes a shoe, the idea (essence) of the shoe is in his mind before he makes it. Man considers God a king-sized artisan who had an idea of man before He made man. Hence, the popular notion that essence always precedes existence. But, says Sartre, there is no creator of man. Man discovered himself. His existence came first; he now is in the process of determining his essence. Man first is, then he defines himself.[3]

Else, says the Existentialists, we would have to assume a creator of man (God), and then to explain God, we must assume a creator of God, then a creator of God's creator, and so forth, ad infinitum. This of course is ridiculous and so likewise is the notion of an uncreated creator. We are left therefore with man who is mere existent, he *is* before he is any particular thing.

In like fashion goes the rebuttal to Descartes and his "I think, therefore I am." What a monstrous non sequitur this has been discovered to be! Why does it follow that I am merely because I am capable of thought? Moreover even to utter the first clause "I think" I must presuppose my existence and my ability to utter it. Unless I existed I certainly could not engage in thought. I therefore must exist *before* I think:

> . . . it is the existence of my body in the world that constitutes me a subject before it is given to me as an object to a subject.[4]

Thus, it is more nearly correct to invert and modify Descartes: "I am, therefore I have one of the prerequisites for thought." We shall see later that Existentialism, in effect, uses neither of these but more nearly "I choose, therefore I am."

    [3] J. P. Sartre, *Existentialism*, translated by B. Frechtman, New York, Philosophical Library, 1947, pp. 16–17.
    [4] H. J. Blackham, *op. cit.*, p. 68.

Thus we behold man, aboriginal man that is, as pure existent devoid of any essence whatsoever. He is not bound by any antecedent or a priori human nature but is completely free to determine his own nature. This freedom is total; man can choose what he shall be. It is this process of choosing and of becoming which describes, as accurately as one can, what the Existentialists believe is fundamental to human existence. If man has an essence, it is literally his freedom from essence and his consequent freedom to choose and become what he will.

Now the concept of freedom has always been a subject of much discussion and dispute among philosophers, and all of the older theories wavered between a position of complete determinism on the one hand and some kind of union of freedom within ultimate determinism on the other. Existentialism refuses to walk this tightrope, and flatly and clearly states the case for complete, undiluted, and absolute freedom. It insists that any attempt at joining or harmonizing the two is merely philosophical squirming, intellectual equivocation in the face of an uncomfortable decision. It is just this necessity for choosing between determinism and freedom which occasioned one of Kierkegaard's major works, *Either/Or.* In summary, his thesis is this:

> "*Either:* the life of the individual person, a microcosm as the image of God, capable of free, responsible action, and therefore . . . a life of toil and much suffering and many dangers; or: the life of an impersonal, unfree member of a collective, without the possibility of independent knowledge and responsible action, a life in the service of unknown forces—, and as compensation for the loss of freedom at best a false, illusory dream of material welfare in an earthly paradise which can never become a reality."[5]

Yes, indeed, "a life of toil and much suffering and many dangers." For to be free one must surrender the privilege of seeking comfort in a supernatural or superhuman authority. We cannot honestly insist on freedom in our successes and then in times of stress suddenly enter "a universe where we can just give up, fall on our father's neck, and be absorbed into the absolute life as a drop of water melts into the river or the sea."[6] If he is merely a pawn acting out the determined thoughts of God, then man's works are all second-hand. He has lost his creativity. He has lost his freedom. He is no longer man. On the contrary, the 'essence' of man is that he is free. He can create. He can choose. And, whether he likes it or not, "toil, suffering, and danger" are his.

Indeed, history is one long episode of man's toilsome struggle to escape from this freedom.[7] In his anxiety and anguish,[8] he has tried the

---

[5] Johannes Holenberg, *Sören Kierkegaard* (transl. by Maria Bachmann-Isler; Basel: Benno Schwabe and Co., 1949, p. 417 (quoted in K. F. Reinhardt, *The Existentialist Revolt*, Milwaukee, Bruce Publishing Co., 1952, p. 36.)

[6] William James, *Pragmatism*, New York, Longmans, Green and Co., c. 1907, p. 292.

[7] See Erich Fromm, *Escape From Freedom*.

[8] This and "dread," "forlornness," and "despair" are favorite Existential words.

religious escape but been turned back. Now he attempts the cultural escape, the submersion of his humanity in the ocean of mass thinking and mass behavior. As Ortega y Gasset has put it, "modern man, afraid of the lonesomeness of his existence, has been trying to steal himself into the anonymity of the social collective."[9]

But this route is also blocked. For, as the Existentialist shows, we cannot claim freedom from responsibility for our acts by attributing them to the conditioning effects of the environment. It is of course true that men have been and are creatures of culture, and once buried in the social collective they find it almost impossible to get out:

> "To battle against princes and popes is easy compared with struggling against the masses, the tyranny of equality, against the grin of shallowness, nonsense, baseness, and bestiality."[10]

But the irrevocable fact is that men do not *have to* follow environment's way. There is nothing in man that inevitably and inexorably drives him to accept one behavior pattern over another. However much the sociologist and anthropologist turn him into a cultural product, man can still oppose his culture. He cannot lay his faulty values, his barbaric politics, or even his personal psychoneurosis to his membership in a given human group—family, community, or national society—for he *could* have had it otherwise. Man can choose which way he will take; and this freedom to choose distinguishes him from all other phenomena in the universe. To be a man is to be undetermined, to be free.

> "No factor outside of a person's own will ever dooms him to follow a certain course. No external condition modifies his behavior in any way. Each person could have taken another course or have chosen another way to act."[11]

We see man, then, as the determiner of his own nature, definer of his own values. He is not the promiscuous and irresponsible scoundrel suggested by the phrase 'every one his own judge of right and wrong.' On the contrary, existential man feels the terrible burden of responsibility thrust on him by the withdrawal of all other supports. Sartre puts it this way:

> My freedom is the unique foundation of values. And since I am the being by virtue of whom values exist, nothing—absolutely nothing—can justify me in adopting this or that value or scale of values. As the unique basis of the existence of values, I am totally unjustifiable. And my freedom is in anguish at finding that it is the baseless basis of values.[12]

Far from being carefree and irresponsible, existential man is continually in the presence of doubt and anguish as to what he should do,

[9] K. F. Reinhardt, *op. cit.*, p. 114.
[10] S. Kierkegaard, The Journals, ed., A. Dru, p. 1317. (Quoted in F. H. Heinemann, *Existentialism and the Modern Predicament*, London, Adam and Charles Black, 1953, p. 35.)
[11] J. M. Spier, *Christianity and Existentialism*, transl. by D. H. Freeman, Philadelphia, The Presbyterian and Reformed Publishing Co., 1953, p. 71.
[12] H. J. Blackham, *op. cit.*, pp. 155–6.

for he knows that when he chooses, he chooses for Man. His life and conduct become his definitions of Man. Each word, each deed, each choice, represents his responsible understanding of what man is, and therefore each becomes a tiny building block in the existential edifice of value. Certainly no reasonable head could call this ethical theory an invitation to rascality.

We have only to develop one additional concept to bring this overly brief sightseeing tour to an end, i.e., the concept of transcendence. This is not to be confused with either the transcendental or transcendentalism, for Existentialists have no outer world, no supersensory, supernatural, trans-empirical region representing the "control booth" of the universe. Transcendence is the Existentialist name for the unique mode of human existence. Since man is indeterminate, since he is capable of choice, he is always seeking to realize himself. He constantly engages in reaching up, struggling for a new and higher definition of himself.

Now this process is, in effect, the process of becoming. In short, to exist is to be engaged in the process of becoming, and it is destined to go on as long as man is on the earth. There is no limit to what man can become. His *rate* of advance is of course always checked by the upper limits of his facility for making free choices, but that he shall advance and that there is no end point to his advance there is no question.

Man's existence is then marked by his reaching up beyond himself, in making himself over, in constantly reordering human nature:

"... human reality cannot be defined because it is not something given, it is in question. A man is possibility, he has the power to be. His existence is in his choice of the possibilites which are open to him, and since this choice is never final, once for all, his existence is indeterminate because not terminated."[13]

Sartre expresses it similarly:

"... man is constantly outside of himself; in projecting himself, in losing himself outside of himself, he makes for man's existing; and, on the other hand, it is by pursuing transcendent goals that he is able to exist; man, being this state of passing-beyond, and seizing upon things only as they bear upon this passing-beyond is at the heart, at the center of this passing-beyond."[14]

Man is thus, unlike any other phenomenon in the cosmos, always oriented toward his possibilities, toward the transcendent notions of what he might be.

In a sense, the idea of transcendence boils down to man's gift of what might be termed dynamic self-consciousness. Not only can man think, but he can think about (and criticize and correct) his thinking; not only can man contemplate but he can contemplate his facility for contemplation; not only can man have feeling but he can have feeling about feeling. This no other organism, so far as we know, shares with us. Thus man is not only conscious, but he is also, and uniquely, self-

[13] H. J. Blackham, *op. cit.*, p. 88.
[14] J. P. Sartre, *op. cit.*, p. 59.

conscious. He can possess a certain quiddity at a given moment and at the same moment be conscious of, and criticize and seek to change, this quiddity. He is, in a sense, always standing outside himself (transcendent) and engaging in thoughtful plans about how to do himself over.

EXISTENTIALISM AND EXPERIMENTALISM

Experimentalism, unfortunately, has not delineated its ontological notion of man anywhere near as thoroughly as have other philosophies, having confined its interests, as Reisner has pointed out, "to the analysis and description of experience, particularly to the problems of knowing and conduct . . ."[15] If it had, there is considerable speculative evidence that it would have come out with a close facsimile to the description just given of existential man. There are many ideas in the two positions which almost if not actually coincide.

For instance, at first glance we can recognize the fraternity of the two positions in their embrace of a dynamic, "open-ended" view of the universe. Both positions subscribe to James' "world-with-the-lid-off" concept and the thesis that reality, whatever it is, is in a process of becoming rather than in a state of being. The Existentialist tends to stress this more with relation to man himself, but implies the extension of this concept to include the rest of the cosmos.

Both philosophies therefore disavow a transcendental deity who rules and governs over all things. If we must have God, then He (or better, It) can be defined in terms which stress the human impulse to seek the better way. Dewey's definition of God in *A Common Faith* shares much with the Existentialist notion of transcendence. In this volume, Dewey has opened up not only the possibility but the actuality of a type of experience which does not rely upon sense perception. In like fashion speaks Marcel: "there must exist a possibility of having an experience of the transcendent as such, and unless that possibility exists the word can have no meaning."[16] This means that "since we respond to external stimuli, the possibility cannot be excluded that we respond to some which transcend the sphere of our sense-perceptions."[17] Or, as one of Jaspers' oft-quoted epigrams has it, "it is thinkable that there should be something unthinkable."

There is also a significant linkage between the Existentialist's transcendence and the Experimentalist's concept of growth. In this case the more accurate term would be self-transcendence[18] since we refer here more specifically to the microcosm of an individual person rather than man as macrocosm, to which the general term transcendence more appro-

[15] National Society for the Study of Education, Forty-First Yearbook, Pt. I, *Philosophies of Education*, Chicago, Univ. of Chicago Press, 1942, p. 30.
[16] *The Mystery of Being*, vol. i, p. 46. (Quoted in F. H. Heinemann, *op. cit.*, p. 138.
[17] F. H. Heinemann, *op. cit.*, p. 138.
[18] For an exegesis of self-transcendance in educational terms, see R. Ulich, *Fundamentals of Democratic Education*, Ch. III (See also Footnote 26.)

priately applies. The very function of living is to grow, to transcend one's present self and become something more, to realize one's possibilities (the familiar notion of self-realization).[19] This is the essence, if you will, of a human life.

> . . . there is, in the human being, a certain amount of elasticity in the gearing of urges or propensities to abilities, giving these urges the possibility of self-realization in a variety of activities. A man who has lost this quality is not normal . . .[20]

This growth, this self-transcendence thus becomes both means and end, both product and process of the human enterprise.

At this point the positions slightly diverge, the Existentialists arguing that growth-self-transcendence takes place through the activity of choosing without any guides or criteria, the Experimentalists linking growth with education and the process of exposure to and study of the alternatives open to choice, the criterion of workability governing the choice finally made.

Here we can discern the beginnings of a wider and more profound difference of views concerning the ultimate nature of man. Both philosophies of course demur from both the Aristotelian notion of man as rational animal and the Thomistic concept of man as spiritual being. The Experimentalist has preferred to consider man as a behaving organism whose behavior, because it reveals purpose, can be studied and, in ever-increasing measure, predicted. The proper study of man's behavior, or of anything, is of course governed by the scientific method. Though the Experimentalist does not ever say so, the implication is that theoretically the scientific study of man will continue to enlighten our understanding of him and simultaneously narrow that area of human action which might be called arbitrary. If the psychologist is correct in saying that "all behavior is caused," then a scientific investigation into causes will theoretically lead us eventually to complete understanding (and ultimate control over) human behavior.

The prospect of reducing man to a completely determined organism is not only uncomfortable but, happily, far from proven, and it is doubtful if even Experimentalists believe it will ever come to pass. Nevertheless, taken to its absurd extreme[21] the unconditional embrace of science seems to point in this direction.

The Existentialist, on the other hand, believes that man, although a purposive, behaving organism, is fundamentally and primordially an arbitrary organism. He can choose. It is true, his behavior suggests causal factors, but the important point is that man *is not compelled* to act in

---

[19] Since our unique freedom opens up a limitless variety of choice, we each have a multitude of possibilities and therefore an infinity of "possible selves" to realize.

[20] R. Ulich, *Fundamentals of Democratic Education*, New York, American Book Co., 1940, p. 140.

[21] We are warned, by Existentialists incidentally, that the absurdity of a proposition is no criterion whatsoever of its lack of validity. Absurd extremes may actually be our ultimate fate. In fact, maybe, as Sartre says, the whole business of living is one colossal absurdity.

any a priori way to a given set of causal circumstances. Alternate behavior is always a possibility for him. A leading Existentialist has this to say:

> Science, it is true, shows us remarkable and highly surprising things about man, but as it attains greater clarity, the more evident it becomes that man as a whole can never become the object of scientific investigation. *Man is always more than he knows about himself.*[22] [My italics.]

We have now, in a sense, come full circle:

> Existential philosophy reaffirms the ancient dictum of the ineffability of the individual. By virtue of its concrete individuality, the self is ultimately opaque to rational understanding.[23]

Clearly, say the Existentialists, science is not going to save the world; indeed it may be its undoing. Choosing their words with care in a final burst prepared especially for Pragmatists and Experimentalists, they can be heard to utter:

> It seems, in fact, that philosophers, in league with scientists, are bent on ridding the world of man's presence. By a sort of fundamental abstractedness . . . they have built up the myth of a world which is primarily the world to the exclusion of personality; it is a purely objective thing with no person in it to make it credible.[24]

EXISTENTIALISM AND EDUCATION

We come now to a consideration of the role of education in an existential world. What does all this mean for the education of man?

At the outset, it seems probable that the existential school will be a place where man's non-rational, i.e., his aesthetic, moral, and emotional self will be much more in evidence than his scientific, rational self. Experimentalists have envisioned a school where youngsters learn by using the scientific method to solve real, genuine problems, by using their reflective intelligence to explore and test possible alternative solutions to the perplexities their environment poses. Existentialists, while no doubt providing room for this kind of teaching, will be more interested in developing the affective side of man, his capacity to love, to appreciate, to respond emotionally to the world about him.

This seems probable because of the Existentialist Imperative—the necessity for personal "involvement" in human situations and the consequent requirement for unguided, unjustifiable but nevertheless responsible choice on the part of the individual person. Existentialists are not so concerned about gathering factual evidence on a problem; science can do that. They are more concerned with what man does with the evidence.

---

[22] K. Jaspers, *The Perennial Scope of Philosophy*, New York, Philosophical Library, 1949, p. 60.
[23] K. Hoffman, *Existentialism; A study of its past and present forms*, Unpublished doctoral thesis, Harvard University, 1949, p. 7.
[24] E. Mounier, *Existentialist Philosophers*, London, Rockliff, 1948, p. 8.

Science does not prescribe answers; it only gathers data. It is the individual who selects the answers, and he does so with no help from anyone. He is not compelled by nature to select any one answer; he can select any. His selection is therefore his alone, and he is responsible for it. He cannot justify it except in terms of himself. He may of course choose in a way in which the majority chooses. But the company of a majority does not make his choice right. He is condemned to live in constant anguish and doubt as to whether his choice was the right one.

Although there is no easy escape from this anguish, it is presumed that the development of the affective dimension of human personality would better prepare the individual for this kind of existence than would the development of his rational and scientific faculties which are after all supposed to be kept objective, neutral, and therefore free of personal preference.

For better or worse, therefore, the Existentialist educator would seem to be committed to the task of developing the choice-making power in the individual, and it seems probable that in working to this end, he will move away from the sciences, including the social sciences, and increasingly turn to the humanities and the arts. For it is here where man's aesthetic, emotional, and moral proclivities are exercised.[25]

By way of paradox, however, the opposite point of view might easily be developed. If the business of living is to be, at least in part, an effort to escape from this anguish, the *deadening* of the affective centers might emerge as a suitable educational objective. In this event, the more dull and insensitive a person became, the more satisfying and certain a life he would presumably lead. I take it however the Existentialists do not consider the amelioration of anguish as either possible or desirable. It is in the very nature of things that we are free; being free we are committed to live in anguish, and we must make the best of a very difficult situation.

As for pedagogy, it seems inevitable that the existential school will become more individual-centered. In a way, it will have to be, since its prime consideration is the individual living unattached in a friendless world. The "group method," so long a friend of democratic Experimentalism, will have to be discarded. You cannot teach the individual the true significance of his unique individualism with group dynamics; the very function of group dynamics is to illustrate the superiority of group decision over individual decision.

In fact, it would seem likely that all forms of cooperative endeavor would atrophy, at least all those in which decisions were sought (as distinguished from those in which factual information is shared). And we would likely find boys and girls working individually with their teachers, assessing the material before them and learning the necessity for making existential choices.

To an Experimentalist, this would of course be an intolerable kind

---

[25] For a similar analysis emphasizing "the culture of the emotions" as the future core of the curriculum, see R. Ulich, *Crisis and Hope in American Education*, Boston, Beacon Press, 1951, Ch. III.

of school, one in which the social and gregarious qualities of human experience would certainly atrophy and die. But the Existentialist does not value gregariousness. Gregariousness is only a transparent excuse for the loss of man's unique existential individuality, only a pretty word for explaining man's unhappy capitulation to the cosmic forces trying to make him a mass animal. If man is to regain that which makes him human, he must be willing once again to stand alone, willing to withstand the pressures of history and culture, and to chart the course of his own life, not only for himself but on behalf of Man.

This is surely a large order, particularly in an age when we cower before the awesome might of man-made instruments of power. To think that men can be expected to stand up to these twentieth-century behemoths may be only philosophic whistling in the dark; but stand up they must, say the Existentialists, if men are to cease being animals and start being men.

One can readily see from all this that Existentialists would hardly be expected to concern themselves, as have the Experimentalists and the Reconstructionists, with the problem of cultural change and social reconstruction. The way to the good life, according to the Existentialists, is not through social reform; that only tends to substitute one kind of social collectivity for another. In both, men are driven by tradition, custom, and public opinion. The way to the good life, or as the Existentialist would put it, the *authentic* life, is instead for each individual human being to begin realizing himself by asserting his individuality and making his own choices instead of being stampeded into the choices of the collectivity. In school, therefore, youngsters would not be encouraged to examine and criticize the cultural tradition they were inheriting with a view to its improvement and reform. They would instead be concerned with developing that integrity in themselves necessary to the task of making personal choices of action, taking personal responsibility for these choices, whether the culture smiles or frowns. Sociologists are always arguing about how to improve society—by improving social institutions or by improving individuals. Existentialists clearly choose the latter.

The problem, therefore, of democracy vs. authoritarianism seems rather irrelevant to the Existentialists. Democrats, they say, delude themselves with the myth that group decision is not authoritarian. But surely there can be tyranny in majority rule. We all live under the oppressive leveling influence of mass opinion, custom, and habit. Is this not tyranny? If democracy means group decision, let us have none of it.

If, however, democracy means individual choice, if the Fourth-of-July speeches concerning the freedom of the individual are to be taken literally and at face value, then we shall be on our way to an existential conception of socio-political life. For the individual is his own best (and *only*) judge of what he should do; any defection from his freedom, whether excused or justified by autocratic fiat, democratic law, or "the cake of custom," thereby subtracts from his intrinsic humanness. The only adequate socio-political order is one which recognizes and values the absolute freedom of the human person. The school in such an order shall be the instrument through which the individual learns how to use this freedom.

Here finally we come upon a most profound divergence of Existentialist and Experimentalist educational theory. We have said that the Existentialist school will not become involved in any particular choices but only in the choice-making process itself. If this be true, it would hardly claim to be a school at all in our modern sense. For schools, as they have been defined by contemporary students of culture, are places where specified values, skills, attitudes, and modes of response are presumably selected out of the multitude open to men as the particular cultural conditioners a given human group has chosen for itself. Civilizations invent and build schools because they have become self-conscious of their own experience and wish to perpetuate it; they support educational systems because they have made choices and wish these choices to become the working equipment of oncoming generations.

All this would become impossible in Existentialist theory. No choice is demonstrably better than any other because there are no external standards by which one may measure their validity. Each man, being radically free, is his own supreme court of value. He cannot look to culture or to history for any guidance whatsoever. His schooling therefore would become, in our modern understanding of the term, quite meaningless; indeed, if education means the selection and acquisition of certain modes of response over others, it seems most preposterous to believe that Existentialists could have schools at all. If, in short, education, as Childs and other Experimentalists have so forcibly stated, is primarily a *social* undertaking perpetuating and interpreting a social system to succeeding generations; and if, on the other hand, Existentialists view society only as a new mode of tyranny over the minds of men, then we might even conclude that Existentialism would have no traffic with education in any shape or form. Indeed, the case might even be developed that Existentialism is the very denial of education as we understand it today.

Toward Dialogue

Toward the close of the foregoing essay, the author spends a couple of paragraphs developing the alarming idea that Existential philosophy in educational thought is a contradiction in terms. Of course, he hedges his argument by scattering phrases like "might conclude" and "might be developed" through his final words and by affecting a hypothetical tone throughout. But, otherwise, his language is rather strong.

If he is serious about this, why did he include Existentialism as a major component of this book?

Further Readings

Greene, Maxine, ed. *Existential Encounters for Teachers*. New York: Random House, 1967.

Herbst, Jurgen. "The Anti-School—Some Reflections on Teaching," *Educational Theory*, 18 (Winter, 1968), pp. 13–22.

Kneller, George. *Existentialism and Education*. New York: Philosophical Library, 1958.

Patty, Austin. "Existential Teaching," *Educational Theory*, 17 (October, 1967), pp. 329–334.

Tenenbaum, Samuel. "Implications of a Phenomenological Approach to Education," *Educational Theory*, 17 (October, 1967), pp. 343–352.

Vandenberg, Donald. "Life-Phases and Values," *Educational Forum*, 32 (March, 1968), pp. 293–302.

Index

Absolutism, false, types of, 122
Adler, Mortimer, 6, 8
Aiken, Henry, 6
Alexander the Great, 3
American Anthropologist, 160
American artifacts:
  baseball as possible artifact, 56
  list of twelve, 42, common character-
    istics of, 45–47, 51–52, 55
Analytic philosophy: (*see also* Seman-
    tic empiricism)
  metaphysical and normative state-
    ments, relationship to, 174–175,
    arguments dissociating it from
    metaphysics, 185–187, 191–195
  propositions in, 173–174, analytic,
    174, synthetic, 174
  schools of, 5–8
Anthropotherapy: 134, 160
  defined, 166–167
  importance of psychotherapy in,
    167–168, 171
  and obstacles to man-in-culture con-
    ceptualization, 160–164
  precautions regarding use of, 169–
    170
  social-self-realization in, 165–166,
    169, 171
  working propositions for concept of,
    164–170
Aquinas, St. Thomas, 3, 111–112, 282,
    314
Archimedes, 175
Aristotle, 3, 6–7, 9, 104, 111–112, 282
Armstrong, Louis, 46
Assembly-line production, as American
    artifact, 42, 53
Austin, J. L., 5
Ayer, A. J., 175, 185, 195–196, 214

Bach, J. S., 75, 205
Bacon, Roger, 17

Barometer problem, 82–84
Barrett, William, 329, 339
Bateson, Gregory, 148
Bavelas, Alex, 183
Beethoven, Ludwig van, 205
Belief(s):
  enabling, 252–254
  evidential and non-evidential styles
    of, contrasted, 244, 246
  primitive and derivative, relationship
    of, 241–242
  psychologically central, 242–243
  systems, structure of, 240–244
Believing:
  and learning, knowing, and teaching,
    217–219, 221–223
  range of, 224–226
Benedict, Ruth, 108–110, 161
Berdyaev, Nikolai, 336
Bergmann, Gustav, 180
Bergson, Henri, 19–20, 295
Berlin, Isaiah, 9
Bidney, David, 96, 103, 130, 164, 168
Blake, William, 325
Blanshard, Brand, 4
Bradley, F. H., 4, 187–188, 196
Brain, need for exercise of, 78–79
Brameld, Theodore, 134, 159, 160, 171
Bridgeman, P. W., 84, 179
Bridges, Robert, 105
Broudy, Harry, 270, 274
Brubeck, Dave, 46
Bruner, Jerome, 20, 278
Bruno, Giordano, 3
Bryson, Lyman, 131
Buber, Martin, 20, 329–330, 340

Caesar, Julius, 183
Calandra, Alexander, 59, 82, 86–87
Calvin, John, 320

Please remember that this is a library book,
and that it belongs only temporarily to each
person who uses it. Be considerate. Do
not write in this, or any, library book.